Memorial Book of Kobylnik (Narach, Belarus)

Translation of *Sefer Kobylnik*

Original Yizkor Book Edited by Yitzhak Siegelman
Published in Haifa, 1967 in Hebrew and Yiddish
By *the Va'ad Yozei Kobylnik b'Yisrael*
(Committee of Former Residents of Kobylnik in Israel)

Published by JewishGen

**An Affiliate of the Museum of Jewish Heritage—A Living Memorial to the Holocaust
New York**

Memorial Book of Kobylnik (Narach, Belarus)
Translation of *Sefer Kobylnik*

Translation Project Coordinator: Anita Frishman Gabbay
Layout: Joel Alpert
Cover Design: Jan Fine

Published by JewishGen, Inc.
An Affiliate of the Museum of Jewish Heritage
A Living Memorial to the Holocaust
36 Battery Place, New York, NY 10280

Printed in the United States of America by Lightning Source, Inc.

Library of Congress Control Number (LCCN): 2019949166

ISBN: 978-1-939561-84-8 (hard cover: 394 pages, alk. paper)

JewishGen and the Yizkor Books in Print Project

This book has been published by the **Yizkor Books in Print Project**, as part of the **Yizkor Book Project** of JewishGen, Inc.

JewishGen, Inc. is a non-profit organization founded in 1987 as a resource for Jewish genealogy. Its website [www.jewishgen.org] serves as an international clearinghouse and resource center to assist individuals who are researching the history of their Jewish families and the places where they lived. JewishGen provides databases, facilitates discussion groups, and coordinates projects relating to Jewish genealogy and the history of the Jewish people. In 2003, JewishGen became an affiliate of the **Museum of Jewish Heritage—A Living Memorial to the Holocaust** in New York.

The **JewishGen Yizkor Book Project** was organized to make more widely known the existence of Yizkor (Memorial) Books written by survivors and former residents of various Jewish communities throughout the world. Later, volunteers connected to the different destroyed communities began cooperating to have these books translated from the original language—usually Hebrew or Yiddish—into English, thus enabling a wider audience to have access to the valuable information contained within them. As each chapter of these books was translated, it was posted on the JewishGen website and made available to the general public.

The **Yizkor Books in Print Project** began in 2011 as an initiative to print and publish Yizkor Books that had been fully translated, so that hard copies would be available for purchase by the descendants of these communities and also by scholars, universities, synagogues, libraries, and museums.

These Yizkor books have been produced almost entirely through the volunteer effort of researchers from around the world, assisted by donations from private individuals. The books are printed and sold at near cost, so as to make them as affordable as possible. Our goal is to make this important genre of Jewish literature and history available in English in book form, so that people can have the personal histories of their ancestral towns on their bookshelves for themselves and for their children and grandchildren.

A list of all published translated Yizkor Books in the project with prices and ordering information can be found at:
http://www.jewishgen.org/Yizkor/ybip.html

Lance Ackerfeld, Yizkor Book Project Manager
Joel Alpert, Yizkor-Book-in-Print Project Coordinator

JewishGen
Yizkor Book Project

This book is presented by the
Yizkor Books in Print Project
Project Coordinator: Joel Alpert

Part of the
Yizkor Books Project of JewishGen, Inc.
Project Manager: Lance Ackerfeld

These books have been produced solely through volunteer effort
of individuals from around the world. The books are printed and
sold at near cost, so as to make them as affordable as possible.

Our goal is to make this history and important genre of Jewish
literature available in English in book form so that people can have
the near-personal histories of their ancestral towns on their bookshelves for themselves and for their children and grandchildren.

Any donations to the Yizkor Books Project are appreciated.

Please send donations to:
Yizkor Book Project
JewishGen
36 Battery Place
New York, NY 10280

JewishGen, Inc. is an affiliate of the
Museum of Jewish Heritage
A Living Memorial to the Holocaust

Notes to the Reader:

We apologize ahead of time for the poor quality of images in the book. Often these images had been scanned from the original Yizkor books which were of poor quality to begin with, being copies of old photographs. Each transfer results in loss of quality. We have done the best we could, given the original material and the resources and technology at hand. Even though images often appear of higher quality on computer screens, that does not transfer to high quality images in print. A reader can view the original scans on the web sites listed below.

Within the text the reader will note "{34}" standing ahead of a paragraph. This indicates that the material translated below was on page 34 of the original book. However, when a paragraph was split between two pages in the original book, the marker is placed in this book after the end of the paragraph for ease of reading.

Also please note that all references within the text of the book to page numbers, refer to the page numbers of the original Yizkor Book.

The original book can be seen online at the Yiddish Book Center web site: https://www.yiddishbookcenter.org/collections/yizkor-books/yzk-nybc313817/zigelman-yitshak-sefer-kobilnik

In order to obtain a list of all Shoah victims from Kobylnik, the reader should access the Yad Vashem web site listed below; one can also search for specific family names using family name option. These lists are continually updated by Yad Vashem, so it is worthwhile to periodically search these lists.

There is much valuable information available on this web site, including the Pages of Testimony, etc.
http://yvng.yadvashem.org

A list of this book and all books available in the Yizkor-Book-In-Print Project along with prices is available at:
http://www.jewishgen.org/Yizkor/ybip.html

INTRODUCTION TO THE TRANSLATION

The undertaking of the translation of the Kobylnik Yiskor Book came after many years of geneological research for my roots, my families that perished in the Holocaust and the inspiration from the late Meir Swirsky, of Haifa, Israel.

It was a labour of love and also pain, my mother, Rasza (Rachel) who survived [see Kobylnik to Bergen Belsen] was not the person she had been prior to the war and therefore I needed to know how she lived, what kind of family she came from, etc. We [second and third generation] will never know the meaning of "loss"! Those destroyed communities were our foundation for love, compassion, learning, brotherhood and Tzedaka…use these Yizkor Books with pride and know the people you came from!

When these Yiskor Books were written, we children in the Diaspora who could not read Yiddish or Hebrew will benefit from the English translations. You will find some stories contradicted or repeated, but the people that wrote them were not trained authors, but read this book and others anyway. Find out how your grandparents lived and how they died. Read about their town and especially about the destruction and the Holocaust. With anti-Semitism rearing its ugly head again, let us remember and never forget those martyrs!

Anita Frishman Gabbay, 2019

In Memory of our families and friends from Kobylnik: Swirsky, Yavnovitch, Gilinski, Rubensteyn, Hadash [Chodosh], Gantovnick, Kudevitski, Krivitski, Todres, Gordon and others

Geopolitical Information:

Located at 54 deg 56 ' North Latitude and 26 deg 41' East Longitude

80 miles NNW of Minsk

Alternate names: Narach [Belarussian, since 1964], Kobylnik [Russian, Polish, until 1964], Kobilnik [Yiddish], Kabylnik [Belarussian, until 1964], Kobilniki, Naracz [Polish, since 1964], Naroch' [Russian, since 1964], Narač [Belarussian], Naročius [Lithuanian], Narutch

Period	Town	District	Province	Country
Before WWI (c. 1900):	Kobylnik	Sventsyany	Vilna	Russian Empire
Between the wars (c. 1930):	Kobylnik	Postawy	Wilno	Poland
After WWII (c. 1950):	Kobylnik			Soviet Union
Today (c. 2000):	Narach			Belarus

Nearby Jewish Communities:

- Myadzyel 11 miles ESE
- Svir 13 miles WSW
- Pastavy 14 miles NNE
- Adutiškis, Lithuania 15 miles NNW
- Lyntupy 17 miles WNW
- Stajetiškė, Lithuania 18 miles NNW
- Mikhalishki 22 miles WSW
- Dunilaviču 24 miles ENE
- Mielagėnai, Lithuania 24 miles NNW
- Švenčionys, Lithuania 25 miles NW
- Nivki 26 miles SE
- Kozyany 26 miles NNE
- Kryvichy 28 miles ESE
- Ceikiniai, Lithuania 28 miles NW
- Kurenets 29 miles SSE
- Vornyany 30 miles WSW

Hebrew Title Page of Original Yizkor Book

ס פ ר

קוביליניק

ע ר ך   יצחק זיגלמן

הוצא על־ידי ועד יוצאי קובי־לניק בישראל

ארויסגעגעבן דורך דעט קאָבילניקער לאנדסלייס־קאָמיטעט אין ישראל

ת ש כ ״ ז — ח י פ ה — 1967

THE MEMORIAL BOOK OF
KOBYLNIK

Edited by Itzhak Siegelman

Published by the Kobylnik Landsleit Committee in Israel
Members: Yitzhak Gordon, Meir Hadash, Meir Yavnai(Yavnovitch), Chaim
Yavnai(Yavnovitch), Meir Swirski, Yaffa Pertzov, (Shainka Yanofsky), Asher Krukoff
Printed in Haifa, Israel 1967

Table of Contents

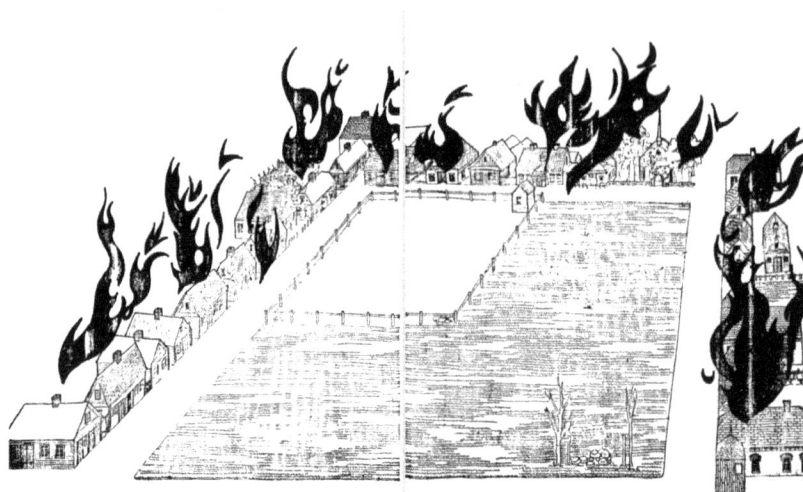

Holocaust

Footnote:

Hakhshara – training in Hebrew – agricultural institutes similar to kibbutzim where Zionist youth would learn their technical skills necessary for their emigration to Israel.

Family Notes

[Page 7]

Remembrance and Grief

A monument to our town
by the Editorial board
Translated by Talya Moscovitz–Klein
Edited by Toby Bird

With a tremor and reverence we approached the sacred work, publishing the book of Kobylnik. Overwhelmed by the burden of grief, bereavement and orphanhood, we carried the terrible burden imposed on our shoulders, though we knew how incompetent and speechless we are to encompass in all its depth the intensity of the destruction and the Holocaust that afflicted the entire Jewish nation.

We are horrified by the bitter role fate has given us, the great responsibility that lies upon us – that we may not deserve it, to try to express the grief of our people and speak for those who are killed in the strange deaths invented by Satan. And if with our own hands we counted the piles of fallen people before our eyes and knew their amazing numbers, we will never know how to estimate the spiritual heritage we lost, or the cultural, moral and Torah life that has been and is no more.

We are stunned by the fate of the precious people who perished, and at the end of 25 years of their annihilation, we, the few remaining who have escaped, are left to build a monument to the town and to its holy people. We will try to describe the history of the people of our town in this book, which was meant to serve as a tombstone, and as a perpetual candle light for the fallen.

These lines will illuminate the path of anguish, in which our loved ones marched their last step towards death. The chapters will merge into a great scroll of fire that will burn the living flesh of the destroyers of our people, and will be engraved forever in the mark of Cain for an eternal disgrace.

And when we leaf through the pages of the book we will discover corners of life that disappeared from the town of Kobylnik at the time, when everything was still standing. We will discuss the lives of the Jewish residents of the town, their deeds and daily struggles, their good and bad, the well–being and suffering they suffered, and dreams that have faded away. The chapters will depict the simple and modest Jews, as they appeared by their sorrow, loneliness, and joy, until they reached the bitter end. The chapters will tell about the death, destruction, and holocaust that afflicted our nation, the moaning of babies who were thrown alive to the grave, the Shema Israel, which Jews shouted on the brink of death, raising their eyes to the heavens.

[Page 8]

These chapters will commemorate the way of life of the town, as it has developed over generations, and the glamorous souls of our holy ones. The people taken from us will be a source of inspiration and pride for us and for our children. We will review this book, and browse it from time to time, unite with the memory of the saints together and in unity, so that their lives and pure sacrifice will be a symbol and a memory for generations to come.

*

Now, after much effort, we can bless the finished and reveal that it was a difficult work because of the meager numbers of those who lived in town that survived the destruction and because of the relatively young age of these people, they did not have enough time to follow and be interested enough in the history of the town. The diary of the town that was kept in the synagogue contained the main events that the town had undergone since its existence was destroyed and we lacked the sources from which we could draw information about the town and its history, and only in concern for the level of the book, we worked to obtain historical material in Israel and abroad.

Efforts were made by us to share the book as much as possible with the members of our town, and indeed more than half of the Kobylniks in Israel gave us their notes and memories. In addition to the main chapter, which contains an authentic and chronological description of the events in the town at the time of the Nazi occupation of Kobylnik from 1941 until the liberation in 1944, the book also contains material written by friends, describing their personal experiences from the Holocaust period, and from the previous period. And if we do not have complete confidence that there were no defects in the book describing the life of the town, it seems to us that we managed to encompass the most important and the maximum under the existing conditions.

As a pleasant duty, we would like to thank all those who helped us carry out the project, first and foremost the members of our town in Israel and some of them in America, who contributed to the publication of the book. We are also grateful to the friends who devoted their time, energy and ability to write things down. We would like to thank the editor of the book, Mr. Itzhak Zigelman, and the secretary of the Committee of the Jews of Kobylnk, Mr. Yitzhak Gordon, who headed the operation to publish the book.

We will bless and thank them all.

[Page 9]

The book editorial board
From right to left: Sitting: Meyer Yavnai, Itzhak Zigelman, Yafa Pertzov;
Standing: Asher Krukoff, Meyer Swirsky, Meyer Hadash, Itzhak Gordon, Haim Yavnai

[Page 10]

Instead of the Orphan's Kaddish

by Baruch Axelrod
Translated by Talya Moscovitz–Klein
Edited by Toby Bird

In memory of the martyrs of the town of Kobylnik who perished and were cut down by strangers

My dear brothers and sisters, a holy community whose bones are scattered all over Poland, with all six million of our pure and holy brothers

I stand at attention on your graves, Kaddish did not say and I will not justify the decree

They also did not hear the prayer of "El Maleh Rachamim" because the heavens were high and the gates of mercy were closed

My soul is bent for the land and my eyes are raised to the heavens, and as then, now there is an empty heaven before me – I knew that you would not listen to my prayer, HaShem.

Because you did not listen to the prayer of infants and babies nursing in their mother's arms. As you have not listened to the prayer of the elders and the holy ones whose eyes were raised to heaven and the Shema Israel prayer on their lips. And as they were united with the Holy Name, HaShem, the O–N–E, they were all cut down one by one.

Are they resting in the shadow of the wings of Shekhinah? No, Elohai! Even the sound of the wings of the Shekhinah will not silence their blood that cries out and rest will not be found.

Land, do not cover their blood! Saints – Your name will be magnified and sanctified, and your memory will never fade from our midst.

And we will build a generation that will remember ... and who will remind our brothers wherever they are, because only here in their homeland – their resurrection. And Here the Jewish nation will be great again.

This will be the living monument in memory and the spirit of our holy ones.

[Page 11]

Eulogy

by Yitzhak Gordon
Translated by Talya Moscovitz–Klein
Edited by Toby Bird

(Was given by the residents of Kobylnik at the first memorial assembly for the martyrs of Kobylnik, held in Haifa on September 28, 1950)

We gathered here a handful of Jews, survivors of fire, haunted and devastated, the survivors of the Jews of our town of Kobylnik, the Vilna district.

A faithful town of holy and pure, tortured and persecuted by the hands of an enemy and oppressor in the years 1941–1942. My heart is with you my parents, my dear brothers and sisters, men, women and children, whose lives were cut down from the book of life, without time or purpose. In the splendor of your fresh blossom, you have mercilessly taken root. And you babies, death caught you up even before you knew what life is.

In the open, in broad daylight, they abused you and harvested your last breath. Heaven and Earth were not shocked at the abominable crime. Everything covered your spilled blood. You were exterminated even though you did not sin, and only because you were Jews. With helplessness you had been led to the slaughter and you had to accept the punishment, because evil had shut you down from all sides. You fell dead and sacrificed on the altar of hatred of the Jews and even for Jewish burial were not brought.

You were buried in your graves and your soul is still in your nose and they have already poured the whitewash on you. In your precious life, you have paid the debt of blood for the grace they have done with you when you are at foreign land. The Gentiles thirstily drank your blood and proved their lust for theft.

You are the sweet and loving ones in your life, fulfilling the 613 commandments, you did not abandon your faith and your faith in the Torah and in the Ten Commandments was not weakened. You opposed the use of violence and coarse force as a solution to interpersonal problems and aspired to justice and justice. Indeed, you believed that in God's image man was created, and in your innocence you trusted them that they were permitted from the beast and were bitterly disappointed. You innocently believed that man was superior to the beast but you were severely burned by that assumption.

Dear Jews, honest and kindhearted, charitable and compassionate you were. No one died of starvation at the step of your door. Your house was wide open and you used it always with great hospitality. At your table you gave a place to the poor, and your shared your bread with an unexpected guest.

[Page 12]

You supported the weak and offered him your help. You have supported the orphan and the widow in distress. You established charities and charitable organizations and, through "secret donations", collected money for the needy for "kimcha dafscha", "kinshet kallah" and for visiting the sick. You had a continuous tradition for generations in the spirit of Torah and Judaism with all its laws and commandments and in this spirit you have educated your sons and daughters. You were careful of assimilation and kept your Jewish consciousness. You were the guardians of the walls of Netzach Israel. Through the windows of your little houses, a light shone from the candles of the Shabbath, and which gave you hope and resourcefulness. Your holidays, though they seemed to be full of melancholy, were full of joy. From your homes came the sounds of your pleasant songs. You concealed your Jewish character in the wings of your clothes and the modest attire you wore. The beard on your face and the Payot testified to your origins. Indeed, even in the delicacies of your food, you were different from your neighbors, who were often jealous of you for that. For countless generations you lived in foreign lands and there rose halachic rulers, and scholars.

The Beit Midrash was a home for you and was a witness to wisdom and Torah and a place for singing and prayer. There you got together with God with devotion and poured out the pleas of your heart; from the Beit Midrash you have taken your strength in the daily life, and it has been your fort against the suffering and distress, which visited you often. In the synagogue, you also found a cure for the things between you and yourselves.

The old argument between Chassidim and Mitnagdim flared up, and they settled into a dispute over who should be the seat of the rabbinate in the town. But at the same time you also gave attention to important and significant issues. You did not object with blind fanaticism to the external education that penetrated your walls and moved from the "Heder" to the modern school, to educate your children, just as you did not oppose and supported the best of your money and your contributions to building Israel. And when the pioneers came to Israel, you did not declare a boycott, in your everyday life. You behaved as common people, as kind people and proud of your Jewishness.

You were healthy and strong in your body. You grew up like a tree and the field grew around. The beauty of the landscape in which you were born was reflected in your nature. Your sources of income were meager and few knew what a bit of abundance was.

[Page 13]

Narach Lake

The common trade and the way you worked as tailors, shoemakers and other professions did not allow you a life of luxury. Many of you worked hard but had to manage with a modest meal. In your homes and in the courtyards of your little houses, love will also fall for the chickens and animals that lived with you. Large and wide families you were. Your homes are crowded with the noise of their inhabitants – the noise of your children and their laughter around them. Indeed, you have been blessed with fathers, sons, and grandsons in the glory of the elders and in the greatness of the wise.

[Page 14]

There is not enough room to describe the extent of the dimensions of wisdom and morality that were hidden in you, the glorious Jews. You were like a tiny pearl embedded in a necklace of Jewish communities in Poland – and you are no longer... Your fate was sealed with the fate of the great European Jewry that was annihilated by the oppressor and their aides during World War II. Your dwellings remained desecrated and nothing was left.

May your memory be preserved in us forever, Amen.

A visit in Kobylnik. Next to the mass grave, 1966

[Pages 15-19]

The synagogue of the town and around it
Written by engineer Meyer Swirsky– Haifa
Translated by Yael Moscowitz
Edited by Toby Bird

There are no more Jews in Kobylnik; with time, the name of the town has also disappeared. Today it's called Narach... there is no trace left of the Jewish community in the town, no one to mention us there. For those who were our neighbors this is convenient, as in their own hand they helped the Nazis to eradicate us and then to delete every trace.

The cemetery was "cleared" of all gravestones and on the mass grave of our dearest, who were murdered, a grave that was outside the town has no sign and no one is coming to visit. The synagogue, the institute that more than anything was a symbol of our small community is no longer there...

The synagogue was built many years ago; "An old man from the eldest people of the town... was the owner of the local estate, the Goy. With his permission, on his land the Jews of the town built their praying house. It was a wooden building. Very often a fire burst and instead of many wooden houses, new brick buildings were built. But the ancient synagogue stayed still despite all. It was a big building in a shape of a rectangle; its width was a bit shorter than its length, with a very high ceiling and many narrow windows around it and a double slope roof. An excellent simple building that characterized all wooden houses in the town.

Although the synagogue was located close to the center of town– the marketplace –it was in a side corner without a street name. The eastern wall was on the border of Todres and Gantovnik gardens. North to it was the Jewish school that was on the border of our family's fruit garden. And so on. Behind the school was the Jewish public bath house and more gardens, the meadow of the priest, the crick and on both sides trees and lots of plants. On the west side to the synagogue were vegetables gardens. Those were owned by the Goys. The south entrance had a wide big square in front of it and the path was leading towards Vilna Street, near the house of the Krivitzkis.

The entrance to the big praying hall was a wide room. On the left there was a library, rooms for accommodations and the rabbis' apartment. In the central room a big square stage was standing proud, for reading the Torah.

In the middle of the eastern wall a holy cabinet high and elegant with a few steps in front of it, on the right– a praying place for the cantor. Seats for the prayers were located around the stage and another row next to the eastern wall.

The western wall had windows from side to side– these were the woman's seats and had a separate entrance.

This was the center of our lives for generations.

Of the "glory days" of our synagogue we would hear from our fathers. It appears that this era was going on until the First World War. The Jews of the town had pretty much an equal status; they were working in craft work and a little trade and were mostly poor. Electricity and light haven't been available and there were no paved roads. Houses without water or toilets, modest furniture... only seldom people have traveled far from the town. Jews excelled at being religious and keeping the purity of the Jewish religion when around there was primitive Christianity. Their integrity, innocence, kindness and keeping mitzvahs united the entire community back in those days. Those were our forefathers for generations and until our grandparents.

The synagogue was the only religious center at the time, without any other spiritual– cultural institute. The only photograph that was preserved from those days was taken in the synagogue, showing everyone with heavy beards, serious and innocent faces.

The belief, faith and sometimes learning the Torah, kept our forefathers more than the crafts and work they were doing for a living. Although there was poverty, our grandparents stuck to the synagogue like a moss to a wall... this is where they thanked God for their existence. This is where they reached joy on holidays. A live evidence for those days was the eldest people on the town who still lived in my childhood days. Those were our grandparents and their main business remains praying, the synagogue and keeping Mitzvahs.

We were educated growing up around the synagogue and our forefathers' tradition. Almost all of our parents, without any exceptions, were highly religious. Keeping kosher, Shabbat, holidays and occasions were common to all. Most of them even prayed three times a day, in their houses or at the synagogue. Nonetheless that was another generation, different, more advanced in trade. We were not educated on Torah only; advanced general education was part of our share as well.

Our parents read newspapers, listened to the radio and knew well about politics. They used bicycles, didn't have much free time and didn't dedicate their lives to the work of God as their parents did. Although there was no grandparent without a long beard, our parents did not grow beards anymore. And yet, the synagogue kept on being our spiritual center. This is where the congregation gathered around on Saturdays, holiday, special occasions, and everything that had to do with the community. Nevertheless this was not our only central place; behind the synagogue they built the new advanced Hebrew school, the youth group of the "Yung Halutz" was getting together, things that were established by our parents.

Lately, people who came to the synagogue divided into three defined groups more or less. The elderly group, those with the long beards, adherent to the Torah and prayers. Sometimes they just sat for some time in the place that was so holy to them. They were mostly sitting next to the eastern wall, the most respected among them. They also sat around the big stage in the center of the praying house; the tiles around the stage were used as a heating system.

The head of the elderly group was Rabbi Einbinder, next to him the most central person in the synagogue and in the entire community– Yeshaya Yosi Gordon. This is where we regularly saw Haim Yankal'e Yanovsky, the porcelain trader, his brothers Avraham It'che and Moshe, Berl Gebtovnik the butcher, Mendel Leib Hadash the teacher, Yeshayahu Vexler the tinsmith, Zternosky the blacksmith, old Glot and the others...

About half of the elderly group passed away before the Shoah and were considered to have a special right from God to be to die naturally and to be buried in a Jewish grave. Our forefathers were the main group of the synagogue; among them we crowd together, us– the children, youth and teenagers.

On the two sides of the stage set the young generation and the parents. On Shabbat and holidays the synagogue was full of people, everyone dressed in the best clothes. Not only on the high holidays, the time of praying was also for mental serenity, time for small talks, catching up and fun pranks by the children.

This part, that stood in contradiction with our fathers' feelings, was the daily occurrence for the younger people and for some of the older as well. Things like those happened mostly while reading the Torah. Instead of following the reading that was performed with much grace and talent by Leib

Friedman or the butcher Avraham Goldzegger, people made conversation about events in the world, or their impression of visiting other villages markets, things about Zionism and the lad of Jews, updates about Kobylnik, jokes and funny pranks like throwing a towel on the head of one of the prayers...

Some literal assassination with the elderly group and the more conservatives were inevitable, and the adjudicator and peace maker as usual was the good and innocent Rabbi. An example that you can see is the case when people told the rabbi that Yankel Beinish is disturbing the prayers. The rabbi came to Yankel Beinish who sat near the southern was among the "Jokers"; everyone stood up for the rabbi (this was custom at the synagogue). The rabbi asked if that was true. Yankel said: "His blood is on his own head, I swear..." the rabbi wondered, turned to the complainant and said: "What do you want from Yankel Beinish? He clearly swore he had nothing to do with this."

There was much joy in the synagogue during the holidays, like Simchat Torah, Purim, Shavuot. Being happy was a mitzvah and even if there were some jokes or pranks, the older generation saw this with understanding. Everyone has a special courtesy to Shaya Yossi. Although he was very old, he still "controlled the yarmulke," calmed every fight, set who will be the prayer leader, who will go up to read the Torah etc. He was also the address for all that was going on outside the synagogue. When he passed away all those issues transmitted to the managers of the synagogue, first to Shlomo Yavnovich and then to David Leib Swirsky.

Upon the arrival of the soviets in 1939, we felt a severe decrease in the importance of the synagogue. Even keeping Shabbat became very hard, because most of them worked in governmental positions, and the young generation that was studying in the state school had to come to school on Shabbat and holidays. And what a wonder; the external difficulties made the Jews want to be even stricter about keeping the Mitzvahs...

My father for example, insisted and received an approval that he will be free of any work on Shabbat and will work on Sunday instead, the official day off. Others followed him if they were able to receive the approval. I remember the time when all the Jewish children (who were attending school on Shabbat without books or pencils) organized together and didn't show up for school in Rosh Hashana. The principle, the Goy, came to the synagogue with his teachers and tried with to force us to leave. He did not succeed this time but it was clear that that the next generation should expect many difficulties in the future to keep those values that were sacred for generations by our forefathers.

The twist was sudden and crueler than anything we expected. The Nazis, yimach shemom, came, and with them the big Shoah of the Jews of Europe, and our town in it. The hardest of all was the idea, that the god of armies, who we believed in and was so sacred, is punishing so cruelly his flock. We had enough admonishment and beating one's breast, thinking that all of this came upon us for not keeping the Mitzvahs strictly enough, while trying to ignore the horrible truth... we were humiliated and tortured before being totally destroyed.

The Synagogue together with most of the Jewish houses were set on fire on 1943 by the partisan Meyer Hadash, one of the few survivors, for the sake that our Goy neighbors will not be able to defile them anymore, most of them had on their hands clean blood of the town's Jewish people...

Jews in the synagogue during the 1920s

[Page 20]

Remember
by Dr. M. Dvorzhesky
Translated by Jerrold Landau

Remember the Holocaust of Israel, remember the loss and the bitterness, let it be fore you as a sign and a lesson for years throughout the generations;

Let this memory accompany you always – as you travel along the way, when you lie down, and when you get up;

Let the memory of brethren who are no more be bound to you forever;

Let this memory penetrate your flesh, your blood and your bones;

Grit your teeth and remember: when you eat your bread – remember; when you drink your water – remember; if you hear a song – remember; when the sun rises – remember; when night falls – remember; on festival days and holidays – surely remember;

If you build a house you should leave a breach, so that the destruction of the House of Israel will be before you always;

If you plow a field, you should set up a mound of rocks – as a monument to brethren who did not receive a Jewish burial;

When you bring your child to the wedding canopy, at the height of your joy, recall the memory of the children who will not be brought to the wedding canopy;

Be as one: the living and the dead: the victim and the survivor: those who went and are no more – and those who remained alive;

Hear, Jewish person, to the voice calling to you from the depths: do not be silent, do not be silent!

[Page 23]

Life and Folklore

The Grandfather from Kobylnik
Moshe Kulbak
Translated by Joseph Leftwich

My Grandmother

When my grandmother died
The birds sang.
The whole world with her kind deeds
And her good heart rang.

When they lifted my grandmother from her bed,
And laid her on the floor,
Everybody wept, because
The kind old lady was no more.

My grandfather walked up and down the room,
With anger in his eye,
Because he had promised grandmother,
He would be the first to die.

When they bore her into the town,
And the Christian folk cried,
And the Greek Catholic Priest lamented,
That such a good woman had died.

Only when the Shamash took his knife,
To cut in their clothes the mourning slash,
My uncles and my father cried aloud,
Like prisoners under the lash.

My Grandfather

My grandfather in Kobylnik is a plain man,
A peasant, with a fur skin coat, an axe and a horse,
And my sixteen uncles and their brother, my father,
Are plain folk, like cods of earth, lumpish and coarse.

They float rafts on the river, haul timber from the forests,
Toil hard like beasts of burden all day,
They eat supper together, all out of one basin.
Then fall into bed, and sleep like lumps of clay.

My grandfather can hardly manage to crawl
To his corner on the stove; he falls asleep there.
His legs carry him on their own to the stove.
They know the way, this many a year

Grandfather Dies

My grandfather came home at night from the field,
Made his bed, and said the Prayer of those about to die.
He stared hard at the world around him,
Saying to all his last goodbye.

My uncles and my father, his sons, stood silent,
Their hearts were heavy; they couldn't speak,
grandfather sat up in his bed, slowly,
And addressed them in a voice trembling and weak.

And this is what grandfather said to his sons,
The big, burly fellows, the sturdy ones:
You, Ortche, my eldest, you are the prop of the family,
The first in the field, and the last to come home,
The earth knows the feel of your plough,
Like in rich soil may your seed grow.

Rachmiel, who can compare with you in the meadow?
Your scythe works like fire in the corn,
The snakes know you in the swamps, and the birds in their nests,
May you be blessed in stable and barn.

You, Samuel, man of the river,
Always with a net and fish in your hand,
You have the smell of the fisherman about you,
Be blessed on the water, and on the land.

Night was falling, the sunset glow
Came through the window. No one stirred.
My uncles and my father stood dumbly,

Listening to my grandfather's last word.

Then my grandfather drew his knees together,
And lay down in the bed,
And closed his eyes for ever,
Not one tear my father and my uncles shed.

A bird sang in the forest.
The sunset glow went out.
And my father and my uncles stood there,
With their heavy heads bowed.

[Page 24]

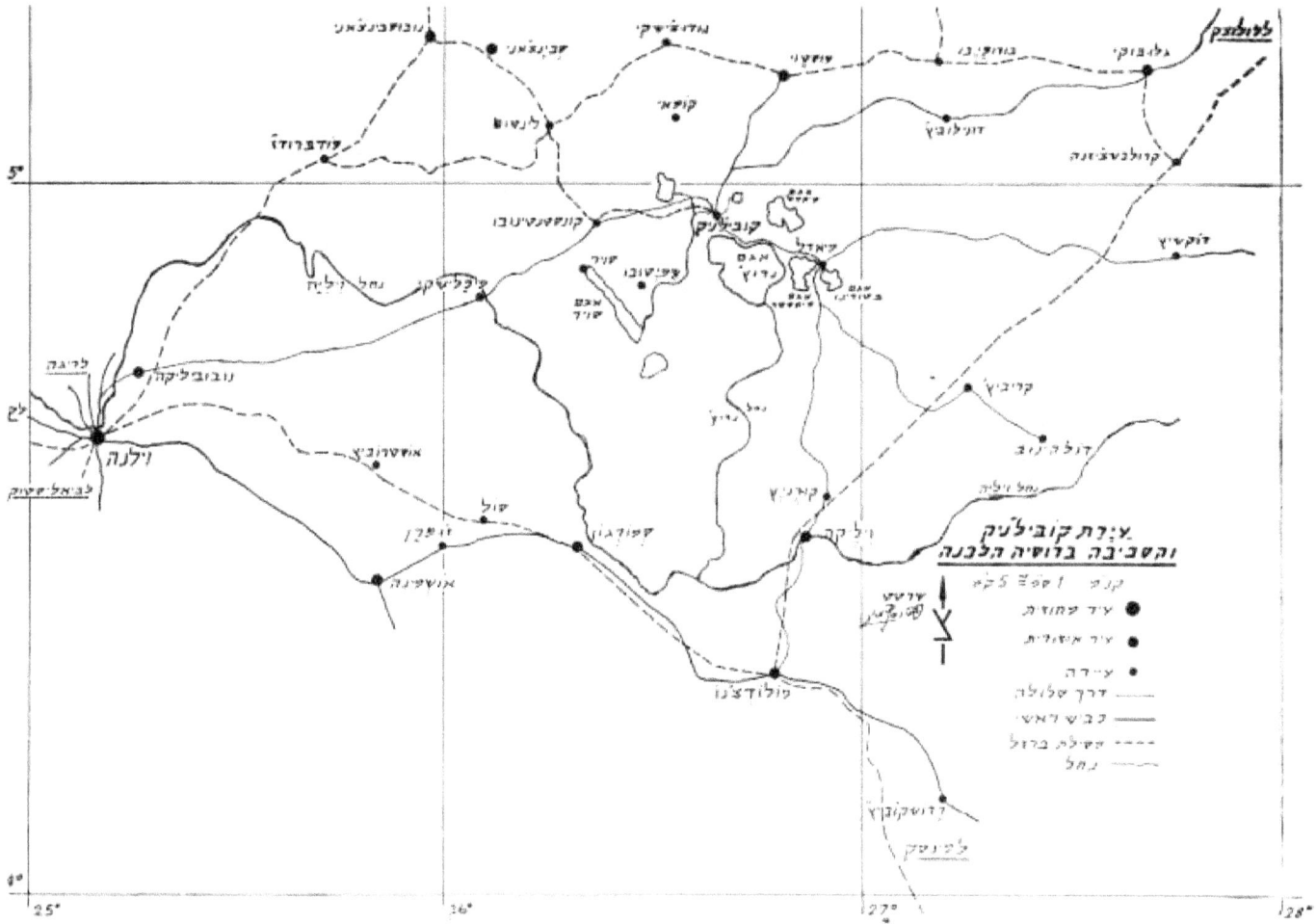

Legend for the map on the previous page:

Town of Kobylnik and its district in White Russia

North ↑

●	District city
•	Regular city
.	Town
_____	Paved Road
_____	Main road
--------	Railroad
~~	River

[Pages 25-29]

History of our Town Kobylnik

by Yitzchak Gordon of Haifa

Translated by Jerrold Landau

In memory of my dear mother Chaya–Musia Gordon.

Kobylnik, is a small town in Soviet Byelorussia (In earlier period, Jews called the district "Reisin"). From the 16th century to the third partition of Poland in 1795, it belonged to Lithuania and the Kingdom of Poland, which were united for 400 years.

After the partition, the district transferred to Russian hands during the rule of Ekaterina II (The Great). Russian rule lasted until the German conquest during the First World War, in 1915. During that war, the Germans occupied the town for about four years. Heavy battles between the opposing armies took place nearby. Kobylnik was under Polish rule during the inter–war period. The town was connected the Vilna region, Postów district. It was 105 kilometers from Vilna. It was on Lake Narach, one of the largest in Poland (with an area of 80 square km.), and on the Vilna–Polatsk Road.

A small river, which flowed into the Viliya River, passed through the town. Kobylnik served as the final stop on the narrow train that connected it with Lyntupy, as well as the broad train that went from Królewszczyzna, through Globky, to Vilna. The Russian–Polish border passed less than 100 kilometers east of the town. The border was broken by the Soviets in 1939, and Kobylnik passed to their rule. With the outbreak of the war between Germany and Russia in 1941, the town was conquered by the Germans, and remained under their yoke until the liberation by the Soviets in 1944.

***

When exactly the town of Kobylnik was founded, what is the meaning of the name, and from where did its first settlers come? We do not have exact answers to these questions, and the facts are clouded in the fog of recent history.

[Page 26]

Nevertheless, we do know the following from historical sources. Jews were already living in Western Europe from the first centuries of the millennium, having arrived via Rome. Other Jews reached Greece in earlier times, spreading to Constantinople and the Crimean Peninsula. However, they did not live in those places permanently, and their rights that they earned were dependent on the goodwill of the kings and nobility under whose protection they lived. From here we can perhaps surmise that the first Jews who came to Kobylnik area arrived because of persecution and deportations that they endured in their previous places of residence.

These persecutions lead to a migration of Jews from Western Europe to the east, which was populated by the Slavic nations. Jews reached the kingdom of Poland during the 13th century. In 1385, Poland and Lithuania united under the crown of King Władisław Jaggiełło. His cousin Witold was appointed as Grand Duke of Lithuania. During his wars with the Tatars, Witold expanded the borders of the country and reached southern Russia. He brought back Jews among his captives, and settled them in Byelorussia, Lithuania, and the vicinity of Vilna.

At the beginning of the 16th century, commerce with the lands of the west increased, especially in the export of agricultural and forestry products. The estate owners, who were not proficient in administrative business, looked for talented people to manage their businesses. They found the Jews to be fitting and appropriate in this area. Even though the Polish nobility was suffused with hatred toward the Jews, and related to them with disdain, they did not refrain from using them as a force against the city dwellers (Meisczinim) to weaken their influence.

Indeed, during that era there were Jews who left the royal cities and accepted the role of managing the estates and farms of the nobility. Others leased the tax depots and the tollbooths at intersections and rivers, which served as sources of income for the landowners. Jews owned taverns and inns in the areas between cities (*Krechemes*). Such a *krecheme*[1] is known to all of us in Kobylnik. It stood near the center of the town. Thy leased the mills, the milk business, the taverns, the fish ponds, the wineries, the orchards, and the like from the landowners. There were also Jews who obtained the rights to move mail from place to place ("Poszters: we all recall, for example, Bentze the Poszter, who lived in our town before the First World War). In addition to all this, Jews were also involved the grain, flax, and pig hair trade in the villages, as well as in the selling of haberdashery to the residents. This is how the Jews and their business endeavors spread in the villages and estates. At that time, official towns were formed from settlements that had once been "private" towns of estate landowners. Most of these towns were named for the landowners and nobility.

[Page 27]

Kobylnik during the era of the First World War

We have found evidence for these names through the names of the towns near Kobylnik. The names identify the family names of the landowners (boyars) of the area. Even our town of Kobylnik is named for a landowner named Kobylnicki. The landowners to whom the towns belonged granted Jews the rights to establish synagogues, inns for housing the poor, bathhouses, Jewish cemeteries, and other institutions that were necessary to conduct communal life in the towns.

The growth of these towns came primarily through the charters that were issued against the Jews during the rule of King Alexander I in 1804. The Jews were ordered to leave the villages in which they lived and move to towns. The deported villagers led to crowding and a rapid growth in the Jewish population of the towns. We find testimony to such from our times: Many Jews who lived in Kobylnik are called by names related to the nearby villages in which they had previously lived. For example, my father of blessed memory was called Avrahamel the Moczanier. Others were called Yisrael the Pasinker, Meir the Skarier, Shlomo the Szloker, Leibe the Wirenker, Zalman the Hatowiczer, Yisrael the Kuper, etc.

[Page 28]

In maps from the era of the "Lublin Unia" (the uniting of Poland and Lithuania in 1569), we find that in the district in which our town of Kobylnik exists, there were already towns such as: Globoky, Dolhinov, Smorgon, Oszmina, Radishkowce, etc. Even if we do not find Kobylnik on that map, we can surmise that the history of our town also began from that period. Support for this theory can be found in the Geographical lexicon of Poland, published in Warsaw in 1883, in which the following is written about Kobylnik: "During the 16th century, Kobylnik belonged to the Duchy of Greater Lithuania, and was owned by the nobility of the Zaborsky family. Later, it was transferred to the ownership of the Abrahamowicz family. Ludwig Bakszt Chominski, a writer and land registrar in the Duchy of Greater Lithuania sold Kobylnik to Marcin Oskrako, the prince of the palace of Oszmina. Later, Kobylnik was sold to Antony Swintorczki. In 1866 we find that, aside from the Swintorczki family, two other families of nobility had ownership in Kobylnik: Zybmunt Sziszko and Wansowicz.

***

Even though we have found general historical material on Kobylnik starting from the 16t century, we have not found any material confirming that Jews lived there during that time. We know about the existence of Jews in the town only from the 19th century. In the Yevreiska Encyclopedia, published approximately 100 years ago in Peterburg, the following is written about Kobylnik: "In 1847, the Jewish population of Kobylnik was 140. Fifty years later, in 1897, the general population was 1,055, including 591 Jews." In the aforementioned Geographic Lexicon, we find that the general population of Kobylnik was 370, including both Jews and gentiles. This number included 190 Catholics, 164 Jews, 7 Pravoslavs, 6 Muslims, and 4 families of "Strobirs. "

In the continuation of the same source, it states that Count Swirski built a wooden church for the Christians in 1651. It also states that there were five annual fairs in the town. In 1966, the district of Kobylnik includes also Swirani, Wierenki, and Chomiki. It had 315 houses, 67 agricultural settlements, and a population of 3,487 farmers.

[Page 29]

In various times Kobylnik served as an export depot for lumber, via barges on the Narach River. In the nearby village of Sciepieniewo, which is surrounded by large, thick forests, they would cut down the trees (especially the large pine trees), collect them on a hill on the banks of the river, and roll the large trunks into the water at an opportunity time. They would tie them into barges, and float them to distant places.

The barge drivers put up a tent in that area, which served as a sleeping place and a kitchen. Through the efforts of the drivers, and by rowing day and night, they floated the lumber eastward until the source of Narach River. From there, they lumber floated down the river until it reached the Viliya River, upon which the city of Vilna was situated.

In Vilna, they would take the lumber to a sawmill close to the city. The planks of lumber were used in the carpentry shops and factories for the manufacture of wood products for use within the country, and for the provision of wood products for export abroad.

Translator's Footnote
   1. A general store.

On the Narach

[Pages 30-50]

Holidays and Festivals in Town

by Meir Yavnai (Yavnovich)

Translated by Gilad Petranker

Edited by Toby Bird

A commemoration for my parents, my sister, my brother and their families who have perished in the Holocaust

Yamim Noraim – The High Holidays are at hand

The month of Elul in our town – as in all Jewish towns that have woven together the special Jewish way of life – moved the hearts of every Jew, young and old, man and woman. The hot summer sun, shining with all its might, brought peace to the entire universe. The wheat ripened; the fruit trees were heavy with fruit that ripened from day to day, and enjoyed the blessing of the sun from above and suckled the essence of life from the ground with their roots. From a distance echoed the doleful song of the harvesters – a song that heralded the approaching of the gloomy autumn days and the end of summer's glory. In the warm and delicate air, a thousand thin threads were woven, like the webs of a spider, which the rays of the sun made silver with their light. These threads were called colloquially "a woman's summer."

It seemed as if this summer peace would never be disrupted. The heart envisioned it as everlasting, imperishable. But early in the morning on the first days of Elul, the town – which had been sleeping and snuggling against the calming serenity of the late summer – was alarmed by the sound of a Shofar blasting lengthily, like a cry, awakening the sleepy hearts and calling them to repent, the hearts submerged in their slumber and enjoying the bright light of this blessed world. This blast moved the heart of every Jew. It announced that it is time for introspection; that the day of judgement is nigh. It cried to us to detach from the vanities of this world and to call for repentance, to face accusing Satan and to equip oneself, facing the Creator who gives life to every living being, with a sack of good deeds and acts of kindness.

And while the entire world is sleeping, and the night's chill of an approaching autumn covers the universe, doors would open and figures would slip away through them, with the sleep still clinging to their eyelids, and all their limbs still weary and craving rest. The warmth of their beds hasn't gone from them. And these figures would gather within the walls of the synagogue. The candles and the gas lamps were lit, and their light broke through the dark of the departing night. From afar rose the voices of children, begging to their Father in heaven: "Oh oh, merciful God, saving His grace unto thousands." In this refrain the voices rose and spread throughout the town which was still asleep. These voices would wake me from my sleep since I was too young to take part in saying the penitential prayers, and perhaps my will was not strong enough in those days to give up the hours of sleep just before sunrise, which are so sweet. Morning came. Each man would return home, carrying the bag of tefillin and tallit under his arm, and in his heart the hope that the prayer sent indeed would reach its destination and would perform the mission it had. And from holiday to weekday – the working day returns. The shops open; everyone goes about their business, to sell and buy, to haggle and bargain. But each one had in his heart the secret of sanctity as well as the hope that the sacred overcomes the secular, good overcomes evil, the advocate of truth overcomes accusing Satan.

Rosh Ha'Shana (New Year)

With the days of Elul approaching their end, the commotion in town grew towards the High Holidays. Their awe was felt everywhere. The number of people waking early to pray grew every day and the voice of people in prayer grew as well. The blast of the Shofar, which pierced the stillness of the universe before sunrise, increased the quivering of the heart and demonstrated more fiercely the approach of the deciding hours.

On the eve of Rosh Ha'Shana the prayer in the synagogue was longer than any other day. Inside the houses, the housewives diligently made their last preparations toward the holiday. The scent of the special food for the High Holidays was carried through the air. The ladder–shaped Challah bread was baked, for the prayers and wishes to ascend to heaven. Care was given to the bowls of honey, brought to the table to taste from, so that the year to come would be as sweet. A slice of watermelon was prepared, called "Kavineh," which had seeds peeking out like black eyes. Everything was scrubbed and polished in silence and moderation, befitting the upcoming serious moments. And when evening came, everyone hurried to the synagogue, illuminated with many candles, in memory of the people gone, whose memory would be mentioned the next day during the "Yizkor" prayer.

And the people pray, wrapped in their white Kittels (robes) and their books of prayer on the prayer stand before them, ready for the signal given by the prayer leader. The prayer pours out in the special melody of the High Holidays, all of which is sadness and purification in the face of the Creator – a melody of crying and supplication, momentarily changing into embellishment expressing joy of hope and security, ending with the blessings of "may you be written for a good year" and "so may you" – leaving the synagogue after the Arvit, after the "first knock" that was sent to the Gate of Mercy, and hurriedly returning to their homes to the festive and solemn dinner. They taste the honey and the special fruit and with an anxious yet hopeful heart they retreat to a night's rest before the next day, toward more penitence with the Creator.

And the next day, early in the morning, again, they flow to the synagogue. After the Shaharit comes the solemn moment when the prayer recited is "The King," and the fear of the King is felt all around; the fear of the judgment day becomes more tangible. And that fear rises and reaches its peak when the prayer is "Unetanneh Tokef" – "Let us speak of the awesomeness" – who for life and who for death, who by famine and who by thirst, who by sword and who by fire. Broken cries pierce through the wailing of the prayer leader; bitter sobbing of women comes from the ladies' section in hearing the horrible words. And with a pronounced emphasis, the entire congregation's voices follow the cantor, the words planting security in everybody's hearts: "and prayer and penance and charity pass over the harsh fate." And when the hour of blasting the Shofar is near, again the solemnity and the heaviness of the occasion grow. When everybody wraps their tallit around their heads and stand on their feet – the sounds of the Shofar pierce the awe–struck silence encompassing everything. Appeased and calm, everybody continues praying until noon. Jews return to their homes with a recovered stride with a solemn countenance. With the blessing of "May you be inscribed for a good year," they enter their homes for the lunch of the Rosh Ha'Shana.

After gathering strength, they would go before sundown to the river for the "Tashlikh." While reciting the prayer "And you will cast all our sins into the depths of the sea" they would shake the pockets of their garments to symbolize the shaking off of all sins and the tossing of all faults to the depths of the river, so that the current would carry them to unknown distances.

And again the Arvit arrives, and the next day would be the second day of the Rosh Ha'Shana, like the first day. The days of the Rosh Ha'Shana have ended, the two first days of the High Holidays, and the Ten Days of Repentance begin, leading up to the most awesome day of all – Yom Kippur, the Day of Atonement.

The Ten Days of Repentance and Yom Kippur

And between the Rosh Ha'Shana and Yom Kippur, between the new moon and the tenth day of the month, grows the air of repentance, prayer and charity. The droning of prayer becomes the basic tone of these days. It's voice is carried in the mornings through all the streets and yards near the synagogue, and these sounds bring with them a sort of sadness to the heart, along with the sadness of the days of autumn, boldly approaching.

And the days grow short. The doleful song of the harvesters at dusk joins the minor harmony, mantling the sadness. Women wearing headscarves and with eyes full of tears hurry beyond the bridge and disappear on the narrow path going between the yards of the gentiles – the Goyim – leading to the cemetery. There they stretch over the graves of their dear ones and call unto them with bitter sobbing or with quiet and broken weeping, to stand at their side at the deciding moments of the verdict. Their lips silently move, pouring out the wishes of their hearts, to come up before their Creator.

The hand opens generously, giving charity to every pauper and person in need. And on the Shabbat between Rosh Ha'Shana and Yom Kippur, the Shabbat of Repentance, the Jews swarm to the synagogue after a short afternoon nap, to hear the sermon of the rabbi about the matter of the day, that is repentance and the fear of the days. And the rabbi would weave into his words sayings of the old sages and parables, along with legends from days of old and stories from more recent times – and all of them are directed at evoking thoughts of repentance and regret, since the modern time has led us astray.

And on the night before Yom Kippur comes the shrieking of roosters from every Jewish home, from the attics or from the alcoves of stoves, roosters which have been disturbed, taken out of their places and tied up for Kapparot – atonement. With a heart full of faith, Jews – old and young, men and women – swing the rooster above their heads and their lips move silently with deep intent: "Men dwelling in darkness and the shadow of death... this is my atonement, this will go to death and I will go to a long and good life, Amen." And from the yard of the Shochet –the butcher – echo the last chords of these poor birds, who are slaughtered for the atonement of the humans, and for the feast ending the tiresome exhausting fast.

At the eve of Yom Kippur, the town resembled a camp that was called for duty. Every deed and every step, the keeping of each and every detail in custom and tradition kept for generations, were directed into a single purpose – to take away the harsh fate, to add floor above floor to the building called Teshuva – repentance, a building which was started on the first day of the month of Elul. And again, the ladder shaped Challah bread was baked. And it was a custom to eat exceedingly before the fast, as it was a Mitzva to hold the fast. And special Jewish cuisines were brought to the table: bowls of soup with meat–filled dumplings and the ladder–shaped Challah. And again, a meal – and they would hurry to the public bath house to cleanse the body well before the day of judgement.

And from house to house the Jews would pass to ask for forgiveness for offences that had hurt somebody's dignity during the year. Bitter rivals who would not exchange a word during the year would make peace on that day. With a serious countenance and an air of importance, the heads of the families would sit themselves at the table for the final meal before the fast, an early meal.

And when they finished eating the delicacies that were carefully prepared, all the members of the family would hurry to the synagogue for the Minha and the "Kol Nidre" prayer. The entire town, even though it was not wholly Jewish, wore the air of Yom Kippur. Even the Goyim felt that during this day, something serious was taking place in the homes of the Jews and, especially, in the synagogue.

And the memorial candles would be brought to the synagogue to be lit. Jews would take off their shoes and would wrap themselves with their Kittles. At the entrance to the synagogue they would put up tables with bowls for charity with signs next to them. In recent years, the bowl of the Jewish National fund appeared next to the other bowls. Everybody saw a holy and exalted duty to donate to the different bowls of charity, each one according to his ability and perhaps above that. The floor of the synagogue was covered in dry hay, letting off its special scent, the scent of a field.

The beadle of the synagogue, the Shamash rabbi Shaya–Yosef would walk around in a manner of dignity, wrapped in his white Kittle and carry a strap, which he used to adminster the customary whips to whomever desired them. Jews would stretch themselves on the floor in front of him, kneeling, and he would count to forty minus one.

The dark would descend over the town. The candles and lamps would shine around. The congregation would hurry to its place. The set of prayers would begin, starting with a whispered "Be'Tfillah Zaka" – "in a pure prayer."

The hour of "Kol Nidre" is approaching. At the entrance to the synagogue, by the door and in the entrance hall, some of the Christians gather up as well, to witness the "awes of this night." Among the people gathering are the dignitaries of the town: the head of police, the head of council, important officials etc. and I remember the hearts of the children would be proud – here, even the Goyim would honor us with visiting the synagogue on this day.

The Shamash would beat on the table of the platform. The "Kol Nidre" prayer is recited with its traditional melody in the breathless silence. The congregation joins the cantor. The Torah scrolls are taken out of the Torah Ark in awe and reverence. The words "Light is sown for the righteous, and gladness for the upright in heart" are heard and from this point the entire congregation would gradually take a more active part in the prayer. The voice of the cantor and of the entire congregation blend with each other. The doleful and pleasant melodies are sung by everyone. The "Yaalu Tachanuneinu" prayer, "May our supplications ascend at eventide; our pleas come in the morning," purifies the heart and soothes; and the prayer approaches its end.

Some of the people praying stay in the synagogue to stand in their place – the place of connection with their Creator – during the entire night, and most of the congregation leaves. Sometimes a light rain, heralding the coming autumn, would start trickling. It seemed as though nature added its bleakness to the bleakness of the moment, accentuating the seriousness of those returning home from the prayer of Yom Kippur. And with total silence they would depart from each other with the blessing of "Le'Shana Tova Techatemu," "For a good year you shall be confirmed," and disappear into the darkly illuminated houses. Bit by bit they would go to the night's rest, to gather strength for the next day, the day of fasting and torment, the long day of prayer from morning till night.

And early in the morning the synagogue would again be filled with people praying. After the ordinary Shaharit, the people in front of the ark would be replaced. The intended cantor would take his place by the ark. "The King" is trilled by the cantor, and the congregation joins him with the traditional melody of the High Holidays. Bit by bit the words of the people pour out, the prayers are loudly recited – sitting down and standing up – and again the congregation is called up during the Musaf prayer when the cantor opens with "Unetanneh Tokef." And with describing the tribulations expecting man, the crying is fiercer than that of Rosh Ha'Shana, all according to the will of the Almighty. Low and heartbreaking wails come from the ladies' section. Children with their curious eyes search for their mothers to see them by the narrow openings in the attic, where they pour their words to the Creator. Their wails grow with the mention of the dead. Some of the people hurry home after an additional Musaf prayer to rest a bit and gather strength.

After the Minha, the marks of the fast are seen everywhere; signs of fatigue and paleness are on the faces, but it seems that everybody is feeling relieved. A pleasant weariness is prevalent as well as the satisfaction of those who have done their work honestly. And maybe the emotion, like a child's, that has been reconciled with his father filled the hearts of the congregation at that time. And in those moments of quiet everyone sits, rests and anticipates the song that has become a part of the tradition of Yom Kippur, like an intermezzo between the Minha and the concluding prayer, the Ne'ila. In a deep and pleasant voice, Rabbi Eliezer, with the gray–streaked black beard, starts singing with a kind smile spreading over his face, and the congregation follows suit, from one melody to the other – the songs would flow heartily and slowly and even "Ha'Tikva" was in repertoire of recent years, if my memory does not mislead me.

The evening has settled. It's time for the Ne'ila. Again, a time of solemnity, but softer than in the commencing of the fast. With renewed energy and with a new hope, takes place the last charge on the Gate of Mercy: "Open a gate for us at the time of the locking of the gate," flows the pleasant voice of the cantor and the congregation. A last request is sent to heaven, before the verdict is sealed. Everybody believes and hopes that the harsh fate is removed, that the prayer and everything done will bear the desired fruit.

And the blast of the Shofar is encouraging and brings hope: a hasty Arvit with "Next year in Jerusalem," the blessing of "Gmar Khtima Tova," "May you be written and confirmed." While leaving the synagogue they quickly bless the moon, and in tired steps the Jews go home to the meal after the fast. In everyone's heart there is a feeling of leaving a heavy burden behind.

Sukkot

And already at the parting of the holiday, after the end of the meal, lanterns were flashing in the yards of the houses: Jews were busy fixing the first pillar for the Sukkah about to be erected on the days between Yom Kippur and Sukkot.

The preparations for the holiday are performed in happiness, feeling relieved after the solemn days fearing judgement. How happy were the children of Israel in those days, especially while erecting the Sukkah. Who could forget the joy of taking part in the work?! So diligently and willfully the toddlers of Israel would present to their father a beam, a pillar or a nail, who was busy with erecting the Sukkah! How joyful would the heart be, in sight of the green canopy, the Schach, that was brought in a wagon from the forest by the Goy or by the eldest son on his own, if he owned a wagon and a horse. The scent of the forest would spread and a homely warmth would enfold everything, when we would huddle between the four shaky walls roofed by the Schach. And the children would rush to cover the floor with yellow sand and the housewife would decorate the walls with anything befitting decoration. A table would be put in, benches or a few chairs. The table would be covered with a white tablecloth, and how great was the anticipation of the children for the evening, for the first dinner in the Sukkah, with the stars winking from above through the crack in the Schach. And anxious would the heart be, that the sitting in the Sukkah would be interrupted by rain, since the time of autumn was at hand and its presence was felt in the air; and more than once the rain poured down on the very first day of Sukkot.

And obviously there is no holiday celebration without a festive prayer. And Jews would stream into the synagogue fresh and with renewed energy, their faces shining, and in their hearts the joy of holiday. The prayer ends with a jolly melody, expressing the joy in the heart. And with the greeting of "Happy holiday," "Good holiday," they would hurry home to the illuminated Sukkah, the family atmosphere, the special holiday cuisines served in the Sukkah. The sound of festive songs breaks out from the meagre looking Sukkot, but a stranger would not understand the elation and the holiday joy filing these four walls from within, covered with branches of fir and willow.

The seven Ushpizin – the Sukkah guests – are invited to come. The children fall asleep and are taken into the house. Another long time passes with the songs and special prayers sounding through the night. It seemed that the world has returned to the wandering of the Israelites through the desert, when they sat in their Sukkot on the journey back to their land.

It's morning. Again, the town wakes up to life. Rabbi Shaya–Yosef is dressed in his black robe, the Bekishe, and his silvery quivers in the wind. In one of his hands he holds a box padded with strands of linen with the Etrog, the citrus fruit, and in his other hand he holds the Lulav, the young palm tree frond, surrounded by branches of myrtle and willow – Hadass and Arava – tied to palm tree branches with strands from last year's Lulav. And how wonderful that Lulav would be for us, the children! I can still remember to this very day: with shaking hands, we would hold the Etrog and the Lulav, Rabbi Shaya–Yosef would say the blessing, and we would repeat and delightfully shake the Lulav to the four winds. Mother is also called from the kitchen to fulfill the Mitzva of blessing the Etrog and Lulav; the rest of the adults hurry up to fulfill the Mitzva as well, and Rabbi Shaya–Yosef leaves the house and goes on to visit other houses.

Now there are the days of Chol Ha'Moed, the intermediate days of the holiday. The rains often pour, heralding the approaching winter, but the air of the holiday still lingers, reigning supreme. A strange chord steals its way into the air of the holiday, a chord forgotten with the passing of Yom Kippur – the day of Hoshana Rabba, the seventh day of Sukkot, which is approaching. We children know – from listening to the grownups – that on that day there is still hope to remove the harsh fate that has been sealed on Yom Kippur. The children delight on this day in the special occupation it summons: the picking of branches of willow trees and arranging them into bunches for the day of Hoshana Rabba.

In the chilly and foggy morning, we would awaken and go to the river and the forest to pick these branches. On the way, we would visit the chestnut trees which would shed their fruit at night. How we would delight with that fruit, still in its green shell which had cracked when the fruit fell from the tree. We would find the fresh colors charming, the brown and the white. This fruit, when still smooth and fresh, would get collected like a precious treasure into our pockets and fill our hearts with endless joy. And from the tree to the main purpose – picking the willow branches. Heavily laden we would return to the town and supply the branches in small bunches to anyone who would desire them, to whip them during the prayer. "Please God, sav – sounds the cantor, and it's time to whip the branches. The whipping sounds fill the space of the synagogue, and the children join the Mitzva with all their hearts and their childish innocence.

And at home, special cuisines are served: again, dumplings like on the eve of Yom Kippur, a white Challah bread, etc. Bit by bit we enjoy the blessing of the holiday, fearing every passing moment. But the main part of the holiday, its center, is still ahead: after the celebration of Beit Ha'Shoeva – which was a big deal, especially for the grownups, and for us children was not completely clear – would come a day all good, filled with the joy of the Torah, a day which we had been anticipating, Simchat Torah. Who will not remember the flag, preparing the stick for the flag and crowning it with a hollow carrot or an apple, a base for the candle?! And unlike nowadays, how many hardships did a boy in town have in obtaining the flag and stick! And undoubtedly that was why it was so pleasing and joyful to have gotten it. We anticipated the fall of the evening, the time for the rounds– the Hakafot– the real reveling in the Torah. Everybody would pride himself in his fancy outfit and flag. The candles would be lit. The flags wave on the hands of children, shaking with joy and fearing the safety of their goods.

Simchat Torah

The synagogue was bathing in a sea of lights, hustling and bustling with people. On this day, the women were allowed to mingle with the crowd. Women, children, toddlers – all stuffed together, with the joy of the holiday gleaming from their faces. The toddlers are carried up, lifted high so they could see what's taking place. The Shamash Shaya–Yosef is running around gleaming, radiating holiday and joy. The prayers are said with joy. Everything is tense for the bringing out of the Torah scrolls – the Hakafot. The verses of

"Ata horeta lada'at"– "Unto you it was shown" – are festively said. The scrolls are taken out and given out to the crowd. The first round starts. The first one parading recites the right verse, and after him come the carriers of the scrolls. Some carry a scroll in one hand, and in the other hand – a little boy. The people going around dance and sing. The crowd all around kisses the scrolls, touching them with a finger and then kissing the finger – kissing the Torah through the finger... and who could forget the rising excitement, the growing joy, and many pranks pulled by the adults, many of whom came to the synagogue properly drunk. Drunk Jews – do not think lightly of it. And the rounds go on and become a whirlwind of circling feet, running and dancing. Everything is swept away with the current of joy and celebration. And I remember, a light sadness would always slip into this joy of mine – worrying about the approaching end of joy.

The next day the synagogue is full of glee again; rounds, and ascending to the Torah: the ascent of the Chatan Torah, the groom of the Torah, the ascent of the children, wrapping themselves with one joined Tallit – "with all of the boys" – and then splitting into Minyans, groups of ten. The Torah scrolls are taken out of the synagogue and into private houses, to Minyans. Proudly and with a calm of holiday, Jews accompany the scroll carried in the hands of one among them to his house. There they spice up the joy of the holiday with brandy and cookies. We remember the stories of the elders, of the true holiday joy that they had seen at their time, when Jews who would be serious year–round, would go from house to house, break open the stoves and take the holiday foods to bring to the town's market square, where they would serve them to the drunken feasters on a yard's gate, that had been taken off its hinges. The food would be eaten, washed down with drinks, and the Jews would break into dance, before the eyes of a crowd of curious people, among which even Goyim would watch.

But we heard of that only from the stories; we did not see with our own eyes. And we remember the joy in the houses. After prayer, groups of Jews would gather, mostly relatives and friends, from the same circle. They would go from house to house and sit around tables set with food and drink, and the drink would be guzzled. "Cheers, Yidden (Jews), cheers!" The housewife would happily serve and everyone would harass one of the drunkards, wanting to see him in his disgrace – then give him cup after cup enjoying his looks and delighting in his senseless drunken talk.

Bit by bit they would scatter to their homes with the family dinner still to come. What magic these moments had! How much the strong connection stood out between the members of the family, between related families, and the whole of Israel. On that day, all the quarrels and fights of the entire year would be forgotten. Enemies and rivals would kiss and the memory of their animosity would vanish, as if it had never existed.

As mentioned, this was a day entirely good, a day of Simchat Torah, the joy of the Jewish person, invested throughout the year with the worries and the burden of livelihood, the trouble of the individual and the whole of Israel. It was such a pity that the day did not stay longer, and with its end came the concern to town, that was brought by the approaching cold winter: wood for fire, warm clothing, stocking potatoes and storing them for the cold days of winter, keeping the apartment against the cold etc., etc. And children were obligated to go back to the "Cheder," the class, after the High Holiday and Sukkot, for the long winter period. Again, being confined in the narrow room from morning till evening, to part with the willows of the river, the charming chestnuts, the wild pears that were piled in crates or in piles, and were stocked in the attic on the dry hay.

The days of rain, a Polish autumn: the mud covers every street, path and trail. Unwelcome days, an autumn sadness veils the meager and bent houses of the town. As if it were from the whipping of the raindrops on their roofs, it seems that these houses are even more sagging. The days grow shorter and the nights are long, endless, infinite. Only once in a while does life pierce through the dark of the clouds and push away the bleakness of the world.

One morning the entire universe wakes up and everything is clothed in white, a cover of snow. The black of the mud is covered in white. The trees are coated with a white cover, the roofs are white and mischievous boys go out to roll up the clumps of snow that was piled overnight and to make it into a snowman. Others have snowball fights, with a mischievous and gleeful spirit. On the street, the sleigh is seen instead of the wagon, which until yesterday had its wheels sunken in mud. The snowflakes keep falling ceaselessly. People clothed in furs or winter coats, wearing boots are seen treading through the snow – winter took hold of the town. The frost, the cold, grow from day to day. The snow creaks underfoot. Sometimes a snowstorm breaks, and no one leaves home. People abundantly feed the stoves and keep warm by them. The double-glazed windows are taken down from the attic and are set in their frames, with the gap between them filled with sand. The cracks are covered with strips of paper and only here and there is an opening left to keep the apartment aired. In the evenings, the housewives sit and knit, weave and repair a sock by the light of the gas lantern and the warmth of the stove. The men gather for the game of cards, which started spreading through the town like an unwanted plague.

On the market days, the town is filed with life. The tracks of the wagons, man and beast soil the white mantle which wrapped the town during the week, but the next day everything will be covered in white again. The trees stand with white robes. Early in the morning white smoke rises from the chimneys in the roofs of the houses; in the chill of the morning the housewives hurry to the well to draw water from the wells, surrounded by hills of ice, so much that the people carrying the water are in danger of slipping. Sometimes the men go and dig through the ice, to allow access to the well. Here and there a sleigh is seen laden with barrels of laundry, hurrying to the river, where they would dig through the ice down to the water, to rinse the undergarments that were laboriously washed at home.

The children of Israel hurry to the Cheder to study from the mouth of their Rabbi. Unlike the days of summer, they are confined to the narrow room for a whole day and strain their minds and talents to come up with various excuses to go out and cause some mischief. At noon, they hurry home for lunch and will come back carrying lanterns with candles inside, to light their way home at dark late at night, through the dark alleys. On the short recesses they go out to have snow fights or slip away to skate on the ice–covered river.

From Sukkot to Hanukah there is no holiday, apart from the Shabbats which will partly be dedicated to prayer and an exam in the Torah that they had learned in the Cheder by their fathers.

Hanukah

A few days before Hanukah the efforts would be to start to get hold of a Dreidel and a few pennies to play. Even cards would not be deemed too lowly if they could only be found. Some try to melt zinc or tin into a wooden mold, to make a Dreidel – but mostly that would not be fit for playing, and they would settle for a wooden dreidel. The menorahs are taken out of their hiding place; bunches of candles appear in the house.

The first Hanukah candle was lit in the windows of the houses. The blessing of the lighting of the candles, "Ha'nreot halalu" and "Maoz tzur yeshuati," are sung by the father, and from the kitchen spreads the smell of the latkes fried in goose fat, which were fattened for weeks and slaughtered a few days before Hanukah, to collect the fried fat and its fried dried bits called Gribenes. Guests are invited to the festive latke feast, and the game of cards, which becomes these days a game acceptable by every Jew, occupies all the members of the family as well as those coming for the feast. And obviously those who have been playing cards all through the winter's evenings keep themselves busy on the nights of Hanukah and stay up late. Sometimes one of the card players might return home to meet the curses and scolding of his wife, for losing his last pennies and so deprived the house of its many urgent needs. More than once this late–night meeting would end with a loud fight between the husband and wife, which would fuel the gossip the next day of those hunting for sensations in the vacancy of town.

Anyone going through the streets of town at night on the nights of Hanukah will see the flames, flickering through the windows of the Jews, piercing the white cover of the glass. The candles of the menorah would wake the warmth of the days of old in the heart, tell of the miracles and the wonders that were done to our forefathers in those days and today.

The eight days of Hanukah have passed and the town goes back to the everyday sleepy winter life, and the mundane businesses, the worries of livelihood, replenishing the wood for the stove that had become scanty through the first months of winter. On these days Shaya–Yosef can be seen slowly striding through the snowy streets, going from house to house to collect the few pennies for the poor, for medical needs and for heating up the houses of the needy. Bit by bit his frozen, shaky hands would write the donation of the week in the wrinkled notebook.

On the 15th of Kislev, there is much commotion among the members of Chevrah Kadisha, holding the annual feast in memory of Rabbi Shneur Zalman coming out of prison. As a boy I couldn't have understood back then – what the business was of this celebration, this feast and these delicacies abundantly given to the people who deal with burying the dead. The happiness of the people who do such bleak work which horrifies both old and young could not be resolved in the minds of the town's children and seemed unbecoming to their work– the work of burying and cleansing of the dead. "Amcha," simple people who did not have the honor of a decent ascent to Torah or a decent place in the synagogue are exalted on this feast, feeling their importance and guzzling the wine until they are drunk, feasting on the many delicacies that were abundantly prepared and which, perhaps, only at this time of year they will be able to enjoy.

And from holiday to weekday. Up until Tu Bi'shvat, the 15th of the month, was a day whose importance only the children in the Cheder felt, with the taste of dried up shriveled carobs and a few almonds which were said to have come from Eretz Israel. In their imagination, they would strain to float from the cold land of frost to the land of warmth, where on this day would be the trees' new year.

Purim

But compared to the dullness of this day, Tu Bi'shvat, the coming of Purim was really felt in town. Sometimes its coming was heralded by the winds of spring, which started blowing through the world, thawing the "candles" of ice hanging from the cornices of the houses. The children expect this day with anticipation, and rushed to equip themselves with various weapons against the bitter foe, Haman. All their talents and tricks were mustered to get hold of the gunpowder, the pistons, the keys and nails, the matches, the rattlers and all the other props.

It's the evening of the reading of the scroll in the synagogue. Set for battle, the mischievous children wait for the reading of the scroll, their ears anticipating the uttering of the name Haman from the reader of the scroll in the traditional melody. When the name is all but uttered, a bellowing thunder of shots and various tools and weapons fill the entire synagogue. And the weapons would be re–armed for the next round... smoke would fill up the synagogue, and joy would fill the hearts of the children of Israel, since they were given – and not often did they have this privilege – to deliver all their mischief with permission, in public and uninterrupted. And the louder, the better. And the next morning the whole scene would repeat itself. I think only the day of Simchat Torah might compete with the day of Purim in the glee it would fill in the hearts of all, especially those of the town's children.

And neither would the adults withhold themselves. The preparations would be made beforehand, for the Mishloach Manot – the sending out of food as gifts– and for the feast of Purim. The feet of those carrying the plate, the bowl of the Mishloach Manot, were treading through the snow, melting slowly on the town's streets, from house to house. And the bowl would be filled with coins: money for the main people who would send out the Mishloach Manot, such as the rabbi, the Shamash and the Shochet, who had the Mishloach Manot as one of the sources of their meager livelihood.

On the feast of Purim, the relatives and friends would gather, drinking and eating, and everyone would be merry and joyful with the air of brotherhood, with the air of a whole Jewish celebration, which did not frequent the hearts and homes of the town's Jews who would be burdened with the worries of livelihood and surrounded by the hatred of Goyim and bitter foes. The memory of that miracle, the memory of Haman's downfall, warmed the hearts of all and brought hope and faith, that that would be the end of all the foes and accusers who rise against us every generation. Even the spring weather added its warmth to the heart, which had become frozen during the long days of winter in the chill and frost. And Passover would be winking from afar, approaching, the holiday of our liberty, coming out of slavery into liberty, the holiday of the Matzos.

Passover

And immediately after Purim the preparations would start for the Passover, that is to the main issue of the holiday – preparing the Matzos for baking, as was the custom in many towns of Israel in those days, manually and together, with mutual help: "Fodredn." And there would no other days like this – with the winds of spring, the melting of the snow, the frost and the ice covering the river – to warm the hearts of the town's Jews, to arouse hidden and unconscious hopes, to encourage them and strengthen them in the harsh war of survival.

But we'll go back to the commotion toward Passover and first and foremost, the baking of the Matzos. The town's people would divide into groups and would agree upon the baking to take place in one of their houses, with a big enough baking oven, and with ample room for all of those taking part in the baking, that is, the dough kneaders, the water pourers, the flour spillers, the Matzah piercers with the dough docker, and the baker, who puts the Matzos in the oven and removes them, and the disperser of the dough, called in Yiddish "Der Meyre Halter." And when they would all agree they would also set the time and place to bake a Matzah Shmurah – a guarded Matzah – a task which was done by men who were specially trained.

And how much joy did the children of town have. Here is a holiday coming, here– in a few days they would be free from the Cheder two weeks before the holiday, free to run to the river to witness the thawing of the ice and the cracks forming in it, and the blocks of ice carried away with the rising water, going up from day to day, putting the inhabitants of both banks in danger. And how great it would be to join the grown–ups in the "fodred" and help with the work of baking the Matzos, according to the capacity and age of each one. The young ones, who had been doing this Mitzva for the first time, get the more minor jobs which they view as important as a rung in the works' ladder.

And this was the order of work according to their value and importance: pouring water and flour into the basin– the first rung in the ladder and the least important. A more respectable level – the Meyre Halter, meaning the dough holder – sitting at the head of the table and dispersing bits of it to the women and girls to roll on the long tables until they become round and flat Matzos. Another level, with doubtful importance, is the receiving of the flattened Matzah from the kneaders and bringing it on a round piece of wood to the table of the docker to be pierced and then to the baking room. By the way, this role was dangerous, since any toddler who might drop the Matzah on the way to the table, or if he would stumble on the bread peel of the "high priest," serving in the most important role– the baking itself, putting the Matzos into the oven and removing them– such a toddler would be severely scolded.

But the most revered and desired role by all children was the role of the Redlen – the piercing. That is a role which requires a great deal of training, agility and special talent. But how could you acquire practice when you are not permitted to the "Holy of Holies," the table of the Redlen, and not be given a chance to test your strength?! And if you did get a break and you finally get the privilege of trying, when the tired piercer feels kind enough to hand you the docker, you need to prove your agility and produce a properly pierced Matzah, worthy of entering the oven and coming out with no blisters and not swollen. And if, God forbid, you failed your task– then the baker would give you a taste of his bread peel, and would shamefully throw you out of the "Holy of Holies" with oaths and curses, to the laughter of the professional piercers. The man who was especially dreaded by those who gave the piercing task a try was Moshe David Dimenstein, God rest his soul. And I remember well the feeling of the long bread peel coming down on my shoulder after my numerous efforts, mostly ending with failure. How happy would be the boy who would overcome the hardships and the suffering after many failures – to produce a properly pierced Matzah. After that he would win the title of "Redler" and could come into the "congregation of God," to be one of the experienced and seniors of the profession. With enthusiasm and great devotion, the happy boy would replace the payed professionals and work for hours next to the table as a resident, who would even be recognized by Moshe David as a professional who was qualified by him – and not by the long peel but by a compliment. Indeed, it was doubtful if there would be a happier man on that day in the entire world.

The baked Matzos would be piled in tall baskets padded with pure white and ironed sheets, and after the quota baked for someone would be filled, the basket would be carried by hand to the house, with the children of the family happily escorting the procession.

And in the houses, in those days, there would be great commotion toward the holiday. After the cold had passed and the spring with its warmth had melted the frost on the windows, the double-glazed windows would be removed and carried to the attic. The cleaning work would commence, thoroughly scrubbing the entire house, every room and every corner. All the portable furniture would be taken out, all the walls painted white, the furniture cleaned outside with warm water, the windows washed – to sum it up: everything was cleansed and polished, as if to welcome a respectable and important guest. The children would run around, couldn't find a place to settle in and would be a nuisance for the adults. When they would appear in one place they would be driven out only to appear somewhere else, to be driven out from there as well.

And when the task of sweeping and cleaning would be over, the furniture would be taken back in and the Passover cutlery would be brought down from the attic; these would be taken for Hagalah, purifying them by immersing them in water. Knives and forks would be tied on a long rope to form a long chain; along with the other dishes they would be taken to the river, that had lately been freed from the shackles of ice, and were dipped in it. The children who were permitted to place the cutlery as part of the Hagalah would be delighted. The ritual of the Hagalah would take place in the public bathhouse where the cutlery would be dipped in boiling water. I fondly watched the plates and saucers, which had golden or silver rims and the cups adorned with golden lines and lovely drawings. What special warmth would fill the heart in sight of these! But one would not get enough of these sights and immediately would be called to the pestle for the grinding of the Matzos. This wooden tool with a deep recess was meant for receiving the crispy Matzos, and a big wooden mortar would be used to crush the Matzos and turn them into flour or flakes for soup. This task was prized by the children who did it, but they soon grew tired of it because of the great effort it required.

And the last day before the holiday had arrived: the eve of Passover – "Put thy shoes from off thy feet." On the evening before, they would start the ritual of Beur Chametz, the burning of the leaven. Earlier, crumbs of leaven would be scattered in various places in the house, and then the father would walk around, carrying a candle, "searching" for them and finding them, cleaning well the places where the leaven had been "found" with a rag. On the next day, a sale of the leaven would be held at the Rabbi's house. On that day, yellow sand would be spread on the floor, white tablecloths would be put on the tables, and very special care would be given, so that not a bit of leaven would be found lest the Passover would be damaged. And since the bread had completely vanished from the house and it is still forbidden to eat the Matzah, we ate a lot of potatoes – a "neutral" food kosher for Passover. Everyone would rush to the bathhouse to wash themselves in the boiling water and to go and sit up on the sweating benches, where the steam would rise from the stove in front of which would be hot stones that had streams of hot water poured on them. Above the top bench came the voices of Jews enjoying the choking heat and the whipping of brooms being brought down on their hot bodies. I especially remember the one who was the bravest in lying up on the top bench, a place where only few would be able to hold on – Yenkel Yanovski, who would growl "ay, oh oh"– in mixed pain and pleasure. Washed and cleansed the respectable heads of families, with their children, would emerge from the bathhouse, and rush home for the final potato meal before the Seder and hurry to the synagogue.

And how great was the light in the synagogue that was also cleaned and prepared for this festive evening! Many lights were lit in honor of the holiday, including the gas lamp, which Shaya–Yosef had skillfully taken care of a long time before sundown, a skill which only he possessed. Light and the joy of holiday was all around. The holiday prayer would be happily recited and with an elated air, with everyone filled with self–importance, mixed with a feeling of a bit of Jewish pride. After the end of prayer, they would greet each other with "Gut yomtov" – "Happy holiday"– and would march home with their families to the tables laden for the Seder.

The pillows to recline on for the father on the bench is next to the head of the table, the bowl in the center, everything in accordance with the custom.

Out of all the houses, the shrill voices of the children of Israel would be heard, asking the Four Kushiyot – the four questions – "Ma nishtana ha'layla haze mikol ha'leylot?" – "How is this night different from all nights?" and after the questions would come the answers with the traditional melody: "We were slaves to Pharaoh in Egypt." The first cup and then again Haggadah, and more Haggadah up to the washing of the hands – and then the festive feast would commence in every house, even in the houses of the poor, who would not be forgotten, since the able would remember the Mitzvah of "Kamcha Depascha." The Kneidlach, the matzo balls, and the Chremslach, the small fritters filled with goose fat practically melting in the mouth, and the delicious chicken soup. The doors would be opened for the saying of "Shefoch chamatcha el ha'goyim" – "Pour out thy wrath on the gentiles." Again, the Haggadah. The song of "Chad Gadya" comes out of every house. The children await the coming of the prophet Eliyahu, but fall asleep and are carried one by one to their beds. Only the head of the family and the grownups go on reading the final chapters of the Haggadah, with their eyes slowly closing. Hush, everything is silent. The town is asleep, with only the dogs barking in the yards of the Goyim breaking the silence of night and holiday. But the peace in the Jewish heart is encouraged and strengthened, because he will remember the verse "U'livey Israel lo yecheratz kelev leshono" – "And unto the people of Israel even a dog would not move its tongue."

On the next day, the housewives would rise early to prepare the dishes for lunch. The young ones also would get up to receive their share of nuts, nuts from Turkey and local nuts, as well as big nuts called "Veleshe Nis." Right after breakfast they would rush to meet their friends and play the game of nuts. A plank would be set against a wall, for rolling down the nuts. The nut hitting another on the floor would be awarded to its owner who collected both and the game would go on. Those who would be lucky would fill up their pockets, and those unlucky would have empty pockets, and they would shamefully return home and beg their mothers to get another share. Others played the game of "odds and evens," with their closed palms holding the nuts, so that their amount wouldn't show. Fights would sometimes start as well, often with children playing, and might even turn into scuffles.

Passover in town: there would be no days like the days of Passover with light and celebration, because along with the celebration of the heart, nature would awaken all around, showing its signs in everything – the rejuvenation of nature and Jewish person alike.

Shavuot

And from Passover to Shavuot. The hot days of summer, the days of the Counting of the Omer, and only one day, Lag Ba'omer, is to remind us that not everything is secular in the world. But that day would go by almost unnoticed in town, apart from the children in the Cheder who would make themselves bows and arrows and would roam the field and forest.

At a certain distance from Lag Ba'omer, the holiday of Shavuot would wink, the holiday of Matan Torah – the giving of the Torah. And dairy foods: "Blintzes," cheese–filled dumplings. The floor of the house would be covered with yellow sand; greens for Shavuot bring the memory of the Bikkurim, the first fruit. The holiday prayer in the illuminated synagogue and the holiday rest – that is the holiday of Shavuot as I have it imprinted in my memory. The holiday did leave a deep impression on the children.

After Shavuot, the scorching days of summer would begin. The children would taste of everything to the fullest. Bathing in the river, picking and stealing fruit, carrying off fruit from wagons and shops of the peasants, going afar to the pea fields to fill up pockets with pea pods and even the inside of the shirt up to the chest. These trips had many dangers involved since the unlucky boy who would be caught stealing would have his hat taken away and even his shirt sometimes. And a group who would be chased by the Goy who owned the field or the orchard with his dogs – woe to them – but it would be worth the risk, worth the labor and trouble, since "stolen water would be sweeter."

Tisha B'Av

And days of grief and mourning are in town – the first nine days of the month of Av, the memory of the destruction of the temple. On the night of Tisha B'Av in the synagogue, the adults sit with their shoes off, sitting on overturned, low benches, and the cantor chants the lament of "Eicha" in a sad melody, but the children do not know the grief of destruction. In a day, their pockets will be filled with the cones of a thorny plant call "shsishkes," and while the laments are sung they will send the cones in clusters or one by one, into the thick beards of the mourners over the fate of Jerusalem. Among the ones taking the shots there would be those who accept the arrows shot at them with indifference and understanding, sometimes with love. And then there would be the ones who get angry, reacting severely and looking for the mischievous brats who attack their beards. The latter ones are a more desired target than others for the mischief, and the atmosphere of Tisha B'Av, an atmosphere of lament of a crowd mourning the loss of what was precious to them, becomes an air of mischief, even happiness and glee, that would not settle with the solemnity of this day.

Celebration days

And the special celebration days in town were wedding days, but these had their scent and taste vanish during recent years, before the Holocaust. I'll bring the memory of the last weddings which kept the original tradition with all its grace and purity. I remember only a few weddings like that – two or three. And they lasted, I think, a few days, and no other days were like it in joy in town. I still remember a Chuppah in town that was held with all its practices and customs until the last of them. The entire town was gathered in the courtyard of the synagogue. Perl–Leah and Sheyne, the old women who knit socks for the members of town, danced at the head of the procession and clapped to the sound of a friendly, delightful and sad melody.

And how much light and joy was in the house where the wedding was held: "Die Kalah Bazetzn," the groom coming to the bride sitting on a chair, the Klezmers playing, the crying of the women, the sounds of crying of the bride, in memory of the missing relatives. And later – "Die Chuppah Vetshere"– the wedding feast, "Sherele" dances and more.

And the next day again holiday and feast. The feasts would last whole days and on the Shabbat of the wedding week – "Sheva Brachot," the seven blessings. But all these, as mentioned, were a way of being that faded away, with their shine dimming; only bits of memories stayed in my heart and even those are partially blurry.

"Bris Mila" – circumcision – that was also a celebration in a small circle in town. In the seven days before the Bris, we children would be invited to the house of the woman who just now gave birth to say certain Tehilim, to drive away the evil spirits. They would paste on the walls Tehilim of "Shir Ha'maalot" for that. The children would be treated with sweets in exchange for this service.

Death in the windows

And from joy to sorrow. A death in town; someone passed away. We young children would be terrified and forget our mischief for a moment. We were called to say Tehilim next to the dead person who would be lying on the floor with candles lit by his head. (Today I am amazed about our parents letting us stay in a house of mourners who had their dead lying in front of them.) The funeral proceeded slowly through the town's streets, the bed carried by the Chevrah Kadisha members. The charity box tinkled, the person carrying it called out loud "Tzedakah (charity) will rescue from death." The wailing sound of the women, a heartbreaking sound, would pierce the silence of the crowd, walking after the bed.

Here the procession would reach the bridge on the river, and stopped for a moment to say farewell to the dead and ask for forgiveness. One by one the people escorting with their lips whispering "zeit mir muchel," meaning "please pardon me, forgive me." The bleak procession would pass through one of the Goyims' yard gate, since that was the only way to the cemetery. And when they would reach the gate of the cemetery and disappear among the trees, the crows' calls "Cra, Cra, Cra" would increase the sadness and pain of the heart. We children would be convinced that the crows would come to the cemetery with full awareness of the significance of the place and their calls were meant to express the pain of death and cessation. we would be comforted by the fact that the soul did not die and just went to heaven. But we would be divided in our views in the arguments we had – did it go to paradise or, God forbid, to hell, to be tormented in its seven sections, in tanks of boiling tar, or on burning embers or maybe on a white–hot iron floor.

I remember the air of death which would pervade town when one of its people would be terminally ill, when everyone would rush to the synagogue to say Tehilim, to add a name and to open the Ark. The wailing of the women of the family in front of the open Ark would terrify the town and would announce that death had risen in the windows.

We do not know what has become of that corner of town, the cemetery, the final stop of every human being, flesh and blood, when their time comes. But at the time it was a part of the everyday life of the town, and we didn't imagine, the few survivors, and definitely our brothers and sisters who were murdered in the Holocaust did not imagine, that even to this final stop the ones murdered would not arrive, that their bones would be scattered all around to be fed to wild beasts, and will not be visited by their children, their brothers or their sisters to come to their graves, to commune with their memory, to say the Kadish prayer in memory of their souls.

Boating on the Narach

[Page 51]

A Wedding in Town

by Dvora Bachman (Gordon), Haifa

Translated by Jerrold Landau

Dedicated to the memory of the sheathes that were cut down, and to the memory of those who did not merit to reach the wedding canopy.

Since more than 30 years have passed from the time I made *aliya,* and was cut off from the events of life in the town; the realities with which we lived years ago are not as clear as they once were, for the passage of time and years has taken its toll and erased from my memory a substantial portion of the events that were our lot in the past. Nevertheless, several memories remain etched in our hearts that are still fresh today, as if the passage of time had no influence on them. One of them is a Jewish wedding in the town. Indeed, this Jewish wedding in the town expresses something fundamental and unique, that typifies that era and the environment in which the Jews lived.

Concern for a Daughter who is Getting Older

The concern to marry off an older daughter held an honorable place in every family. There was no shortage of factors that prematurely added to this worry. Most of the families of Kobylnik had several children, and the marriage of the oldest daughter did not free the family from this concern, for after the oldest daughter comes the second or third daughter, who were also waiting for their wedding day...

Furthermore, the daughter in a family was the weakest link in the economic chain. Most of the girls did not learn a trade, and were not economically independent. They remained dependent on their families even after their marriage. In general, they became successful household managers, dedicating most of their time to the care of their family. This fact increased the concern of the parents, for they knew that their meager means would not be sufficient to provide full support to all their children for their future lives. In general, the ideal age of marriage for a male was considered to be 30, and a bit lower for a female. However, there were many cases where that age passed due to the poor economic status of the family. There were also exceptions, where the parents were able to provide all the clothing and other necessities for the couple at the right time, and to set up the economic basis of their children for the future. It is unnecessary to explain the uncomfortable situation of a girl in town whose marriage was delayed. Such a situation was discussed by everybody, and became a target for the arrows of the members of the town. People spread rumors to their best of their ability regarding the reasons that the daughter of so–and–so was not yet married. In short, marriage became a public topic upon which everybody trampled, and this exaggerated curiosity only ended when the daughter reached the wedding canopy.

[Page 52]

Before the wedding, there was an extensive, very practical exchange between the two sides, with the central aim being the size of the dowry that the parents of the bride would present the groom on the wedding day, as well as their agreement to support the young couple and to provide them with livelihood after the wedding if the groom wished to continue with his Torah studies. When they came into contact, each side of the family praised the bride or the groom to the best of their abilities, describing their special qualities. They would discuss the wonderful traits of the bride, her beauty, her charm, her expertise in running the household and maintaining cleanliness, her capabilities in the kitchen in cooking and baking, and her interpersonal success with her friends. On the other side, they described the groom's handsomeness, his good health, his success and abilities to become a good supporter of a family, and his diligence in business or some other endeavor. They also talked about his dedication to tradition, his expertise in the small letters[1], prayer, and scriptures. The age of the groom also served as a key point of discussion between the families.

Pedigree...[2]

Another very important stage was confirming the family tree of the families. Serious and exacting work was done to investigate the past and lineage of each side of the prospective couple. There were also cases where they dug back for many generations to investigate the past and status of each family in great detail. This was easy when both sides of the family came from Kobylnik. In such cases, everything was known, and the investigation was superfluous. It was more difficult, however, when the proposed match was from outside. In such cases, they had to dedicate time to find the connection and contact with the town from where prospective bride or groom came.

[Page 53]

The main point of attention in this investigation of the pedigree of the couple was: who were the maternal and paternal grandparents – were they Hasidim or *Misnagdim*; where there any family members who fell into a bad crowd or who abandoned Judaism, heaven forbid, bringing shame on the family? Or, on the contrary, were there in the family scholars, Yeshiva students, scholars, intelligent people, who were a source of glory to the entire family? It was also important to know whether there were businessmen, forestry or wheat traders, suppliers, agents, and the like; or merely small-scale merchants who were involved in peddling or trading with villagers; or whether they were tradesmen such as tailors, shoemakers, etc. All of these factors contributed to the positive or negative fate of the marriage. The young couple were not always asked for their opinion on the marriage, even though the choice was at times not to their liking. As in all towns in the district, Kobylnik did not suffer from an excess of love amongst the youth. As their parents, the wedding was the fruit of the labor of the matchmaker, who knew how to forge matches. It is difficult to ascertain how many of these couples were happy, and how many suffered all their lives became of the lack of minimal compatibility between themselves.

A New Custom Comes to Town

After the First World War, a significant change came across the way of thinking of the people, including the youth. Fundamental changes also took place in the realm of love and marriage. A new factor appeared over the skies of the town – the youth movements, where boys and girls would meet each other under a common rubric, and many previously held concepts would be weakened. The call to the youth to change their ways of life, to would participate in summer camps, venerate the work ethic and to draw close to nature also contributed important concepts to the realm of marriage. The youth would go out on excursions in the bosom of nature. They would spend time in the forests near the lakes near Kobylnik. They and go out to *hachsharah* points far from home. They would spend the late–night hours dancing at the chapter headquarters. All of these factors deepened the connection between the sexes. The result was marriages through direct connection, without matchmakers and without middlemen...

The Wedding Ceremony

Nevertheless, everything related to the wedding ceremony remained unchanged. This was a joyous, happy day. Aside from the bride, the groom, and the families — most of the townsfolk, both Jews and gentiles, took an active role. Preparations for this day were noticed very well already several days previously. Already on the Sabbath prior to the wedding, the family with the groom went to the synagogue, where the groom was honored with the reading of the *Haftarah*. As he descended from the *bima* after the reading, he passed through a shower of nuts and sweets that were thrown down from the windows of the women's gallery. The children in the synagogue gleefully gathered the loot into their pockets. At the same time, the family treated the worshippers with wine, cookies, and other baked goods. At the end of the good wishes in the synagogue, the entourage returned home with the groom, where they found a table set for Kiddush. The gathering once again raised cups of liquor and blessed the groom. The atmosphere was exalted and full of joy.

[Page 54]

In the bosom of nature

For several days prior to the wedding, care was taken that the bride and groom not meet, and not even be under the same roof... Both remained in seclusion with their respective families. The families were also careful that the Jewish laws that applied to the wedding day would be observed meticulously. Both would fast on the wedding day. If, heaven forbid, either the bride or the groom had lost a parent, they would go to the cemetery on that day to supplicate at the graves, so that they pure souls would beg for mercy on High for the success of the young couple, and that the Creator would grant them good fortune and a happy life.

[Page 55]

Close to the time of the wedding, the bride already sat in her home on a chair decorated with flowers, wearing her lovely dress and a white veil on hear head. A band conducted by Alexei the gentile played fiddles and trumpets inside. Alexei used to play at the weddings in town. The bride's friends who gathered in her house bedecked her with countless kisses. Pious women groaned and shed tears from great joy... There were cases where the jester stood on the porch and greeted the guests who came to bless the bride. He would announce the arrival of the guests in a festive voice to the best of his ability, and tell jokes to entertain the celebrants. The tension grew until the groom arrived at the bride's home along with his parents and attendants for the bedecking ceremony and covering the face of the bride (bedekins).

The ceremony here was very short. All the participants then walked from the bride's house to the synagogue, where the wedding ceremony would take place in the yard, under the open skies. This was a very joyous procession along the main street of the town, headed by the band, which was playing wedding songs. Behind the band, two elderly women, Sheina and Perl Leah, danced the "mitzvah dance" as everyone accompanied them with joyous hand clapping. The groom walked nearby the dancers, pale and emotional. His parents and attendants marched next to him. The crowd walked behind them with drums and dancing, all of them were singing amidst a very large bustle. The local gentiles (*shkotzim*) were also not absent, adding to the bustle and noise.

The wedding canopy (*chupa*} was already set up in the synagogue yard, supported by four poles. Another group, who had already gathered there, sang loudly and repetitively, "He will bless the groom, He will bless the groom," asking G–d to bless the groom. The entire gathering sang this incessantly, repeating it over and over, for close to half an hour until they saw the bride approaching the canopy with her parents and attendants. Then the gathering changed the words of the song, and added the word "the bride" – that is "He will bless the groom and the bride." Small candles were lit net to the canopy, and everyone waited for rabbi to intone the betrothal blessing and to read the *ketuba* [marriage document]. Yeshayahu–Yosef Gordon assisted him, taking care of all other matters, and giving the bride and groom the cup of wine to drink under the canopy. With the resonance of the breaking of the glass by the groom, shouts of Mazel Tov echoed throughout the gathering. The ceremony concluded.

The entire gathering, accompanied by the band, returned from the synagogue to the house of the bride. Prior to entering the house, the new couple was greeted by a bucket of fresh water and a decorated cake – as a sign of a full, happy life that should be their lot in the future. Tables were set in the house full of sweets (a zisser tisch).

[Page 56]

It was primarily the young people who went to enjoy this table. Other tables were set up for the family and the older invited guests. A festive meal with "gold soup" (the well–known fat, clear soup) was served on those tables.

When this gathering was literally at the pinnacle of drinking and eating, the jester began, as best he could, to announce in a loud voice the gifts {*drasha geshank*) that each of the invited guests was prepared to give to the bride and groom, whether money or gifts. The jester called out the name of the giver, and the crowd of celebrants applauded him. Of course, the titans of the community, including relatives, came first. The givers of bog fish or tin sheets came at the end.

The meal finished, and the rounds of dancing began. If the wedding took place on the eve of the Sabbath, the dancing would be postponed until the next day, after the Sabbath. The crowd was enthusiastic and tipsy, and they danced with anything that came to hand: they mixed a stormy polka with the solid waltz. The Cossack dance came after the Sherele[3]. Of course, the tango, quadrille[4], foxtrot and other dances that were popular at that time were also not lacking. In general, the dancing continued until dawn. In the meantime, someone made sure to prepare a nearby side room for the bride and groom so that they could spend a bit of time together, away from the hustle and bustle, before the crowd dispersed.

The celebration, called *Sheva Brachot* continued during the Sabbath after the wedding. This would usually take place at the time of *mincha* amongst a gathering of relatives and friends, including the local rabbi and other notables. They would enter to worship and partake of the third Sabbath meal, as was usual on the Sabbath afternoon toward evening. They would preach words of Torah and sing together until well after the Sabbath ended. Thus ended the wedding, which raised the level of life in the town. There were weddings that did not reach this level, but this was different, for it was celebrated in a higher fashion than usual, and was conducted with great splendor.

I have described a specific reality of life in the town. However, Jewish life has perished and is no more. All that remains are gloomy memories, lamenting in our hearts.

Translator's Footnotes

1. Referring to the rabbinic commentaries written in small font in the Talmud.

2. The Hebrew word is "*Yichus.*" The English translation "pedigree" does not do it justice. See https://en.wikipedia.org/wiki/Yichus

3. See https://en.wikipedia.org/wiki/Sher_(dance)

4. See https://en.wikipedia.org/wiki/Quadrille

———

[Pages 57-65]

Hechalutz in Kobylnik
by Yitzchak Gordon
Translated by Jerrold Landau

It is very hard to delve into the roots of the matter and to determine precisely how Zionism reached our town of Kobylnik; from where did its first buds grow, and who were the news–bearers who began a fundamental change in the spiritual reality of the youth of the town.

After the First World War...

The First World War, with all its horrors, fundamentally changed the outlook of the world in the areas of morality, family, and society. The liberation movements of oppressed nations in Europe, which found an opportune moment to liberate themselves from the mighty yoke of the empires and attain political independence, left a heavy impression on the national minorities in those countries.

The Jewish nation, suffused with suffering and bitter experiences, always bore in its heart the powerful hope and desire for the Land of Israel, where they would be able to live a life of independence and freedom in the future. The Jewish youth, who internalized these ideas, were prepared for daring action and for a change in the values of the life of the nation – and this was immediate. The dismal reality in which the Jewish public lived during those times in Poland was also a key factor and moving force for a revolt against convention and the old way of life that disappointed. It gave a push toward forging new routes for the future.

In Kobylnik, as in any small town in Eastern Poland, there was great poverty, and the economic possibilities were limited, without sources of livelihood and income. Many lived in a meager fashion and in want, without hope or possibilities for the future. It is no wonder, then, that under these conditions – with worries about forced unemployment and a cloudy future – the town was ripe for bitterness and dissatisfaction among the youth. The feeling was hard and oppressive, as if the ground was being pulled from beneath one's feet. There was nowhere to escape, for very few could continue their studies in a large city or succeed in immigrating oversees. The youth who lives in the town searched for a means, at any price, to effect a change of the dark, depressing reality that was the lot of the masses. Indeed, these factors as well as others that typified those times in Poland formed the background for the sprouting of the Hechalutz chapter in Kobylnik.

[Page 58]

The Founding of the Hechalutz Chapter

The Hechalutz Chapter was founded in Kobylnik in 1923. The following were among the founders: Baruch Akselrod, Yosef Todres, Gershon Kribicky, Shalom Yavnovitch, Liber Kirmalinsky, and others who joined them. When the chapter opened, efforts for preparation for *aliya* to the Land of Israel began. Special stress was placed on agricultural work. Some of the members went to *hachshara* [*aliya* preparation] in agricultural farms in the area of Vilna to learn how to work the land, and to gain experience in hard physical labor, of which most of them had never had any experience. They leased a large vegetable garden from Mrs. Anyuta Klumel, the town dentist, to grow all types of vegetables during the summer. In the manner of the farmers, who would bring their produce to sell in the town, the first *chalutzim* also appeared and sold cucumbers, radishes, cabbage, leeks, beets and the like in the market. This was an uncommon experience in the eyes of the gentiles and the Jews: Jews selling agricultural produce that they grew on their own!... The *chalutzim* treated this as holy work, working with great dedication and enthusiasm. They excited all the people of the town, young and old. Toward evening, many of the townsfolk would gather in the yard of the garden to help the *chalutzim* in their work. The means of work and irrigation were primitive: The water was drawn from the well and brought to the garden in pails. The plant beds were watered with a hand sprinkler. They also had to hoe, prune, and weed. Of course, with the bustle that surrounded the *chalutzim* in the town, there was no shortage of people who spent much of their time trying to make their own vegetable gardens...

[Page 59]

There was also no shortage of Jews with time on their hands who came out of curiosity, as well as pessimists who helped the *chalutzim* when they came, but spared no negative investigation about the essence of the strange endeavor to which these *chalutzim* were attached. The types of rough work that these *chalutzim* were prepared to do did not agree with their way of thinking...

Hechalutz in Kobylnik

There were also Jews in the town who looked upon the lads in amazement, and did not understand their objective. They regarded them as crazy or wanton people, going beyond the bounds of Jewish tradition. Indeed, it was only the youth who internalized into their hearts the footsteps of the new era, which brought in its wake a revolution of Jewish communal life in the Diaspora. These were the first signs of the transition from spiritual Judaism disengaged from the reality to a new Judaism, which aspires to base itself upon productive work and individual and national honor.

The *chalutzim* drew this influence from the realities of the Land and the life on the kibbutz. Newspapers that arrived from Warsaw, such as Heint and Moment, or newspapers that came from Vilna – all provided a great deal of news on what was happening in the Land. The life and death of Joseph Trumpeldor[1], the life and teachings of A. D. Gordon[2] on "the religion of labor", became the ideology that forged and directed the hearts of the youth in the town.

This impetus pushed the best of the youth of Kobylnik to abandon the tendency toward small–scale business as a future profession. Instead, they began to learn productive trades. It is difficult to define exactly the meaning of a proper and appropriate productive trade within the economic realities of that period. It was also hard to define which trades would be needed in the future in the Land. Under the accepted conditions of the time, all hard, backbreaking work was considered to be productive labor. Therefore, many preferred to study carpentry, shoemaking, building, and agriculture. They signed up as apprentices in these fields. The pioneering Zionist consciousness deepened step by step among the youth of the town. The circles broadened more and more, and the relations with the movement grew more serious. Even the adults who previously displayed some hesitancy lessened their opposition and went with the new reality.

[Page 60]

Connection with the Land

The living bridge to the Land, established with the *aliya* of the earlier ones, also did its part in the strengthening of the ties with the movement. The first of the *chalutzim* of the town to make *aliya* was Baruch Akselrod. The elders among us can describe the day of his *aliya* to this day, a day which is unforgettable until today. On the day of his *aliya*, the warm Jewish heart, with its love for the Land, was displayed, bursting forth from its hiding place. The vision of all the townsfolk, adults and children, accompanying comrade Baruch the distance of two kilometers to the railway station was impressive. Of course, there was no shortage of tears and weeping – not only by his family members, but also from the entire gathering of people.

[Page 61]

This connection with the Land continued to strengthen, and withstood the test when other political parties tried to discredit the Land in the eyes of the people. There were factions that stormed through the hearts of the youth: particularly the radical Bund, which was opposed to the Zionist camp. However, it did not take hold in Kobylnik. Even the Communist movement failed to gain adherents. There were also other Zionist parties, from the right and the left, but the youth ignored them. Only the Chalutz movement, which was pioneering in its vision and path, found faithful supporters among our townsfolk.

In addition to the organized pioneering *aliya*, some residents of Kobylnik succeeded in arriving to the Land through personal connections, whether through invitations that were sent from the land, by registering as students in the university in Jerusalem, or even through fictitious marriages and forged documents. All of them strengthened the connection with the Land.

Hechalutz chapter in Kobylnik

The bloody tribulations of 5689–1929 shook all Jewish hearts in the Diaspora. As a young child, I recall how all the residents of Kobylnik would gather each evening in the market square in the center of the town to discuss the events in the Land in groups. The newspapers that arrived from Vilna in the evening, and were snatched up from hand to hand, did not lack detailed descriptions of the atrocities and destruction that were perpetrated against the community in the Land. As the emotions increased, so did the awakening. A streak of zealotry was ignited within the Jewish youth, who began to prepare en masse to make *aliya* to the Land.

An assistance fund was set up, and Jews donated money for the rebuilding of the ruins. The tragedy that had taken place caused most segments of the town's Jews to gather around us. Nevertheless, only a few people succeeded in making *aliya* from Kobylnik at that time, for the gates of *aliya* were quickly closed by the Mandate government.

The Closing of *aliya*

The 1930s arrived. Even though the gates of the Land were locked, the youth did not give up on the chances of *aliya*, and many went out to *hachsharah* kibbutzim in Poland. My sister Devora Gordon (today

Bachman), Gita Klumel, Chana Yavnovitch, Yosef Yavnovitch, Asher Krakow, Pinchas Kribicki, Sheinka Janowski, and others went out to *hachsharah* at that time. New youth joined the chapter and replaced those who had left for *hachsharah*. In 1933, the writer of these lines along with other members, including Tzvia Chormecz joined. I played an active role in the chapter until I went to *hachsharah* in 1935. I was given I remember that in 1934, a regional convention was announced for Dunilowicze, 40 kilometers from Kobylnik. The convention was to take place close to Passover, and there were obstacles on the routes. The snow had already melted in some of them, and the snow was still lying on others – so we did not know what vehicle to use for the journey. We contacted three gentiles and convinced them to transport us: The decision was that we should set out in tow trucks. We set out toward morning. We walked for most of the time, for the horses dragged the wagons with difficulty. It was already toward evening when we reached Dunilowicze. We wanted to shorten the journey so that we would arrive on time. A straight, smooth path spread out from before us. It was frozen. This was a large lake whose name I do not remember. We took council about whether we should cross the pond in the tow truck. We supported ourselves on the ice, and we began to advance in the lake. The tow trucks skated properly, and we were all happy... Suddenly we realized that the leg of the horse got stuck in the ice, and could not be moved. We began to feel the ice breaking below us, and we all began to sink... I traveled in the first wagon. Aharon Chadash, Yafa Janowski, and two others were with me. We immediately jumped out of the wagon and began to save the horse. We succeeded in extricating it from its trouble. We retraced our steps, and reached the convention in a roundabout fashion. We were wet and exhausted, but our hearts swelled as we saw the masses of youth gathered in the movie theater hall. The hall was filled to the brim, and the audience thirstily drank up every word from the speakers who spoke from the podium. This served as an encouraging source, promising good.

[Page 62]

The Work Branches Out

With time, we saw the need to raise the cultural level of the members. We began to make efforts to study the Hebrew Language, history, Judaism, the Zionist annals, and political economy. We also studied about the workers' movement and knowledge of the Land. Indeed, one of the foundations of our work was physical labor, to which we all aspired. We organized a group of woodcutters in the town, and we dedicated the income to the welfare of the chapter. We attempted to carry out this work displayed no less skill than did the gentiles, whose hands were expert at this trade.

[Page 63]

***

At that time, a chapter of HaOved arose in town. This organization was directed toward the professionals, who did not have the possibility to go out to the *hachsharah*kibbutzim as did the pioneers, whether because of their age or because they were busy with a family and children. At that time, the Mandate government was dependent on the working element in the land, and they allowed the immigration of HaOved members drop by drop. The members who joined HaOved in Kobylnik were mainly adults, and the form of the organization was foreign to them. I recall how I gathered them at meetings and instilled in them material regarding the workers movement and knowledge of the Land. Their approach was very realistic and practical: they saw in this organization a way of life and a solution to the difficulties in which they found themselves in Kobylnik. They hoped for the possibility of immediate *aliya*. To our great sorrow, none of them could make *aliya*, for the gates of *aliya* were closed, and they did not have the patience to wait for better times, as did the *chalutzim*. HaOved continued to exist even after my *aliya* in 1938. It only disbanded after the outbreak of the war in 1939.

We regarded he activities of the Jewish National Fund in our town as especially important and valuable work. We were all united in the opinion that the collecting of money by the masses of Jews in the Diaspora will lead to the redemption of the Land of Israel from foreigners. Indeed, the blue box of the Jewish National Fund caught my eye in every Jewish home that I entered. Every month, we would bring the donations to David Swirsky of blessed memory, the representative of the Jewish National Fund in Kobylnik, to transmit to Warsaw. It is worthwhile to note that he exhibited exceptional dedication and trustworthiness. He found free time for the Jewish National Fund even though he had a family and children.

Aside from the donations through the boxes of the Jewish National fund, we also organized the annual memorial observance of Herzl on the 20th of Tammuz. It was a mourning gathering or a "sorrow academy". We collected donations there as well. In later years, the memorials for Herzl and Bialik were conducted together. On the eve of Yom Kippur, a propitious time, we would place a plate in the synagogues for the benefit of the Jewish National Fund, among all the other charitable plates. The Jews of the town did not, Heaven forbid, embarrass us. Rather, they responded to this cause willingly. During the years of the Zionist Congresses, we would distribute shekels [tokens of membership in the Zionist organizations] among the resident of the town, all for the Working Land of Israel block.

[Page 64]

A severe crisis afflicted the Hechalutz movement in the wake of the shutting down of *aliya* by the Mandate government, as well as the bloody events that began in the Land in 1936. Thousands of members were stuck in the *hachsharah* places in Poland, which were scattered in hundreds of locales, without any possibility of *aliya*. The despair and oppression began to affect the masses. There were those who did not have the patience to wait for the gates to open, so they left the *hachsharah* places and returned to their homes. However, most of them maintained their stand and lived with the hope of *aliya*. There were also attempts by various members to go in an illegal fashion or through some other route, but that took great means, and the majority did not have such means.

Hechalutz Hatzair

This severe situation also affected the existence of the chapter in town. The members who already went out to *hachsharah* still hoped for *aliya*. However, only few new members joined the chapter. We understood the difficulties and causes that lead to a decline in the movement, but we did not give up on the path that we had forged for ourselves. We knew that there were good youth in potential, who could fill the ranks and would be idealistic for the Land, although the time was not appropriate for *aliya*. We felt it appropriate to organize the youth, so we set up a chapter of Hechalutz Hatzair [Young Hechalutz] in town. As a young counsellor, I did not have any experience in counseling youth of that age. We always struggled with the problem of which activities to conduct with the youth. We preferred hikes in the field, meetings in the forest, and spending time in the bosom of nature. We devoted a great deal of time to basketball, swimming, and sailing in the nearby lake. Our aim was to strengthen the muscles of the youth, to forge their character and to firm up their image. This path attracted the youth to us. We placed our hopes for the future in this youth.

[Page 65]

This chapter continued to exist literally until the outbreak of the war. After I went out to *hachsharah*, Yehoshua Janowski led the Hechalutz Hatzair chapter in Kobylnik. He displayed immense talent and dedication to matters relating to the youth in our town. Unfortunately, he did not succeed in making *aliya*, and he met the same fate as the rest of the natives of Kobylnik.

***

The second World War passed, and Jewry was annihilated, including all the youth. Only a few survived, including some who had belonged to Hechalutz and Hechalutz Hatzair in the past. These few found their way to *hachsharah* and kibbutzim that were set up in Italy. They immigrated to the Land instead of going to other places. The vast majority of alumnae of Hechalutz and Hechalutz Hatzair continue to affiliate with the labor movement in Israel, and play important roles in all branches of labor and creativity.

Let these lines serve as a monument to our dear comrades whose hearts were directed to the Land, but who perished in the Holocaust without meriting to come to the homeland. May their memories be a blessing.

Translator's Footnotes

1. See https://en.wikipedia.org/wiki/Joseph_Trumpeldor
2. See https://en.wikipedia.org/wiki/A._D._Gordon

———

[Pages 66-69]

With the Actualizers in the *hachsharah* Movement

by Aharon Chadash of Petach Tikva
Translated by Jerrold Landau

This severe situation also affected the existence of the chapter in town. The members who already went out to *hachsharah* still hoped for *aliya*. However, only few new members joined the chapter. We understood the difficulties and causes that lead to a decline in the movement As a lad of the era, during the 1930s in Poland, I also found my way in the ranks of Hechalutz in Kobylnik. It is difficult for me to explain today the true obstacles that hindered my participation in Hechalutz. There were certainly many reasons for this. Some have already been forgotten or blurred with the passage of time. Only the goals that we strove toward remain etched in my memory to this day. These are: actualization, *hachsharah*, kibbutz, and *aliya*. To my good fortune, when I recall that era today, I am full of satisfaction that I was one of the first in the Hechalutz chapter, as well as one of the first from Kobylnik who went to a *hachsharah* kibbutz. Aside from one or two others, I was the first to succeed in making *aliya*.

For me, going out to *hachsharah* was a significant experience. As a youth who grew up in a small town far away from the wide world, I was afraid to leave the bounds of the town and the family circle, to which I was bound with all strands of my soul. Nevertheless, I marched toward the future with my head held high, full of hope that my path was proper and just. I arrived at *hachsharah* with such feelings.

My first stop was Szczuczyn. This town was not large. *hachsharah* groups were organized in that place. I arrived in the town, and, without much effort, found myself within the walls of the kibbutz. It was the afternoon, and the members had not yet returned from work. I only found a few female members in the kibbutz, working in the kitchen and in cleaning the house. They greeted me warmly and joyously. This was a very pleasant experience for me, for I had never received such a "reception" organized by ordinary Jews whom I had met along the way while I was walking from the train to the kibbutz. They said in front of me, "So, another fresh sacrifice..." They said this in jest when they realized that I was a "green" kibbutznik.

[Page 67]

Members who gathered around the tables after work in the evening, also made jokes at my expense. This was not plain rudeness, but rather mocking of the reality in which we lived. It is also impossible to hide the fact that there were factions and movements on the Jewish street that operated against Zionism and the Land of Israel in general. Aside from the difficult conditions that pervaded I the land, the conditions in the *hachsharah* kibbutzim were also difficult and unbearable. Every situation of going out to *hachsharah* seemed like utter craziness in the eyes of many Jews. When the gates of *aliya* were closed by the Mandate government, despair began to affect the interior of the movement itself. Many could not continue, and returned home.

Despite these conditions, thousands of members remained in the *hachsharah* kibbutzim and continued to struggle under difficult conditions, hoping for the opportunity to make *aliya* to the Land. I was one of them. I was set up with work already on my first evening there. There was no shortage of working hands in the kibbutz. Apparently, however, I gave the impression to the comrades that "one cannot just leave him alone." I already had broad shoulders, and I was not lacking in energy. This certainly was decisive, for I was already among those who went to the sawmill the next day. I was stationed beside the edging machine. My task was to stop and gather the planks that the machine ejected. I was a strong lad, and it was not difficult for me to fulfil this task. The girls brought a warm meal form the kibbutz for lunch. I ate it with a great appetite even though it was not completely to my taste... I worked at this job for a long time, until I became an assistant to the driver of the transport truck. This is how I entered the circle of labor in the kibbutz with full energy. I exchanged several times according to the demands and the need.

The males and females who I found in the kibbutz from all corners of the country were for the most part "mommy's children," who were not used to hard physical labor. It took great effort for them to get accustomed to it. Therefore, it was not long before many comrades became ill and could not continue their work. The economy was also low, and the living conditions led to a weakening of the comrades and a decline in the workforce of the kibbutz. Considering that the types of work carried out by the comrades were the basest, such as: porting, wood cutting, and other types – and not only were they difficult and backbreaking, but the pay for them was meager – it is easy to understand the difficult conditions of existence. Indeed, the income was insufficient to cover the minimal level of cost of living. There was also lack of experience in conducting the economy under the unique conditions related to hired work. All this lead to seriously difficult conditions in the life of *hachsharah* kibbutz.

It is proper to note that there were various fluctuations in the state of work in the kibbutz. Just as we suffered from a shortage of work, we also suffered from an overabundance of work on occasion, and we had insufficient workers. We did not have regular workplaces, so all our work was provisional on what came our way. Despite all this, we succeeded, step after step, to improve our living conditions when we obtained a larger dwelling, to improve the economic situation of the members, and to improve the clothing and shoes – for the interim, the clothing that we brought from home had enough time to become torn. With great effort, we also succeeded in arranging hospitalization for the members who had become ill.

[Page 68]

At that time, we also began intensive, wide–branched cultural activities. We stressed the learning of the Hebrew Language. We read newspapers that arrived from the Land. We had sessions about the history of the labor movement in the Land and in the world, sessions on political economy, and lectures on topics relating to the life of the nation and the Land. In the evenings, we spent a great deal of time at meetings dealing with actual problems, but we also knew how to sing, dance, and rejoice... These things deepened our recognition and connection to the path in which we were walking. Our faith increased that we would be able to fill our life with them.

Chalutzim (Zionist pioneers) in Kobylnik: wood choppers

This severe situation also affected the existence of the chapter in town. The members who already went out to *hachsharah* still hoped for *aliya*. However, only few new members joined the chapter. We understood the difficulties and causes that lead to a decline in the movement.

[Page 69]

After close to a year and a half of live on the kibbutz in Szczuczyn, I left with a small group to Neman to strengthen the group that was organized there. I did this voluntarily, for I felt that I had gained experience where I was, and I would be able to give something to the new group. However, since the new place did not have the power to absorb new members due to lack of work, we returned to Szczuczyn. From there, I went to the kibbutz in Lida.

This kibbutz was much more firmly based than its predecessors. The members of the kibbutz had become involved in many branches of work, I among them. I worked at all types of arduous work until I was certified for *aliya*. My turn came to make *aliya* to the Land.

"Hechalutz" in Kobylnik

[Pages 70-77]

The Education in Our Town, Kobylnik

In memory of the children of Israel in Kobylnik, who were killed by the persecutor

by Meir Yavnai (Yavnovich)

Translated by Gilad Petranker

Edited by Toby Bird

One of the foundations of Israel's existence living among the Goyim was undoubtedly the education of the younger generation and its training to the well– set life accustomed for generations.

And it is therefore clear that in the weave of life that the Jewish people had created in the Diaspora, the deep concern and devotion for education stood out. It is therefore impossible to describe the life of a Jewish town in the Diaspora without giving education its rightful place. But this task would not be easy when I come to outline the education in our town Kobylnik, since I would have to rely on one single source– remembering the things from 20–30 years ago, and more.

In is obvious that many of the things have become blurry in our memory over the years. The deeds and things which will be told, are bound to be lacking or have a surplus in them; even their sequence would be hard or even impossible to set. And along with all of these serious flaws it would be impossible to remove our attitude to things, which with time changes and obtains a manner of a subjective admiration for the past, sometimes with a sentimental hue. Even in normal days this is the situation, then in our times, after the Holocaust and the destruction, after everything we cherished was lost and completely destroyed, our words would definitely suffer from the mentioned attitude.

And along with all of these, it would be difficult for us to give a true and impartial description of the tradition of education in town owing to the lack of clarity and instability of the time which we are about to describe. This time of the past twenty years before the destruction was a transition, when the foundation and patterns of life that were set solid for generations were destroyed and left derelict. It was a time of change of values, but the new ones did not yet consolidate and did not yet take the place of the old; even the content and the trend of aspiring for something new were not clear enough.

And of course, it is hard to describe things which are in motion, taking form, whose shape is not set and clear.

There were many towns, including our own Kobylnik, that conducted themselves on a far–off, side path, away from the main road of the general Jewish life. Only distant echoes from what was being done and what was changing in the general Jewish life had reached these towns, and had left a very small impression on what was taking place in them. Indeed, in slowly and even slacking steps, the town walked on the path of changes. Numbness and weakness marked what was being done. And these things are not said as an accusation, but in order to give the facts as they were and as I view it through the mirror of time.

The purpose of educating the generation

And to the matter of fact: the subject of education is composed of a set of different problems, and each generation sets first the purpose of the education itself, according to the way of life and to their aspirations. For many generations, the purpose of education in the Diaspora was clear– to educate the generation on the lap of Torah and the practical Mitzvas, so they would keep on weaving the well–set tradition of life, based on the foundations of the Torah in practice. The instruments to achieve this purpose are also properly and well–set for their task.

The path led the boy from the Cheder for the toddlers, through the Cheder for the advanced in studying the Torah and from there to the Yeshiva– the university or the high school to train the professional students of Torah, rabbis, spiritual leaders and sages, who embrace the world of written and oral Torah. But not every place in Israel had a whole set of these institutes. It depended on the number of residents and the talent of the place's leaders who took care of the education.

And what did things look like in our town Kobylnik?

I remember that when I turned five years old, I was one day put into the Cheder with an old woman named Channah was working as a teacher, the wife of my uncle Avraham. I'm trying to explain this to myself today: why did a woman have a role of a teacher, a Melamed? These were the days of chaos after the first world war; there was not enough time, probably, to establish a Cheder to educate the children who were wandering around aimlessly; everyone was looking for a way to bring their sons into the schooling of Torah.

This Cheder was in the apartment of the teacher and was the only one fitting for the living of the family. In this Cheder boys and girls studied together and there I had the experience of taking my first steps in reading in the method of those days: Kamats – Aleph–Ah, Kamatz – Beit – Bah etc.

The Melamed Rabbi Chalvina

The second Cheder, which definitely occupies an important place in the memory of that generation who were lucky enough to stay alive, was the Cheder of rabbi Chalvina, at the house of Rabbi Avraham Yitzhak Yanovski, first on Ahuzza St. and then on Pastov St. not far from the bridge. In this Cheder the studies were conducted using the system predominant in all the Cheders of Israel at the time, that is reading out loud by one group of students while other groups would memorize their lesson with a whisper. There were few groups – according to the level of their knowledge. Group A for those learning how to read and group B for the more advanced– who already knew how to read and were brought in to the hall of the Chumash. In this group, they would read verse by verse, or word by word, and translate it to Yiddish. This method was called back then "Ivri Taitsh."

As for the relationship between the teacher and his students: Rabbi Chavilna did not divulge his teaching pleasantly. For "persuasion" this Melamed would often use his hand, or he would grab a stick, or a whip that was especially prepared beforehand for this purpose. Indeed, we were amply whipped.

There were two main offences which we would be whipped for: 1) not listening or not knowing the material for any kind of reason; 2) other "occupations" or games during the lesson while the mouth utters out loud the verse and its translation – and the hands are busy with exchanging buttons or any other kind of notions, for peas or any other way of payment.

Nevertheless, despite the severe system and the many punishments, the Rabbi was unable to suppress the natural urge of the children to play, and to make all kinds of mischief. The urge to play and the joy of life set in the soul of the boy found different outlets, sometimes good and healthy and sometimes destructive and making the Rabbi's life miserable.

The Cheder of Moshe–Zelig

Another Cheder which many probably remember was the Cheder of the town's resident Rabbi Moshe–Zelig Chaddash. In his Cheder they would learn Chumash as well, the laws of Israel according to the "Chayei Adam" and "Shulchan Aruch" books. Furthermore, in Rabbi Moshe–Zelig's Cheder the foundations of writing and arithmetic were given.

The studies in the Cheder were conducted all through the year and during the entire day, in two seasons or two "Zmanim," each having a short break of two weeks: after the summertime– during the High Holidays and Sukkot, and at the end of wintertime – about a week before Passover and up until the end of the holiday.

On the days of winter, going to the Cheder we would equip ourselves with lanterns to light up our way going back home from the Cheder late at night. In the room of Rabbi Moshe–Zelig the studies were conducted in a narrow and elongated chamber by the kitchen, as it says in the folk song "a small narrow and warm room…," but the problem was that this chamber was not always warm, which is so charming to us when today we hear this folk song with its sad melody, a song which brings us memories of childhood. This chamber was also used by the Rabbi as a chicken coop and a warehouse for all kinds of tools and objects for which he couldn't have found a better place. At night, after the pupils left, they would take the chickens into this room for their night's sleep. More than once, we would find in the morning physical evidence of the birds. After they would be driven out, evidence that was left on the tables and benches, that would soil our clothes, and the special smell of the birds and their litter that were not always taken out, would often welcome us. But Israel had been educated for years to accept torments with love, and the children of Israel were also educated in this spirit and were commanded to be quiet.

Learning and discipline

The educational means in the Cheder of Rabbi Moshe–Zelig were not much different form the ones I mentioned in the Cheder of Rabbi Chavilna. Physical punishments were widely dispersed in big portions and mainly at times of anger and rage. The physical damage was substantial, but even more severe was the damage to the spirit of the boy since it was not always just and proportional. It is no wonder therefore that there were many to "break through the fence": the more the Rabbi was harsh, the more incidents of breaking of discipline occurred. Let me demonstrate with an example, one out of many. It was most difficult to study in the long hot days of summer. In those days, the Cheder was an isolated island in the beautiful world of God. All around – lovely wood and field, stream and river, songs of birds, and gardens of fruit trees. Countless temptations would draw the heart of the boy from the narrow suffocating Cheder to the outside world. Yetzer Ha'ra, the "evil urge," would rise in the children's hearts especially on market day, which was held every Tuesday. On one of these market days, in the beautiful warm summer, I asked permission of the Rabbi to step out for a few moments– that is, to go to the bathroom, because that was the only way to be permitted out and to have a few minutes of a break. I flew like a bird out of its cage. I dashed straight into the marketplace with its crowd and noise. My feet carried me between the wagons and shops that were full of the good of the earth and its produce. My eyes could take their fill: here are the peasants in their special costumes, the wagons and the produce; here are the buyers and sellers and their tumult. How different was this world from the world of the narrow, suffocating Cheder. The child's spirit, yearning for freedom and experiences, couldn't have its fill on those moments. I wasn't the only one who desired to break out of the Cheder, out to the open. One by one, many others could break out like me and joined the group of wanderers in the marketplace. But everything must come to an end... how dear was the price we had to pay for submitting to the bad urges!

That Rabbi, after seeing that the Cheder had become almost empty, understood that he has been deceived and prepared the young delinquents a proper welcome. I, the first offender, hurried back. I just opened the door of the Cheder, and a resounding slap from the bony fingers of the Rabbi landed on my face, with many more to follow. I saw stars. I was shocked and didn't know what happened to me; only my feet acted in the right direction and carried me to my place by the table. But the Rabbi did not settle for this natural weapon, meaning his fingers, and took the whip and with it was able to make me forget the pleasure I cunningly won. I sat by the table weeping and only comforting myself with the suffering of the other pupils. As it was said, "Misery loves company." One by one and out in the open, unlike in Bialik's poem "without being seen," the rabbi, lurking behind the door, would welcome them with his blows, whips and slaps, which grew in strength with the entrance of every new offender. We accepted what was coming to us as obvious, not to be disputed, and I have no doubt that the rabbi was also content with himself and with his well–used means of education, which he partook to keep the discipline in the Cheder, to set an example.

I did not say these things to persecute the performer of the deeds or his actions; neither will I judge the justice in the acts, since this is not the right place for it. Nor will I judge the efficiency of these means. I just set out to present this fact in order to illustrate the general ways of education, as they were conducted in most of the Cheders of Israel. It is obvious we cannot judge these ways by modern criteria.

New winds

And new winds started blowing in our world. As mentioned, the new cracks in the wall of the old education were seen. Life demanded improvements in education, its expansion and adaptation to changing needs. And in those years, the years of values beginning to change in our town, the one who started spreading knowledge in town was Rabbi Eliyahu Almog, the son of Rabbi Eliezer, a soft Yeshiva student, wearing glasses and well–liked by the children. His speech was calm and his nasal voice poured like soft oil on the spirit of the children, who were used to the harshness and severity of the Melameds. In the room of this Eliyahu we learned grammar, also, as well as Hebrew, using special readers, writing and arithmetic, and if I remember correctly, also Russian, the state's language. Arithmetic was often taught with Russian books, which were filled with hard and complex problems that had no relation to actual life. I don't remember how many years or "times" the Cheder of Rabbi Eliyahu existed; neither do I know today how and why his Cheder ceased to exist.

The days came of wandering around aimlessly. A boy's education was usually not taken care of after coming out of the mentioned Cheders. Once there was a rumor that in the neighboring town of Globoki they had opened a Yeshiva. Some of the teens headed to that Yeshiva to absorb Torah, but because of the harsh conditions and the new winds blowing from all around, their sitting inside those walls did not last long. This fact proves how helpless and lost were the graduates of the Cheder. And today I cannot comprehend the notion of helplessness and weakness in town in those days toward the continuation of education past the first years of the Cheder.

The corrected Cheder and beginning of school

And in the meanwhile, the cracks in the Cheder widened until it collapsed completely. The word "school" started sounding through the air of town. On the ruins of the Cheder, two teachers – and not Melameds – who arrived from one of the towns in the district, started a kind of school, or a "corrected Cheder." Indeed, by our modern standards this institute, which resided in the synagogue, was far from a modern school. At the head of the institute stood the teachers, Isaac Lifshitz and Arie Friedman. (The first one is today a teacher in Uruguay, and the second is in America serving as a Gabbai and Shamash in a synagogue.) There were a lot of students in this school at first, but with the passing days the excitement vanished and they became fewer and fewer, until the ladies' section was enough to have all of them. In this school, new subjects were taught, which had names that were not commonly understood, such as geography and nature. The study of arithmetic was according to the Russian arithmetic books mentioned before. The main novelty was teaching Tanakh by the new method of Hebrew through Hebrew, by the commentary of the "Mikra Meforash." But even this novelty was not very efficient according to modern views, since the study of the Nevi'im Rishonim and Nevi'im Aharonim was completely literal, with neither life nor soul. The main emphasis was put on finding the meaning of the Hebrew word in Hebrew, but the spirit of the prophecy, the vision of the prophets and the content were trivial and had no place in this teaching.

However, this school was a step forward from its predecessors, although the physical punishment reigned supreme there as well, and the degrading words used for students by the teachers are still echoing in my ears to this very day.

The one specializing in degrading words in Russian was the teacher Lifshitz, but it should be said in protection of the teacher Friedman, that he was well–liked by his students, even though he would lose his temper with his students more than once.

The fate of this school was similar to the ones that came before it. I don't remember how it vanished. One of the teachers, Isaac, left town after spending two or three years there, and the other teacher, Arie Friedman, went on privately tutoring individual students or groups in his house. Many of the children of Israel in town started flowing to the Polish school; I who am writing these lines, studied at this school for a whole year, which was called "Powszechny" in short, meaning "general". Of course, the children of Israel were driven away from the Israeli culture by this, went astray from its values, and were educated in a foreign, hostile atmosphere.

The school and its various colors

And in those days the Hebrew school of the "Tarbut" administration started putting down roots in the Jewish towns in Poland, but did not reach our town. Also, many schools of the Tzisha company were established in many towns (schools which taught in the Yiddish language). There was a fierce war raging between the two types of school, as part of the more general war between Hebrew and Yiddish. But in our town, the neglect was evident in the field of education, with only faint echoes of this struggle reaching it. A few young people, both boys and girls, wandered far to higher institutes of education; the word Gymnasium started have its charm, but only a few, as mentioned, could get to that hall.

In the last years before the Holocaust, our town, Kobylnik, won its own actual school, in a special building that was initiated by some of the town's leaders. This school, which was established by the "Scholl–Colt" company, belonged to a new Yiddish chain of schools that was established at the time by nationalist Jews who'd had enough of the nature of the Yiddish Tzisha schools. The people of Scholl–Colt did not accept the Yiddishers' attitude to Zion and to the Hebrew language; with all their loyalty to Yiddish, they were nationalist Jews who were positive in their stance toward the Zionist movement and the Hebrew language and gave them a proper place in the new schools established, especially in Vilna. The early days of the Scholl–Colt school in our town were very hard, struggling against financial and social adversities throughout its existence, and indeed– it did not persist.

Toward the bitter end

In the meanwhile, the hatred toward Israel grew constantly. Echoes started coming of what was being done to our brothers in Germany. The anti–Semitic venom infiltrated forcefully through the streets of the small town. The hatred and animosity brought a financial boycott on the Jewish shops, which were struggling, and the sages had already said: "If there is no bread there is no learning." The school did not hold on in the town, which grew poorer and was struggling to survive– and perished. Again, the spiritual and cultural neglect returned, after it was driven out for a short while.

The war broke out. The town was conquered by the Russians and the end came for all Jewish culture and all its facets. And with the German occupation and the Holocaust– everything came to an end.

Chorev School in Kobylnik

[Pages 78-81]

The Economic Life of Jewish Kobylnik

by Chaim Yavnai

Translated by Joseph Schuldenrein

Edited by Toby Bird

How did the Jews of Kobylnik support themselves? What was the community's social fabric, its economic base?

Kobylnik's economic as well as its spiritual source emanated from Vilna, some 105 kilometers to the northeast. The district seat was Postov [currently Postavy in Belarus] 26 kilometers to the north. Postav was the administrative center and housed the governmental agencies including the office of the district commissioner, the Tax Bureau and similar departments. As noted, however, it was Vilna that served as our regional cultural capital, as it did for the entire network of towns in the district. Our commercial connection to Vilna was by train. At that time, the railroad ran along the "narrow tracks" to the town of Lintup; from there the "wide tracks" continued all the way to Vilna. Wagon drivers frequently shuttled from Kobylnik to Vilna for commercial purposes; in the summer they transported their wares on wagons and in winter on carts attached to the rear of the wagon. The round trip generally took five days.

The town's population was a third Jewish (65 families, 300 people) and two thirds Gentile. The latter included Poles, White Russians, and a number of Greek Orthodox. There were also a few Tatar families. Most of the non–Jews were in the farming sector (alternatively peasants) while most of the Jews were either merchants or shopkeepers.

The Jews owned grocery stores (they carried anything from heating oil, flour, and cooking oil to sewing needles and thread, and shoelaces); there were also fabric shops, shoe stores, and butcher and fish shops. The local apothecary was Jewish–owned. Besides the flour mill–that belonged to my father Shlomo and his brother Dovid— there were no factories or any type of industry in Kobylnik.

The Jewish shops were closed Saturday and Sunday. Sunday was Poland's official Sabbath. On that day the local farmers crowded into town for church services and ceremonies. The Jews did not observe Sunday and business was performed informally and inconspicuously. Since most of the Jewish shops were adjacent to the owners' residences it was possible to conduct business easily and without outside interference.

The town had a small number of families (5–6) whose livelihood was fishing. Kobylnik was only 4 km from Poland's biggest and best–known river, the Narach. Jewish families in the fishing business owned both summer and winter nets and their fishing enterprise was operated together with the village farmers and peasants from the nearby towns Kupa and Psinki.

In the later years, the (Polish) farmers bought their own nets and eventually the Jewish families abandoned fishing altogether.

A number of families, amongst them Yanovski and others, leased fruit orchards seasonally (in summer) from the local noblemen, and they supplemented their incomes that way. It should be noted that orchard leasing was extensive and attracted Jews from as far away as Vilna and even central Poland; they competed for rights with the locals. The competition often bordered on the combative. Arguments for leases grew especially fierce when the trees began to bear fruit, around Passover, even before the extent of the season's yield and productivity was known.

Almost every Jew had a vegetable garden and a barn cow on his property. The animal waste (fertilizer) was sold to local farmers in exchange for equal quantities of potatoes (after harvest).

Other Jewish families simply tilled the soil. Those Jewish families (Glot, Milkman, Yanovski, Gordon–Joshua) leased parcels from local farmers and worked them. Typically this work was not a primary, but rather, a supplementary form of income. The Yanovskis, for example, sold pottery to local farmers during Market Days. And David Glot was the representative for the Singer Sewing Machine Company. He would travel from town to town, trying to convince the farmers' wives to purchase the newest models.

What forms of work and sources of income did Jews almost deliberately avoid?

During the winter and summer seasons they would buy chickens and eggs from the peasants; in winter the farmers brought to market dried (smoked) mushrooms, pig hairs, flax and flax seeds, foal (horse) hides, fox furs, rabbit skins, and the like. and the vendors found a willing clientele amongst the Jews. Kobylnik's Jews, in turn, assembled parcels for shipment and sale to Vilna.

The commerce in fish was not solely retail. Kobylnik, as noted, was situated near the banks of the river Narach and became a commercial center for fish sale and distribution. Local farmers came in from the countryside bringing fish into town and sold them to Jewish merchants. As in the case of other items and wares, Kobylnik's Jews repackaged and redistributed the goods to Vilna. In winter the ultimate destinations for the fish supply extended as far as Warsaw. Along with these standard shipments there were also deliveries of Poland's dietary staple, apples.

Tuesday was the designated weekly "Market Day" in Kobylnik. Farmers, peasants, and locals from all over the area descended on the town in their wagons and assembled in the Market Square: sellers and buyers alike. As expected, the Jewish merchants looked forward to this day all week.

There were Market Days in most towns in the vicinity. In Postov that day was Monday. In Myadel and Hidotzishok [now Adutiskis], closer to Kobylnik, it was Thursday. The local merchants typically checked out all the local markets during the designated Market Days of the week.

At a general festive gathering in town

The butchers bought beef, lamb, and veal on Market Day and sold largely to two main groups: to the local Jews and to local (district) government workers (chiefly police, teachers, and postal agents).

On special occasions Market Days were combined with street fairs. Kobylnik, like other regional towns, hosted a number of them. These were especially prominent affairs. They attracted large numbers of peasants and villagers. The Jews anticipated these days with baited breath and counted the days until the next such event.

Of course, Kobylnik also numbered many artisans in the town. These included shoe–makers, tailors, and tinsmiths; there were also two blacksmiths.

The majority of Jews derived their income from the local rural folk and their economic situation, with very few exceptions, was depressed. I would note that the situation of the Gentile population, economically engaged in tilling the soil and crop agriculture, was also quite depressed. The main reason for this was that the soils were rocky and largely unsuited for high yield crop production.

There was yet another economic activity favored by the Jewish community of Kobylnik. It was very noteworthy. Almost every family in town had relatives overseas. And these relatives, who had left their families years earlier, never forgot their kinfolk (in the "Old Country") and sent them money and consumer goods on a regular basis. For this reason the town's residents held their overseas relatives in the utmost esteem.

Until the entry of the Red Army to Kobylnik, in September, 1939, the town sustained a Charity Fund ("Gemilut Chasadim") which was linked (with collected proceeds) to the network of collection charities centered in Vilna (called "YaKaPa"). Later the administrative center of the Charity Fund was moved to Warsaw (referred to as an "Interest–Free Center for Credit").

The YaKaPa was run by an elected Executive Committee, that managed lending and credit matters on a volunteer basis. The Committee was headed up by my brothers David and Sholom. They ran it for years, and my brother and I took care of the accounting at the time. We all gave unstintingly to this organization.

Almost all of Kobylnik's residents were members of "Gemilut Chasadim". The Fund would issue loans up to 250–300 zlotys, with a bi–weekly dispensation of up to 10–20 zlotys, all interest–free. For this reason the Fund assumed a unique position in the town's legacy.

[Pages 82-88]

Memories From the Old Home

by Pinchas Kariv (Krivitzki)

1. Remembering Shaye Yoshe the Beadle–a Person of Unusual Character

Translated by Ann Jaffe

Edited by Toby Bird

One can't remember everything after so many years, but some episodes about a one–of–a–kind individual remains engraved in my memory. One such individual was Yishayahu Yosef Gordon. In town he was called Shaye Yoshe the Beadle. Young and old knew him by this name. Why was his title Beadle? I don't know. If they would have asked me, I would have called him president. Why not? I am not sure if a president would have taken upon himself so many obligations than the so–called Beadle did, all this not for pay, but for the sake of Heaven. Everything and anything that needed to be done in town he did, without being asked. He was always the first one to do it and his initiative energized others.

At a wedding in town, he was the first guest (mechuten) to arrive, more dedicated than the real relatives. He put up the Chuppa (wedding canopy) on four poles near the synagogue and he sang the wedding songs and the prayers. If, God forbid, someone got sick in town, he was the first one to visit them. If a tragedy happened and someone died, he was the first one to come and make the burial arrangements. If money was needed for the poor to celebrate the holiday of Passover, it was he who collected the money for support. If a woman remained an old maid because she did not have a dowry, it was Shaye Yoshe, who saw to it that money for a dowry was gathered. If a poor maiden married and did not receive gifts, it was he who went door to door and gathered wedding gifts for her.

When someone fell on hard times and had no income and could not heat the house in winter and the family was cold, it was Shaye Yoshe who clandestinely dropped off a wagon of wood so that a Jewish family with little children would not freeze to death.

He looked like a birch tree in the forest – straight, tall and with his long legs constantly marching from one end of town to the other. One could see him everywhere: Passover, in the Matza baking place and in the bath house where Jews made their dishes kosher. He was the only man in town to whom anyone in need could turn. If someone was ailing and thought it was an evil eye, they call on Shaye Yoshe.

He had a long white beard and looked like a patriarch, the way we imagined our patriarchs looked when we were young children in grade school (chader). His presence evoked respect and humility (derech eretz). In the synagogue he was king. Everything was done according to his requests. During Sabbath and the holidays he would decide who will conduct the morning service, who the additional service (musaf), who will be called up to the Torah, and who will do the other parts of the service. Everything was properly and carefully calculated and arranged.

Before a holiday one could see Shaye Yoshe in his fullest glory. Dressed in his holiday attire, he sparkled with happiness. It gave him special pleasure, before the special prayer the evening before Yorn Kippur, when the so called nicest (richest) men in town would prostrate before him on a straw–covered floor and he would give them lashes in the right place (for their transgressions–an old symbolic custom).

When he entered the synagogue, silence would fall. All the mischief-makers would close their mouths and become quiet. I alone had a special privilege to get to know him better than all my friends. Since we lived near the synagogue, he often took me to help him light the big gas lamp that hung in the middle of the synagogue. And so, before every Shabbat and every holiday, before the worshipers gathered to greet the Sabbath, I was his helper because he couldn't do it himself. His fingers were getting stiff and began to shake. I was good at it and did it relatively fast. Later on, I had something to brag about to my friends, telling them stories about Shaye Yoshe.

As long as I can remember, he did not have a wife. She probably died earlier. I remember that he had two daughters in Kobylnik, neither married. Their names were Bertha and Chava. If I am not mistaken, a young son of his died after WW1. Two of his daughters emigrated to the USA. Shaye Yoshe had the privilege of dying a natural death in 1938 before the German murderers occupied Kobylnik and murdered most of the Jews.

Translator's notes:

To us Shaye Yoshe was known as uncle Shaye Yoshe. He was my grandfather Hertzl's brother. Since my grandfather died very young (he was in his mid-thirties), and my grandmother Rivka was left with five little children, Shaye Yoshe became a surrogate father to my mother Chava and the rest of her siblings. My mother was three years old when her father Hertzl died of pneumonia. I was seven years old when uncle Shaye Yoshe died. I remember him very well. My mother was a very close friend of his daughters till the last days. We have a couple of pictures of Bertha, Chava, my mother's older sister Slava, and my mother (also named Chava).

I, Ann Jaffe (Chana Swirski) and my brother Joshua Swirski often reminisce about our old home town of Kobylnik.

For the title I chose Memories as opposed to Remembrances.

2. Cultural and Social Activities in the Town
Translation by Janie Respitz
Edited by Toby Bird

This was the end of the 1920s. The town's youth were idle. A few went to work every day and the rest just hung around. There was nowhere for them to spend their time and the time passed slowly. In the autumn and winter, when it was dark and the mud in the streets came up to your knees, they all sat confined at home feeling sad. It was during these times that a group of young friends in town decided to found a library to enrich the consciousness of the youth and raise their cultural level.

In order to carry out this idea we needed a source of funding to buy books. We had the idea to use our own "artistic" talents, and put on a show. We would sell tickets and from the money we would raise, we would buy books. We also realized that the monthly fee of our members would bring in some money as well.

On the Narach

Although we were not actors, we took on all the roles of the play. For our first performance we chose "Motl and Kopl" written by Sholem Aleichem. The Participants were: Boruch Axelrod, Bayla, Michal and Yitzchak Yavnovich, Dobke and Liber Kirmelisky, Ite Raize and Yechezkel Todres, Gitl Klumel, Dvoshke Yanovsky and others. It goes without saying we chose the best we had, all the young, beautiful kids, actors each and every one. The teachers from the Yiddish school helped us out, as did Yitzchak Levitan and Chaim Lipe Svirsky, who were a lot older than we were, but they considered our goal worthwhile.

We worked very diligently. There was a lot to worry about, beginning with decorations, sets and other behind–the–scene preparations. I remember until today how we went from house to house collecting tablecloths for the curtain. We also collected wood for the stage and benches to sit on.

Another issue was to find an appropriate venue for the performance. The Poles in town had a Folk–House, but Yiddish theatre was not permitted there. We had to manage with what we had. After a lot of searching we found a large place that belonged to Shepsl Berger. It was used as a warehouse for produce like potatoes, apples and other things. We had to empty the place and prepare it for a theatrical production.

Slowly we arranged everything, and after many long rehearsals that took place in the evening there was one thing left to arrange – to obtain permission from the authorities to perform. Since we could not get it, we decided we would still go ahead without it, but unfortunately, we were mistaken. The night of the performance, tickets already sold, the audience was seated and awaited the curtain to go up – a policeman came and ordered everyone to leave. In short, our complaints didn't help; we were forbidden to perform and we had to refund the money from ticket sales.

But despite this failure we were not giving up. After many attempts by Noach Todres to the authorities in Postov, we received permission. The performance took place a few months later and it was a great success. We managed to raise money and buy books; the library in Kobylnik was founded.

The library slowly grew until – until the big fire on May 1st 1930. The entire library went up in smoke.

But we did not give up. After the fire we turned to the surrounding towns – we even went to further ones – and asked for help in the form of books, in order to rebuild our library. And really quickly they sent us books, and the library once again existed.

Parallel to the library endeavor that instilled great enthusiasm among the youth, we found another branch of work – sports and football. If I remember, our football team was made up of Jewish boys and a few non- Jews; together we competed against other teams from the area. Sometimes we would be the guests in another town like Svir, Pastov, Sventzion and others. Social activities with non–Jews in those days were still possible.

Also, a wind orchestra was founded by the fire fighters, also together with non–Jews. We gave concerts and had solemn events which were very successful.

And now there are only sad memories for those who survived, and an emptiness gnaws deep in our hearts for the life which has disappeared and will never return.

Football players in Kobylnik

A general celebration in Kobylnik in the 1930s

[Pages 89-96]

Kobylnik's Landscape and Characters
by Yehoshua Svidler
Translated by Janie Respitz
Edited by Toby Bird

Kobylnik, which was situated on the road between two large cities – Vilna and Pultusk – was quiet all week; the town was cut off from the outside world. It was rare when a free thought entered. Our parents lived according to their understanding: raw and primitive like nature, pious, good and modest, happy with their fate and not worried about a thing. Time went on at a natural pace. From time to time a peasant's wagon would lose its way and end up in our marketplace. The squeaking of the old wooden ungreased wheels and the wild screams of the peasant to his horse woke up the shopkeepers of our town from their dreams. All faces were now turned in the same direction.

Kobylnik Goats

Meanwhile the peasant stops, like a nobleman, in the muddy marketplace. He unharnesses his horse and gives him something to chew and majestically walks through the mud. The first to take advantage of this visit are the goats. They fall upon the wagon and help the horse eat. They waste a lot of hay and make a big mess. While searching, they find a bag filled with oats. The horse stands naively and helpless with his head down. Meanwhile the goats eat with zest. The peasant notices what's happening and comes running with anger. The goats sense the danger and run away.

Kobylnik is known far and wide for its goats. Even the residents received the nickname "Kobylnik Goats." They wander through the streets freely, in the marketplace, eating from the peasant's wagons, straw from the roofs...yes, every poor man had a couple of goats and a lot of children.

We kids couldn't stand the pigs. We persecuted them bitterly. Their central place was in the middle of the marketplace. They would spread out in the mud and enjoy sun bathing. For pleasure they would close their squinted eyes, spread their piggy little legs and oink happily. What can you compare this to?

My friends and I would hail stones on these guests. Not living and not dead they would run in panic squealing like pigs.

The Flock Comes Home

The town looked different in the evening, the sun setting in the west, behind the church, the flocks coming home. The sleepy town would awaken for a short time from its dreams. The clamour and noise fill the air, the dust blocks the sun. The four legged creatures bring a bit of life for a while.

The first to arrive are the pigs. They always have to be first...running as if they were coming from Hungryland. Their long ears hang down over their small eyes. They can hardly see. Their little feet carry them quickly so they can get to their food as fast as possible.

After them the sheep come running, trembling. Frightened and helpless, they jump on top of each other. Sometimes they just stand still, look around and cry with such a pitiful voice that it tears your heart, then continue running. Then the goats come but it is more difficult for them to run as their udders are full.

The cows appear different. They walk slowly with measured steps, half sleepy and lazy. They stop and stand around at each gate, look around and begin to moo; they let everyone know: they are arriving.

Night

Night falls. Nature sleeps. Everything has sunken into a deep sleep – the forest, the town. It is quiet all around. You can only hear the water running in the river. The waves are playing joyfully. From far away you can hear the croaking of frogs; they are singing their requests to the night kings.

The night queen rules with her charm. From a nearby forest we hear dull voices. A mild wind blows through the grasses in the field and caresses the flowers in the garden. The whole world sleeps. Our little town sleeps as well.

At Night in the House of Study

In the long winter evenings the elderly would sit in the House of Study (Beit Midrash), reading a page of the Gemorah or "Eyn Yakov" warming their cold limbs. It was a pleasure to spend a cold, frosty winter night by a warm stove and listen to the interesting stories people told. Here is where you could hear and learn everything; of course, no gossip was lacking either. One would learn that Yankl's cow was about to give birth, whose wife was about to deliver and whose potatoes froze in the cellar.

Meyer the dyer sits at an open Gemorah, the pages soiled from milk. He sits and learns. His melancholy voice rings through the entire House of Study. The crowd absorbs every word. From time to time Shaye Yoseh hands out a sniff of tobacco from his twisted tobacco pouch that is on the table. Sometimes, the learning is disturbed by a loud bang on a book. This is the beadle demanding the crowd to be quiet and not disrupt those wanting to learn. The silence would resume. You could hear the clock on the wall ticking.

In a corner, beside the Holy Ark, Shabbatai sat and read to himself. He swayed with great zeal, and the wooden bench moved with him. His voice was sad, soaked in troubles and prayer; this was carried through the whole House of Study.

In another corner, Yakov –Yosef sits and tells stories. He was a smart Jew and people liked listening to him, a fine little man with a scant white beard, with happy, laughing eyes. While recounting his stories he always held his beard, as if explaining a difficult law. With eyes half shut and with a quiet voice, he measured and calculated each word. He was capable of keeping his audience in suspense.

He would always begin with the phrase "What else do you need"? "This is what happened to me..." – and he would begin his story with such great enthusiasm, his audience would swallow every word. Silence prevailed. You could only hear the melancholy ticking of the clock. The memorial candle flickered like a man about to die. The shadows strode secretly on the walls. A pale shine from the candle barely lit the big building. The frost outside crackled. You could hear it clearly. The windows were covered with ice.

"It was a hot summer day," begins his story. That day I was at the fair. In the evening after everyone already left, I set out for home. The road led us through a thick forest. The peasant was sleeping. The horses pulled us slowly along the sandy road. I was deep in thought. It was dark; we could not see a thing; we could only hear the panting of the horse. It is unwelcoming. A shiver crawls on my skin. Often, the horse perks up his ears as if he hears something. I wake up the sleeping peasant and ask: 'Where in the world are we?' It appears the horse went in another direction, off our route. The peasant got down from the wagon, tapped around in the darkness and felt a living creature, and what do you think it was."

But Reb Yakov Yosef doesn't rush. He keeps his audience in suspense, and a little while later he continues: "It was a sheep. We were both able to put the sheep in the wagon... "

Until the listeners heard the end, that the sheep was in fact not a sheep, but a ghost in the shape of a man, and that they suddenly began to laugh loudly, jumped off the wagon and disappeared –they sat spellbound, as though they experienced it.

The little flames from the candles flicker. Shadows of people swinging like phantoms, the hands of the clock are not standing still. They remind the people that it is time to go home.

Simchat Torah Rhymes

Simchat Torah has arrived – Firstly, we must thank our beadle Shaya – Yoseh. He was a joyful and happy Jew; and a great Hasid. He excited everyone with his songs and attitude.

But he was not alone. As the whisky poured like water, many of our respectable Hasidim showed us what Simchat Torah was all about. Eliyahu the shopkeeper, a fine, respectable Hasid, showed in his way, what Simchat Torah means. He sang and made merry, although it was difficult to understand him: he spoke through his nose, and not clearly, but came out with such rhymes that made people roll with laughter. " Jews are blessed – Goyim have malaria."

When Simchat Torah fell on Shabbat the Kobylnik housewives were not sure about their Cholent (Sabbath stew). Black Leyzer together with a few other Hasidim removed everyone's Cholent from the ovens and ate in the middle of the marketplace. And there, while everyone was eating, Shaya – Yoseh would show off his rhyming talent; a few have remained in my memory. The song was sung according to the alphabet and everyone joined in the refrain:

Workers who are hard at work, drink wine and make a blessing.
Wagon drivers travelling along, drink wine when they are afraid.
Thieves sitting in hiding, drink from clay pitchers.
Judges who pass judgement drink the best sorts.
Merchants who go to the market drink from a full jug.
Women who sit at home drink wine and eat olives.
Cantors who stand at pulpits drink wine from a pretty jug.
Jews who partake in Torah drink wine when they are scared.

And so on.

A – All are dressed like the rich.

B – Barefoot are the poor.

C – Cooked chickens are eaten by the rich.

D – Doubts and worries belong to the poor.

E – Eating chicken soup is enjoyed by the rich.

F – Full of pains are the poor.

G – Garments of satin are worn by the rich.

H – Huts are inhabited by the poor.

I – Intricate clothing is worn by the rich.

J – Joy is unknown to the poor.

K – Kingly chrome tanned calfskin boots are worn by the rich.

L – Light woven hemp boots are worn by the poor.

M – Men are obviously the rich.

N – Numbskulls are the poor.

O – Ornate satin clothing is worn by the rich.

P – People who are meek are poor.

Q – Quality plush is worn by the rich.

R – Ragged are the poor.

S – Shershevesky's cigarettes are smoked by the rich.

T – Titon Machorke Polski cigarettes are smoked by the poor.

We also sang songs in three languages like this:

Candle – in Hebrew Yiddish and Polish
An Oven– in Hebrew Yiddish and Polish
And so on...
This was Simchat Torah.

Shaul– Yonah and Shlomo – Meneh

Shaul – Yonah was a mid– sized man. He fancied himself to be an educated, modern person. He was always well dresses, clean shaven, with a pair of gold glasses on his red fleshy nose, which he was always blowing. He walked around like a puppet. This is how he was referred to in the town. His steps were measured. He spoke matter–of–factly and calmly; he actually calculated his words. He was deaf and filled his ears with cotton, in winter and summer. When he spoke to someone he always held his hand to his ear to hear them better. He earned his living at a tavern where he was the lessor, but the real boss was his wife; he could really depend on her. He was able to have fun with his neighbour Shlomo – Meneh.

Shlomo – Meneh was an intelligent man with a grocery store. Besides his business he was a writer in the rural district and sent his books to the administrative office. He wrote petitions for the authorities, contrary to all the functionaries. He managed the books of the community, inscribing marriages and births. In one word, he was the guy the functionaries dealt with; the police superintendent himself would come to visit. He would walk around, in those days of the Enlightenment, in a short jacket and a trimmed beard, with a gold pince–nez on his long nose. He would sit with Shaul– Yona by a boiling Samovar and play chess.

Esther Chaya the Cupping Placer

A Jewish woman who always did what God asked of her. Her job was cupping, particularly among the Christian villagers. This was not extremely hygienic. Her medical instruments were tin cups and a rusty little knife. Before she would place her cups, wet or dry, she would already receive a basket of potatoes, or a pot of peas – and both parties were happy.

———

[Pages 97-100]

Blood Libel
by Meir Yavni (Yavnovich)
Translated by Gilad Petranker
Edited by Toby Bird
The spiders of hatred

It was toward the end of 1934, the days of the "flirting" between the rulers of Poland and Nazi Germany. A sun of late summer shone and warmed the world, which started declining on a slope of calamity and evil. The evils of the world started planning their evil thoughts, like the prophet had said (Yeshaya 59 5): "They hatch cockatrice' eggs, and weave the spider's web." But the world did not yet know that "He that eateth of their eggs dieth, and that which is crushed breaketh out into a viper."

Concealed and in the open, the spiders of hatred weaved their schemes against the free world, and especially against the Jews. The fruit of this hatred started ripening. On those days, a wild inciting for boycott started against the Jews. In the marketplace, watches were marching next to the Jews' shops to prevent any kind of bargain or commerce with the Jews. The audacity of the various persecutors of Israel and their call "Jews to Palestine" accompanied us everywhere.

The story of a Christian peasant

On one of the first days of autumn I happened to go to the post office. And that time, a Polish or Byelorussian woman from the neighboring village came in, and worriedly said that her six or seven–year–old son was lost and missing, and asked the post office clerk to call the Strusta (the district governor) in Potzbi and ask for his help in searching for her missing son. In her story, she emphasized one detail that interested me, that on the day when her son disappeared there was no stranger in the village, apart from a yellow Jew, a peddler, who was buying rags. I couldn't hold back and I asked what did that Jew have to do with her missing son. She replied with mock innocence that she meant no harm by that, it was just that no other stranger happened to be in the village that day, no one she could suspect that might have any connection to her son's disappearance. Her intentions were crystal clear despite her so–called innocent attempts to avoid the problem. The post office clerk replied that it was not his job to call the district's governor and that she should go to the police about the matter. She claimed again that she was indeed sent to the post office by the policemen themselves, who advised her to do take that action. The plan was probably set beforehand, and the woman was directed to act that way by the foundations for whom this incident acted as good material to incite against the Jews, as they did at the time. And as for the clerk– he did not comply to the woman's request and insisted that in his view this was not the correct way to take care of the incident.

The libel

At that moment I understood that a plot was being made against us, but I did not imagine that this would grow into an actual blood libel that would upset the entire town and the area, a libel that would be used to grease the cogs of the hatred for Israel, which started turning quickly in those days. The rumor of the missing boy spread fast and the tale about the yellow Jew who kidnapped the boy went all around the district. Of course, the intention of kidnapping the boy was his blood, needed for baking the Matzos of the Jews in the upcoming Passover.

The hatred for the Jews grew from day to day; it was felt in the air. In the evenings, incited thugs would gather on the streets of the town. There were also incidents of glass shattering in Jewish houses and it was dangerous for Jews to go out at night. The libel was "adorned" by the inciters with details, letting their imagination and hatred flow freely. They even named the names of the wealthy house owners in town who donated their money to bribe the authorities so they would not act against the committers of the "crime."

After a week or two from the day the woman appeared, the boy was found in the forest, dead, sitting under a tree, with one of his arms gnawed, probably by birds or an animal. In her investigation the woman said that on that day she went to the forest to gather up wood and the boy followed her. She sent him away several times and ordered him to go back home but the boy kept on following her. When she went into the forest, he disappeared, and she thought he went back home. But apparently, he went into the forest as well and couldn't find his way back home nor find his mother, who went farther from him. In an autopsy, a government doctor determined that the boy had died of fear and hunger, since leaves were found in his stomach which he tried to eat to deal with the hunger. The boy was re–buried and it seemed that everything would settle down after the libel was proved wrong, but that was not what happened. The hatred for Israel grew stronger every day, nursed in a well devised plan by the anti–Semitic foundations in town, whose main purpose was push away the Jews from their financial positions and to take their place in commerce and craft. These foundations included teachers, policemen, officials, who held a poisonous incitement and went on nursing the hatred with the use of the libel, a weapon which they were not happy to give up. So, they spread rumors, that the government commission, which was set to determine the boy's cause of death, was bribed by the Jews of town and of neighboring towns and even named the sums and the names of wealthy Jews who donated large sums for the purpose. The venom of hatred went on spreading and gave its signs. On the market days, there would be an air of Pogrom, a mass lynching. The peasants of the area would stream in to town with sacks for the loot, and "blunt" weapons like axes and knives to wreak havoc on the Jews. Things came to a point where every week the authorities had to draft the entire police force of the district in order to keep the peace, because it was not in their interest back then to give complete liberty to the incited mob.

The incitement goes on

On one of the days the district governor happened to come to town, the Jews of town sent to him a delegation, which I took part in as well, since I was proficient in the Polish language. I extensively talked about the state of things in the ears of the governor and asked him to protect the lives of the Jews in town and their property. The governor promised to do everything in order to keep the peace and to stop the incitement.

Again, a governmental committee of inquiry was set up, this time on a higher rank, by the regional governor in Vilna. The corpse of the boy was once again dug out of the grave and meticulously checked in the presence of Polish citizens from town. The ruling was identical with the one of the first committee and was made public on the billboards, along with the warning to stop all acts of incitement and spreading false rumors. But the incitement did not stop; this was organized by anti–Semitic foundations in the place and drew its inspiration from above. Even the persuasion of the town's Jews by the priest, who had a critical influence over his Christian congregation, didn't yield anything; the priest was also anti–Semitic. And more market days went by with the fear of riots, and reinforced police forces kept the peace in town. The accusations of libel kept up for about three months and subsided only with the approach of Christmas. But the hatred for Jews and the incitement for boycott went on, and it was well known who were the ones pulling the strings, but no restricting action was taken against them because plain hatred of Jews and incitement and boycott was a formal line of action of the authorities in all of Poland, inspired by the nonaggression pact between Beck, the Polish foreign minister and Hitler, damn his name. It should be mentioned that years after the incident, a teacher from the government school would take her class, among whom were children of Israel, to the Christian cemetery, to visit the grave of the mentioned boy and would explain how the boy was murdered by the Jews.

The opinion of enlightened and friendly Goyim

About the libel I remember the version of one of the Goyim who used to visit us. He was the Soltis (the representative of the civil rule and its messenger, a sort of official), who one day came to our house and wanted, as an enlightened friend, to sweeten the bitter story of the libel. And so he said with great importance, that he does not believe, God forbid, that we, the enlightened and advanced Jews have a part in using Christian blood for Matzos, but it is known that there is a dark and zealous cult within Judaism, and they performed the kidnapping of the boy, and even us Jews did not know who they were. So he tried to speak positively of us. But my mother, who had civil courage, threw harsh things in his face: "I hope dogs will lap the blood of the haters of Israel, and have no need of the blood of Christians." The "friend" heard these things and parted shamefully.

***

We did not know in those days and did not imagine where this poisonous hatred would lead. We hoped that this murky wave would pass, as it did more than once in our history, and the haters of Israel will be lost – but "They hatch cockatrice' eggs" and the Jews of the world ate from these eggs and died; died in multitudes, when they were led by the vipers and the cockatrices – to be slaughtered.

[Pages 101-102]

The Great Fire in Kobylnik 1930
by Yehoshua Svidler
Translated by Janie Respitz
Edited by Toby Bird

Kobylnik was blessed with fires. A legend circulated in Kobylnik that older people would tell, that a curse hung over the town, cursed by a righteous man who lay buried in the cemetery forgotten by the community.

The legend said that Kobylnik must burn every twelve years. Who knows if Kobylnik burned because of its wooden houses and roofs made mainly of straw, or because of the curse of the righteous man. Facts are facts – every twelve years the town burned. We heard about the fires of 1894 and 1906; the fire of 1918 we witnessed as children – but the great fire of 1930 was clear in our memories. (By the way, Kobylnik burned again in 1942.).

It was a beautiful summer day, Thursday May 1st. Many of us were by chance at the market which was taking place in the neighbouring town of Myadel. It was very early. The town was just waking up from its sleep. The houses were standing as if dreaming. Silence ruled. No one could even begin to imagine that soon the devil's dance would begin that would bring fear, pain and despair.

The fire began on the "other" side of the bridge, from Postover Street. The town now awoke from its dream and everyone ran to help. To our great surprise the fire was carried to the centre of the market, a distance of 400 metres and jumped like a wild animal from one courtyard to another. The wooden homes covered with straw and shingle roofs flared up like torches. The crowd was wild and scared and ran to save their belongings – but the town was surrounded by a sea of fire and no one knew what to do. The mayor immediately told the surrounding area that Kobylnik was burning on all four sides.

Meanwhile the fire spread more and more and consumed one house after the other; the wild flames were like turbulent waves in a stormy sea that raged undisturbed. The giant pillars of smoke and flaming sparks tore towards the sky and blocked the sun shine. The crying and wailing and crackling of the burning fire mixed together like a wild concert.

Soon fire fighters from eight surrounding towns arrived, but unfortunately, there was nothing left to extinguish. They were able to prevent further spreading, but they lacked water – the river was depleted. It was also difficult for them to approach the burning streets due to the terrifying flames that the storm winds were enlarging. The flames rolled on the soil like poisonous snakes.

We were then notified that our study house began to burn! From the shingled roof there were small flames like little candles. We ran with all our strength not to allow our synagogue to burn; if this had not been successful, the other half of the town would have been in danger.

The fire lasted until late into the night. The town looked like a cemetery; the black smoking chimneys looked like tombstones; everyone was frightened. The houses on the other side of the market stood helpless; in the window panes one saw the red sheen of burning houses. The fire did not want to calm down – and in some places grabbed the opportunity to claim more victims. The half–burnt embers shone and gave out a greenish–yellow flame, and with a devilish little tongue searched and waited.

People went around broken and embittered. Everyone stood by his ruin and poured tears on the hot stones. People strode around among the destruction and mourned as if for the deceased.

It took a long time for the town to return to its former self, and was rebuilt – this time not from wood, but from stone and brick.

———

[Pages 103-106]

Yeshayahu–Yosef the Beadle
by Meir Yavni (Yavnovich)
Translated by Gilad Petranker
Edited by Toby Bird

This was the way everyone called him – Yeshaya–Yosef the Shamash (Shaya Yoseh Shamash). He was tall with an upright stance. He wore his white beard long, dressed throughout the year in a faded gray Bekishe and wore a sash that had its ends loose on both sides, in the custom of the time.

He was called Shamash by everyone, but in practice he was the spiritual leader of the town for many years, an unanointed Gabbai who has never been elected. With the changes taking place in the life of the town, so did his position start to wane in the last years before the Holocaust. But I can still remember the days of his glory, when he was still the leader or ruler of town.

****

As a little boy, I would follow all his actions at the synagogue, that was almost under his ruling alone. With great curiosity, I would look at him while he was standing next to the cabinet in the corner of the synagogue, where its treasures were hidden, such as wine for Kiddush and Havdalah, cups, candles, siddur, a box of snuff with which Shaya Yoseh would like to treat the people coming for prayer, Tallit and Tefillin for guests who might need them, a "Besamim Biksle" – perfumes – for smelling and other objects of ritual.

With envy, I would stare at him, with his hands taking care of the various objects in the cabinet, wanting to go into the secret of the treasures hidden in the cabinet. But I looked at him only from afar, since a stranger might not go into the realm of Shaya–Yoseh, who would terrify the mischievous brats trying to cause trouble in the synagogue. Indeed, his upright stance, his angry glare, his scolding would remove any desire to perform such acts, and when he would approach to put everything back in order, the children would flee full of fear.

***

I remember he gave me the privilege of having a conversation with him, in which he revealed his conservative views. He had harsh things to say against the "Bibliateke," the library, against the "foul" books, that he saw as Terefah, an abomination. He completely denounced the importance of both the words and authors who wrote them – Mendele, Shalom Aleychem, Peretz and others. What value does their writing have, what point? All their writing is useless and empty. What are they worth, compared to the sacred books, which contain the living words of God, which will stand forever. And the writing of these authors is heresy; they are foul and their writing is foul, unworthy things which spoil the generation. Only one path stands before the Jew– the path of Mitzvas and Torah, while the "Bichlech" – the booklets – came to destroy our world. I listened silently to what he was saying, though not in consent, but I dared not go against him and argue, because who was I, the little boy, in front of the tall white–bearded Shaya, who everyone deemed important.

***

As mentioned, Shaya–Yosef was the unanointed leader of the town, unlike other Shamashim who had the other roles in the synagogue, such as feeding the stove, bringing water, lighting candles, cleaning the bathroom etc. He was a Gabbai who was never elected, with a constant uncontested authority, which did not expire after the end of his term. The simpler roles of the various services were conducted by his deputy, Yosef the fisherman ("Yoseh der Fisher"). Shaya–Yoseh was an owner of the synagogue of sorts, handling the finances and the orderly conduct, the rituals and all the capital it held. The leaders of prayer were often at his mercy. Will they be allowed to pass in front of the Ark or not? Will they get a decent portion like the Musaf prayer on Shabbat or on the High Holidays, or only a weekday prayer of Minha or Shaharit? His determined intervention and ruling in this matter, as in in other subjects, would often cause resentment and would be even a source of fights, especially on Shabbat and holidays, but Shaya–Yoseh would insist that it was his right to rule on these matters.

On Shabbat, he would sometimes delay the reading of the Torah when he thought there was an urgent public matter to be resolved, or when he thought that someone had done something abominable, to his view. He would go up on the platform, give the table a strong pat, and announce: "I am delaying the reading," and loudly lecture about the reason for the delay. His stance would sometime arouse opposition and plenty of resentment. Heated arguments would arise, but usually Shaya–Yoseh's opinion would get accepted, or the controversy would end in a compromise that would be to everyone's satisfaction.

The distribution and selling of the ascents to read the Torah would all be managed by Shaya–Yoseh. He would fight a bitter battle when he thought there was a need to help those in need in town who were deprived, the sick or other unfortunate people. He would firmly demand that those in need of help from the majority would not be left alone. I remember that he once harshly attacked those heading a charity fund – Gamach – that was operating in town at the time, and that was headed by my brother Shalom, God rest his soul, for refusing to take out money to help a poor family to help treat a baby who was terminally ill. He would not be convinced that the fund was for loans and not for charity, and yelled out: "One soul in Israel has to be sustained, even if it is a baby, because it is unknown what will become of this baby; and it is written – one who revives one soul, it is as if he revived the entire world."

True to this view, in recent years he started to regularly go from house to house collecting charity for treating the sick. In a squished notebook, he would write the names of all the heads of family, and divided the page into columns according to the week's Parashah. In summer and in winter, in autumn and in spring, in snow and in mud, in heat and cold– he would march from house to house collecting the few pennies for "Bikur Holim," treating the sick. He would write down the money he collected in shaky hands, with his head shaking as well, because in the last years he had Parkinson's disease.

***

On times of holidays, the figure of Shaya–Yoseh would shine, and he would have a countenance of joy.

Then he would be of good spirit, wearing his black satin Bekishe, put on a special sash, and on the eve of the holiday he would come early to the synagogue, preparing the gas lamp. This job was somehow very important to him and did not belong to his deputy. He would do this job very carefully. On his normally angry face would spread a wide and hearty smile; when his hands started shaking he would call in his neighbors to help in the task.

Like a commander over an army he would go every morning from house to house with a linen–wrapped Etrog in a special box in one hand, and his second hand holding the Lulav. With great importance, he would march through the town's streets, visiting every Jewish house, greeting with the holiday's greeting when he enters the house with a special delight and immediately inviting for the Mitzvas of Netilat Lulav and Etrog everyone present – young and old, women and toddlers, with a wide smile on his face; he immensely enjoyed the fact that he was able to merit all of town with this Mitzva. After Sukkot, he would put the Lulav and Etrog in his special cabinet; from the Lulav he would pull strands to wrap the Arba'at Minim, the four species, the next year, and the Etrog he would keep for jam. On Purim his feet would tread through the melting snow and mud on the streets of the town holding a plate of Mishloach Manot.

His actions and importance were great on the eve of Yom Kippur in the synagogue. He would set the table, which held all of the charity boxes. Wearing a white Kittle and holding the whip in his hand, he would call in the heads of family to stand behind the platform, and they would come one by one to stretch on the hay–covered floor, receiving the whipping in the custom of those days. He would count his whips one by one, with a smile hiding between his mustache and beard. Along with the whipping he would also receive his salary.

One could not imagine a wedding taking place without Shaya–Yoseh being actively involved. He was the sovereign of the synagogue next to which the wedding ceremonies would take place in the courtyard, and of course he was the chief director of the ceremony, the head guest; his voice was heard out loud when he would call the parents of the bride or groom to bless their children.

And from joy to grief. He was the head of the Chevrah Kadisha; without him no funerals would be held. All the preparations involved in the funeral, setting the place in the cemetery, purifying the dead, the order of the funeral – all these were done under his direction. And so he would write down the date of the passing in his special notepad, which he would keep in the mentioned cabinet. Indeed, he was also the first in the feast that the members of the Chevrah Kadisha would hold every year on the month of Kislev.

Even though he was arousing against him the opposition and resentment of the heads of families in his severity and his extremity with his stance which they did not always appreciate, he was well respected by all, and would be forgiven after the anger would subside because Shaya–Yoseh was a part of the view of town, a part of its flesh and blood. It is hard to imagine the character of the town and its view without this tree, without his white beard, his raging eyes, his tall figure, his smile in times of holiday, his voice delaying the reading, his direction of the holiday rituals, the funerals and his firm opinion on various public affairs. If he would have gone from town one day, while the life of town was still shining and vibrant, it would be as if the soul was taken out of a living body, as if one of its limbs were cut off.

And this tree fell off the body of town before the break of the Second World War which brought the Holocaust; so he was spared the horrors of the Holocaust and all the bitter trials that his flock experienced – those who stayed alive. May his memory be blessed and reside deep in our hearts with the memory of all the other sons of town.

———

[Page 107]

Daily Life in the Town

by Yafa Pertzov (Sheinka Janowski) of Ein–Carmel
Translated by Jerrold Landau

Life in town began early in the morning. In the summer, when the night was short, and dawn appeared early in the east, the town shepherds would also arise early to lead the flocks out to pasture. The mooing of the cows and sounds of the sheep and goats blended with the creaking of the gates through which the animals went out to pasture. The bustle all about woke the townsfolk up from their deep sleep – aside from a few who were undisturbed by all this, and continued to sleep. At that time, the blinds moved from their places, and heads of people could be seen here and there through the windows of the house, as they breathed fresh air into their lungs and refreshed themselves from their morning weariness. People began to go out to the streets from various corners, and everything came to life in the market square.

Everyone was hurrying to their jobs, such as the shoemakers, smiths, and locksmiths, looked as if they were in a rush. Wagon drivers hitched their horses to their wagons, so that they could get to Lake Narach, about three kilometers from town, as quickly as possible, to load up the fresh fish that had been caught a few hours previously and transport them to the big city of Vilna.

In the Market Square

The market square was the center of the town, surrounded by shops. Business was quiet all week, and the earnings were meager, except for Tuesday, the regular market day. That day, farmers streamed in from the nearby villages. Jewish merchants from the region also came to conduct business as peddlers, stall–keepers, or in any other form. I recall that when we were small children, we waited impatiently for the market day. The screeching of the stall keepers announcing their merchandise out loud, and all the other bustle around, left a deep impression in us. It was a unique experience.

[Page 108]

Preparations for the Sabbath

Preparations for the Sabbath began as the weekend approached. Mothers would send their children to the rabbi to purchase yeast for the baking of the challos for the Sabbath. The following day, the aroma of fresh baking would waft from the Jewish houses, heralding the onset of the Sabbath.

In the afternoon hours, at candle lighting time, the Jews of the town would be wearing their festive attire, and a festive splendor would radiate from their faces. Even the children were clean and tidy, and they would be wearing their Sabbath clothes. They accompanied their parents to the synagogue. The feeling of the Sabbath enveloped the entire town. The appearance of the streets changed.

Without Class Warfare...

Even though we cannot escape the fact that there also were more wealthy and less wealthy Jews in Kobylnik, most of the Jews were poor, living in a meager situation, and lacking livelihood. Nevertheless, none of them reached the conclusion that there must be a change of the social and economic order. Even though there was a wide gap between the different groups of Jews, there was no room for class warfare. On the contrary, the relationship amongst all the Jews of the town was quite heartfelt and honest. Rather than a battle, people felt a sense of a common fate. All residents of the town, without exception, felt connected. These feelings of solidarity came to expression at times of individual sorrow, as well as with the full participation at times of joy. We must especially note the mutual assistance offered by the community to anyone in need.

*

This reality disappeared and will never return. Only deep agony and sorrow rest deep in our hearts.

[Pages 109-111]

With the Sense of Farewell
by Y. Gordon
Translated by Jerrold Landau

It was the pleasant and elongated end of summer of 1939, the time when potatoes were harvested from the fields and the late apple harvest for those apples that have ripened in the interim. I enjoyed the splendor of the nature around me and the beauty of the atmosphere in Kobylnik.

At that time, I returned to my parents' after a long period of absence, which I spent in several *hachsharah* kibbutzim in Poland. It was also after a long period of activity in Hechalutz, Heclahutz Hatzair, and HaOved in Kobylnik, preceding my time in *hachsharah*. It was good, therefore, to be at home once again, and to rest. The brief vacation that I received was designated for the preparations for my *aliya*, and to bidding farewell to the members of my family. My free time enabled me to calmly summarize the recent past and to wait with anticipation for the unknown future.

With the telegram that I received, stating "make *aliya*, and succeed," my new reality for which I had waited many years draw closer. From that time, I knew that the time had come, and that a change in my way of life would take place with my *aliya* to the Land.

[Page 110]

It is difficult to describe the feelings of joy that overtook me at that time, and it is difficult to describe the emotions of my family. I still recall the face of my mother, of blessed memory, with tears flowing from her eyes, and how her stare accompanied me wherever I went. The question as to whether we would see each other alive again certainly afflicted her. Indeed, her suspicions were not in valid... My dear father acted as if he was in control, and did not allow himself to show any weakness in his diligence to prepare and pack my belongings... When we parted, he said with tears in his eyes:"Remember, my son. Do not forget us. Succeed in your new path." My older brother patted my shoulder and said,"Be strong, and do not worry!" He expressed his hope to see me in the Land. To my sorrow, his hope did not materialize.

It was Friday afternoon, before the Sabbath entered the bounds of the town. Some people were still busy working. Since the time was brief, I used a bicycle to ride through the whole town to bid farewell. I went from house to house, not skipping any door. How could I leave the town without bidding farewell to everybody? Everything there was so close to my soul. We were literally like one family. Small barriers disappeared within a moment. I clasped the hands of my friends, and bid farewell to the all. It was a day of blessings for me. My heart was overflowing with joy and emotion... Along with this, the expressions of sadness and lack of faith that were clear on their faces were no lost on me... Just recently, there were many who related to *aliya* to the Land with skepticism – indeed, what happened?...

On the Narach

[Page 111]

Indeed, new winds began to blow over the Jewish street in the cities of Poland at that time. This was after incidents and anti–Semitism burst forth from every corner.

***

More than two decades have passed since then. When today I think about the past, about all those who once were and are no longer, I recall that sense of farewell that I felt on the day of my *aliya*. Visions of the town, of brothers and sisters, flash before my eyes incessantly. I see them all, hear their voices, and sense the expressions on their faces and the look of wonder in their eyes.

Just like then, I wish to pass by every house in the town, without skipping over any door, and to tell them all about the small and big things. All of them are so well guarded and fresh in my mind, as if time stopped moving... All of them appear before my eyes with the individual story of their lives.

I remember them with trembling, awe, and love.

[Page 112]

From the Minutes of YIVO in New York
Translated by Jerrold Landau

A copy of the minutes of the meeting of activists for the Yeshiva in Vilna, that took place in Kobylnik in 1938

Minutes

From the meeting that took place on Wednesday, 24 June, 9 a.m., here in Kobylnik. Organized by the executive committee of the center of the committee for the Yeshivas of Vilna.

1. Elections: a local committee of twelve people was chosen: chairman Rabbi Shlomo the local rabbi, his son–in–law , Reb Chaim Yaakov Janowski, his son Reb Eli Yosef, Reb Shmuel Kaplan, Reb Yitzchak Mashitz, Reb Shabtai, Lishnecki, Reb Shlomo Jaowicz, Reb Leib Swirsky, Reb Yitzchak Krowczinsky, Reb Leib Kahn, The executive committee, the supervisory committee, and the activists

    a. For the executive committee: chairman – the local rabbi may he live long, treasurer – the rabbi's son–in–law, secretary – Reb Yitzchak Mashitz

    b. Supervisory committee: 1) the local rabbi 2) Reb Zelig Swirsky, 3) Reb Yitzchak Krowczinsky.

2. The work of the committee and the activists:

    a. The chairman is responsible for supervising the budget, and ensuring that the collections will be sent out in a timely fashion, under the supervision of the committee.

    b. The treasurer is responsible for supervising the treasury balance.... (???)

    c. The secretary is responsible for all announcements.

    d. The supervisory committee is to receive a report on every activity

    e. The boxes (i.e. charity boxes)... are to be emptied out. The money collected is to be given to the treasurer. The treasurer is to also be given the keys to the boxes. He is to include the proceeds along with the account of monies received.

    f. Every member of the committee, and the activists, are to participate every half year and to receive an accounting of the work that has taken place, and to prepare themselves for the upcoming [work].

3. Types of income

    a. An accounting from the boxes should be made every two months

    b. ???

    c. ???

    d. Private donations

    e. Various ?

    f. ???

    g. ???

Chairman (–) Rabbi Leib Einbinder, local rabbi; representative of the headquarters (–) Rabbi Yaakov ???; treasurer (–) Tzvi ???; secretary (–) Yitzchak Mashitz(–) the local rabbi

[Page 119]

Holocaust

The Destruction of Kobylnik
by Yitzhak Gordon, Chuna Dimentsztajn, Asher Krukoff, Yosef Blinder
Translated by Jerrold Landau

A festive gathering of the entire population in the market square

Words of introduction from Yitzchak Gordon

The final days of Polish rule in 1939 were accompanied by increasing anti–Semitic incitement: pickets outside Jewish businesses, a semi–official government boycott on Jewish business, attacks by hooligans upon Jews on the streets, and heavy taxes imposed on the Jewish population, including the special war tax. These afflicted the masses of the Jewish people and created a difficult, oppressive atmosphere already on the eve of the war of the Germans against Poland.

The population of Kobylnik was Byelorussian and Polish, and occupied themselves with agriculture. There were farmers who were of the Roman Catholic religion, and zealous in their faith. They regarded themselves as Poles by nationality. They formed the majority of the population, and cooperated with the Polish authorities. On the other hand, there were farmers of the Greek Catholic religion. Some of them had a Communist outlook. These farmers, who were oppressed to now small degree by the Polish majority, conducted underground agitation against the government. They were not anti–Semitic, and at times even formed mutual friendships with the Jewish population. In contrast to the outlook of that group, the Polish farmers had a strong anti–Semitic outlook. Therefore, in those days, the Poles began to incite anti–Semitic politics, and took on a clear Nazi outlook, with all its symbols.

[Page 120]

In 1935, the Poles set up a large resort on the banks of Lake Narach (the largest lake in Poland). This resort, located in the village of Kupa, 3Â½ kilometers from Kobylnik, later became one of the most famous summer resorts of Poland. Among the many Poles who streamed to it from all parts of Poland for a vacation with cruises and bathing in its clear waters, there were extremist elements who took the opportunity to incite anti–Semitism there. The local population was quickly poisoned with Jew hatred. The lake itself became "outside the pale," and entry of Jews to that place was constantly fraught with danger of attacks by hooligans and a good chance of being beaten. Despite all this, the Jews did not forego bathing in the lake. They continued to enjoy its waters, albeit at farther point.

*

September 1, 1939

On Friday night, September 1, 1939, the Germans attacked Poland. Within two weeks, they put an end to the existence of the institutions of independent Poland. The eastern districts of Poland, including Kobylnik and its area, were annexed by the Soviets, in accordance with the prior agreement with the Germans. The first Soviet tanks that appeared in the town on September 14, 1939 heralded the end of the Polish government and the beginning of a new period in the region.

The Jewish community, which suffered difficulties under Polish rule, welcomed the new regime with appreciation, and almost with open joy. Many people became immediately accustomed to the new life conditions, received employment in various professions, and penetrated the administrative offices of the new government. The new government also served as a shield against Polish anti–Semitism, and especially assuaged the fear of the Jews of a Nazi occupation, which had lately threatened them.

[Page 121]

In contrast to the Jewish population, the Poles had difficulty in adjusting to the new regime. This regime was strange to their spirit and way of life. They were zealous for their religion, and were bound to the influence of the church in the previous regime. The collectivization of agricultural production also contributed to the dissatisfaction. In addition, they also had hard feelings when the Jews received equal rights of citizenship, benefited from the good relations with the authorities, and obtained honorable government positions. All these were like thorns in the eyes of the neighbors, who continued to deepen their hatred of the Jews. Indeed, Soviet law forbade anti–Semitism, but it pulsated in their hearts, and waited only for the first window of opportunity, when they would be able to take revenge against Jewish brazenness...

And the window of opportunity was not long in coming...

The Holocaust Approaches...

On the night June 22, 1941, when the Germans attacked the Soviet Union, they bombarded cities and towns in Poland and cruelly murdered the peaceful population. Hundreds of thousands of refugees had already abandoned their homes, set out on their path of aimless wandering, and went from the fire to the knife. The Jews of Kobylnik were still sleeping peacefully, and the entire town was still immersed in the quiet of night. The sun rose, and heralded a bright summer day.

Chuna Dimentsztajn Tells (recorded by Y. G):

As I did every morning, I woke up and went to work. People met and greeted each other, without knowing what was awaiting them within the coming hours. I was only told the frightening news when I came home for lunch at noon. My wife was weeping bitterly as she said that the radio announced Molotov's speech. The speech announced that the Germans attacked the Soviet Union, and bombarded and destroyed cities and settlements. This news fell upon me like thunder on a clear day. I immediately felt that something very dangerous a serious was taking place, and that a great tragedy was coming upon us. Memories of the previous war immediately came to my imagination: the troubles, hunger, and oppression that were our lot during the German occupation. That was during the day of Kaiser Wilhelm, who treated the Jews kindly – what would be now during the regime of the wild beasts of prey?!

[Page 122]

I went outside. I wanted to hear what people were saying, and to find out their reaction to the events. The news spread very quickly in the town. I heard the sounds of weeping. People were wringing their hands over the great tragedy.

People gathered in groups in the market square. They spoke, screamed, debated, and consulted together – what to do?!... The light on people's faces disappeared and was replaced by deep sadness. Everyone felt like an animal caught in a trap, and everyone sought a means of salvation, how to escape from the situation – but nobody knew how to do so exactly, and what means should be taken to that end.

The situation became increasingly tense. The question became clearer for everyone: should they escape to Russia or remain in Kobylnik under the German yoke? A few people felt that they should escape, and not remain under German rule, for that regime implies certain death. The majority claimed, "Jews, where will you flee? Here – at least everyone has a small house, a garden, a cow. Should we turn them over to the Germans! Can we give up our property for the gentiles to pillage, so we can wander around in strange places and die of hunger? And if we die – it is better in our place than in Siberia or some other remote place in Russia."

The Soviet officials in the town did not hesitate very much – they packed their suitcases and prepared for the journey.

*

At 4:00 p.m., army units, armed with light weapons, began to march toward Kobylnik from the direction of Vilna through Postavy. These were retreating units of the Red Army, who were retreating from the conquered areas to the interior of Russia. A stream of refugees accompanied them, some on foot, some with vehicles, and some riding on horses, with meager luggage on their backs... adults, elderly people, children... Many were Jews. A few youths joined them in Kobylnik – especially those who were not bound down by families, and who had no wives and children.

Most of the Jews of Kobylnik remained in the place, without knowing what fate would bring – despite the clear information on the fate of our Jewish brethren in the areas that had been conquered by the Germans a year or two earlier. Indeed, nobody could have imagined that the "cultured" Germans would be able to perpetrate murder like wild beasts of prey.

[Page 123]

We found out about the German attack from the mouths of refugees that had filled the town in the interim – how they bombed Kovno, Vilna, etc. without respite, and that the Soviets had not yet mounted any meaningful resistance. The Germans were advancing incessantly, conquering city after city. Vast amounts of military equipment were falling into their hands. The German radio was inciting incessantly against the Jews in various languages. We indeed understood that this incitement would not be for naught – we would pay with our blood...

The Poles were in good spirits. They received all this news with open joy, and proudly awaited the arrival of the German army.

A few days and nights passed in this manner, with tense anticipation of the unknown – until the first Germans entered the town.

The First Germans in Kobylnik

Toward evening on Friday June 27, 1941, two Germans from the battlefield gendarmes arrived in speeding vehicles. They stopped near the former Soviet kitchen, and found massive quantities of beer, wine, and food that remained after the departure of the Soviets. Crowds of local gentiles immediately gathered around them – some out of curiosity, and others to enjoy the new regime that had arrived in town.

The first cups were filled for the crowd. After they realized that the beer and wine were appropriate for drinking, they began to enjoy themselves. They drank to the point of drunkenness. The few Jews who worked in the kitchen were immediately chased away. The mood of the crowd became very high.

From afar, I heard the sounds of exuberant singing. I approached the place through a back route so that the gentiles would not notice me. I tried to see what was taking place. An amazing site appeared before me. Before my eyes I saw Krulak Abshiok standing and speaking Yiddish to the Germans. (He learned Yiddish from the Jews, with whom he had business relations.) After he greeted the Germans, he turned to them all, stating that they must bless the new situation, and asking everyone to offer assistance to the German Army, who had come here only to free and save the Christians from the yoke of the Jews. Everyone cheered in joy that the Jewish regime had passed from the world, and that a new life was now starting.

[Page 124]

After the Germans interrogated the community regarding details of the Soviet Army, when they left the city, etc., they quickly left the place.

In the meantime, after the Soviets left and before the Germans arrived, the gentiles set up a provisional militia that ruled the city until the arrival of the German army. Their first act was to start to pillage Jewish property, to beat, and to oppress. The Jews immediately took note of the beginning, and of the gloomy prospects for the future. They closed themselves into their houses and did not appear on the street. When somebody wanted to meet their friend, they would slink through the gardens so that the gentiles would not notice.

This is how they lived for six days until the German army arrived.

Under the German Boot

The German army entered Kobylnik on the morning of Wednesday, July 2, 1941. The provisional civilian militia immediately placed itself at the service of the army. They wore red band with swastikas on their sleeves. There was a large pit in the yard of the town market that was dug when the Soviets dismantled the gas station that was located there, and removed the large benzene tank. Now they herded together all the Jews of the town to fill the pit with earth and cover it. The cruel people forbade them from working with spades and pails, and the Jews, young and old, were forced to dig the sand with their hands and nails and carry it to the pit. The gentiles came and saw how we were working – and were filled with satisfaction... Some whistled and threw stones at us.

Anyone who was not working quickly enough was slapped on the face by the German soldiers. Their beards were also plucked. At times, the Germans also attacked the working Jews with beatings and slaps without reason – threatening that the German government would liquidate all the filthy Jews – who had declared war upon Germany...

At the end of the first day of work, ten Jews had been beaten and injured. This was the beginning.

The First Murder

We were all freed when we finished covering the pit. After some time, the police arrested four Jews in town, including one woman. The next day, they hauled them outside the city and shot them. At an early hour in the morning of July 3rd, they came to wake us up, so we could take the bodies of the four Jewish victims. We found bodies of the victims on the route to Postavy. They were Yeshayahu Wexler of Dunilowicze, and Chaya Gordon, the wife of Avraham Gordon of Glubokie Ruchani, a village seven kilometers from Kobylnik. We found the other two Jews next to the "Skobik" on the road leading to Vilna. These were the teacher Solomon, a refugee from Congress Poland, and the writer Shimon Tzafnat, a Jew from Vilna, who had lived in the town for the previous several years. We buried our dead in the places where we found them. A few months later, after interceding with the police, we succeeded in bringing them to a Jewish burial, along with the victims of the aktion of Sukkot, 1941.

[Page 125]

Without Respite Written by Asher Krukoff:

Our situation worsened from day to day to the point of being unbearable. All sense of security ended, and our lives were made wanton. Every gentile could pillage everything from you if he wanted to. All wellsprings of hatred opened wide with the gentiles, and they began to take revenge upon the Jews in a sadistic manner. Even those who had been known to this point as peaceful, proper gentiles now behaved as criminals and wild people...

The Jews sat in their houses in secret. They did not put on lights at night. Everything was done in darkness. They did not dare sleep next to the window for fear of stones that would be thrown into the houses of the Jews. We slept in our clothes, for we were prepared to flee for our lives at any moment.

The danger was especially high on Sundays, when the gentiles were free. They would wander about the streets of the city with smiling faces. At such times, a great fear would fall upon us, and we would hide in any hole so that they would not, Heaven forbid, notice us and commit murder.

We were ordered to wear the patch already on the third day after the arrival of the Germans, without being informed of its exact shape. The first patch was white with the letter J in the middle.

[Page 126]

After a week, a new ordinance was issued that the patch must be yellow, and must be worn in the front as well as the back. A few days later yet another edict was issued: the patch should not be larger than 8–10 cm, and must be shaped like a Star of David. Even this form was not final... After some time, the patch was set at the size of 12 cm, also in the shape of a Star of David, with the letter J in the center in black. Therefore, we quickly suffered a lack of yellow cloth... We cut up various articles of clothing at home with the correct color, and we helped each other with the raw materials.

Aside from the yellow patches, other restrictions were proclaimed, with the aim of oppressing and degrading the Jews. Jews were forbidden from walking on the sidewalks – they could only walk on the road. They were forbidden from travelling by bus or train. Jewish houses were marked with yellow Stars of David. A special edict forbade the Jews from leaving the town. Jews were completely forbidden from shopping in the stores and the market. Anyone transgressing these edicts was liable to a serious punishment. At the same time, Christians were forbidden from having any contact with Jews.

The source of all these edicts was the district commissar Bavilaika. They were posted on all streets of the town. Thus, Jews were forced to live in isolation from the outside world; oppressed and persecuted to the neck. It is no wonder that a deep despair quickly overcame us, and every person searched for ways to escape somehow and to ease their daily difficulties.

The Burning of Holy Books

On the Sabbath morning of July 12, 1941, the police began to chase the Jews out of their houses and concentrate them in the market square. From them, the police selected a group and commanded it to bring all the Torah scrolls from the synagogue and place them in the center of the market. They also brought two chests filled with books of Gemara, Mishnah, Chumashes, Siddurs, Kinot, and other holy books.

Another group of Jews was commanded to bring wood and kerosene... When everything was carefully arranged – first the wood, and then the Torah scrolls and other holy books on top, and the kerosene was poured on them – Rabbi Makowsky, the son–in–law of the rabbi of the town, was ordered to set the pile on fire. When he refused to carry out the order, he was beaten before the eyes of all present. Then, with murderous blows, they forced a certain lad to light the fire and carry out the act of vandalism of the "cultured" Germans and their local assistants.

The fire quickly ignited the parchment. From all the books, only a heap of ashes remained. A fit of trembling overtook us all when we saw this. We remained frozen in our places as our eyes shed tears, our hearts were torn with agony over the holy books that were desecrated before everybody – as we stood their helpless...

[Page 127]

After this deed, we gathered the holy ashes and buried them in the yard of Anyuta Klumel in the town.

*

Jews still came to worship in the synagogue even after the burning of the Torah scrolls until... one Sabbath night the police, with the assistance of the residents of the town and the nearby area, attacked the worshipping Jews and beat them cruelly. From that time, we could no longer worship in the synagogue. Chaim–Yaakov Janowski and Leibe Hadash of Myadel suffered the worst of the blows. We were forced to carry the latter home by hand, since he fainted.

Blood Libels

There was a district jail in nearby Vileyka. Prisoners who had been imprisoned since the Soviet times were serving their sentences there. When the Soviets left, they brought with them the prisoners who had been sentenced to long sentences, whereas those who had shorter sentences were left in the jail. When the Germans conquered Vileyka, they murdered the prisoners and desecrated their bodies: they cut off their tongues, removed their eyes, cut off their genitals, and perpetrated other such fine deeds. At the same time, however, the Germans spread terrible rumors throughout the entire district that all these deeds had been carried out by the Jewish N.K.V.D. (the Soviet security police). Indeed, the aim of this Satanic game became clear to us very quickly...

When the matter became known, Mrs. Kristofowicz of Kobylnik went to Vileyka to identify her brother who had been imprisoned there. After she inspected the corpses, she "found" that one of them was definitely the body of her brother, and brought news of this to Kobylnik. Indeed, her brother later returned to Kobylnik quite alive. In the meantime, however, a pall of fear fell upon the Jews of the town. We found out from gentiles who still acted as friends that many of them were planning on carrying out a pogrom in the town on the upcoming Sunday. They advised us that it would be best to escape from the city, for mortal danger was awaiting us.

On Sunday morning, July 27, 1941, farmers from the area streamed into the town with their family members. The atmosphere immediately became electric. Danger of death hovered above our heads. We approached the

Catholic priest in the name of the entire Jewish community of the town and requested that he influence his flock to refrain from attacking the Jews – but we were answered with a definitive refusal. He refused any possibility of offering assistance. We also made a similar request from Pope, (the Pravoslavic priest), who promised his help. However, the Germans shot this priest a brief time later in a prison in Vileyka, and killed him for his assistance to the Jews!

[Page 128]

It was necessary to quickly examine the situation and decide on the most urgent means we could use.

Shalom Yavnovitch approached the German commander of Kobylnik directly and bribed him. The commander sent a group of soldiers to quiet the masses and ensure calm that entire day. The soldiers scattered the incited farmers. The certain destruction of the entire Jewish town already at the beginning of the occupation was averted due to Shalom's astuteness.

From then, Shalom Yavnovitch served as the emissary of the Jews of the town to the German government. All German commands to the Jewish population went through him. Therefore, things became a bit easier administratively from that time. With the help of other Jews, they organized the forced labor, and divided up the obligations in a manner that was fair and just to everyone. The weak and the sick remained at home. The wealthy also worked, and were not able to pay ransom to the police in exchange for their work.

Forced Labor told by Chuna Dimentsztajn (recorded by Y. G.):

A German communication point was established in the village of Shemtovo, 18 kilometers from Kobylnik. There, Jews were taken out to forced labor, to cut down and chop trees of the forest. They were forced to make the journey from the town to the workplace by foot. In the winter, early in the morning in the greatest cold, everyone had to be prepared to depart. We did not receive any food: everyone concerned themselves with their own morsel of bread. We returned from work late at night, tired and worn out.

They would also take us to other places of forced labor: to clean latrines, clear the snow, and perform other similar jobs. The commands were issued by the Germans, but the local police attempted to carry them out with full exactitude. The fist and butt of the gun were in constant use. Jews with certain professions were transferred to various places and employed in their professions.

[Page 129]

Once, when I was cleaning the latrines, the German taskmaster commanded me to grab the pail which I had filled with excrement, not with my hands, but rather with my teeth. (It was a full pail!) When I did not carry out the command quickly enough and I fell down faint, he approached me and beat me with the butt of his gun. I got up and continued with the work with my last strength.

With Constant Threats of Death Written by Asher Krukoff:

In the village of Globoky Ruchai near Kobylnik, the Germans murdered the entire family of Avraham Gordon (his wife was already murdered earlier, a day after the entry of the Germans) – he, his three young children, and his parents. This was on the Sabbath, a day before the aktion of Sukkot 1941. When they came to take the family and haul them to the place of murder, the eldest child bid a heartfelt farewell to his gentile neighbors in the town, with whom he had lived together for many years. The child waved the handkerchief in his hand toward them as a sign of blessing and a wish to see them again. However, to our sorrow, the family never returned, and they never got together again.

Two Jewish families were murdered that same day in the village of Pasinka. We received tidings of Job from nearby towns regarding the murder of masses of Jews. The first refugees, who had succeeded in escaping from the knives of the murderers, reached us from the towns of Podbrodze, Święciany, Hoduciszki, Ignalina, and other places, where the liquidation had already commenced. In Polygon, near Święciany, 8,000 Jews were brought from those towns, and forced to dig pits with the help of the Lithuanians. When the Jews asked about this, they were told that these pits were military excavations... However, after the end of the digging, they were all murdered by shooting.

The Lithuanian population earned the complete trust of the Germans. Already with the outbreak of the war, the Lithuanians turned their guns against the Soviets, and greeted the German conquerors with open joy. Therefore, they received broad powers to do what they wanted to the Jews. Indeed, these Lithuanians helped the Germans to quickly liquidate the Jews of the Lithuanian towns. At that time, no more Jews remained in the small towns. Jews only remained in Kovno and Vilna. During those months, the German hangmen succeeded in murdering most of the Jews of Lithuania.

[Page 130]

The following fact testifies to the nature of the strong cooperation between the Lithuanian population and the Germans:

Next to Lyntupy, about 20 kilometers from Swięciany, the partisans killed the German commissar. As a punishment for this deed, the Germans and Lithuanians gathered up 850 Poles and shot them. From that time, the Polish population began to realize that the danger of liquidation was hovering over them, and not just over the Jews.

In the meantime, rumors spread in Kobylnik that a substantial portion of White Russia would be given over by the Germans to the Lithuanian government. This rumor added further pain to the oppression of the soul. At that time, we were prepared to flee for our lives at any moment. Even a portion of the Christian population had packed their bags and were prepared to leave the area that the Lithuanians were to receive. Only after a half a year did it become clear to all of us that the plan was cancelled, and our town would not be included in the proposed autonomous region.

This fact was accepted with great satisfaction, and eased the minds of the local population. The Jews also began to breath a faint sigh of hope – perhaps better days would come despite everything... There were Jews among us who "proved" almost definitively that the downfall of the Germans was approaching. Already in the first winter, they believed that the German army would be defeated, and would not be able to escape from the fate of Napoleon, who was defeated near Moscow. We therefore waited for a difficult winter with cold and ice that was to come to our aid. However, to our sorrow, the difficult winter tarried, and the hopes that we placed in it did not materialize... In the meantime, the population was fed news the opposite of what we had hoped for. We were informed of the victory of the Germans in Russia, on their constant advance and large conquests. Indeed, we were unable to confirm the situation, for we were cut off from the world, and lacked any means of communication to find out what was happening on the front. It is worthwhile to note that the Germans confiscated all radio receivers immediately upon entering the town. They also threatened the Christian population with death if they were to listen to any outside news. Despite all this, the natural sense directed us, from which we were able to surmise the situation on the front: for example, when we saw the movement of a battalion of the German army numbering tens of thousands of German soldiers passing through Kobylnik in the direction of Polocki, going to the front without stop, seemingly going toward death, and many returning along the same route severely wounded, we were of course encouraged and hopeful. We also had a bit of comfort when Soviet airplanes roared over the area dropping flyers that explained to the civilian population their great responsibility that they had taken upon themselves by cooperating with Germans in the occupation zone. There were also flyers that stated that all traitors who kill Soviet citizens will pay with their heads and blood... In addition, they infused hope by stating that the day of victory was approaching, and the end of the German occupation would be that they would be expelled from Russian soil. There is no doubt that these flyers had a significant impact on the residents. Signs of fear of retribution for crimes could be seen on some people... It is only too bad that these types of flyers were only distributed rarely.

[Page 131]

The Large Aktion

At the outbreak of the war, we immediately began to search for way to secure our property and possessions. We dug hidden pits in our yards at night, in which we hid everything that seemed valuable and useful, and should be stored for the future. However, when we realized that the war would last for a long time to come, and the objects in the ground were liable to rot and become unusable, we all looked for a "good" gentile acquaintance whom we could trust, so that we could give over our property to guard until after the war. Every Jew in town found a "trustworthy" gentile to whom he gave over his objects for safeguarding. Indeed, this was the thought of the Jews. This is not what the Christians thought... As soon as they took the objects from the Jews, they thought about how to free themselves from the bonds of trust of the Jews as quickly as possible. To this end, they made every effort that the Jews who gave over their property to them would be the first candidates for murder, with the "pure" intention that they would remain as the sole heirs to the Jewish property that had been given over to them...

In the wake of this pernicious intention, a list of 48 Jews who owned property was compiled and signed by the mayor Wanczkowicz, confirmed with Christian acquaintances in the town, and given over to the local German captain. The pretext was that only Communists appear on this list, and revenge must be taken upon them with the full force of the law. To "take care" of this request of the Christians, a group of German S.S. men arrived in Kobylnik on the eve of Sukkot, October 5, 1941, and began to arrest Jews the following day. We only found out about this list after the aktion. A general commotion arose among the Jews on the town with these arrests. Everyone left their homes and ran with all their energy at top speed to hide: through gardens, paths, and yards, as they tried to disappear until the wrath passed. However, the Germans and their assistants chased after the Jews and captured 48 people, who were imprisoned in the town jail on Dom–Ludavy.

[Page 132]

At that time, twelve other Jews were drafted for excavating pits near the town. Everyone received a spade. German taskmasters supervised them. They were brought to the area of the Catholic cemetery along the route leading to Vilna, where the Germans urged them with cruelty and deathly blows to dig the pits as quickly as possible. We immediately understood the purposes of the pits that we were preparing.

Told by Yosef Blinder – an eyewitness (recorded by Y. G.):

When the digging ended, we began to recite the confessional, for we were certain that we too, the 12 excavators, would be liquidated along with the rest of them. At the end, we were commanded to stand at the side and wait. At 3:00 p.m., we noticed from afar a group of people who were being brought toward us. When we approached, we saw many people, including a woman with a young child in her arms. This was Chaya Botwinik. When she saw the open pits, she burst out in sobs, and approached the S.S. man with a plea to free her because the baby. As a response to her plea, the man immediately removed the baby from her arms by force and cracked its head on a tree. Streams of blood flowed in all directions, and the trembling body of the baby was tossed into the grave, with blood flowing from it. They shot the mother on the spot, before the eyes of all those gathered. Another girl, who had arrived in Kobylnik as a refugee from Baranovichi and was brought to the pit with everyone else, did not hold back. She removed her shoe and tossed it straight at the face of the German with all her might as a sign of anger and disgust. She too was shot on the spot. After this, the Jews were made to stand next to the pit. They were ordered to remove their shoes and coats, to tie them together, and organize them carefully in one row. They were all ordered to stand on their tiptoes, and bend over next to the pit. Then the Germans shot them in their backs. The unfortunate people fell straight into the pit, in accordance with the order that the Germans had set out from the outset.

Zelig Narochki, a native of the town, saw everything that took place and escaped from there at the last minute. He fled far in the direction of the forest, but the Germans who were guarding the event directed their guns at him. A bullet hit him from a distance of half a kilometer. He fell and sunk into the bog. We later removed his body and brought it to a Jewish burial.

Yaakov Beinish Greenberg, who was one of the 12 excavators of the pit, witnessed the atrocities and murders. He could not control himself out of great anger. He burst out in terrifying, hysterical weeping, and uttered curses. The Germans immediately brought him to the pit and shot him.

[Page 133]

When Shlomo Yavnovitch was ordered to kneel down before being murdered, he turned to us, the pit diggers who were standing at the side, with pain and screaming," Jews, avenge the pure blood that is being spilled!"

When the terrifying atrocity ended, and all the Jews who had been brought in groups had been shot before our eyes, an order was issued to cover the pits. Before that, we were commanded to straighten the corpses in the pit. I began to move the corpses with trembling hands. When I touched them, they were still fluttering with their final death throes. I will never forget this moment! I shuddered when I noticed the wife of Tzafnat (a barber in the town), who still displayed obvious signs of life in the pit. As I approached her body, a pair of large eyes gazed at me, as if she was begging mercy from me, asking whether I could help her or save her from the murderers. Thus, we became witnesses to the great atrocity that the Germans perpetrated upon 48 Jews of Kobylnik, whom they murdered in cold blood. When we finished covering the pits, we were surprised when we were given permission to return home. Tired, and broken from everything that we endured that day, we walked clumsily through the town, and returned to our homes with broke hearts. From then, no doubt remained in our hearts that the Germans were going to continue to murder us until there were no more Jews in the town. This was the feeling of all of us.

Asher Krukoff writes:

With the terrible blow of the murder of 48 Jews of Kobylnik in one aktion, we could no longer bear the suffering. Almost all of us were weakened by the tragedy that affected the depths of our souls. We hid in our holes like mice, as our lives were consumed with bitterness and despair. We could not even weep. Only anger and curses laid on our lips against the beasts of prey, the Germans and their helpers. We remained powerless, without any energy in our souls to stand up against the snares that we encountered daily. Therefore, let me first record the unusual strength of spirit displayed by two women in the town – Beila Hadash (nee Yavnovitch), and Chava Gordon. On that same day, once the murder had finished, they approached the German police chief in the town to complain to him about the act of murder. Of course, his response was smooth and singular: it was not his fault at all, for the act was perpetrated through the word of the mayor Wanczkowicz and other gentiles, who demanded the murder of Jews, for they were all Communists. It was they who presented the list of people that must be liquidated...

Shalom Yavnovitch also stood up to the difficulties and was not subdued by them. Thanks to his wise involvement, we succeeded in receiving permission from the Germans to transfer the bodies of the victims to a Jewish grave, three months after the murder. This was a large funeral, rending the heavens with the grief and agony that enveloped us all. All the Jews of the town participated, including the elderly, women, and children. Everyone came to honor their relatives after their deaths, and to fulfil the final act of mercy. We removed the disintegrating corpses from the pit. We were only able to identify them by their clothing. Indeed, children recognized their parents, husbands recognized their wives, and mothers recognized their sons and daughters. The screams of those attending the funeral penetrated the heights of heaven — bitter weeping and wailing.

[Page 134]

Since we were unable to obtain carts to transfer the bodies from the place of murder to the Jewish cemetery, we were forced to carry them the distance of two kilometers on our shoulders. In the cemetery, we buried them according to families in the large communal grave that we had prepared. Some of us sensed the great merit of the victims in that they were able to be brought to a Jewish burial. On the other hand, those still living – who knew where our bones would end up?... Indeed, to our sorrow, this feeling turned to reality. At the time of the second aktion, when they slaughtered everyone in that same place, in "Skabik" on the road to Vilna, their bodies were not brought to a Jewish burial. At the end of the war, we were only able to identify their burial place with great difficulty.

Winter of 1941

About two months after the first slaughter, we felt that the sharp sword was still resting on the neck of everybody, even though we wanted to hope that there would not be such a slaughter again... For the pretext of "Jewish Communists" no longer existed, for the Communist "suspects" had all been taken out to be killed – therefore, perhaps they would leave us alive?... Jews thought of vain consolations and wanted to ease their hearts with words of hope.

Meetings and conversations between one Jew and another were only possible in the darkness of night. To discuss the situation, people would crawl through the gardens, side paths, and bogs so that the gentiles would not notice them. They broke fences and removed partitions for this purpose. Debates between neighbors about land demarcations, which had at time lasted for decades, were decided themselves... These things became ownerless, just as our entire lives had become one big abandon.

The winter of 1941, that we had awaited so much, so that we could see the downfall of the enemy, was indeed very difficult. Our clothes were not appropriate at all for the strong cold. The Germans had pillaged all the warm clothing of the Jews already when they first arrived. Any Jew who still had warm clothes was forbidden from wearing them. Anyone wearing furs was liable to death. It was also forbidden to wear boots if they were whole. If a Jew was caught wearing boots, they would be removed in the middle of the street, and the Jew would be forced to run home barefoot... However, we took comfort when we saw units of the German army passing through Kobylnik–Postavy–Vileyka, half frozen... Then we desired and hoped for even deeper cold...

[Page 135]

Burden of Contributions Told by Chuna Dimentstein (recorded by Y. G.):

There were very few Germans in Kobylnik itself. Their commander lived in Myadel, 21 kilometers from Kobylnik, and edicts were issued through him. The edicts included expropriations of property from the Jews of Kobylnik. The district commissary, in old Vileyka, 55 kilometers from Kobylnik, was where the edicts were hatched – primarily expropriations and contributions.

In the winter of 1941 we received an urgent edict with a list of belongings that we had to provide the Germans. These included bedding (pillows, covers, blankets, and sheets), warm linens, cots, furs, closets, tables, sofas, beds, benches, chairs, sewing machines, hides, prepared shoes, woven goods, and other such objects. Aside from this, we were ordered to provide 1,000,000 Russian rubles in checks and 25,000 golden rubles.

We immediately began to gather and collect all the aforementioned objects, with the hope and faith that this would postpone our deaths and that we may perhaps remain alive. Therefore, we collected everything that was possible. We left everyone barefoot and naked during that harsh winter. Jews gave over their last covering and the clothes that they were wearing. We managed to collect everything except for the 25,000 gold rubles. We loaded everything up on the 25 sleds that were given to us. We had to present the objects at the command center in Vileyka along with the contribution that was also collected in the town of Myadel. Here an internal discussion began – who would drive on the mission?... Everyone sensed the danger fraught with this journey. The task fell to me, the writer of these lines, and Shalom Yavnovitch. We set out on the journey.

We arrived in Myadel. The Judenrat there had not yet finished gathering the objects, and we were forced to wait an entire day until the task was finished. The Jews of Myadel also did not have gold rubles. Therefore, they removed their rings, bracelets and other jewelry to give over the ransom for their lives.

[Page 136]

We found out from the Jews of Myadel that there was no longer even a single Jews in Vileyka. The Jews of Myadel did not want to travel to Vileyka to give over the objects, for they had a suspicion that they would never return... Therefore, what should be done? Shalom said to me, "If fate fell upon us to be the sacrifice of the Jews of Kobylnik, we cannot refuse. If we refuse, they will murder all the Jews there!" I stopped asking when I heard his words. We ascended our sled, took six loads of belongings from the Jews of Myadel along with the belongings from Kobylnik, including the jewelry – and we set out for Vileyka.

It was a freezing night. The snow crunched under our feet, and the full moon lit up the way. Shalom traveled with the first sleds, and I went with the latter ones. The horses ran with difficulty. Nobody urged them on... Our thoughts afflicted us – how would the district commander receive us?... Would he accept the objects and reward us with a bullet, or would he leave us alive, letting us reach home in peace?

The night dragged on, gloomy and sad. Dogs from the surrounding villages barked at us and accompanied us for some of the way. Here and there a light shone from a window of a house, as the farmers slowly got up for their work. Morning arrived. At exactly 9:00 a.m. we arrived in Kurenitz, a village 50 kilometers from Kobylnik and 8 kilometers from Vileyka. We went to the market square with our sleds, and we noticed a farmer hanging in the square. They did not notice the Jews, for everyone was hiding in their holes.

Two hours later, a Jew noticed us, approached us, and said, "If you wish to survive, under no circumstances should you go to Vileyka. They have already shot everybody there. You will be no exception. Go back!" However, the news no longer frightened us, for we had already heard this news in Myadel. We continued our journey with the full knowledge that we were responsible for the fate of the Jews of Kobylnik.

In Vileyka, we also found a man hanging in the market square. Since the Jews and the Judenrat, with whom we might have been able to consult, no longer existed, we set out directly for the district commander. We approached the high fence, and the wide gate immediately opened for us. We entered the yard with all the sleds laden with the objects. The commander was not present at that moment, and we were ordered to wait.

We stood silently, without uttering a word. Every moment felt like an hour... Until the door opened, and two tall, corpulent Germans came out. This was the district commander and his deputy. The commander turned to us and asked, "You have come from Kobylnik – did you bring everything according to our command!"

[Page 137]

Neither of us answered. I peeked at Shalom, and saw that he had lost his voice. His face was as pale as a corpse. We received a command to bring all the objects up to the second floor. Shalom and I began the work. With our last strength, we brought all the closets, tables, benches, chairs, bedding, and other things upstairs. The farmers who owned the sleds stood at the side and did not come to our assistance. We were also ordered to count the items and place them in their right places.

After we finished, we were ordered to bring the gold rubles... Then Shalom answered that to our sorrow, we were not able to collect the gold rubles, but we brought gold jewelry instead. Shalom took out the jewelry that we received in Myadel. When the commander heard these words and saw the jewelry, he slapped Shalom over the cheeks twice, and pushed him down all the stairs, accompanied by kicks from his boots. He turned to me and told me to take the jewelry back. If we do not provide the gold rubles within two weeks, they will slaughter all the Jews of Kobylnik. Then he kicked me out of the room. He tossed a travel permit to return to Kobylnik out the window to us. We quickly picked up the paper, and set out on the journey, distancing ourselves from Vileyka. Getting far away was our only desire at that moment.

Ransom Written by Asher Krukoff:

Aside from the contributions to the district command in Vileyka and the military division in Myadel, the Germans in Kobylnik with any rank also imposed contributions – expropriations and ransom for the Jews of the town. The primary demand was for gold rubles. Every one of them acted on his own behalf and attempted to steal anything possible from the Jews. We already understood that they would not ever be satisfied with the giving over of items. The more we gave, the more they would demand... Their intention was to obtain all the Jewish property that had been buried in the ground, as well as all that had been given over to the neighbors for safekeeping. More than once a German approached a Jew demanding that he give over the name of the gentile with whom he had deposited his gold. He would get it, and they would divide it up piece by piece...

The S.S. men did this in a different manner. They demanded that the towns provide workers. The murdered them after a few days. They did this in Krivitz, Smorgon, Svir, and other places. We received the same command from the S.S. in Kobylnik and Myadel as well – to provide 20 workers for them. A pall of fear fell upon everybody. We knew that they were going to a sure death. In the meantime, we began to intercede with the authorities to lessen the quota. We traveled to the district commander in Vileyka for that purpose. The writer of these lines went from Kobylnik, and Tovia Hadash went from Myadel. When we arrived in Kurenitz, we found out that there was a group of S.S. men then who murdered 8 people. They broke into the house and shot anyone they wanted.

[Page 138]

With the assistance of a girl from Kobylnik who worked for the Germans, Tzipka Hadash, the daughter of Moshe Mirem, we proposed a ransom to the German murderers in Vileyka – and we succeeded. This is how we saved the

20 Jews. Jews from other towns did the same thing – in the meantime, Jews were saved through ransom.

For Tomorrow We Will Die...

The winter cold let up a bit. The snow began to melt, along with the great hopes that we held for the winter – that it might hasten the downfall of the enemy, may its name be blotted out... The atmosphere became oppressive, and despair hovered in every corner. Everyone was enveloped in darkness, and not one ray of light could be seen. The Germans again advanced along the fronts and conquered vast areas of Russia. The situation was unbearable. Many began to drink, overeat, and play cards out of despair, with the adage, "eat and drink, for tomorrow we will die!" We sold everything possible so that the least possible amount of goods would fall into gentile hands. Indeed, many families were already penniless, with nothing to live on.

Shalom Yavnovitch, who maintained connection with the Germans and divided up the work, would send the poor Jews to workplaces where they would be able to benefit from food provisions in a roundabout manner. The central wheat storage warehouse of the army was located on the estate of a landowner of Kobylnik. Jews worked there, and brought several kilograms of wheat in their clothes when they went home at night. "Experts" would bring home up to 20 kilograms at one time in the pockets that they sewed for this purpose. This helped them greatly.

Once we received a command that the all the Jews from ages 7 to 70 must come to the police. A death pall once again fell upon everybody. The commander informed us that the local farmers had complained to them that the Jews were buying all the cream brought to the town, causing inflation. According to the law, Jews were forbidden from eating cream, fats, and other nourishing foods. The edict now was that it was forbidden for Jews to appear in the market among the Christian population.

[Page 139]

It once happened that Gershon Krivitsky, a Jew of the town, purchased a chicken from a Christian on his way home from his job of chopping trees in the forest. The commander of the gendarmes noticed the chicken even before he succeeded in arriving home... The commander arrested the Jew, and summoned Shalom Yavnovitch, who was responsible to ensure that Jews do not do such things. "You Jews are still short of meat," shouted the commander to Shalom. As a punishment for the first offence, the Jew was given 30 lashes, and Shalom only 25. Krivitsky was bedridden for three weeks because of these lashes. Yavnovitch continued to fulfil his duties toward the Jews even that same day, even though he suffered pain. He was forced to stand on guard day and night, because danger was lurking from every direction.

The Refugees from Krivitz

Most of the ghettos in our area were already liquidated by the beginning of 1942. Ghettos only remained in a few towns: Postavy, Myadel, Kobylnik and Svir. After the slaughters and liquidations in the towns, various refugees would arrive in Kobylnik. Even though harboring refugees was forbidden under the threat of death, the Jews of Kobylnik took in tens of refugees, who later perished with the rest.

On evening, two refugees arrived in Kobylnik from Krivitz, who had spent a few days in Myadel. In Myadel, people explained to them how to find a Jewish house in Kobylnik, so they will not fall into the hands of the gentiles... They were given the address of Chuna Dimantsztajn who lived on Koszbaczyzna Street. But this is what happened: By mistake, they knocked on the door of a gentile who collaborated with the Germans. The next day, that gentile reported him to the police...

When Chuna found out, he and his wife left their home immediately. The police broke into their home claiming that these two Jews were partisans. Shalom Yavnovitch immediately began his intercession and wanted to pay ransom to the police, but he did not succeed. The police turned the matter over to the German gendarmerie: that they had captured two Jewish partisans in a Jewish home. The gendarmerie immediately ordered the arrest of Chuna and his family. If they could not be found, they would arrest five other Jews. That day, Chaim Reider, Yosef Jablonowicz, Reuven Steingart, Yitzchak Yavnovitch, and Yisrael Binyamin Berger were arrested as hostages that day. The Germans announced that the five Jewish prisoners would be shot if Chuna does not present himself.

At first, the Jews of the town did not think that the matter was so serious, especially since some people from the police promised them, on purpose, that the hostages would be released in the evening, of course in exchange for money.

[Page 140]

In the meantime, the Jews spread out throughout the entire area to search for Chuna and his wife. Yosef Hadash found them in the village of Radki, informed them of the chain of event, and appealed to their conscience to appear at the police. Chuna agreed, and they set out for the police. Along the way, Yehoshua Gordon and I met Chuna. We also told him about everything that had taken place in town. His response was, "To hell, of course will not live until the end of the war, and of course we will fall into the hands of the enemy. Therefore, I do not want anyone to suffer because of me, so I have decided to go to the police." I left them after these words, but, in the end, Chuna did not arrive at the police...

I met Shalom and Aida Akselrod next to the police station. Aida held a gold watch in her hand and said that the commander promised her that he would immediately free her husband Chaim in exchange for the watch. In the meantime, 6:00 p.m. came – and Jews were forbidden from appearing on the streets after that time! Of course, the police preferred that Chuna Dimantsztajn would not be brought in at all...

At night, the police found Chuna's wife, and she was arrested. In exchange they freed Yitzchak Yavnovitch. However, toward morning, the police took out the five hostages to be killed, including Chuna's wife, as well as the two Jews from Krivitz. Two days later, a command was issued to arrest the wives and children of the murdered hostages. First, they arrested Ida Reider and her two children, and then Mona–Chana, the wife of Reuven Steingart.

Mona–Chana had two children. The oldest was nine years old. The child fled from her pursuers and hid with a certain gentile. The police immediately arrested five Jewish women in her stead – including Chana's sister... We realized that the game was becoming increasingly dangerous, and that the noose was being pulled tighter around our necks, for the children of the new hostages also had children, and the German command was to arrest the family members of anyone who does not fulfil their commands...

In the meantime, heartbreaking scenes took place at the police station. The screams of these prisoners pierced the heavens. Through the windows, they pleaded for us to recite Psalms on their behalf – perhaps G–d would have mercy. Children hugged their mothers, and their weeping could melt even a heart of stone. However, the police, as well as the gentile neighbors with whom we had lived together for many years, did not pay attention to us. On the contrary: they even mocked us and laughed heartily. They enjoyed our tears.

Gedalyahu, the father of the imprisoned Mona–Chana, was in a state of despair. They arrested his two other daughters in place of his nine–year–old granddaughter who had disappeared. One of them was married with two young children... In order to save them, he went and removed his granddaughter from her hiding place, and brought her to the police as a sacrifice... They released the hostages, and brought Mona–Chana and her children, as well as Ida Reider and her children, to slaughter. They did not harm the two families of Yisrael–Bina Berger and Yosef Jablonowicz.

[Page 141]

We saw how the women and children were hauled to the cemetery – the place of slaughter. Ida's daughter Estherl asked her mother, "Where are we going, Mother?" "To Father," was her answer... They shot the women and children in the cemetery. We gave them a Jewish burial there.

The Dream of Natural Death

This last event completely broke the final strength of spiritual opposition of the remaining Jews in the town. The hope of surviving was almost completely obliterated. The police began to pillage in an increasingly stringent manner. They would summon Jews to their station and accuse them of various crimes that they had apparently committed. They would beat them cruelly, stating that they were doing this because the Jews were apparently pleased that the Germans would be suffering a defeat in battle. They also said that the Jews would say, "With their heads (i.e. of the Germans) we will pave the streets," etc. They would publish brochures stating that the Soviet airplanes were bombing, and they would blame the Jews for this, claiming that they were spies who enticed the Soviet airplanes to fly over Kobylnik. They would beat the Jews every day. In addition, they were ordered to be quiet, so that nobody would know about this. The beaten people were required to bring items of gold and jewelry as a token of gratitude for the beatings.

The police, who registered countless criminals, added crimes to these criminals. They decided to annihilate the entire Jewish population, without leaving any survivors who would be able to testify against the murderers at some point. Indeed, doubts began to arise in the hearts of the murderers when the Germans were defeated near Moscow and other fronts: what will be if the Germans are defeated... There is no way to justify such deeds – therefore, we must murder the entire Jewish population, erasing all signs and covering their traces.

The rabbi of Kobylnik bore their mockery, torment, and beatings. They would often summon him to torture him. they would gather old men and women, and torture them badly. They would force them to undress and dance naked in front of everybody... They would force these women to urinate in front of everyone, and force the men to drink it... On one occasion during these public torments, a crazy gentile entered., The gentile beat the Jews, and the Jews were forced to return the beatings... The policemen sat down and enjoyed the performance...

[Page 142]

Yosef Hadash was imprisoned a few days later. They beat him with deathblows during his investigation, on the pretext that he was a Communist, and that he was required to disclose the things that he was hiding from them... We managed to save him with difficulty. We bandaged him with wet sheets all that night to cool his wounds. His consciousness slowly returned. He asked that nobody be told about this...

This entire provocation was perpetrated by the Pole Sarafin, who was in charge in of business for the money borrowers, in which the aforementioned Yosef Hadash was a partner. After Sarafin liquidated his first three partners, he concerned himself with freeing himself from the fourth partner, so he could take ownership of the entire treasury of the organization. He stated to the police that Yosef Hadash was a Communist, hoping that he would be liquidated...

The next day, even before Hadash had managed to recover from the beatings, he was again summoned to the police, this time with his wife Beila and their daughter. Their son succeeded in escaping. They also arrested David Glatt and the shochet [ritual slaughterer] Avraham Goldzeger along with them. At first, they beat them all with death blows, and then murdered them in the Catholic cemetery. This was on Friday, 3rd of Av, 5702, corresponding to July 17, 1942. David Glatt's wife escaped, leaving her two children behind. The police took the children, led them to the Jewish cemetery by hand, where they murdered them. We then gave the victims a Jewish burial.

Death came to our windows and became a daily occurrence. The desire of everybody was to die in bed in their house. It was considered a great merit.

Indeed, we dreamed of death as a redeemer, which would save us from all tribulations... Those who merited such a death included Riva Gordon, Ezriel Jablonowicz, and Sima Hinda. They died natural deaths. Nobody wept for them, not even their closest relatives. Everyone knew that their own deaths would be fraught with greater spiritual and physical suffering.

Bringing the dead to burial in the Jewish cemetery forms a story unto itself.

The old path to the cemetery was sealed off when the Germans arrived in town. The Christian Adam perpetrated this. The new path, which was the only one through which one could reach the cemetery, passed through the bridge parallel to the river. You should know that during the autumn and the spring, when the water of the river overflowed the banks and cast mud all over, we required at least 20 people to transport the coffin of the deceased, so we would not slip and drop it, causing a desecration of the dead.

[Page 143]

The cemetery itself was also destroyed and desecrated. The gate had been taken down and stolen. The gentiles had removed the bricks of the graves. They also made use of the gravestones. The grave of Leib Todres, which was built of bricks and protected with iron chains, was destroyed, and its materials were stolen. Goats, horses, and cows grazed in the cemetery. Nobody could complain about this. We were forced to be quiet.

Autumn of 1942 – Partisans

The partisan movement in White Russia had already begun at the beginning of the summer of 1942. At first, this movement was small and weak, but it developed greatly during the years of 1943–1944. Here and there, we heard about fierce acts of revenge conducted against the Germans and their helpers. The partisans attacked German brigades, bombed bridges, derailed trains, and threatened any German movement, even when they were in small groups. Entire areas were conquered by the partisans. They also set up an administrative government, and collected taxes from the residents as in normal times. The farmers were forced to pay and give them everything that they demanded – because of the strength of the partisans. They especially threatened those who collaborated with the Germans. The partisans would capture such people and take revenge upon them. They would liquidate the entire family of the traitor. Many gentiles fled to the areas which were still under German control. The mood of the town improved somewhat with the rise of the partisan movement in 1942. People had the idea to escape to the partisans in the forests. However, the fear that all the remaining Jews in the town would be murdered if individuals escaped to the partisans prevented such steps. The general thought that, after all, nothing would help, was also one of the factors leading to the certain destruction.

The partisans were in strong contact with the Jews in certain towns of the area. On the night of Yom Kippur, 80 people escaped from Myadel with the help of the partisans. The escapees included several Jews from Kobylnik who had moved to Myadel. The next day, the Germans gathered the rest of the Jews of Myadel, hauled them behind the city, and murdered them.

Several natives of Kobylnik who were among the escapees came to our town the next day and told us the details of the escape. These included Eliahu Moshe Gordon (the son of Avraham Gordon), and Yitzchak Yavnovitch. The farmers of the area later murdered Yavnovitch and tossed him into Lake Narach so that they would not suspect them. "It would be better" if it appeared as a suicide. However, the deep holes in the head, as were seen by certain gentiles who later informed Shalom and me, left no doubt that this was a cruel murder.

[Page 144]

The Final Aktion Yom Kippur, September 21, 1942

The day after the murder of the Jews of Myadel, a command was issued by the gendarmes of Kobylnik that all the Jews must gather in the market square, for they were going to set up a ghetto... Some Jews who sensed the extreme danger and realized what was going to take place, escaped. The Jews who came to the market square were brought into the House of the People (Dom Ludavy) and imprisoned there. The windows of the building were sealed with boards, and the building was completely surrounded by German police. It became clear that the bitter end of all the Jews had arrived!

A few hours later, 48 people deemed useful by the Germans were freed. These were professionals, with their families. Yehoshua Janowski was among those freed, along with his sister and her two children. Janowski explained that they were his wife and children.

The agitation of impending death pervaded amongst the prisoners. People sought means of salvation – but there were none. There were attempts to jump over the walls and escape. Others tried to escape through the windows. Tovia

Fogelman broke a board, burst outside, and escaped. The police pursued him and shot him. Great and bitter outcries emanated from that building all day. The recital of *Shema Yisrael* penetrated the hearts. Women parted from their children forever.

They were imprisoned for an entire day. Toward morning, all of them, men, women and children, were taken out, arranged in rows, and marched to the Catholic cemetery. One Jew, Eliahu Moshe Gordon, who was identified as a "useful Jew" by one of the Germans, was taken out from the death row at the last minute. His parents, who were with him, remained and were hauled off to their bitter end.

Several Jews attempted to escape as they walked on their death march. The lad Leibel Solomon, a refugee from Warsaw (whose brother, the teacher Solomon was murdered by the Germans at the time of their arrival in Kobylnik) jumped under the bridge as they were crossing it. The Germans shot at him, and missed their mark. Yeshayahu Tzernockii and Chaim Leizerowicz also escaped – but the Germans killed them both by shooting.

The pits were already prepared... They lined up the people next to the pits without undue delay, and shot them! One girl, Beila–Dovka Kirmoliski, was only shot in the leg. When the shooting stopped, she pleaded to the policeman Kobilniaki, who stood near her, to have mercy on her and let her live. His response was curses and invective – and a bullet in the head... After the bloody job was over, the excavators filled the pits with earth and flattened out the ground, as if nothing had happened... More than 150 people perished in this manner. They did not merit a Jewish burial.

[Page 145]

After the police and the Germans completed the murder, they immediately began to take possession of the belongings of the murdered people... They pillaged all the Jewish houses. Yehudit Frajdman's mother did not go to the gathering place, because she was ill. The police found her in her bed. They tossed her onto a horse drawn carriage, hauled her to the cemetery, and shot her there.

The Hand of Destruction was Outstretched

Many who survived this final aktion met their deaths in the forests at the hands of the anti–Semitic Polish partisans from the A.K.A. (National Camp) movement, whose aim was to fight against the Germans and liquidate the

Jews. They fulfilled their second objective faithfully... Indeed, their cruelty was no lesser than that of the Germans.

The blind Jew Moshe Janowski and his son Pinchas, were murdered in the forest near ChwaÅ‚owice by the Polish A.K.A. murderers. These murderers also murdered Akiva Kribichki. Shmuel Janowski, who was also a blind lad, escaped with the help of the young boy Herzl Swirski. The latter led him by hand for a distance of many kilometers in the forest. The Germans captured them and murdered them along with a Jew from Vilna in Ponary.

Several Jews of Kobylnik fell in Postavy, including Yosef Yavnovitch and his wife. Chaina Krukoff, Chava Gordon, Esther–Leah Swidzler and her children, Yisrael Chernocki, Sara Toronczyk, and others were murdered on April 4, 1943 in Ponary.

*

The surviving Jews of Kobylnik were brought to Myadel. From there, some were brought to Vileyka. Kobylnik Jews who remained in Myadel were freed one evening by the Russian and Jewish partisans, who surrounded the Germans in Myadel by force. The partisans then transferred all these survivors to the forest.

[Page 146]

And Who by Fire...

Jews of Kobylnik who survived in Vileyka along with a group of Jews of Kurenitz, approximately 130 individuals, were imprisoned in a bathhouse that was later set on fire. They were all burnt alive on November 7, 1942.

Here are the details of this atrocity: The Jews of Kobylnik who were sent to work in Vileyka, were in two ghettoes. The writer of these lines, Eliahu Gordon, Yisrael–Leib Gordon, Kaganowicz, and Esther the daughter of Yankel–Beinish Grynberg were in the ghetto of "Bebits Comissariat." This ghetto held only individuals without families. The remaining 48 people with families were in the ghetto of the S.D. These included Yosef Steingart, his wife and two children; Shaul Gordon, his wife and two children; my brother Yisrael Krukoff, his wife and son Leib Michael; David Yavnovitch and his wife; Yehoshua Janowski, his two sisters and their children; Shlomo Leizer Janowski, his wife, and two children; Avraham Keibaski, his wife and two children; etc. All of them, along with the Jews of Kurenitz who were in that ghetto, were imprisoned in the bathhouse near Vileyka and burnt alive. I saw with my own eyes the pillar of smoke rising from the bathhouse.

That day, Yisrael Leib Gordon, I, and 14 other people from Kronitz escaped to the partisans. It is interesting that the remaining Jews in the ghetto were not punished for our escape. The continued to exist there for another two months.

With the help of the head of the ghetto, Schatz, the remaining people succeeded in forging connections with the partisans, as well as in providing them with weapons that they purchased from the Germans. The weapons were transported to the partisans in wooden crates. The partisans would come to the carpentry shop in the ghetto dressed up as farmers, and load up their wagons with the boards, which contained dismantled weapons inside.

By coincidence, the situation ended in a tragic manner: One day, when such a wagon was loaded up and prepared to depart, a German appeared and ordered that the boards be unloaded so that they can use the empty wagon to transport a sick person. Schatz, the head of the ghetto, did not understand the intention of the German and was certain that he came to capture the weapons, so he issued the command "Escape!" The Jews began to escape. Most were caught and shot on the roads, but a few succeeded in hiding. Only Kaganowicz and Esther Grynberg remained in the ghetto, but they were also murdered one day before the liberation, when the Germans left Vileyka.

With the Partisans

Only a few Jews of Kobylnik escaped to the forest, where there were a few Jews from nearby towns who had escaped from the sword. Life was difficult to bear. People arrived there during the harsh winter, naked and barefoot. The sun warmed things up a bit during the day, but a fierce cold pervaded at night. Everyone crowded around the fire and warmed their dry bones. There was no food. The Russian partisans assisted to some degree, but it was not sufficient. People sat entire nights in a half faint, immersed in themselves. Only the eyes sparkled... Lice took over the entire body, and it was impossible to rid oneself of them. There were also many cases of typhus. The situation was unbearable, and no solution was in sight.

[Page 147]

However, the drive to exist did not disappear. We searched for ways to maintain life under the most difficult circumstances in the forest. We dug pits to protect ourselves from the cold. At night, we would break into villages to request bread and potatoes from farmers, so we could survive. Some people paid with their lives for such a "journey." The Germans ambushed them and killed them by shooting. There were cases where the gentiles turned people over to the Germans.

The situation of the women and young children was even more difficult. There was a young woman from Myadel with a ten–month–old baby among a group of Jews in the forest. (There was also a similar baby from Kobylnik, Zundele [Swirski – ed.].) The members of the group once asked the woman to leave their group because of the child – for the baby's cries endangered them all. Having no choice, the woman went deep into the forest with the baby, closed its mouth, and left it to itself... The next day, Russian partisans found the child. They returned it to its mother with a stern warning: If you continue to do that with the baby, we will shoot it... The mother received the baby with joy and tears in her eyes, and guarded it carefully.

The Russian partisans transferred the Jews who were wandering around the forests of Kronitz to the other side of the Russian front, hundreds of kilometers away. The people, including several from Kobylnik, made the journey on foot. Many fell along the way. The Germans as well as farmers who were collaborators also followed after them. Nevertheless, many Jews succeeded in crossing the front and arriving in Russia.

The Siege of the Partisans

The siege of the partisans began on October 20, 1943. The Germans invested strong forces in the battle, and organized fierce attacks against the areas in which the partisans reigned. Their intention was to liquidate once and for all any elements that were inimical to them, who gathered in the forests and disturbed the orderly movements of the German army who were streaming to the front. The partisans were indeed thorns in the eyes of the Germans. The Germans attacked with a battalion of 22,000 soldiers, and conducted aerial bombardments wit firebombs. The bombs set many villages in the area on fire.

[Page 148]

The partisans fled for their lives and did not organize any opposition. Everyone searched for a corner in which to save himself. The young farmers who were captured were sent to Germany to work.

This attack lasted ten days, and brought destruction upon the partisan ranks. Several tens of Jews hid in the bogs. The Germans did not reach that area for fear of sinking in the bogs. Nevertheless, many Jews fell in this attack, including several from Kobylnik: Shalom Yavnovitch, Matla Gilman, Nechemia Miznowicz, and the pharmacist Kowarski with his son. Matla Gilman had arrived from the Vilna Ghetto only one day before the attack.

The Partisans Reorganize

When the attack finished, the partisans regrouped and returned to their former places. They once again attacked and ambushed the German forces. They bombed trains that transported soldiers, set warehouses of merchandise and grain on fire, and bombed bridges. Small groups of Germans could not move at all without the assistance of tanks. The partisans quickly learned how to attack tanks. The partisans crushed a group of tanks next to the village of Pasinka, and the Germans did not reach their destination.

At that time, a Polish partisan group was organized. The was an element that had previously collaborated with the Germans, and had perpetrated many iniquities, especially against the Jews. After they realized that the Germans were losing the war, they began to direct their weapons against the Germans, but also against the Jews. They murdered many Jews that they found in the forests. At the end, the Russian partisans surrounded them and forced them to submit. The Russians killed most of them. Those who could prove their innocence were drafted into the Russian ranks as fighters.

Sparks of Hope

Sparks of hope began to appear at the end of 1943. The feeling got stronger that some might witness the day of liberation. News began to reach us about German defeats on the front. This inspired up with hope and strength that we might be able to swallow up the enemy. Jews bean to feel more secure. The Germans did not prepare new traps against the partisans. Their will and resolve weakened. The Christian population, which had so greatly collaborated with the Germans, began to shake themselves off from them... The Germans no longer succeeded in obtaining the assistance of the local gentiles during their various final actions in the area.

[Page 149]

The partisan ranks grew. New brigades were added daily. Buildings of mortar were built in the forests, in which they were housed. Not all the Jews belonged to fighting brigades. The elderly, women, and children were separate from them. At a certain time, there was an elite group of Jewish fighters, called by the Hebrew name "Hanokem" [The Avengers]. Later, the Russians shut it down and distributed its men into other groups.

At the same time, groups of Jewish tradesmen were organized: tailors, shoemakers, bakers, tanners, and other tradesmen. The partisans provided them with food, and they worked for the partisans. This group, whose purpose was military, continued to exist until the liberation.

Many Kobylnik natives participated in the group of tradesmen, especially in the group of fighters who fought and took revenge against the Germans. It is a holy duty to mention the partisans in particular; Meir Hadash, who was injured twice in fighting against the Germans; Herzl Gordon (both are in Israel today); Chaim Sztajngart (today in the Soviet Union); Peretz Krupski (in Israel); Avraham–Yitzchak Hadash (died in an accident); Heshel Krukoff (fell near Smolensk on April 17, 1943, when he crossed the front for the fourth time in transporting weapons); and Chaim–Asher Gilman (later fell on the front).

*

At the beginning of 1944, we already knew clearly that the Germans were retreating. It was also clear to us that they would want to liquidate any Jew that they ran into, and that they would organize local traps so that no person who might later testify to their crimes against the Jews might survive. Therefore, we began to prepare bunkers in which to hide in the event of a German attack. We also found means against search dogs: we scattered tobacco along the routes and hid pieces of meat in the ground, causing the dogs to lose their way. We carried out all these actions without anyone seeing. We made sure that anyone who does not belong to the specific hiding place would not know about it. The reason was that sometimes a German would capture an isolated Jew, and torture him to the point that he would reveal the hiding place...

The Front Approaches

On the first days of the month of June 1944, we heard powerful cannon shots in the forests. We were all shaken up. Many of us thought that the Germans renewed the blockade against the partisans–and the final end of the survivors who had withstood so many dangers was approaching. However, to our great joy, we were mistaken. The Red Army arrived in the forest on June 5, 1944, and the Germans fled for their lives. The partisans destroyed roads, dug trenches along the roads, and hid mines so that the Germans would not be able to escape, but would rather find their graves in the same forests in which they pursued us like animals.

[Page 150]

After the Liberation

Only now, after the Red Army liberated us, could we appreciate the tragic sum of our torments, of our destruction, of the great tragedy, and of the families that were slaughtered. Very few of the town natives survived. We went from the forests to the town with lowered heads. All of Jewish Kobylnik was one ruin. Only the weakened frames of the Jewish houses could still be seen here and there. Not one Jewish family remained whole. A fear and pall overtook us as we arrived there.

When the gentiles of the town saw us, they looked upon us as people who had returned from the world of truth [i.e. from the dead] ... We were also afraid to approach them. Those who had collaborated with the Germans were afraid of revenge. Many were forced to return our pillaged property. It made sense that we would have to be very careful about our lives, lest they attack us and kill us. Indeed, many Jews were murdered after the liberation in many town.

After returning to the town, we first went to the place where most of the Jews of Kobylnik were murdered in the final aktion. We fenced off the area, and wept bitterly over our tragedy. In our imaginations, we saw the countenance of all our Jewish relatives who were burned at the stake in such a cruel fashion.

May their memory be blessed.

[Pages 151-182]

Kobylnik, the Destruction
Yehoshua Swidler
Translated by Jack Smuckler and Janie Respitz
Edited by Toby Bird

June 22, 1941

We were fearful about the shocking news that Germany has attacked the Soviet Union. It's difficult to describe the moment without grasping that it is confusing and that we worry for the coming days. Even worse, it impacted us how much disorganization there was in the ranks of the Red Army, who were so sure of their strength and all at once they became so impotent and weak. They ran away in such a great hurry and disorder that they didn't take everything with them and left behind so much ammunition and machinery for the use of the enemy.

All of this caused great panic for the Jewish population. We were left helpless and didn't know where to run or what to do. The enemy appeared to advance quicker than the Russians retreated. For us, a life of pain and fear began.

Every one of us wished to survive if it were not too late- but where do you run with small children and the elderly?

Who knows what awaits us in Russia? In the meantime, we sat in our homes and the days dragged on like an eternity. Our neighbours, in the meantime, left us in peace. They were too busy looting whatever the Russians left behind. Each day that passed peacefully, we thanked G-D. Far worse, was when night approached. Every sound of the wheels over the stone bridge rang out so loudly in the silence of the night and this really affected our nerves.

June 27, 1941. The first German forces advanced to Kobylnik. A part of the Christian villagers greeted the Germans with great hospitality, and we, the Jews, hid ourselves in holes and whatever hiding places we could find. It was a very warm evening and the air was suffocating. It was Erev Shabbes.

There was not a visible candlelight from any Jewish home. Everyone was hiding and we were scared of our own shadows. Later in the evening, some of us were brave enough to step out and gather with some of our neighbours. We couldn't believe that such a tragic situation befell us.

Suddenly, in the distance, we saw a German soldier marching towards us, tall and skinny like a herring, loaded with all sorts of weaponry. He strolled along leisurely and inspected everything around him. We remained standing in our places and decided when he got closer, that we should engage in conversation with him and gather as much information from him as possible- How will they treat the Jews. Gitl, the butcher's wife was amongst us and she spoke a little German. As he approached, we greeted him very hospitably. He was eager and willing to engage in conversation with us.

His first words were: "We've come to free you from the Jewish Communists that oppress you so badly. Our Army will bring you provisions and work. You will be able to live in peace and enjoy the fruits of your labour. We are not like the Anglo Saxons that bomb your houses and take away lives of innocent people. Consider yourselves lucky that we have freed you." With those words, he gave us an emotional wellbeing. "What about the Jews?" we asked. He answered like a poisonous snake: "Jews, Jews," he screamed wildly, "We destroy them!" And in order for us to understand his message clearly, he took out his bayonet and drew it across his throat. "This is how we deal with the Jews."

I broke out in a cold sweat and silently, without another word, we all retreated to our homes and the German left on his own. When I arrived back home, I was restless and could not find any comfort. I lay down in my bed, but it took some time before I fell asleep. From that evening on, our days were filled with fear and tension.

Bloody Wednesday

Wednesday the 2nd of July 1941 the first German mechanised division appeared and continued for several days and nights. The army was streaming in from all directions. Wednesday the 9th of July we experienced the first step of the German might. They commanded all Jewish men to come and fill in a huge hole in the middle of the market place which previously served as a reservoir for petrol. A large crowd of Christians, mainly "vastachne" - former Russian jailed criminals who worked on the air field and were left behind after the retreat of the soviet military - greeted the Jews with a hail of stones, defamatory comments, mocking laughter and anti-Semitic remarks. They began to beat them up and forced them to move faster, and ridiculed and mocked the frightened group of Jews. They selected 4 men against whom the local Christian residents had a grudge, led them to a little forest near the town, and shot them. This brought out in us a terrible rage and bitterness. We were very depressed and couldn't stop talking about it. We called that day bloody Wednesday.

Name of the victims: Shimon Tsefanes, Rivka Gordon from Gluboki Rotshay.

From that day on our positions became even more horrific and sorrowful. The greatest source of our suffering came mainly from our neighbours who shed our blood and could do with us whatever they pleased. No one stood in their way and they carried on unrestrained in their bloodletting. I have to say that that we would have had a much longer period of quiet, almost several months, if not for our bloody neighbours who didn't miss an opportunity to betray and persecute us. Many a time they were worse than the Germans. They embittered our lives without let-up. They taunted, jeered and made our lives a living hell. Power was taken over by the nationalists who longingly awaited this opportune moment. They readily forgot the enemy of yesterday who decimated their nation and country. They chose to serve the Nazis.

Pogrom and the Burning at the Stake

Friday the 11th of July 1941 the local Christians organized a Pogrom against us. Friday evening they forced their way into the synagogue and fell upon us at prayer. It was a murderous assault sparing no one. They destroyed everything , damaged/defiled the holy ark, tore up the Sefer Torahs and trampled them underfoot in the middle of the street. The lectern, the wall clock, the chandeliers, even the windows and doors – they destroyed everything. The ferocity of the attack took us by surprise. We could not believe that past neighbours whom we had known all these years could do such a thing.

But that was only the beginning of our persecution. The following day they forced more Shtetl Jews to collect the remainder in a pile and set it alight. With wild laughter and hysterical joy they looked on at the flaming pyre. The glowing ash and blackened leaves flew off far into the sky and we, the observant Jews, had to witness this shameful act. Every day they thought of something else for us to endure. Outrage followed outrage till they broke our morale to such an extent that we accepted what they meted out and prayed to God that the situation shouldn't worsen.

Shameful Badge

With each change of administration, which happened quite often, we had to carry out something else, without knowing what they wanted from us. Shortly after we were forced to wear the yellow patch/badge of shame which so terribly humiliated us. We were thus marked immediately as though we were the biggest criminals. Soon after we were forbidden to walk on the pavements but had to walk in the road like all four-legged animals. In addition, we had to work very hard and be at everyone's beck and call. We were like slaves: wherever anything had to be done we had to be ready. They worked us day and night without respite. We had no say in the matter. Furthermore, we were not allowed to leave town on pain of death – or be seen at the market making a purchase. We were forbidden to talk to Christians or have any business dealings with them. The Christians were also liable to be

punished for any contact with us. Those were the circumstances in which we
had to live, harassed and persecuted.

Every Day Brought New Outrages

Before we could regain our composure from all the forgoing worries/
tribulations we had to face our incorporation into a ghetto. This truly
distressed us terribly. We walked around, broken and stressed out. We tried to
revoke the decree but at this point a strange coincidence happened. It was
necessary for us to occupy a certain side street and the Christian residents of
that street refused to leave their houses. They objected most vigorously and
thanks to that we were left in peace. But because of that all the richer Jews
were driven out of their houses and they jammed 2 families into each house.
Also we had to paint a Mogen-Dovid (Star of David) on each house to indicate
that a Jew lived there.

We were very upset, because every time there was a change in military
command we had to be ready to accept all sorts of mischief. Still, we were
happy with the fact that we were not thrust into a Ghetto. Our wives could
come to us and discuss things concerning our livelihood. Also, we were able to
sneak out of our houses and organize our lives. At that time we were also able
to help the various refugees who escaped from the Lithuanian murderers and
were looking for a place of safety. Many of them hid out with us; others were
sent to neighbouring Ghettos.

Hooligan Greb and His End

Even so, we were able to control some of the streets and we enjoyed some
peace and quiet because the Gestapo hadn't established themselves and the
military was still in charge. For the most part we had to endure our
murderous neighbours. Outstanding in this respect was a certain hooligan
called Greb. He spoke a good German and because of it he had connections
everywhere. More than anyone else he embittered our lives. He was avoided by
every one of us. He would extort from us as much as possible. He would
approach one of us and say that we were, on the list to be killed, but he Greb,
intervened on our behalf and would like something in return for his trouble.
We tried not to give but, of course, he was given.

In particular he was a frequent visitor at the tailor Joseph Steingart. He
had everything done for nothing. In addition, he was to provide information

from the Judenrat. Greb also demanded certain amounts of money from the Judenrat and they had no option but to give. We just didn't know what to do about him. We tried various ways to get rid of him because of our dejection. It was difficult to confront him openly.

Nonetheless there was something we could do. I once suggested to Yavnovitch "may he rest in peace" that there wasn't any point in bribing the pig. I gave him various suggestions but he only laughed at me and said, "If you are such a hero go and do something." Everyone can be a hero, literally "a hero behind the oven," an armchair hero. Obviously, it wasn't easy but in the end they accepted what I said at that time. At that time the commandant was former Polish police officer. He could be bought. Furthermore, he had a personal grudge against Greb, because he and the Polish hooligans couldn't communicate with the German murderers. Greb ruled the roost. They even began to fear him and that sickened them. It was decided that when Greb came to the tailor to ask for things from the Judenrat he should bring a request in writing because the Judenrat did not believe the tailor. And that is how it really happened. Friday evening he came with a prepared list of clothing which included riding boots, a warm lumber jacket, laundry linen for the wife, felt boots and galoshes, and many other things. He was plied with drink and became quite inebriated and cheerful. He began to curse the police and the Germans in the strongest terms. As he came outside, loaded from head to toe with all the items, the police were waiting for him and grabbed him and sent him off to the ends of the earth. All our enemies end up this way.

Blood Libel About Vileyke

For a short period we were able to breathe more freely. But that didn't last very long. The bloodthirsty enemies were always on the lookout for ways to disturb and embitter our lives. At that time libellous and false rumours circulated. When the Soviets were in power there were many prisoners in the old Vileyka jail. When the Soviets retreated and left the town, they killed off all political prisoners in the most horrific way. So the rumour was that this was done by the Jews.

The locals said it was time to settle scores with the "Zhids"- the Jews. A huge worked-up crowd went to visit Vileyka, hoping to find friends or family. We awaited their return anxiously. We tried to appeal to the local priest, but he didn't promise anything. Sunday, the 27th of July 1941 we were expecting a bloody Pogrom. The local hooligans were roaming the streets, armed with knives and iron bars. Many gentiles from the surrounding villages joined the locals. The enraged mob was only waiting for a sign. So we hurried to the German military commandant who was stationed just outside the Shtetl. He sent off 2 soldiers armed with rifles, and they dispersed the wild enraged mob. We managed to get a short breathing space, and this time had to endure the only trauma of fear. In any case our fate was sealed.

Pain and Rage

Saturday evening the start of the 9th of Av "Tisha B' Av," 2nd of August 1941, we once again experienced a scary moment. As usual we stood around our houses chatting and hoping to get things off our chests. There was a constant march of military towards the front. All of a sudden there was turmoil and chaos as the local police went chasing Jews and every man captured was taken to the first station building. Every one of us scattered looking for a hiding place. I was chased by a policeman on a bicycle but I was fortunate enough to avoid him by closing myself in a toilet. He searched for me everywhere but I, thank God, was lucky and only suffered a moment of fear. All those who were herded into the first station were beaten and tortured. In the morning they were forced to march to work and sing. Some prominent Gentiles intervened on their behalf, for which they were well paid. After a few days and more suffering they were freed.

A short time after, they arrested the ritual slaughterer Abraham Goldzeger. A hooligan from the Shtetl was especially harsh on the ritual slaughterer and bugged the life out of him. We tried every opening to have him released, showered money and jewellery on them. Eventually, he was freed.

There was great joy in the Shtetl for we knew that we had saved him from certain death. In this way we had to endure daily terror, daily libels, and anxiety for the coming day. In addition, we had a heavy work load. There was no end to what we had to give away as bribery. Everyone had to be paid off, everyone had to be bribed. Even so, we thanked God for each day that we found ourselves alive and well. The festival days were drawing closer, but who had time for festivals. They were marred and awash with our blood. We were forced to work on Yom Kippur. The evening we were holed up in our houses and didn't dare to poke our noses outside. Many of the houses had their windows broken by the hooligans, and the children were terrorized/ frightened out of their skins. We shed bitter tears over our sorrowful fate and begged God to have pity on us. This is how we passed our Yom Kippur. In spite of that we were thankful that we were still all together.

A Horrific Murder

As if we hadn't had enough, we had a horrible Sukkoth. That happened on 5th October 1941. It was a Saturday evening. A day earlier, that is Shabbat, we heard a rumor that a punishment detachment arrived from the nearby Shtetl of Svir – nobody knew why – but our instincts told us that it didn't auger well for our community. Regrettably the Jews of Svir did not tell us who we had to deal with. It later transpired that they had paid a large sum of money to buy themselves out.

The majority of the Jewish population stayed at home, because to walk the streets without being employed was extremely dangerous. At night the exhausted little town slept well enough. For us the night was a very short respite. The Shtetl gentiles, led by the mayor, gathered in the hall and decided our fate - who is to live and who is to die. Who could possibly imagine this diabolical plan they were about to carry out? Who could possibly believe that today, for many of us, it could be our last Shabbat? Early on Sunday I went outside to see what was happening in the Shtetl, for I didn't have a restful night. I am sure the same held true for others because whenever we met in the street the standard question was, "What did you hear today?" To my surprise I saw exactly what I had anticipated. A large band of armed German murderers made their way to the Jewish homes and dragged the Jews out onto the street. They weren't allowed to take anything but a small package. In answer to the question where were they being taken they were told that they were just waiting for special wagons to take them to work at Poligon around Podbrodz. In the meantime they led them to the fire station and shut them in. The rest of the terrorized crowd ran away wherever possible. I didn't even bother to return to the house. Dressed in a thin shirt I ran across gardens and fields straight into the forest. We were chased by the police and the soldiers. Many of us hid out in the little village of Kupe/Kufe, at a certain Mr. Galvatsky's, a Pole who helped us enormously. A former chairman of the "ocean league", a Polish patriot, he harboured a passionate hatred against the Germans. For several weeks he hid 2 Jewish families who came from Warsaw. He was reprimanded, told not to stand up for the Jews, and was forced to withdraw his help. Personally, I had no intention of running with the others. I found a hollow amidst the tall grass and saplings in the forest and lay there till night fall.

Broken and drained I lay in that hole. I had lost all feelings in my limb. Terrible and disturbing thoughts occupied my mind. Where was I to go? What was I to do? Not willingly the thought came to my mind that today is Sukkoth, that wonderful holiday.

Evening fell. I came out of my hiding place. I crawled on fours so no one would notice me. I stood up and ran and didn't feel the soil beneath me. I go into the village looking for my Christian friend. When he saw me, he was more frightened than me and didn't let me in because he was afraid. He told me to go into the barn where he was not responsible. Go find his barn. It was pitch black. I tried to go back. Wandering through the gardens I found a hut on four poles. I went into the hut. It protected me from the wind, but even more important, from people.

I remained in the hut for 24 hours until the next evening. I didn't think I would make it. The cold, hunger and lack of sleep were torture.

I was very worried. I had no idea where to go. I struggled with my thoughts and heard barking from my hut. A dog was chasing a cat and ripping the world with his barking. Hearing the noise, the farmer came out to see what was going on. He searched until he found a man. He calmed me down, and told me not to be afraid; he told me to remain there. He brought me a piece of black bread and told me to eat it. Now I had no rest. He now knew my hiding place. No more secret.

Since it was still night, I left immediately. I went to my farmer and told him what happened to me. He let me in and told me to climb up on to the oven. I could warm up and he would bring me food. When it got really dark he took me to his barn and told me to climb up into the hay and bury myself deep so no one could see me. He gave me something to cover myself with and I tried to go to sleep; unfortunately I couldn't because big rats were running around. I covered myself so I couldn't hear them and fell asleep.

In the morning, when the Christians brought me a basket of food, I asked if the woman could do me a favour. I asked her to go to the Shtetl and see what was doing there and to find out what happened to my household. She promised she would go and I waited with great impatience to hear what news she would bring. At noon she came and told me what transpired in town. She calmed me and told me not to fear: everything was as it was; people were going to work as usual. She told me who was killed and told me now I could calmly go home. I went home through side paths and fields. When we met, it was as if

I returned from the other side. The joy was great, but the pain in my heart was greater – How long will this tragedy last?

The Slaughter

The people who were led into the fire station were killed behind the town near the Christian cemetery. Everyone had to get down on their knees facing the graves. They opened fire and shot from behind. Those who were later forced to cover them recounted horrifying scenes. Many were still alive and suffered great pain before they died. Children ran around half shot in the grave and wailed bitterly. A mother wanted to save her 3 month old baby. She wrapped him up and placed him among the trees. Maybe someone would have pity on him. But he began to cry. A murderer heard and ended his life.

The horrible events broke us so badly, we could not recover. The despair, the destruction was so great. No words to describe, no comfort.

Here is a list of the martyrs who perished in the first massacre: Itskhaq Kravtzinki, his wife, mother-in-law, parents and children. His son Efroikin saved himself because he was part of the group who dug the mass grave and covered it up. He literally saw his whole family perish.

Kumel 3 persons

Shnayderowitch 4 persons

Todres Yehudit and child, 2persons - her husband ran away

Mosheh Botvinik, Chaya Leha Simes, and 2 children: 4 persons

Levitan Fride, 2 children and the brother - her husband managed to save himself that time but later on perished in the Glubok Ghetto.

Meyir Gantovnik, his wife and child: 3 persons

Kasovsky, the Rabbi's son-in-law, his wife and child: 3 persons

Shapiro Shrage the teacher and his family: 4 persons

Yavnovitsh Shlomo;

Grinberg Yankl Beynish wanted to take the place of his son at the graveside, so they shot him as well.

Khadesh Mine and her daughter, 2 persons

Freydke the Baker

I don't remember for certain the names of others. A few days later we were forced to collect the clothing of those who were killed. The better clothing the murderers took for themselves. Furniture and various other household items, wagons full were taken to the community hall and sold off to the gentile population for next to nothing. The gentiles were only too pleased to buy the items. They fell upon the clothing like greedy flies. Where could you get such bargains.

Monday the 13th of May 1941 several groups of Gestapo arrived and demanded from the Judenrat that in 20 minutes they should hand over gold watches, a bag of sugar, a few kilos of leather and various other things. They threatened to kill 3 men if we wouldn't comply. It goes without saying, we made the effort. What we didn't have, we bought from Christian speculators for jacked up prices. Besides that, we had to make special uniforms for the Shtetl police and for each of them a pair of boots. This is what every day cost; we were sold out. We sold all we had and bargained as much as possible.

Job's Announcement

Our sad life became worse when the White Russians took over. It was impossible to bear. Black clouds were descending on our heads. A new bloody wave spread through the region and one town after another was wiped out. Horrible news came our way. No pen can describe the horrible atrocities perpetrated by the White Russians murderers. If the first time the unfortunate people were running from murderous persecution that took place in Lithuania and sought protection from us, now people were running from slaughter that was happening here in White Russia and looked for protection from yesterday's murderers. Refugees arrived telling of terrible events that were taking place in Dokshitz, Dolinov,Krivitch and in many other towns. They told of the gruesome things that were done to the helpless Jews. This had a great effect on us. We knew our turn was coming; the bloody current that inundated the other region would not evade us and from that day on we trembled, how far are we from that hell? In what way are we better than those unfortunate Jews? We didn't sleep entire nights. We went around black like the earth. Everyone spied on our naked lives: Poles, Russians, Ukrainians, Lithuanians and Germans. And like this, in fear, the summer disappeared.

A very strong, difficult winter arrived. With the frost, snow and storms we hoped perhaps the winter would conquer the enemy. Things did become a bit easier. They left us alone for a short time. We heard they were falling like flies by the thousands from the cold on the front. We were comforted by this. We were hopeful that we would soon be redeemed.

Friday, January 2nd, 1942 we received an order that everyone had to go clean the road that goes from Minsk to Vilna. For us this was a sign that they were retreating. We had to fight hard against snow storms and frost until late at night! As diligently as we worked, we had no idea how to fight the wild storm winds – after a few minutes there was no sign left of our hard work, just mountains of snow! But we were happy that our suffering would soon be over! But the winter passed and our hopes faded.

A Case With a Priest

This case happened with the local priest. He took various things from Dovid Leyb Svirsky to hide. As much as they tormented and tortured him, the priest did not betray him and thankfully nothing happened to Svirsky. They sent the priest to old-Vilayka and tortured him until he died. Nothing helped. Not even the interceding of the entire parish.

Spring 1942

We were ordered to work for the Gestapo in Myadel. No one wanted to go voluntarily. It took a while until the right amount went. I also had to go.

It was just before Pesach when we made our move. Our families shed bitter tears and bemoaned our fate as though we were already dead, not knowing our fate. I worked as a painter which was my trade. The others had to do all sorts of menial work. After a week I was returned home, the others remained to carry on their work. Spring arrived and with it fresh worries and fears.

Power was handed over to the murderous White Russian authorities and our fate was in their hands. Neither money nor our tearful entries moved them. Our lives and fortunes belonged to them and we depended on their mercy.

The Story of Refugees and Horrific Murder

The 30th of May 1942 a week after Shvues (Shavuot). At a time of glorious summer days, beautiful days of sunshine and warmth. For those unfortunates who were driven from their homes, the warm summer brought some short relief. It presented them with opportunities to escape their horrible fate. Anyone who possibly could, did so. Among those who were in search of a safe haven were a number of Jews from Krivitch, who arrived in the middle of the night from Myadel, over the lake of Narach, hoping to stay with Khone Dimentshtein. However not knowing where they lived they happened to knock on the door of Aaron-Leib Naratzki, asking where Khone lived. Instead of taking them there he gave them directions and they went to look for him themselves. Eventually they found a close neighbour of Khone, a gentile by the name of Mazur, who showed them where Khone lived. The same Mazur later betrayed them to the police and himself became a policeman and boasted about the atrocities he committed against us.

Saturday after lunch the Shtetl was shocked to learn the news that Khone's house was surrounded by a group of policemen. The house was locked but they broke the door down and

found 3 frightened Jews who they immediately, took under strict guard – their hands held high – to the police. We tried to do something. We poured out money, ran from one to another, to the mayor, to the commander, that he should have pity and should end this before the Gestapo arrived. But talking to them was like talking to the wall. They took advantage of the opportunity. The commander, Smolensky, may his name be erased, was a horrible tyrant – "You and your money belong to me," – he would say. The Shtetl Jews did not sleep all night. Sunday afternoon the Gestapo arrived. They immediately ordered us to take five hostages until Khone was found. They gave a deadline until the next morning for him to appear.

This is where the tragedy began. We ran through the fields looking for Khone and couldn't find him anywhere, just his wife Esther. The entire night the Shtetl was wrapped in sorrow. Neighbours were running from one to the other in despair, tearing their hair out, crying and wailing. Not caring it was late at night, they knocked on all doors where they thought there would be an opportunity to help. One more hour and the executioner would begin his rule. We had already lost hope.

The five hostages were: my brother-in-law Reuven Shteyngard (he was sick and they pulled him out), Yitzchak Yavnovich (he was later freed in Esther's place), Yosef Yablonovich, Khaim Reider, Yakov, Yosef's son-in-law, and Berger – a young boy.

At dawn, when the shepherd let us know it was time to bring the cattle to the field, the murderers slaughtered 8 young Jews. When the Shtetl awoke, it was all over.

Infanticide

As it appears the murderers were not yet satiated with our blood. Three days later they demanded the wives and the children of those killed because the men were Communists and they too should be killed. There was great despair. Helpless, we had to watch in silence. Women and children also had to fall to the demands of our killers: Adke Reider with 2 children and Muneh Khane with 2 children. We tried to hide my brother-in-law's children and when the murderers couldn't find them they came up with a devilish plan. They took my wife and two children and if we didn't deliver my brother-in-law's children, they would kill my children and my wife.

Monday, June 8th 1942. My brother-in-law's 2 children were shot. Who had the strength to endure this?! We spoke about this tragedy for some time. There was a lot to say until the next tragedy. The sad times got worse. We didn't know what tomorrow would bring. Without a future, without hope, physically exhausted with swollen eyes from tears, with broken hearts, we walked around. A murderer named Arshe excelled in his cruelty. He was the substitute for commander Smolensky and wanted to stand out among his friends. Every evening he fell upon the Jewish homes and pronounced they were hiding partisans. He bloodily beat his victims. Everyone was afraid to stay home. He particularly put a tight squeeze on Yosef the butcher's old father. He lived in Shul and Arshe would come there every evening, drunk, to harass and extort with a variety of vexations. He would ask him for money and other things every day. He didn't give him any rest. If Yosef's father managed to hide and couldn't be found, the next day would be worse. "Where were you"? – was his question. "You were taking food to the Partisans." Once he asked him to dance on the table. After, the scoundrel peed on the table and made the old man lick it. This is how, as a beast, he tortured his victims.

Summer 1942

The month of July brought in the glorious summer days, but how could we enjoy that when we were harassed and forced to do hard labour. Many worked for the Gestapo in Myadel. Some worked with the administration but most of them worked in the adjacent courtyard. Everyone who worked hoped that the work would save him. Everyone was looking for a more secure workplace.

Those who worked for the admin commander were quite well off. But an infernal fire started and sparks were flying everywhere.

On a certain day the Germans sent one of their people, David Glat, to the former Polish commandant, Srafin. They entrusted him with a firm dealing in silver foxes that previously belonged to the Jews Joseph Khadesh and Leyb Gilman. They requested a fox hide but instead of handling the hide, the Polak chased the Jew out and came back empty handed. The Germans came themselves and took many more hides. From that moment the Polak harboured great anger especially against Khadash. He got together with the police and asked Khadash and Glat to come to the police station. They beat them up so badly, they were unrecognizable. Glat went to work the following day. When the Germans saw his condition they began to interrogate him. They wanted to know how it happened. He was reluctant to tell them fearing what the Poles might do to him. But they insisted and in the end he told them everything. Enraged the Germans hurried to the Pole and asked: "What's going on? You dare to beat up one of our workers." The situation caused great concern. The mayor immediately called the Gestapo to come and stabilize the situation. As soon as they arrived the Poles pretended to be investigating the incident. The mayor twisted the facts, implied that it had to do with Communism, and they were allowed to do as they pleased.

They really showed what they could. Thursday afternoon they began to romp and run around the Shtetl, and anyone they caught they brought to the police. They brought Gliyat and Khadash again and this time they almost killed them. Yosl's wife and daughter were also arrested; Gliyat's wife ran away and her children remained with her brother-in-law Avrom Kievski, a professional tailor. With him were a little boy of 3 years and a little girl 6 months old. Every minute the panic grew.

I then lived near a Christian in a back house. I couldn't see anything that was going on in the Shtetl. One Christian woman called me in to her home to stay with her. From there I could see everything through the window. I remained glued to the window. This had a huge effect on me. I became ill from nerves and I had to lie down for a while. I don't know how long I lay for. The Christian woman woke me up. She stood beside me. She was very pale and asked me to leave as quickly as possible because they were going from house to house – and if they found me there, she would suffer.

This was fate. I could have easily gotten out of this situation but I became confused. I lost myself and fell into their hands. My wife and children were also with me but I didn't strike anyone. I was very scared. As I went I walked and thought that I won't let them kill me easily.

In the Chambers of the Inquisition

They brought me to a small, dark room. The windows were covered with bars, the door was locked tight. In the room lying on the floor and suffering were Yosl the butcher and Mendl's Dovid Hirsh. Also Yosl's wife Beylke and her daughter stood nearby and were consoling the unfortunate. The girl cried bitterly. This scene quickly sobered me up. I saw where I was in the world.

I tried to talk to the men about how to save ourselves, how to disarm the 2 guys that came in, and run away. But unfortunately they were more like skeletons than men. A few minutes later they brought in a certain Zelig Naratsky, a refugee from Podbrodz, who was saved from the last slaughter. When I saw him, I felt a little better. I presented my plan to murder the two. There was a brick oven beside us. I took two bricks and planned to honour them. Just then, a policeman named Hilman enter the room. He examined our pockets. Zelig gave him a pocket watch and was let go; I remained, but my plan failed.

Sitting worried and broken, a deathly pallor filled the room. We could only hear the heavy sighs of those beaten. A short while later they brought in Yosl's father and Yakov the tanner; they also brought in a few women and soon after the ritual slaughterer. The slaughterer appeared pale and depressed, but he tried to console us, to have hope in God. We all sat on the floor, waiting in fear, not knowing what would happen next.

A half hour later we heard heavy footsteps in the corridor, and the jingling of keys. We all gathered together. They entered and began to lead us one by one into a side room. Soon it was my turn. I was extremely depressed and hoped the end would come soon. After a short pause, the murderer Arshe came and told me to go with him. They took me to a room and asked me to stand by the wall. The other guy hit me from behind and I fell with my face to the wall. (That was the murderer Mitke.) They hit me from left to right, and I was confused. They let go of me and threw me with wild outrage into a cell. Broken, beaten and ground up like apples, we lay on the bare ground. Some recited confessions of Yom Kippur. Again, we heard wild drunken voices and again the two murderers were in front of us. Here began the frightful inquisition. They carried out the most vulgar, twisted acts. They commanded the old butcher Yosl's father to stand and we had to rip the hair from his beard. When it was my turn, I pretended to pull hard. This did not please the murderer. He beat me viciously and tore the beard himself.

The old man stood motionless, didn't even groan, and the murderer stood with a handful of silver hair. When this ended they ordered Dovid Glat to pull down his pants, and if you'll excuse me, we all had to kiss him. The bandit stood and watched to make sure we all really did it. After this, another scene. The old men were forced to dance with women. Who can even explain this horrible indignity?

Satisfying their wild instincts, they let us be. A dead silence filled the room. No one dared to break the silence. Suddenly we once again heard voices and keys jingling. The same Arshe came in and began to look among us. He pulled me out and told me to go with him. Petrified, nothing mattered to me, as long as the end to this suffering came quickly. He took me to the back door and told me to quickly disappear and never tell anyone what took place. I couldn't believe what was happening, if this was true. Without feeling my pain, I ran home. No one was home. The door was open. I closed it from outside. I went in through the window. I lay down on my bed and applied cold compresses on my body. I didn't sleep a wink due to pain and fear. I lay there and thought about the whole experience I just lived through.

The next morning Yosl, his wife, child and the ritual slaughterer were all shot. The murderers were not satisfied with this, so they demanded Dovid's wife. They ordered a search for her; they went to look throughout the villages. When they didn't find Glat's wife, they took her two children.

We experienced more difficult sad times. We didn't feel safe sleeping at home. My wife came a few days later; she was hiding in a cornfield with 2 small children, didn't eat and became faint from thirst. She had to give the children water. They drank from a shoe instead of a bowl.

Tuesday afternoon my uncle had to take his niece and nephew to the slaughter, a 3 year old boy and a 6 month old girl. He had to sit, witness it and bury them. It wasn't easy to shoot the boy. They had to throw toys and when he ran after them, they shot him in the back. It was easier with the baby. They lay her on the grass and put a bullet in her head. This was all carried out by the murderer Mazor.

Dark Clouds Over Head

A short time later they called Sholem Yavnovich, the eldest on the Judenrat to a regional council. We were all very frightened. Who knows what they will do with him? He brought us sad news. The picture he presented was that the last group of Jews in Vilayke were living in conditions impossible to describe. Suffering, hunger and poverty ruled. You don't see any Jews in the area. All the towns that once had such a vibrant Jewish life were devastated. The regional commissioner ordered we give money – a lot; this overtook all previous contributions. With the best intentions, we could not raise the money.

At that time a few Jews remained in towns in the area like: Myadel, Kobylnik, Fastov, Glubok. We understood well that our turn had come.

The situation in Myadel worsened. The Kobylnik Jews who worked there let us know in a variety of ways. One wrote to his wife that he's going to collect berries in the forest, an insinuation she should know what to do. A second person recounted that the local mayor confided to the Myadel Judenrat that soon the turn will come for the 2 towns and they should be saved. Thanks to this, many Myadel Jews were saved.

This was sad because we did not know what to do. Saturday, September 19th, a day before Yom Kippur, we were once again trembling. The Jews of Myadel ran to the forests, but the Kobylnik Jews came home. We were helpless and didn't know what to do. Some ran to Christian friends. They hid them at great cost. The rest awaited their fate.

We were awake all night, everyone sitting on his bags, sad and exhausted. We asked God to let the night last as long as possible. It was a cool night. The moon shone through the window. Somewhere a baby awoke and woke up the dreamers. The other side of the street was brightly lit, and from there we heard wild, drunken laughter.

In the morning the town looked like after a battle. You didn't see anyone. Some people were at work; some families ran away. My wife went out to see what happened but she had to quickly turn back. She heard from my good Christian friends that today would be the final slaughter in our town. My wife took the children and left town. We didn't know if we should believe them. Perhaps they just wanted to make us feel bad? I went to the yard. Those who saw me realized something was wrong. I told them what was in store for us that day. They were petrified, indifferent.

Extermination Day

Ten o'clock in the morning, a resolution was passed. White Russian police and Gestapo surrounded our town. They asked the Jewish elders to go from house to house and tell everyone to gather in the Shul, because they were going to make a Ghetto. They also came to the yard, told us to stop working and help people move to the Ghetto. Sadly, the people blindly followed the orders.

I immediately escaped to the forest with three other Kobylnik Jews: Golda's Feyge, Shloyme's Rashke and Moishe's Pinke. Soon after, we heard the shooting at the people who tried to run away.

Now the question before us: What's next? Where do we go? What do we do? We tried to find a place to spend the night. We wandered from village to village. No one let us in. Everyone feared us. We had to lie down in the middle of the field because all the barns were locked. The Christians were ordered to do this, so we could not enter and hide. It was cold. We barely closed our eyes, and we were awake again. One of us was missing. Moishe's Pinke left to find himself a place.

I remained with two girls. We wandered an entire day through the village Sirmezh. The village magistrate pointed out that we should hide because they will catch us and shoot us.

The next day my wife arrived with our 2 children and another girl, Yisroel the blacksmith's daughter. We decided to go to the Svir Ghetto. My wife told me what was going on in our town. They shot my brother-in-law Tuvye. He was working then in the bakery. He escaped through the window and they shot him. The whole town gathered in the marketplace. The professionals and their families were sent to Myadel and the rest to "Dam Ludavi"- to the slaughter. My dear sister Khaya-Soreh together with her daughter Rokhele, a ten year old girl, submitted. She was hiding, but when she heard her husband was shot she totally lost it and went to the murderers: What happens to everyone, will happen to me.

Where Does One Find Strength?

Where does one find the strength to describe everything? Where can one find the courage? I will share a few tragic episodes.

At the time of the selection, right and left, in other words, who lives and who dies – the despair was enormous. No one wanted to die. One man, a glazier by trade, Yohushua Yanovsky, remained as a worker and was able to bring a wife and children. He has three sisters and an old mother. Everyone wants to live. Everyone is dear to him. Menukha has three small children. A few days earlier her husband was shot. The second is pregnant. The third also want to live. He doesn't know what to do. Time is running short. No time for deliberation. Everyone's eyes are on the brother. What remains for him to do – you be the judge.

A second case: Eliyahu-Moyshe Gordon, a harness maker by trade, has parents. He could take with him a wife and children. Everyone stretched out their hands toward him for help; he must struggle with the desperate crowd. Everyone wants to live, begging him with tears to save them. Who knows who will be among the fated?

A brother took his sister as a wife. A brother-in-law took his sister-in-law, all to save a life. The lucky ones judged themselves on the way. The unfortunate, ended up in "Dam Ludavi." People bid one another farewell and asked those who may manage to survive to take revenge for their blood. Remember that bloody Yom Kippur, Monday September 21, 1942.

In the Svir Ghetto

When night fell we set off for Svir. Twenty kilometres from Kobylnik, we slept over at a farmer's house. The next morning we arrived at a small courtyard in Lithuanian territory. It was quiet. Here the Jews worked in the yards and didn't know from hunger and fear. We rested for a few hours. They cried bitterly over our catastrophe and then we continued on our way. In the evening we arrived in Balkeve, 3 kilometres from Svir. Here we also came across many working Jews. They did not live too badly and they did not have to endure the fear of the Ghetto. The next morning a girl led us along side roads to the Svir Ghetto.

Arriving in the Svir Ghetto I became very sad. There beside the lake was the whole Jewish "Centre" with its poverty and suffering. There were small wooden houses with three families per house. There was also no lack of Jewish oppressors and guards who blindly fell into the hands of our executioners. The Jews of Svir were not very happy with our arrival. They were afraid and constantly reminded us to leave. It became worse when the amount of refugees from Kobylnik rose.

There were four of us from my family, Kagan, Mendl Leyb's son-in-law, Bene's Sorke with 2 chidren, Kipke, Libe Malkeh, Khiene Krukov, Shmulke Yanovsky with the ritual slaughterer's son, Herzl, Dovid Leb Svirsky's child, Yisroel the blacksmith with his daughter Shloime's Raitze, my 2 sisters-in-law Khane-Khave and Sheyne Basha.

Every day I went to work in Balkeve digging potatoes. Others did the same work. I settled in and perhaps could have lived, but it was not permitted.

Saturday September 10th

At work in Balkeve, to my surprise, I saw all the Jews from Kobylnik worried and desperate. I believe, this was a made up prank, how to get rid of the unwanted refugees. Someone who worked for the Lithuanian police told the Judenrat that the police know everything, and they are warning the Svir Jews to get rid of the refugees; if not, they will carry the responsibility for the consequences that might emerge. Understandably, this was a way to get rid of the Kobylniks. We had to leave Svir and everyone left looking for a place to go. The majority went to Mikhalishok. Me and Kipke stayed in Balkeve for a few days to work. But this became more difficult due to a denunciation and we faced grave consequences. In the evening, a young man took us with a boat to the Svir Ghetto.

Perpetual Wandering...

While in the Ghetto I never met anyone from Kobylnik. Everyone disappeared except my 2 children and Khiene, an older woman. When the Judenrat saw me, they would not leave me alone and told me to leave the Ghetto immediately, even though it was very late at night and leaving meant for us a sure death. How many times did I ask them to let me stay the night and I would leave first thing in the morning. Nothing helped. A policeman accompanied us. There was a boy from Warsaw with us. He had been in Kobylnik and now did everything with us. I don't know how I managed to get out. We went into a nearby house, went right up to the attic and spent the night. In the morning I received a saw and an axe, and we went to the mill. There were a few Svir families working there and we told them the Svir Judenrat sent us to work. We settled in but not for long. There was a woman,

Shaya Yose's Khavke. She knew what kind of "criminals" we were and told everyone. That evening we were told to disappear. We went to a woman farmer, but we were asked to leave there as well. We had no idea what to do. I decided to go to Mikhalishok to look for "luck".

In the Mikhalishok Ghetto

Taking side roads through fields, forests, and far off paths we set out searching for a new "home." At nightfall we arrived in Olkhovke, a few kilometres from Mikhalishok. There were many Jews working there in a paper factory, and thanks to them, Wednesday, October 15th, I arrived in Mikhalishok Ghetto.

In the Ghetto I found Kagan and his family, Benie's Soreh and her 2 children. Later, when the Svir Ghetto was dissolved, Khiene arrived along with Herzl the ritual slaughterer's son, Svirsky's son and also Moishe's Shmulke.

I continued to have experiences suffering as a Jew and as a refugee. The crowdedness was catastrophic. It was good that it was winter, as a great plague would have surely broken out.

Jews from the area were forcibly rounded up and brought to Mikhalishok Ghetto. There were many refugees from Vilna and other places. I received a small room for me and my family. There were already 3 families living there. We slept on the table and under the table. I slept on the floor in the corner. It was filthy and cramped. We all had lice and scabies. It was unbearable. It was not a peaceful household. People fought for a small spot. They fought over a pot. Everyone was nervous and exhausted. Even in Mikhalishok we had no rest. They wanted us to leave the Ghetto. I went to work every day just so they would leave us in peace. After work I had to go earn our bread. I served everyone. I sawed wood, emptied toilets, heated baths. We had enough bread.

This is how we spent our time. Our situation worsened when the front got closer. They brought the Jews even closer together and the overcrowded conditions got worse.

Friday November 17, the Judenrat ordered us to leave Mikhalishok. "Is Mikhalishok the only Ghetto?" "Go," they said. Nobody wants us anywhere. With tears we offered our apologies, but thanks to the powerful blows the murderers received from the Russians, the front moved even closer.

The horrible news we received really embittered life in Mikhalishok. We heard what had happened to the 12 thousand Jews in Gluboki Ghetto. We heard about Bialystok and about Warsaw. We were also frightened when we heard about the Oshmien Jews. Four hundred were killed by the Vilna Jewish police under the administration of Gens. Heads were demanded and they had to deliver. Gens was supposed to visit Mikhalishok Ghetto. I feared the day. I went to work just not to stay home; who knows why he came?

He came to calm the mood. He told us to go to work and do everything demanded of us, not to run to the forests, not to give our enemy the opportunity to kill us – also not to have children. We needed to have patience. Mikhalishok Ghetto is known by the regime, and we can be assured that nothing will happen. But it was clear to all that neither Gens nor all the other providers could help. They talked in order to mislead us, so we wouldn't have the will to save ourselves.

The Judenrat and the police meanwhile did their own thing. Sent people to work, kept order, took away the will of the executioners. But here they already prepared the gallows. A short time after Gens' visit they ordered the Mikhalishok Judenrat to come to Vilna. The Ghetto was worried and nervous about what could be planned. We counted the days and did not count on good news.

Saturday February 27th they told us that Vilna Ghetto needed from us 100 men to work. Again, a panic ensued. Who knew who would be among the 100. No one wanted to go. Thus began the protection, searches and bribes. People were prepared to pay, just not to have to go. The panic lasted an entire week. Meanwhile the police went from house to house deciding who would go. Me and Kagan were among the 100. We knew the refugees would be the scapegoats. Poor people and other unfortunate Mikhalishok Jews, took their hands off their hearts. Everyone received some flour or peas, felt boots and a short jacket. As it happened, it was good. For us it was luck, because the fate of Mikhalishok Ghetto had already been sealed when Gens was there. A short time later they were supposed to take 5 thousand Jews from Mikhalishok to the Kovno Ghetto. At the last minute, they took them to Ponar and killed them all.

Saturday March 6th a few trucks came for us from Vilna with members of TODT Organization[1] and a few Jewish police. The chaos was great. They dragged us from the houses and beat us. Zagar couldn't say good bye to his family; it was an angry rush.

On our way various thoughts came to me: Vilna! - I didn't share this with Zagar- another Ghetto, different worries. What lies ahead?

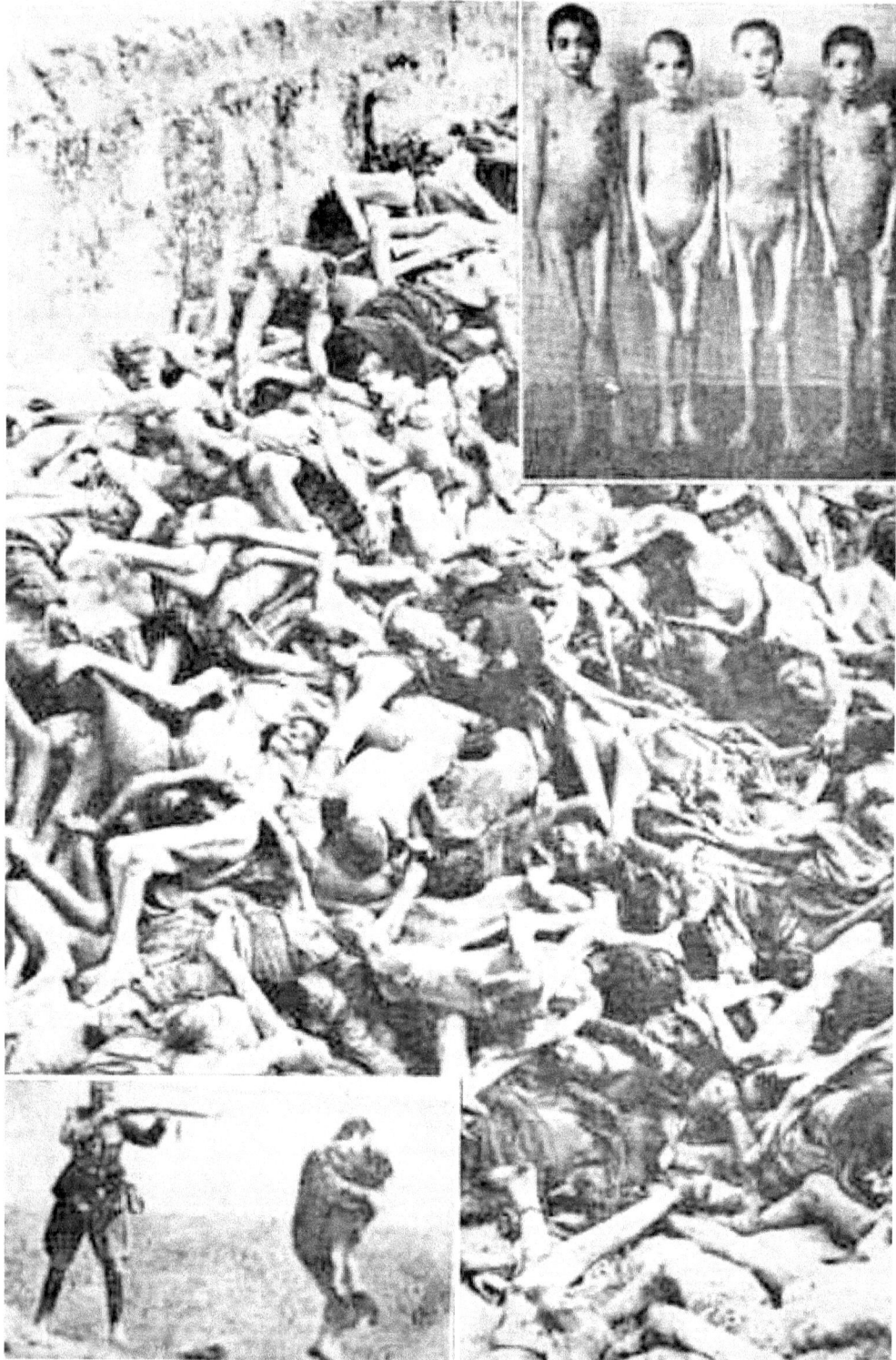

[Some] of the Nazi atrocities

———

Footnote

1. TODT Organization was a German construction firm founded by Dr. Fritz Todt. As a loyal Nazi sympathizer, he used Jewish slave labour for his extensive construction projects in all the occupied territories, including miles of Russian railways.

———

[Pages 183-186]

Murderers – Murderers of Children
by Meir Swirsky, Engineer – Haifa
Translated by Janie Respitz
Edited by Toby Bird

It was a beautiful summer day in Kobylnik, July 1942. No Jew in town was in any condition to describe the beauty of this place once called home. People's heads were not there, nor their thoughts or hearts. All we see with our eyes are bitter feelings and broken hearts. Over our heads hover dreadful black clouds, which totally block the natural sunlight!

A week earlier the town experienced sad days; our town's non–Jewish police bandits showed us how capable they were in annihilating their neighbours with full independent initiative, without German help.

After days of great suffering the following were shot: Avrom Goldzeger, the ritual slaughterer; Yosef Hadash with his wife Bayle and daughter Khayke; and also, Dovid Glot. At the last moment, Dovid Glot's wife ran away from their house. Also, Yosef's son Itzik was successful in avoiding the slaughter as he was warned by Andreke, the one handed, who came specifically for this purpose to the village heap where Yitzchak was working with me. Dovid Glot left behind two small children who were taken by his brother in – law Kayevski.

Yesterday we buried our martyrs. The old cemetery now has an addition of two rows of graves – that is the new cemetery, the graves of our earlier martyrs. In continuation of the rows, we buried the most recent victims. The last one lying in the row is Dovid Glot.

This affair did not end here: Yosl the butcher and Mendl's Dovid Hirsh (the ritual slaughterer) died "outside the row." The local barbarians were not yet satisfied, and looked for more blood; this fate fell upon Dovid Glot's children.

In the above mentioned day, early in the evening, on Fastover Street – the street that leads to the cemetery and the street we live on – Avrom Kayevski appeared; in one hand he was holding his six–month old niece, with the other hand he was leading her three–year old brother. They are being led by the known murderer Mazor.

We see this through the window. People are dying, our breath is taken away, it's impossible to believe that our eyes are seeing this gruesome scene: the children are being led to martyrdom.

The little boy, who a year before didn't know about playing in the street, and for sure, in his short life was never there, walks his last path appearing overjoyed. The whole time he is jumping over the pavement and is happily talking to his uncle, nodding his head with his blond curls; he's not confined to his house or even his yard, but the heavy kicks from the murderer's boots silence his voice, and we see, with tears in our eyes, his movements and sweet smile.

We were witnesses to more events that took place near our house: shooting Jews in the cemetery. This was always at dawn; there would be many murderers with guns in their hands ready to shoot. Now for the first time they were bringing babies. The murderer Mazor was alone, his gun on his shoulder; he had no fear that the children would run away. He walked slowly so everyone would see his heroism; with great joy he was going to carry out his orders.

They passed our house and for a short time we saw Kayevski's face: it was totally black. The little boy is playing; but they are only 100 metres from the cemetery.

Meanwhile at home it is a very sad Yom Kippur; we are no longer hoping for miracles; none of us can help; none of us can stand it.

My mother and father who had six small children had to witness this. I am 14 years old, the eldest, my little brother Zundele just turned a year. Our fate was also sealed. This is now clearer than ever. Mother pulls Zundele to her heart. She hopes that the merits in heaven of my great grandfather Zundele will protect the small child. My father goes into another room, so we would not see his mood. Our neighbours come over. No one can look the other in the eye. A dead silence rules. Everyone is in a cold sweat. The adults are smoking potato skins; there is black smoke in the house.

The silence is broken by the first shot which hits us like thunder; our hearts are broken. Then come the second and third shots, and again a dead silence, together with deep sighs from the people who have lost hope and the will to live. All are sitting motionless.

Everyone is sure that the third shot killed Kayevski.

Night fell quickly. No one was out on the street. Life, even when it is so sad, goes on. People are returning to themselves. We even hear a word spoken. The first thought is to bury the victims so they would not lay prey for the dogs. But how does one dare go out of the house when the hooligans are drunk and celebrating their "victory" and are looking without doubt for more blood? Together with my cousin, Herzke Gordon, we go out quietly to the yard, we take shovels and we go through the gardens to the river. We go under the bridge and remain unnoticed by the murderer, the police who was standing above us on the bridge. We walked along the river to the cemetery.

The light of the moon lights up the horrific scene: the little boy is lying on his side, his hands stretched out, trying to catch the breath that was taken away from him. His smile remains on his face, his eyes are open. It seems to me as if he is resting after his playful walk. The yellow marrow spilled out beside his head of curls leaves no doubt – the little boy is dead.

His little sister is lying beside him, exactly like in her cradle. A bloody mark on her diaper shows the exact spot of the murderer's bullet. Our hearts shout out: Murderers – child murderers!!

We did not find Kayevski; he suddenly came to us while we were digging the grave; the third shot was a victory shot over the children.

Together with Dovid Glot, now lie two dear babies, the beloved and pleasant in their lives will not be separated in death.

Let all their wickedness come before Thee; and do unto them, as Thou hast done unto me... Lamentations 1:22

[Pages 187-190]

The Day of the Slaughter

by Khaya-Lube Svintelsky (Tchernatzky), Brooklyn

Translated by Janie Respitz

Edited by Toby Bird

Danger Hangs Overhead...

Yom Kippur morning, 1942. My three brothers, my mother and I are at home. We move like silent shadows on the wall; none of us dare to open our mouths and destroy the dead silence, which is sitting like a stone on our hearts. Even our mother, who is very pious, doesn't make reference to the fact that today is Yom Kippur. She doesn't speak about fasting or going to synagogue.

Perhaps because it seems silly, to ask for a good year, when every day is borrowed. Since the Germans occupied Kobylnik, our lives have become chaotic, hanging on a hair. It is the antithesis of the meaning of Yom Kippur when it is decided and sealed who will live and who will die. We already had quite a different. This decision could be made by every Nazi criminal, whenever he wants and whenever his heart desires.

But today, more than ever, we felt the danger that hung over our heads. The air was electrifying, knowing that any moment the cruelest thing can happen; this can decide our fate forever. We awaited bloody guests from the town of Myadel – the German S.S. We knew they would not bring us good tidings. And that is how it really was.

The Devil's Orders

Nevertheless, like every other day, I went to work. This was in the nobleman's estate of Kobylnik, a few kilometres from town. Our work was to dry tobacco. I remember it as if it was today: my mother looked me over before I left the house; she accompanied me part of the way, and asked me to return as quickly as possible after work because she will be very anxious about me. Today she was different than always – her heart was telling her that we will be separated forever and never see each other again. With slow steps she returned home and I stood for a while and watched her walk away.,

A while later, when I arrived at work, I learned the Germans had given an order – all the Jews must leave work and return to town, each to his own home, because they were about to create a Ghetto for the Jews; everyone had to be in place. When I heard this, it was as if I felt a jab in my heart: I understood, the Germans were trying to fool us as before.

I didn't think for long and quickly ran to hide, not far from the estate. Meanwhile I noticed many Jews who worked in the wheat storehouse, were walking back to town obeying the German's order. I ran towards them and with all the commotion grabbed the hand of my cousin Aryeh-Leyb Naratzky, and asked him to escape with me. He didn't even look at me. He shook his head – and continued walking.

I remained alone; I did not know what to do. In the end I decided to go home and see what was happening to my family. I ripped off my yellow patch so I would not be recognized as a Jew, and ran home. While running I noticed how Germans and local police were gathering around a barn in the middle of a field, and looking for, most probably, Jews; I almost fell into their hands. I quickly orientated myself and began running back, but one of the Kobylnik Police – Kola Yanines was his name – noticed me and began to chase after me.

Out of breath, I barely made it to the palace and shouted that they were going to shoot me. Luckily I met the wife of the estate manager, who knew me from before – she quickly took me in and hid me in her bedroom. The bandit came running with great fury, searched everywhere and didn't find me.

A little later, the Christian woman, frightened from what had happened, led me from her room and told me to quickly climb up to the attic. Tired and distressed, I threw myself onto a pile of tobacco leaves that were there. Suddenly I noticed another person was hiding there in another corner; it was Reyzele Naratzky from Kobylnik. She told me her sister and other girls from our town were with her but no one wanted to hide and escape like she did.

In a Predicament of Death

Late at night the gardener of the estate came up to the attic with his friend. They knew we were there and came to tell us the sad news that they confined everyone to the Folk-House (Dam Ludavi), near the church, and the following morning they will shoot everyone, except the few that will be sent to Myadel to work.

Hearing this, Reyzele wrung her hands and cried. I asked the gardener to go to town to find out what happened to my family. When he returned he brought me a sad answer: no one remained in our house; the neighbours robbed us of everything. The doors and windows were open; the furniture was already removed. The bandits captured my two brothers Yankele and Dovid-Leyzerke and, together with our mother, were led to the slaughter. The only one who was saved was my older brother Feyvl, who was hiding in a neighbour's attic and witnessed everything.

For a long time we wandered from place to place in great danger, perpetually wandering, on the way to Myadel in the direction of Svir and in the Mikhalishok Ghetto. The further experiences of suffering and danger I endured with my uncle Khone Dimentshteyn who more than once was prepared to sacrifice himself to save my life. I was also with him in the Vilna Ghetto. Everywhere we went we faced great danger, until we returned to the forests where there were Russian partisans. This is where we lived to see liberation.

———

[Pages 191-194]

How did we burn Kobylnik?

by Meir Khadash

Translated by Rivka Augenfeld

Edited by Toby Bird

In the ranks of the partisans

Spring 1943, several months after the last liquidation in Kobylnik, not one Jew could be found in the town; everyone was murdered and there was no remnant left. The few who were able to save themselves had run away to wherever they could. Each person tried to save himself and survive until liberation.

I, like the others, went through a lot during that period, wandered from one place to the next – until I arrived in the Vilna ghetto; but I didn't stay there for too long. I and two friends from Kobylnik, Kayim-Osher Gilman and Herzl

Gordon, and along with two more friends from Svir, reached the forests of Zanarocz, in the district of Kobylnik. There we met Russian partisans and they agreed to accept us into their ranks as fighters. In this way I very quickly participated in combat which the partisans conducted against the Germans: in several diversionary actions, like blowing up bridges and railway lines, and other attacks which we carried out against the enemy.

Destroying Kobylnik as a military base

Once, while I was resting in the partisan base after a successful action which we had carried out against the Germans, I was suddenly called to his headquarters by Commander Zhukov. First he asked me if I was familiar with Kobylnik and her roads. Naturally, I answered 'yes'; I was born in Kobylnik and I know every pathway. Then he told me that our assignment was to burn down Kobylnik, and to blow up the entire military base which was located there and was being used by the enemy. Then he added that this must be done immediately and very precisely.

I left the headquarters very upset, and impatiently I began preparing for the action. I couldn't tell anyone how much this news surprised me, and my blood was boiling in me. I wanted to get to the town as quickly as possible in order to get revenge against our bloody neighbours who had murdered everyone and robbed their property. I was one of the first to grab my gun with aching hands, quickly pack my knapsack and report to carry out my duty. And thus, with other partisans, we started on our way.

On the road to Kobylnik

For security reasons the whole action took place in secret; even the partisans who were with me did not know what their assignment was until we reached the outskirts of town. I was assigned to the leaders who were responsible for the action. After I informed them about all the roads around Kobylnik, they decided that we would arrive through Sirmezh on the Myadel Road.

It was still light outside when we arrived in Khotovizh, not far from Myadel. There we rested a bit and mobilized horses and wagons in the village, and in the evening we all left in full force directly to Kobylnik. The horses dragged along slowly and various thoughts and memories of past times swirled in my head. Near the road the Narach lake gleamed like a mirror in the moonlight, and the beauty of nature awakened various episodes in me that I now remembered. I remembered the hundreds of Jews, merchants, tradesmen and youth who, before the war, traveled on this road to Kobylnik on a daily basis – and now not one of them remains; I am the only witness who knows the sad truth.

We reached the village of Kupa, three kilometers from Kobylnik. The convoy which came behind us stopped moving; only I and two other scouts went to learn what was being said in town. Slowly we rode through side roads until we reached Lesnietshuvka Street, about a kilometer from town. We knocked on a window and a gentile we knew opened the door. This was the former agronomist Lvov and his son, with whom I had studied together in school. We asked them all about what was happening in Kobylnik, and at the same time warned them that, if they gave us false information, they would pay with their heads. They told us that during the day there were Germans as well as Belorussian police in the market.

Understandably, this information was not enough, and we decided to sneak into town and find out what was happening.

The thirst for revenge

Without much thought I left my horse with my comrades, grabbed my weapon and started walking to the town. Dead silence all around, except for the barking of dogs and the croaking of frogs in the mud. First I came to Klemantovich's house on Myadel Street. The man quickly recognized me and was frightened to see me. They told me the same news about the Germans, but added that in the evening the Germans left on the Postov Road; it was also possible that some Germans from the Luftwaffe were to be found in Dubovski's house.

Very pleased with the news I had received, I ran back to my comrades and from there quickly to the convoy. After conferring briefly, we made a detailed plan for attacking the town. A group of riders went first, and we reached the center of the market. I looked around again, and it was hard to believe where I found myself. I saw all the Jewish homes around the market, but without any Jews. I told myself that now was not the time for feelings, since the action had to be carried out carefully and quickly.

From the market we spread out around the town at several points where we prepared for the arrival of the Germans; we took all the necessary precautions. A larger group of us went quickly to the train station as well as to Dubovski's house where, according to our information, there were Germans inside.

As soon as we heard the explosion at the train station we began to set fire to the town. First we ran to Vantskovich's house where we hoped to capture him. He was the mayor of the town and also the one who initiated the destruction of the Jews. Unfortunately, he had already escaped. We set fire to his house and ran to burn down others. The fire surrounded the town from all sides. The Gentiles (goyim?) ran around like poisoned mice wanting to save their property, but the fire was stronger than them. We also opened fire on those trying to escape, and that only increased their panic.

Watching the raging flames, my heart rejoiced and felt revenge against the Gentiles for the spilled Jewish blood. The rocket shot into the air was the signal for the partisans to pull back into the forest, and as I looked back at Kobylnik, completely engulfed in flames, I did not have the slightest feeling of compassion for our neighbours and their suffering.

———

[Pages 195-198]

We Survived in the Forest

by Yosef Blinder, Haifa

Translated by Janie Respitz

Edited by Toby Bird

After the murder of the last Kobylnik Jews Yom Kippur, 1942; after we, the removed Jews, useful due to our professions, had to bury our dead – we were sent , approximately 30 men (among whom there were a few families), to Myadel Ghetto. We were under the supervision of the S.S Gendarmerie whose commander was Kyle Brosh. Every day, he took roll call and frightened us. A few weeks later, they sent half the Jews from Myadel to Old-Vilayke to the regional commissariat; they soon killed them there.

In Myadel Ghetto we remained 70 people from four towns. In September we received news from our friends in the forest that they were preparing for an attack on the Gendarmerie, to free us from the Ghetto where we were confined.

The partisan group in the area was called "Narodni Meshchichel". From our side our contact was Sholem Yavnovitch from Kobylnik and the tooth technician Kusevitsky from Ashmene. The attack was carried out on the Germans November 5, 1942. The result: 2 Germans, 3 Poles and 2 Lithuanian Gendarmes were killed.

The partisans set the Ghetto on fire and all of us, with the small children, escaped to the forest. While running, one woman was injured; we took her with us. The only one who remained in Myadel was Raitze, Sholem Yavonovitch's wife. She was very weak and could not escape with us.

Bare naked, we entered the forest. At that moment we began our new chapter of a difficult life in the forest. It's important to point out that each of the families that escaped had to rely on their own initiatives and strength.

I was helpless with no means to live. Day and night we lay under the open sky. At night we slept by the fire. When winter came we were covered with snow, my weak wife and 2 small children. We were in a situation of hunger and death. The hunger tortured us so much that we faced the greatest dangers just to obtain food. At night I wrapped my feet in rags, said goodbye to my wife and kids and went to the village in search of food. I knocked on the windows of Gentiles' homes and asked pitifully for a piece of bread. Often, others paid for going on such a walk with their lives.

We found ourselves in this sad situation until February 2, 1943, when the Germans made a blockade and attacked the partisans in the forest. Many Jews hiding in the forest were killed. They fell like flies because they had no weapons to fight with. My family and I fled deeper into the forest where the Germans could not find us. A few days later, we returned to the old place, frozen, hungry and barefoot. Our hut had been burnt. Not noticing how dangerous the forest had become, there was no choice but to remain until Passover 1943.

During that time my wife and children got sick with typhus. Despite great danger, I had to go looking for food. One day, upon my return I found my wife with a burnt foot. Because of weakness, she fell into the campfire and the children managed to save her; she suffers from that pain until today.

I remember once on my way back from the village I fell asleep on the road because I was so tired. My little daughter came running and shouted: "Daddy, they're shooting!" She woke me up. I ran quickly, grabbed my sick wife on my shoulders and ran to where my eyes led me. The small children followed me until we crawled into a marsh up to our knees and waited there for the shooting to stop. We couldn't move from the place and take another step. We lay in the mud hiding and trembling hoping the murderers would not capture us. It was simply a miracle that we were not noticed and we were saved from death.

When the shooting began, all my friends who were with us ran away. My family and I were forced to remain because my wife was sick.

When it got quiet, we crawled out of the mud and returned to the small forest where we had previously been. Arriving we saw a horrible sight. All around us were Jewish corpses. I buried a few of them. We remained in that forest until August 25, 1943. On that day, the German bandits once again made a big blockade of the forest, the Jews and the partisans. The blockade lasted for two weeks. They persecuted us like animals, if not worse. We couldn't manage to get any food; our only nourishment was raw mushrooms and grass that we found in the forest and in the mud. We no longer appeared human; we wandered around like shadows the wind could have knocked down.

Meanwhile, winter 1943-44 was approaching and our situation was unbearable. We dug caves underground in order to survive the difficult winter. From time to time new people arrived in the forest escaping German bullets. Our group grew to 160 people; we were suffering from hunger and pain. This continued until the month of May.

Despite all the difficulties there was already an air of hope, that the days of the enemy were numbered due to the big defeats they suffered at the hands of the Red Army; with this hope we survived to see the day of liberation.

———

[Page 199]

My Time with the Partisans
Hertzka Gordon (1922-2006)
Translated by Hassida Shmoelevitz

After escaping from the Vilna Ghetto and recovering from sickness, I decided to join the partisans to fight the Nazis. Unfortunately, because they knew I was a Jew, my first encounters with them were not warm meetings between friends, but were cold and calculating. After a short time, though, I managed to get accepted as a fighter.

I was assigned to a commando unit. My job was one of the most dangerous-- to sabotage and bomb the railroads that carried ammunition and supplies to the Nazi army fighting at the front. To carry out this task, I had to first find the materials to make a bomb and fuse. Often, it involved stealing from non-Jewish peasants or forcing them to give them to me by threatening to kill them.

I remember my first mission. As I put the bomb in place on the rails, my hands and feet trembled with fear and excitement. I lit the fuse and quickly ran away as far as I could.

After the explosion, I realized that I had been left alone. The partisans who had been with me had fled in all directions. But since the surviving Germans were coming out of the train, I immediately regained my composure and started moving towards the nearest village. When I got there, I forced a non-Jew to show me the way I wanted to go by pointing a gun at him. He had no choice but to help me.

As time passed, I got good at carrying out the tasks assigned to me. When bombing trains, the safest way was to put the bomb on the track and leave the area long before the blast. But that method only blew up the engine and the troops and supplies would remain. It was more effective to bomb the middle of the train because the blast would kill more Nazi soldiers and if lucky, destroy their supplies. The problem was that to bomb the middle of the train, I had to hide next to the tracks and wait to light the fuse when the bomb was below the middle of the train. That meant I was very close to any Nazis who survived the blast who came out like hornets and began shooting and I was lucky to escape a number of times.

In spite the considerable improvement in my performance, the partisan commander's attitude toward me did not change. He knew I was a Jew and made no attempt to hide his hatred of me. It had an effect on me. One night, we were drinking vodka in my village we had stolen from some peasants and decided to visit an anti-Semitic Polish priest who was a Nazi collaborator. As a joke, we tied him up and put a glass of water on his head, telling him it was nitroglycerine and would explode if he moved. Then we laughed and left him. The commander heard about it and decided to execute me. I was led before a firing squad but at the last minute, someone convinced the commander that I was valuable to the mission. Instead of killing me, the commander took away my boots, my gun and food and told me I had to blow up a train to be allowed back in the group.

Losing my boots and food was the worst because it was a cold winter. Starvation and cold were to the two main killers of those who survived the first wave of Nazi murders. Hunger, cold and fear were always with me. I was lucky enough to quickly obtain boots, food and bomb materials. I blew up a troop transport using the middle of the train method which destroyed supplies and many Nazis. I was accepted back in the unit. But the commander's attitude did not change and he decided which missions I would be assigned to. This was too dangerous for me.

After a number of attempts, I was fortunate enough to join a partisan company under the command of Major Podolny. When he saw how I could ride a horse, he assigned me to be a tracker.

At this time, I heard that some of my cousins and my younger brother had survived the Nazi murders in my village and were hiding in a place I knew in the swamp with others. I had thought they had all been killed and I received permission from my commander to ride my horse there. I took some potatoes in a sack for them. I was just in time. The other Jewish survivors had given my cousins a choice-- to kill their youngest child, Zundel, who was 18 months old, or leave the hiding place that day. These Jews were afraid that Zundel would cry and the Nazis would find them and kill them all. Moving to another "safe" area in the forest with a child was very dangerous. I gave them the potatoes, put Zundel in the potato sack and kept him until my cousins moved to another safe area of the swamp, returned him and rejoined my unit. I heard later that the Nazis had found the place where my cousins had left and killed all the Jews.

Even with Major Podolny's group, my situation as a partisan was not so simple. I had to protect myself not only from the Nazi soldiers, but also from the Polish partisans who were organized under the name of A.K. Army who sometimes fought with Major Podolny's group. These Poles had been Nazi collaborators until they realized that the Nazis were losing the war. Then, they formed groups that fought against the Nazis but also against Jews. Many of them were guilty of the murder or betrayal of hundreds of Jews and wanted to destroy evidence of their crimes-- by murdering the surviving Jews.

Once, on my way to my town of Kobylnik, I met a group belonging to the A.K. Army. Before long, they asked if any of us were Jews. We said there were none but made up an excuse to quickly separate from them.

In 1943, in parallel with the German defeats at the battle level, the areas of partisan activity expanded. We began to attack the Nazis far from the security of our battalion's normal meeting place.

One day we learned that in the area of Schwintzien, German craftsmen were staying in bunkers and repairing broken telephone lines. I was now assigned to a navigational unit and joined a group of partisans on intelligence mission. Our task was to report on the roads surrounding the base and to mark the entrances and exits from the bunkers where the craftsmen were working. After walking for a few days in the forests, we approached the base and performed our task. We passed the information to headquarters. On the basis of our information, the plan was set.

Our forces numbered about three hundred fighters, commanded by Colonel Tserkov. He divided the forces into three groups. The first group was stationed at the entrance to the camp. The other 2 groups dug in to set up an ambush at the rear of the camp. The first group opened fire. The Germans returned fire with all of their weapons. As planned, the first group of partisans fled to the positions of the other 2 groups and most of the German fighters left their bunkers and chased them. When our first group passed our ambush point, the other two groups of partisans came out of hiding and began firing at the Nazis. During the battle, an order came for us to return to the bunkers. Only few Germans remained and we easily finished them off.

I was involved in number of operations like this. Not all of them were as successful. Once we set up an ambush by hiding under the snow on the side of a road. We had to wait for more than a day under the snow before the Nazis came. During this time, we could not move. I was freezing and hungry and was hoping my feet would work when the time came. I also had to keep my rifle dry. When our commander finally saw the Nazis approaching, he saw that they had a tank. He ordered us not to attack because we had no way to stop the tank. We were forced to lie there silently under the snow, hoping we would not be discovered.

Another time, we were waiting to attack a Nazi unit at the top of a densely forested hill. The Nazis must have been informed by villagers that we were waiting there for them and began to surround the hill to ambush us. The commander saw from the numbers of Nazi troops that we had no chance if we stayed there. Instead of retreating behind us where the Nazis were waiting in ambush, he ordered us to charge forward at their main force and we ran down the hill shooting with everything we had, hoping to kill as many Nazis as we could. Luckily, the Nazis were not expecting this attack and in their confusion, we broke through their lines and most of us survived. But I lost some good friends in this battle, and in others.

Our partisan regiment was called "The Destroyer" (Instrubital in Russian). Late in the war, our regiment was attached to the Red Army.

———

[Page 205]

We Lived to See the Liberation

by Tzvi Dimenshtein

Translated by Janie Respitz

Edited by Toby Bird

On the day of the slaughter, Yom Kippur 1942, I was working in the Kobylnik yards. I was warned by Herzke Gordon, who escaped while the police were chasing him, that they were capturing Jews in the Shtetl. I hid at the yard manager's all afternoon and evening. The manager later brought me a fur hooded cape, a piece of bread and some tobacco. He helped me, despite the fact that the police were in the yard, to sneak through the fence and escape into the forest.

I was out and heading toward the forest. I came across a Christian acquaintance named Boris, near the small village Nanas, about 10 kilometers from Kobylnik. For 2 full days I lay in the forest, not far from his house, and the Goy, from time to time, brought me some food. At night I would climb into Boris' cabin and spend the night. I would light a bit of kindling to see.

From Boris, I left toward the Stakhovtsy houses and went to another Christian acquaintance. He advised me to hide in the sand dunes near the Narach swamp that the Russians had built for artillery during the First World War. He said no one would come to look there.

I listened to him, but I hoped that, nevertheless, I would make it to Myadel where the Germans had sent the last workers from Kobylnik. I hoped to join them and work together.

I knew a Christian in Skok who worked in the Carp ponds. I went to him and stayed with him for a few nights. I asked him to go to Myadel and speak to Sholem Yavnovich from Kobylnik and ask him to add me to the remaining Jews. He replied that not only should I not go to Myadel, I should not be found in any part of the region.

Having no choice, after a few days I returned to Stakhovtsy. Once again, at night, I knocked on the door of a Christian acquaintance. When the Goy saw me, he crossed himself. Apparently, I looked like a ghost. He woke up his wife and his eldest son – he had a lot of kids – boiled two pots of water, brought a large washtub into the house, and told me to wash. The son cut my hair and beard, took away my dirty clothes, threw them away, and gave me different clothes.

After I ate and drank, the Goy said to me:

"Now go hide where you want, but don't tell me where, because if the Germans come and beat me, I'll have to tell them where you are; If I don't know, I won't be able to tell them. And something else. It is now Fall; the holes are still open. Take as much food as you can. Later, when the peasants close the holes they won't give you any food.

I left him and began to search the fields. To my good fortune, I found an old German trench in a corn field from World War I. The trench was made of cement. One couldn't stand up in it, but it was not difficult to sit or lie. I went to another close Christian acquaintance and asked if he would, from time to time, bring me some food. He agreed, but asked me not to go to another Goy because he believed his son was a German spy and he was afraid of him.

So every week, Saturday night, I went to him and he left for me a jug of milk, a piece of bread, kindling, matches and clean clothes. I would leave the dirty clothes, eat and drink. This continued all winter.

One day, in the middle of the week, I cleared the snow covering my head, and saw the surrounding villages burning. I quickly closed my hole and lay for a few days. A few days later I emerged from my hole and ran to my friend and asked what had happened. Seeing me, he crossed himself and told me there had been large movements of Germans and Partisans. As punishment, the Germans set fire to the villages. He was sure the Germans found and killed me, because they searched all the fields. He actually sent his son to search for my corpse so he could bury me. They searched, but didn't find me. Erev Pesach, when the snow melted, I left my hole and went to another place. Together with a Friedman, a Jew from Kobylnik who I met accidentally, we returned to Kobylnik, and went to see a friend of the Jews, Tunkevich. There we found many Kobylnik Jews, among them, my brother Khone. I didn't want to remain there. It was now summer, and I wanted to return to the forest. A group of us went to the forest and joined the Partisans in the Narach forest. I survived there until liberation.

———

[Page 208]

A Hiding Place in the Pig and Chicken Pen

by Efraim Krobchinsky of Petach Tikva
Translated by Jerrold Landau

At the end of 1942, during the time of the great slaughter in Kobylnik, I lived with my relatives – Frydman. They built a secret hiding place on the property of a gentile in the town, but they did not tell me about it. I saw that they maintained good relations with the Polish neighbor Jan Walaj. I once asked him, "If they come to capture me, where can I escape?" He answered me, "Go along with your relatives."

When the great slaughter began, and they began to hunt for the people of the town, I ran together with the Frydman family and did not separate from them. They went to that gentile's property, and entered the hiding place under the floor of the storehouse. We could not sit down there due to the low ceiling, so we lay down. The farmer brought us food only at the time that he brought food for the fowl and the sheep.

We were there for about two months, in October and November. Then I felt as if I was imposing on my relatives. Since I had a large sum of money that I had received from Yitzchak Javonovich, which he had taken from my grandmother's clothing when they transported her body to burial along with other bodies – I approached the farmer when he brought us food, and asked him to find me another hiding place. In exchange for money, he transferred me to the sheep and pig pen in the same yard. He dug a pit under the tree, and placed the chicken coop on top of it. I lay down there without moving. I got air through a hole in the base of the pit with the diameter of a nail. Once I did not feel well and permitted myself to open the pit, which had been sealed completely to that point. At that time, the farmer's father entered the pen. He was an old man, who did not know of my existence until that time. He noticed human excrement in the sheep pen, which I removed from the hiding place. He began to search in all the corners, for he felt that somebody was there. He indeed found me as I was hiding in a corner to get some air. Then he fainted from fright! As I saw this I too fell to the ground from weakness. The farmer came by later, lifted his father, calmed him down, and told him the entire bitter truth about me.

[Page 210]

*After a few failures, the farmer searched for a different, more secure, hiding place for me. In the meantime, the partisans came to Kobylnik and burnt it down. The fire literally reached the pit in which I was lying. I escaped then, as I was still breathing, and went to another gentile whose name was Tunkewicz. I found a few Jews with him, including Dimentsztajn and others. They transferred me to the forest, where I remained until the liberation.

From the City of Death

In great wrath of the stormy winter
And in the grief, between the walls
Listen O stubborn children
To ancient legends.

There is a different daily discussion:
When will the end come, when?
How was there a gas chamber, a killing field?
And regarding revenge – we are still alive! – –

{Herman Adler, from the Book of Ghetto Fighters)

[Pages 210-212]

We Joined the Partisans
by Meir Chadash of Tel Aviv
Translated by Jerrold Landau

In 1943, the Germans rounded up all the Jews who remained in the area – from Michaliszki, Svir, Kobylnik, and other towns – and sent them to the Vilna Ghetto. 100,000 Jews were concentrated in a small area. At that time, news reached us about the setbacks that the Germans suffered at the fronts, and it was already clear to us that their downfall was approaching. For us, every day was precious. We knew well that we would not be kept in the ghetto for many months.

At that time, news that there were partisans in the Kobylnik area reached the ghetto. The problem that faced many of us was – how to get to the forest, to save ourselves from annihilation, and to take revenge on the enemy. Actual details about these partisans reached us from the actions of Commander Markov in that region. Markov, a teacher from Święciany (Švenčionys) and a Communist from before the war, retreated along with the Red Army at the outbreak of the war. He was sent back through the enemy lines in 1942 and reached the area with the objective of setting up a partisan movement.

We began to prepare for our departure to the forests so we could join the partisans. We would meet together in the evenings after a day of backbreaking work: Chaim–Asher Gilman, Herzl Gordon, Berl Reznik, and Chaim Meltzer of Svir. We knew that the partisans do not accept anybody unless they have weapons in their hand. Therefore, the acquisition of weapons was the primary concern of the moment. I had a school buddy named Hershka Warszewczik who served in the Jewish police of the ghetto. He got us our first gun. How great was joy when he brought us that revolver!

The month of April arrived. The cold dissipated and we began to prepare for our departure to the forest. How does one leave the gate of the Vilna Ghetto? Zalman–Baruch Yoel of Svir worked as the head of a group of workers who went out to work in Novo–Vileka every morning. He agreed to join us to his group, from which we could set out on our journey to the forest.

Through that Warszewczik, we also succeeded in arming ourselves with a forged permit from the ghetto police, confirming that we were deported to work camp in the forest near Lawaryszki (Lavoriskes), about 30 kilometers from Vilna.

**

[Page 211]

We were the first ones to leave Vilna on May 14, 1943. The Germans drafted workers that day. The five of us, along with other workers, arrived, and were permitted to go through the gate. We went out to the Vilna truck station. We arrived in Vileka already during the morning. We received our work implements there without any problems, since they saw the yellow patch on our clothes. We continued secretly to the forest without arousing any suspicion. It was impossible to hide. At one place, we ran into a Lithuanian policeman riding a bicycle, who shouted to us to halt. We immediately decided together that we would approach him and explain that we were on our way to the work camp in Novo Ruski. If he leaves us alone – good. If he does not leave us alone – we will liquidate him on the spot. The policeman claimed that this work camp had already been liquidated, and requested a permit. We showed him our document from the Vilna ghetto police. Since he did not know how to read, he let us be.

With great difficulty, we reached a certain gentile near Michaliszki. At our request, the gentile obtained a gun for us. Its year of manufacture was 1917. We paid a large sum of money for it. He also drove us to the Vilya River. However, how were we to cross the bridge, with the guard so stringent?! We knew a different, roundabout route, but it passed through a known village of murderers. We crossed the Vilya at night on a barge with great difficulty.

**

We reached the vicinity of Svir. We obtained information from Misha's sister, whom we had met, that a group of partisans had crossed through the area two days previously, and was about to come back through at any time. We ran into our first obstacle at the meeting place. Hertzka Gordon got a high fever, and we were forced to remain there for an additional night. Suddenly, we heard a scream. At first, we were startled, but then we understood that the partisans had arrived!

There was one Jew in the group of partisans. We explained our situation to him, and he promised us that he would take us into the forest if no additional partisans arrive. He was enchanted by our weapons. We finally went with them. That means – they traveled in a wagon and we ran behind them on foot. They promised to obtain a wagon for us.

We reached an isolated house after running for several kilometers. An elderly gentile came out and gave us something to drink. We suddenly heard the women's voices coming from the depths, from the cellar. It was dark outside. I recognized one voice in particular — Sara Krovechki! She told us briefly about all her tribulations. We explained to her that we must move on. We met her later in Partizanka.

[Page 212]

We approached the area of the partisans, near the Narach and bogs. We arrived at the base. We found Jews there, but the command informed us explicitly that they will not accept us. This was the era after the long siege of the partisans. They did not take our weapons from us.

We found out that certain Jews from Kobylnik were living in the forest. We reached the place, near Rusaki. There indeed was a camp there in which there were also Jews, but we did not find it. We called out in Yiddish and Russian but nobody answered us. The place was abandoned and desolate. Later, we found out that the Jews left and were hiding somewhere else. We searched for them and found them. It is difficult to describe the meeting. This was in the Birurka Forest. We found shadows of people: ill and dirty, with their feet covered in rags. Their hair had fallen out. They were all ill with typhus. Their appearance was unnatural. We remained there for a few hours and continued our journey.

We also found Jews in another place, near Krunis. We remained in the area for a few days. We gathered food at night. The partisans of Mizor Cherkasov operated in the area. He fought against the Germans, but did not accept the authority of the Russians. The man was a great anti–Semite. One day these partisans found us, and told us to raise our hands. They accused us of being German spies... They took our weapons and removed our shoes. We were left naked, without anything...

***

We searched for other partisan groups. We found the man who made the connections. This was on the main road between Myadel and Vileka. After we told him everything that had happened to us, he told us that there are Jews in the area, but he was not willing to tell us the location. After much urging, he brought us to one bunker. The family of the rabbi of Myadel was there. It is difficult to explain the emotions of the meeting. Their situation was better than the situation of the earlier ones. Their only food was black beans.

***

After days of despair, we found out about a partisan brigade whose commander was a Jew from Moscow. When we met the commander and informed him that we were Jews, he greeted us with *"Shalom Aleichem"* He accepted us into his brigade and warned us that we were required to fight. We joined the brigade the next day. The weapons that had been taken from us were returned. Our brigade was nicknamed "Istrobital" (The fighters). He taught us how to use weapons.

The era of partisan rule in the area and large–scale military activity began. We joined these activities, and continued with them until the liberation.

[Pages 213-217]

Episodes From Hell

by Zila Charmetz

Translated by Janie Respitz

Edited by Toby Bird

A small Shtetl in Vilna county; similar to many other towns, but a little different. Perhaps it was prettier because of the surrounding forest? Perhaps particularly the Narach?...Fresh air? Through memories, people remember their daily worries, struggling to exist. But they continued to observe the Jewish Sabbath, holidays and Friday nights. Sabbath candles and lamps shone from the Jewish homes in the market. No one seemed to notice what made the week easier or harder...but the celebration of the Sabbath emanated from all the houses. Sabbath, holidays and Friday nights. Sabbath candles and lamps shone from the Jewish homes in the market. No one seemed to notice what made the week easier or harder, but the celebration of the Sabbath emanated from all the houses. Yes, all was fine and good until the outbreak of World War II, September, 1939. Until July 9, 1941, it was relatively quiet; that was the end of autonomous rule. The same day, the first German detachment marched in and immediately we saw the first sacrifices:

Tsapnas the barber, Vexler the tinsmith, Chaya-Rivka Gordon and Solomon the teacher. The other 12 were White Russians. In general, it's hard to bear these wounds. Those who experienced it, reading this will remind them of their troubles; those who did not witness it, will find it very hard to believe, that people could carry out such deeds. After July 9th, we lived in tension. We went to forced labour where everyone would meet their fate, in the fields, on the roads, washing laundry, cleaning houses, sweeping streets, cleaning the marketplace or tearing up grass with their bare hands. We were happy; we hoped, believed and waited for something better...but nothing better came. Erev Tisha B'Av, as usual, they gathered 50 men in the Polish school for work. Right after head count, the beatings began. They beat all the Jews, the communists and the Zionists. This was just a game; the lucky ones came out that night; the rest remained to sleep in confinement.

The following day, when we arrived for work, we found those who were abandoned: forgotten and bloodied. It was good that this "game" had no fatalities. Hitler's army advanced. They moved closer to Moscow, Leningrad and Stalingrad. In fear and torment, we existed until Sukkot 1941. Friday, a few days before Sukkot, an S.S division arrived in our Shtetl with the skull insignia on their sleeves and caps. I, as usual, had no luck and was immediately sent to work with them; the work was impossible. This was a group of animals dressed in the uniforms of Hitler's army. They prepared bags of dirty laundry and said:

"You Jews are too dirty to serve us here; take the bags and have everything ready by early Monday morning! March!"

Saturday evening, the leaders of the division were taking a walk with Burmitch Vantzkavich, may his memory be erased, and with the military police. They walked through the marketplace, but it did not occur to anyone they would carry out the death sentence on everyone! Sunday morning, the S.S came to the police with a list. We didn't know what to Do - to run, or rely on fate. Sarah and my brother-in-law Nosn and I remained at home. Meanwhile, they assembled 48 men and led them to the Polish school. I can see it in front of my eyes, as if it happened today: Rabbi Makovsky and his family, Freidl Levitan with her children, Meir Gavtovnik with his wife and child, the Ratvinik family, the Kravchinsky family. Also: Rabbi Pulik, Kaplan (who lived with Levitan) Greenberg, Yakov-Beinish, Shloyme Yavnovich, Zelig Natzky with his wife from Fadbrodz with his old mother, Gilman and others. This lasted until 10:00. At 11:00 they came to collect more Jews, now only men. No one knew where they were taking them. It appeared they were taking the last group to dig graves. My brother-in-law, Nosn Zar was at the slaughter.

I remember Batia Shteyngart came to us screaming: Help! Yosef is in shock! Save him! I went straight to him and gave him a tranquilizer which I had received from Dr. Dubovsky. She told me they would be useful. We assembled together (through the gardens; 5:00-6:00 because in the evenings, Jews were not permitted to be in the streets!) Jews gathered all their strength to give hope to one another. We hoped they would not exterminate all the Jews, and we would live to see their end. A day later, Avrom Goldzayger, may he rest in peace, came to us and said:

"Remember, we Jews were slaves in Egypt. When it was terrible for them they said: 'And the people shouted out.' They were able to carry the burden of their suffering. But it passed and they said: 'Sighs of relief – their cries went up." Compare them to us! We have to have strength to cry for our wounds. An end must come to our suffering." But the end did not come quickly or easily. Every day we struggled against death; every day, every week, we bought life. The little accomplices would throw stones through the windows of some houses, they would surround the Jewish houses and demand payment for not breaking their windows. We would pay these little Shtetl Christian boys. The Gentiles from the villages would come to buy Jewish goods. "What do you need them for. They'll take everything from you anyways."

They compared us to hunted animals. Very few displayed any sense of humanity. From there, to an event that occurred in the forest: One evening, in our mud hut, Shmerl Kacherginsky, may he rest in peace, came to us with Avrom Sutzkever. Through the light that came through the slats of wood, they read us their war poetry. This was the hut of Khasia Krukov. Our eyes were filled with smoke from the fanned kindling, but they were also filled with hope. Perhaps the persecuted, broken Jews will one day be people again?

About the Mass Grave Near Kobylnik Forest

In 1954, people arriving in Kobylnik said they dug up a mass grave in the forest. I went there immediately and saw a separate grave and 2 people sitting in the grave, picking through the sand, searching for valuables. I went to the local authorities and asked for militia and a bloodhound; they refused. I then called Patov and asked for Feyvl Tchernatsky. He came and we covered the grave. The end of that week, I had a dream. I dreamt that Gedalya's Esther-

Laya came to me and asked: Have pity. Make sure they cover us. We are cold."
The next morning I organizes the Kobylniks that lived in Pastov. Lazar
Dimentshteyn gave us a car from his work. Once again we found the grave
open. Understandably, we covered it again. A week later, my sister Sarah
found the grave open again for the third time. This time, I approached the
appropriate authorities. This result was, a certain Russian captain (who was
searching the grave for gold), received a ten year sentence. From then on, the
grave went untouched. A few years later, Feyvl Tchernatsky, Boruch Naratsky
and Lazar Dimentshteyn cemented the mass grave. In 1958, before leaving for
Israel, we encircled the entire cemetery with wood. This is how our life in
Kobylnik ended.

———————

[Pages 218-220]

Wandering During the War

by Chaim Gantovnik, Ramat Yitchak

Translated by Janie Respitz

Edited by Toby Bird

A Teacher for the Russians

The German –Polish war of 1939 found me in Kobylnik. Without looking around or trying to make sense of this created situation we heard that the Germans were bombing Vilna - a small group of us decided we would ride our bicycles closer to the Russian border. But this was already superfluous because on the 7th of September the Soviet Army crossed the border and "stretched out a brotherly hand to enslaved brothers".

A new life began under new circumstances. A life that the "big" accomplished ones from a small town were not prepared and couldn't gain any satisfaction. The youth took it a little lighter and slowly began to acclimatize.

Not knowing the national language (now Russian and White Russian) I was sent to teachers' courses, and after learning for six months I begin to work until summer vacation in a school in the nearby village of Ridufle, in a not exactly elevated atmosphere of peasants, both in attitude and power, both to me as a "representative", from a not so beloved people. But again the same – without any choice they had to get used to me.

After the vacation I received a promotion and was sent to be a manager of a school in Jejse (a village not far from Kobylnik), where I don't work very long, because on the 20th of October 1940, I'm called to military service, and after a long journey, ten days later, I arrive in Baku (Caucasus) in a military school.

In Caucasus

It is hard to part with those nearest and dearest, with friends and acquaintances, with everything that for years you were intimate and connected. I long for all of it. I write often and receive letters. Who would have thought I would never see any of them again, and after wandering and returning home not finding anyone among the living.

The war finds me in the army near the Persian border, arriving at the Iraqi border where we meet the English army. We were not there for very long because the armies move forward ravaging everything on the way. They throw us on the front, but also here we don't remain for long. They find among us terrible criminals and they send us deeper into the hinterland to do hard labour. In order to be more isolated than necessary – they send us to a deserted penal colony on an island in the Caspian Sea. The sky covers our heads and the four sides of the world – are four walls.

On the Penal Colony Island

We work twelve hours a day at hard labour; we build reinforcements in a hot climate with minimal food. After a few months the new "inhabitants" on this deserted island look like the living dead, the rows become sparse, but war is raging and there is no time to think about such criminals. I become ill with Malaria; I lie in quarantine (a tent with a wooden floor) and get sent to the city to recover.

After spending time in the hospital, I had no energy to return, and remained to work near the city. Hunger, suffering, barefoot, naked, diseases and troubles to no end accompany us to the end of the war. The only hope is to return to my town and maybe find someone beloved and dear.

Unfortunate! My father, mother and little brother were all killed in Kobylnik; my sister and her husband – after wandering, were liquidated in Pastov Ghetto. A few survivors from the destruction of Kobylnik told about the cruel days and the cruel destruction.

I had nothing more to do there, so I settled in Vilna. I begin anew, and with the first opportunity I left Vilna to begin a new life.

I went to Poland and from there to Israel. An end to my wandering – a calm life for me and a future for my children.

———

[Pages 221-239]

The Hell That Was Ghetto Vilna
by Yehosua Swidler
Translated by Janie Respitz
Edited by Toby Bird

Gate of Hell

I arrived in Vilna Ghetto after experiencing bitter events in Kobylnik, Svir, Mikhalishak and other places since the Germans occupied our area.

It was evening when the crowd streamed en masse from work back to the ghetto.

This scene left a lasting impression on me. People frozen, young and old, women and men, walked powerless with their heads down, as if sentenced to death. They walked four in a row with sacks and utensils hanging by their sides and stuffed with rags they collected. There was great congestion and upheaval at the entrance guarded by Jewish guards with rubber clubs. A few Lithuanians examined everyone, and woe to the person who had concealed something. This was my first glance at the Ghetto.

Our car drove along Osmianer Street where a place was prepared for us. They sent us to an unheated cellar that was once a warehouse. Water ran from the walls. It rained from the ceiling and the chimney smoked. We regretted our bitter luck.

The police guarded us to make sure nobody smuggled anything into the Ghetto.

Later, we waited a week for a bath and after that we became "citizens" of the Ghetto together with everyone else.

Hard Work

They quickly put us to work, which was very hard. Every day, we had to wake up very early for roll call. Then they took us to work like slaves. In camp, the discipline was very strict. We were beaten for the smallest transgressions. They disciplined us with various forms of punishment like jail and other things. Besides the physical suffering, we were also torn away from our families. We didn't see the sunlight. We worked very hard from darkness to darkness; the hunger was painful and we had no hope for better times.

At this time, rumors were spreading that they were about to liquidate Mikhalishak Ghetto, where my family was. The Judenrat said whoever has a wife or children in Mikhalishak can bring them to the Vilna Ghetto. Understandably, everyone did all they could to bring their families to Vilna. Later we learned that they actually murdered the Jews in the Mikhalishak Ghetto like savages. Thousands of people were slaughtered like calves, and everything was taken away from them. A few individuals managed to escape and tell the sad truth about what happened in Mikhalishak.

Our group in the Ghetto received an order to wear numbers around our necks like dogs. Anyone caught without a number would be shot. Even children were not exempt. Their hands were numbered with ink, like criminals.

Today We Live

The regular actions embittered our lives. The "Providers," like the police and Judenrat, lived better than everyone. They ate well, guzzled and had various orgies. They knew that today they were alive and tomorrow they could be dead.

Many of the youth were demoralized and delinquent.

They sent us to work in rows. If you missed one day of work, you had to spend a night in jail. If we were sick, we needed a certificate from a doctor and these papers were very hard to obtain; we needed protection and luck. Mostly, the healthy sat home and the sick went to work. People took it upon themselves not to go to work. The Lukiszki Street jail was filled with people who failed to show up for work.

In Jail

An inquiry began in the jail as if we were the worst criminals. Everyone was confined to a locked cell and had to lie on the dirty soil. The walls of the cell were covered with writings and slogans against the rulers of the Ghetto. I too was confined a few times in the Lukiszki Street jail for the same "crimes." Later it would become even more strict and the people held back because they knew the first people they would exterminate were those arrested and sitting in jail, together with the real criminals.

The worst off were the refugees from the provinces like the Jews from Sventian, Mikhalishak and Smorgon who were in the Ghetto; they filled all the holes with them. There were groups of provincial Jews that wanted to leave the Ghetto, but this too wasn't easy. Passing the gates proved to be a great danger because they were well guarded. Besides that, if someone was caught, his entire family would be punished. So, very few people took this great risk. Only those who had no family could enjoy the luxury, although their housemates would be punished.

Once escaping began on a large scale, for every 10 people, one was made responsible to guard the other nine friends.

The Struggle for Weapons

While in Vilna Ghetto I met the following Kobylnik Jews: Chaim Asher Gilman with his sister Matle, and Feivl and Benchko Shteingart. Chaim Asher and his sister later left with the Svir gang to join the Partisans in Narach forest.

In those times, it was becoming very important to obtain weapons. Not once did one pay for this work with his life.

There was once an incident when a guy from Svenzia wanted to smuggle a revolver into the Ghetto: a Jewish policeman caught him, and the struggle between life and death began. The young man shot the policeman. Gens himself, the leader of the Judenrat, was almost shot. They disarmed the boy and shot him.

The Gestapo could never learn about this. They secretly buried the boy. Dageg, the policeman, "enjoyed" a large funeral where Gens himself delivered the eulogy. After that day, there was even stronger control, especially of the provincial Jews.

But all the restrictions could not deter those who were miserable and wanted to search for a way to bring weapons into the Ghetto at any cost.

A new phase of uprisings emerged when Keitel, the famous mass murderer, took over control of Vilna. From then, all strove to escape as quickly as possible into the forest and abandon the Ghetto.

A group of youths took it upon themselves to organize an uprising. Another group began to organize escape to the forest. Some began to build bunkers and "Raspberries" underground. [Translators note: Raspberry was a code name for hide outs in the Ghetto].

Keitel the murderer was the liquidator of the Vilna Ghetto as well as the fighter against the Partisans. He appeared ordinary and refined and masked his criminal plans. Before coming to Vilna, he had on his conscience thousands of murdered Jews. In Gezdan camp alone, he murdered 1,100 Jews that were confined there.

Transports to Letland (Latvia) and Estonia

In 1943, Keitel ordered six thousand Jews from Vilna to be transported to work in Letland (Latvia) and Estonia; the situation was extremely tense. Keitel wanted the Jews to voluntarily board the trains, but this didn't happen. Jews understood what was in store for them and those who could, hid in the bunkers or anywhere else they could hide. It didn't help matters, when Gens himself went through the courtyards and demanded the Jews, with kindness and anger, volunteer to go.

When no one listened to him, he threatened to rip out the bunkers. The Jews remained headstrong.

In order to carry out the plan the Jewish police had to go from house to house and capture people with force. They also captured Jews from work and stuffed them on to train cars. Through trickery they managed to get a few victims. They sent off one thousand people.

Now the situation worsened and people were afraid to go to work. Life in the Ghetto was paralyzed. A week later, they began again to try to get people to go to Estonia. When they didn't succeed, they blocked the entire Ghetto and the Jewish police, with their own hands, sent those remaining to Estonia.

Panic and Self-Defense

In the first days of September, 1943, the worst days of the Vilna Ghetto began. A dangerous panic ensued, a stampede in the hunt for victims. They searched in all the bunkers, holes and attics. At the same time, many thought if they helped to reveal the bunkers, they would be freed from this turmoil. In time, some showed where the bunkers were. But in the end, the traitors were sent away with all the others who were captured. At this fateful time the youth were creating self- defense organizations. On Strashun Street, house number 12 where I lived, the entire residence was destroyed because it was believed that a shot from the self- defense fighters originated from there.

I was then hiding on Shovelske Street in a "Raspberry." I knew absolutely nothing about it. Later I learned that another group of fighters blocked and occupied two residences, and on the balcony of the children's kitchen, set up a machine gun.

The surrounding people were armed with bottles and stones and were ready for any event. But Gens knew what type of consequences could result from this. He evaded the two residences in order to prevent a huge bloodshed and validate the fall of the Ghetto.

The situation became more confined. The Ghetto was locked. Hunger was on the rise; a kilo of bread now cost 150 Ruble. Whoever had the chance to run away from the Ghetto did. There were even rumors that Gens himself was helping people escape from the Ghetto, maybe due to pressure from the Partisans.

The Story of Itzik Vittenberg

In those days the resistance movement was becoming less clandestine, no longer a secret. Shootings and fights between the Ghetto police and members of self- defense organizations were now in the open. I remember the tragic event that happened to the heroic worker Itzik Vittenberg, the commander of the fighting organization in Vilna.

He was betrayed to the Gestapo as a member of the underground movement, and the Gestapo demanded that at any price, Gens should give him up. A life and death struggle began. He wouldn't be taken so easily. The police pursued him, but it was pointless. The Germans demanded the Ghetto residents capture him, and if they didn't, the whole Ghetto would suffer. Vittenberg disguised himself as a woman and no one was able to find him. They knew he was armed with two revolvers and it would be hard to approach him. This death game could have continued for a long time, but he himself decided to give himself up to the Gestapo so the rest of the Ghetto would not suffer sanctions on his behalf. After a day of horrible suffering at the hands of the Gestapo, Itzik Vittenberg gave up his young heroic life.

The Chase of Victims Persists

The Germans continued to capture people and began to tear apart bunkers and other hiding places. The destruction was huge. We saw doors and windows ripped open, window panes smashed, roofs and balconies hung in mid-air. Piles of nails and debris blocked the way. All the streets were strewn with nails and various other items. It was hard to save people lying under the destruction. The chasing of people persisted. You had to be careful not to fall in the hands of the kidnappers.

The provincial Jews were the worst victims. They simply captured them and their families with force and sent them away to Letland (Latvia) and Estonia. I remained for a while hidden in an attic, but the last days of the Ghetto were quickly approaching, the end of the sad life we were living.

Gens' End

It was Tuesday evening, September 14, 1943. Gens was called to the Gestapo and never returned. They shot him in the yard. The news caused great distress throughout the Ghetto. Immediately, various stories and legends began to spread. People deified him and praised his strength and patience. In general it was hard to have a clear understanding of his character. He supported varied politics and hopes in the attempt to save Jews and survive the difficult Hitler years. But unfortunately, this did not work out and his calculations were wrong. He had been a captain in the earlier Lithuanian army, an assimilated Jew who had married a Christian woman.

After Gens' death, Dessler became the leader of the Judenrat, but only for a short time; the Germans killed him too. Later it was Benia Kansky who remained until the liquidation of the Vilna Ghetto. With the change of leadership in the Judenrat, nothing changed in our lives. The destruction and disturbances continued. In time, our block was also ripped apart and I moved to the German street. My wife worked in the children's kitchen so we had some food, which played a big role.

Thousands of people were concentrated on the Hospital Street. We called it the Stock Market. It was here where we could hear and learn about things in the outside world. Many things were made up. There was no shortage of provocateurs and agents who roamed around and spread rumors about the Ghetto. There were two Cafes in the Ghetto which were always filled with people until late at night. This was also a source of lies and gossip. Much of this eventually became true. I wandered around the Hospital Street for many hours, heard so many stories my head could no longer think. With no way out of my difficult situation I began to think about escaping from the Ghetto. To do this, one had to have a revolver and the price of a revolver was 25,000 Rubles. I did not have so much money.

Liquidation!

Wednesday September 23, in the evening, nine days after the death of Commandant Gens, the Ghetto was trembling from the announcement that the day of liquidation had arrived. We were given until noon the next day to voluntarily assemble on Rudnitsky Street. Everyone understood what this meant.

It is difficult to describe that moment. I needed nerves of steel to carry this out and remain with clear judgement. One could see heart-rending scenes everywhere. Hopeless and broken, people were running around with no idea what to do. Many who were weary from hunger went on a wild chase through the warehouses, bakeries and kitchens; they broke the locks, tore the bars, destroying and trampling on everything. Everyone grabbed what they could. The police and Ghetto authorities chased after them like wild animals and murderously beat whomever they caught. Women were having spasms; children were crying bitterly. Everyone took their packages and families and gathered at the meeting place. Those who had a bunker hid. Seeing what was going on, I too went with the crowd with a few loaves of bread, and ran home to figure out what we would do.

In our yard there was a Raspberry that belonged to the chimney sweeps. It was the best and the surest, equipped with all the comforts, including big beds and water. The entrance was man made and we got air from a chimney. There was a string attached to the chimney which allowed us to go out and see what was happening outside. The chimney sweeps were really specialists. Who would have thought that they would suffer our greatest defeat the very next day. As I later found out, one of the people in the bunker had no patience to sit underground and crawled out through the chimney to get some air and check what was happening around; the murderers noticed him from above, surrounded the yard and eliminated the bunker. They made everyone surrender voluntarily and captured everyone. They sent a few away to the camps. I remember a few days before they destroyed the bunker, the chimney sweeps demanded all the parents in the bunker who had children under the age of three suffocate their children because they feared a child's cry may put them all in danger and everyone would be killed.

We're Searching for a Bunker

My youngest son was six months old, but besides us there were many parents with small children. It's superfluous to describe the misery of the parents who received this order. My little boy was actually quiet and did not cry, but the others did not agree that he should remain with me. They all said I was no better than everyone else and neither was my child. But there was no way I could suffocate my child with my own hands; so, together with my family, I left the chimney sweeps' bunker. We went into the streets looking for a new hiding place, but it was pointless. There was not a lot of time. I saw people streaming to the exit on Rudnitsky Street. My wife and and I and three children dragged ourselves through the yards, cellars and attics but couldn't find an acceptable place to hide. We finally arrived at 8 Shovelsky Street, where we hid before the big round-up to Estonia.

Here we found a bunker where they let us in. The bunker was built on three stories. The entrance was concealed in a wall in the neighboring cellar.

When I entered I found a packed bunker, around 100 people, among them many women and children. It was stifling. Down in the cellar it was a bit cooler, but it stank because that was where the toilet was where everyone came to empty their needs. This was the spot where I had to lie with my family on the bare earth, but I was happy with this too.

"Suffocate the Children!"

Thursday September 24 at night. A dead silence looms; everyone was afraid of his own breaths. It was very hot. People were lying half naked enjoying cold water. The air was scarce, without oxygen; it was hard to breathe. The children were crying bitterly. Nothing worked to calm them: not kindness or anger. They cried without stopping. Everyone was losing patience. Everyone's nerves were shot and they feared for their naked lives. We heard the desperate and bitter orders to suffocate the children. If not we would all be in danger. Mothers desperately wrung their hands and with heartrending cries asked: How can we suffocate our innocent babies with our own hands?! But the complaining was pointless. The distress among the frightened people was growing. The children didn't want to understand and continued to cry, not with their own voices. It was decided that the parents take their children, bring them to an empty room nearby and leave them there.

One can imagine the tragic desperation of the parents, how with their own hands, they had to abandon their own children, their flesh and blood, for a sure death. It's difficult to judge; no one can comprehend and understand that fateful, insane moment when everything was chaotic. Time was running short. There was no time to think. We took our children and left the bunker. Remarkably when my child felt the fresh air, he became lively and started to laugh, and looked around.

My wife, the desperate mother, stood frozen and mute, without words. With a bloody hot stream of tears she separated from her child forever. A long time passed before we could calm down. Our thoughts were there where the children were lying down and crying: my child, a boy, a rare beauty, 6 months old, my brother's child, 1 year old, and another child who I don't know who he belonged to. We left them all to die.

We Are Suited For...

Friday morning, September 25th. One hundred shadows linger between life and death. One hundred shadows are being hunted by the murderers at any cost.

Everyone is worried and broken. We try to figure out what will happen next. How much longer will be able to sit like worms in the ground, in a dark grave without light or food? We had no choice. We began to adapt to these conditions in order to overcome the time.

Whoever had an electric pan was able to cook. But for most the problem was, why them yes, and us no?! It was decided one can only cook for children and the elderly because the heat and the fumes were unbearable. After sitting locked up for almost three days the air became so stifling it was unbearable. The children became pale, temperamental and everyone suffered from headaches. It was much worse in the cellar. Big blood-thirsty flies appeared. On top of this we lost light due to a short circuit. You could feel the darkness with your hands. We tried to find ways to get rid of the plague. Some people took a potato, made a small hole and poured in some oil with a wick. This provided a bit of light. It was a sad light and a sad life. People lay stretched out on the boards without movement, without life, without hope. In addition, a child got sick with a lung infection. The suffering of the child and the unhappy parents is impossible to describe. The child is running a high fever. His lips are burning. His mother sits desperate over his thin, pale body and bathes him with her bloody tears. She has nothing to refresh him with. No medicine or warm water. We all sit motionless. Heavy sighs are heard from everyone breaking the silence. A weak light shines in our bunker and dark shadows sweep over the walls. The child moans. His parents do not know what to do. They are bitter and prefer to leave, no matter what. The others hold them back from these terrible steps.

I personally have joined the unhappy group in our senseless suffering. Who knows how long we'll have to sit. We have to find a solution. We should try to go out to see if there are still any Jews in the city. We also have to repair the light and open the door to let in a little fresh air. If not, we will surely die.

Sunday night we risked opening the small door. The stream of fresh cool air made us drunk. We stood and swallowed the fresh air. Everyone came alive and had a new outlook. We swallowed the air like a fresh stream of water. A cool breeze came in and the stifling heat left the bunker. The bolder ones crawled from our bunker into other rooms. It became more comfortable and freer.

The night was covered in a thick darkness. We fixed the light and got rid of the darkness which had lasted three days. Our little household took on a whole new look. The children were happy with the light.

We forbade cooking with electricity, and from that day on, every night we allowed a fire to be lit in the adjoining rooms. Everyone cooked what they had and we really revived. We were also now permitted to go to rooms a bit further away. We looked for food and other useful items. I found an expensive library with rare books and a little rare Torah. I had it with me in the camp and I don't know how I lost it. I read entire nights to help pass the time.

Slowly, the people in the bunker became used to the bitter conditions. We began to live a night life. At dawn, when the whole world was waking up, went to sleep, and late at night we began our lives. We were our best when the damned slept.

The men collected wood, food – the women cooked. This is how we spent the sad times. Torn away from outside the world, we forgot what daylight looked like and didn't know what was going on.

Tuesday, September 29, 1943. Totally unexpectedly we received a death – knock.

We lost our important lifeline – water. When we noticed it, we froze. Water! Water! We couldn't live without it. What could we do? The only thing was to give ourselves into the hands of the murderers. Confused and worried with great aggravation, we sought advice on what we should do. As great as our fear was, we had an idea. When night fell, we all schemed where we could find a bit of water to quench our thirst. Some of the braver ones went around to the other rooms, toilets and tea houses searching everywhere. People worked together. It was decided that we had to go to the yard to look for the faucet which decidedly closed. Nobody wanted to go out into the yard. Everyone was sending the other. I volunteered to go and needed to take someone with me. We discussed it for a long time and then a brave woman said she would go with me. Slowly and carefully, like criminals going to do a terrible thing, barefoot, we tiptoed out into the yard. We searched and tapped around in the dark until I found a little iron door deep underground. Unfortunately, the murderers closed all the water. We returned with nothing.

This sad reality left a sad impression on everyone. We had no idea what to do. I believed that if fear is exaggerated, we don't see or hear anything.

There were two places in the Ghetto where we could get water, in the bath on Strashuna Street, and in another courtyard from a pump. Some brave ones went away with buckets and found cold fresh water. Everyone was very jealous of this treasure.

Everyone worried about getting water. It was our biggest problem.

Thanks to our will to live, we permitted ourselves to go through the Ghetto in search of food. We found various products like potatoes, turnips, cabbage and other produce and we would meet people from other bunkers near the water.

They did exactly as we did. We knew they were cooking and baking, even bread.

We also knew that due to carelessness a house burned down in the Ghetto. We were sure we would survive these sad times. We had no idea how refined our enemy was, what vulgar ruin they were directing toward us. They knew very well that taking away our water would force us to crawl out of our holes. They waited for us near the water.

Every night at a set time, Lithuanian and Polish murderers came dressed in civilian clothes. They talked to us and offered to sell us bread and promised to get us out of the Ghetto. This is how they spied on us. The next day, they came to the same places, plowed down every corner, revealed the bunkers and killed everyone.

I Go Searching For Jews...

Wednesday I decided to go to the German Street to the Raspberry of the chimney sweeps to learn what was happening in the world, were there still any Jews left, and was there still a chance to be saved. With great effort I found someone to go with me. With great difficulty, and very carefully, we set out on our way because every unsure step could be tragic. When we were finally in the yard, we heard heavy footsteps behind us. We barely managed to crawl into an attic. We then saw two men looking for us with flashlights. They were angry that we disappeared as if into thin air. On my knees I approached the chimney. I knew the entrance. I touched the rope, tried to pull, tear, call out but no one responded. I sensed that the rope with all its force was torn away. We remained lying down in the attic for a few hours and waited for it to be quiet. With great fear we headed back. I then said I will never undertake such a mission again. The mystery remained who pulled away the rope from me, because as I said, the next morning after the action, they were caught and killed.

Thursday evening we were preparing for Yom Kippur. Because Friday evening we had to fast, we feverishly prepared food for the next day. I remember well the sad moment of how the holiday appeared underground. The children ran about the room happily that tomorrow they will have better food. My wife even prepared Tsimes. We were busy all night preparing food. They men took care of everything. They brought water. The wives were busy at the ovens and it didn't dawn on anyone that this would be our last night all together. The children demanded food and we promised that tomorrow they would receive good things.

Who would have imagined that we would not live to eat this food?

Discover the Bunker!

Friday at dawn, Erev Yom Kippur a sign was given that everyone should enter the bunker. Everyone crawled on their stomachs through the door with the hot prepared food. The heavy iron door was locked and we all went to sleep. I was already asleep when my wife woke me. She stood beside me, pale and scared to death. Every muscle in her shook. "Get up! A horrible tragedy has happened to us.

Our bunker has been discovered." Frightened by the sudden news, I jumped up from my bed to see what was going on. I went up to the third floor where I found everyone in horrible confusion. The women were crying and wailing, calling for their children and grabbing their bags. The children realized the great danger.

They clung to their mothers. The men stood despondent. I thought about what to do. The murderers were in the next room waiting for their victims. They commanded we surrender otherwise they would destroy the bunker. I tried to break a wall in the cellar that led to a closet but it was pointless because we were surrounded on all sides by Lithuanian, Polish, Ukrainian and German S.S.

We did not stop to ponder. We gave up. The door was opened and two S.S men came and began immediately to take us out. "Out! Out! Everyone out!" I tried to hide under a bed covered by potatoes. When everyone had left the bunker a Ukrainian searched under the beds. He even shot under a bed, but to my great fortune, in another direction. I was scared and came out on my own. He hit me a few times with his gun and led me to the group.

Walking there, I did not give up hope. Like always, I tried to think how I can get out of the murderers' hands. Utilizing the narrowness of the stairs from the third floor, as quickly as possible, I snuck into a side room and hid behind the furniture.

I entered a small buffet and remained there from ten o'clock in the morning until ten at night, wiggling like a worm. I was afraid of my own breath. I couldn't move or turn around. Time felt like an eternity. Horrible thoughts frightened me. The wound was still fresh. They captured my wife and children and were taking them to their death.

Later a few Poles came into the room to collect the furniture. I lay still and asked God to protect me because they could find me at any moment. They crawled around and rummaged through everything. I heard them joyfully announce that they found something valuable and how happy they were that they were stealing so greedily. I heard one say to the other: "What would we do if we found a Jew here?" The murderer replied: "If we find a local Jew we will hand him over to the Gestapo!" This is how I had to spend 12 hours. Every minute my life was in danger.

Suddenly, I froze. I sensed I few steps away from me a Pole was rummaging around. He opened every door and searched. I closed my eyes so I would not see anything. I clenched my teeth and imagined the great celebration they would have discovering me. I hid in a corner. My heart was pounding. My blood was boiling with noises in my head. My lips whispered a prayer and I was covered in a cold sweat. He was approaching my row, but didn't come to the little door. I heard a voice yell "Lunch!" (in Polish), and everyone left the room. I then breathed more freely and straightened my limbs. When I returned to myself, I began again to think about all the unfortunate ones who would soon be killed. My heart was exploding from agitation. But I tried to comfort myself, and I didn't know what would happen to me. I pulled myself together and told myself I can't lose because so much still lies ahead.

When it got dark I left my terrible unsafe spot and went to look for a hide out.

Here began my martyr's path: Where do I go and where do I look? A broken man, persecuted, I wandered around the quiet dark Ghetto streets looking for a place to hide. I wandered around searching for a long time through the court yards, empty rooms and cellars and could not find a suitable place.

Everywhere and in every corner death loomed. Every step I took could seal my fate forever. The Polish, Lithuanian and Ukrainian criminals, together with the Germans would hide among the ruins and search and rummage in order to catch Jews, if in fact anyone was still hiding and out of their hands.

My troubles did not end there. Besides the Vilna Ghetto I went through all seven gates of hell, also in Germany – until I lived to see liberation.

[Pages 240-243]

The Pain and Grief After the Liberation

by Yitzchak Tchernatsky, Kfar Aviv
Translated by Janie Respitz
Edited by Toby Bird

On the way from Kobylnik to Myadel

1944 – We crawled out of our holes like mice and with our hands protected our eyes from the glare of the sun. Like shadows on the wall we wobbled with trouble balancing.

Death was our best friend, but it neglected to find us.

During three years of war death did its work, but left us very lonely. It took our nearest and dearest to the other world – but here and there left a vestige. But even the remaining few pierced the eyes of the enemy. They looked at us with murder in their eyes and each step we took burned. They couldn't figure out how we had the audacity to survive.

It was, a pity on them, too cheerful to see us wandering around as living witnesses who knew all of the "good deeds" they brought upon the Jews during the war.

They wore stolen possessions they robbed from us that tightened when they saw us. They really wanted to get rid of us as quickly as possible.

Angry from our tragedy, we sought a place to sleep and rest our weary heads. Like cats, we clung to those who shared our suffering. This is how we trudged through the villages. Perhaps we would find a good Gentile: this was very difficult.

Our sad experiences, which were still so fresh, did not provide us with any hope.

Unfortunately, we had no choice because what remained of our homes was ruin and ash. With every day that passed we had to answer the question: "What will happen next?"

I looked for work. I came to the Village Kupa, 3 kilometres from Kobylnik. I was very familiar with the village. Situated on the banks of Narach, it was the lake I would bathe and swim in every summer. In the evenings, we would take boat rides on the quiet water under the moonlight. We were naïve and did not realize what awaited us. But now, as I stood on the shore and remembered the past, I had experienced enough to know that my fate was void of sentiment and sweet dreams.

Coincidentally, I came across a Gentile acquaintance named Anton Baluvke who took me in to his home. He suggested I stay with him and offered to find me work.

As I later learned, during the war he was in contact with the Russian partisans that were nearby. He would bring them news about the Germans. After the war, the Soviets recognized his efforts and made him a big boss in the smoked fish factory in Kupa, near Narach.

Knowing I was a Jew, he required my trust. Knowing I wouldn't betray him, he gave me a job to be responsible for guarding the factory. We received guns and other weapons from the war commissary. Together with a few others, I had to guard the factory day and night. I became the security officer for the factory.

Despite the fact that the Soviets had freed the area and were in power, there were still various groups in the forest who would ambush the Soviets and particularly the Jews. This was the coming together of various bandits who only a short time earlier were collaborating with the Germans and carrying out hundreds of murders and assaults.

Now they were afraid to return to the villages in the event that the Soviets would discover them and sentence them, they preferred to remain in the forest and attack whenever they could. Some of them were deserters from the Soviet army and they knew what awaited them. They were called the "Green Legion" – they romped through the entire region ruining a sense of security.

I was pleased with my work, but I always had to be prepared for attacks from the outside. I was also never quite sure about our own guys with whom I worked – never knowing if they would "accidentally" let a bullet fly from their gun in my direction. I always had to remain alert and sleep with my eyes open.

Around the same time, the boss of the factory came to see me, the same Baluvke.

He told me I would go together with him to transport an order of smoked fish to Malodechne and deliver it to the local fish cooperative. This was about 80 kilometres from Kobylnik.

We left the same day, and this would prove to be my greatest luck. The next day when we returned I received the news that saddened my soul: The day we left, in the evening, the factory was attacked by gunfire. The bandits who attacked stole the weapons from the farmers and demanded they deliver me to them because they had been searching for me for a long time. They demanded to know where I was and said they wanted to make me "a head shorter." I then learned the entire "celebration" was on my behalf. It appears I was missing from their list of murdered Jews that they killed during the war.

After this incident I was awake thinking entire nights and slowly began to drill into my brain the idea that I was superfluous – most of all, what was I looking for among these Gentiles?

At dawn, as I watched the sun rise, I knew where I should turn my sights and aspire to go, as far as possible.

I found some other jobs until I abandoned all this luck and came to Israel to be a free Jewish farmer.

———

[Pages 244-251]

Memorable Days of Kobylnik's Liberation
by Meyer Swirsky
Translated from Russian by Edward E. Jaffe
Edited by Toby Bird

I was residing in Stalingrad for several months, a city located along the shore of the Volga River. It became progressively clearer that the Nazi monsters will ultimately be conquered. Stalingrad, which became the symbol of resistance to the Nazis, was slowly recovering from its ruins. I was among those who were engaged in the restoration and rebuilding of a tractor factory. We just celebrated the delivery of the first tractor.

After the defeat at Stalingrad at the beginning of 1943 the Germans were driven westward by the Red Army. Thereafter, every day, reports were coming in about new victories against the enemy, about liberated towns and territories. The Red Army was successfully moving forward. News reports were informing us about the savage destruction by the Germans in the liberated territories.

The press slipped through hints about the massive destruction of Jews by the Germans and their collaborators. I was actually an eyewitness to such destruction about two years earlier. In the liberated cities and towns there were no more Jews. It was also reported that the White Russian front was breached. With great anxiety, I was catching all broadcast news. The Red Army was moving forward with a series of bloody fights. With every liberated city or town my hope was heightened that the day was near when the town of my youth, Kobylnik, will be liberated.

Two long years of painful ignorance about my home town was changing into a ray of hope that some of my close relatives may still be alive. How soon will the day arrive when I will have to face reality? Suddenly the ray of hope may be extinguished. How will I continue to live? Frequently, during the last two years, I felt isolated and lonely. Will I receive confirmation of what I am afraid to think about? Is it possible that I alone from my family will remain in this world? One after another I see in my imagination images of my dear home, parents, brothers, sisters, relatives and friends. I see them all alive and happy awaiting quick victory over the vicious enemy. But my dreams are not continuous.... I cannot rely on them... reality is quite cruel and leaves no room for Illusions. Yet there was hope, otherwise despair would have overwhelmed me.

My thoughts turned to August 1942 when I left Kobylnik. Since that time I heard nothing about my family and the 250 Jews who were still among the living. The Jews of Kobylnik then received an order to send six more people to work in the town of Myadel (21 Kilometers west of Kobylnik), after several Jews of our town were already dispatched to Mydal. We understood that upon completion of the work nobody was likely to return. The dwellers of Kobylnik could select only four people, among them my father, David Leib Swirsky, a father of six children. With great difficulty, it was possible to persuade the head of the local bureau, Vantzekovich, to send four instead of six Jews. None knew how this would be received by the Germans in Mydal...And thus the four were set to go. The horse drown wagon pulled up in front of our home where total despair reigned – mother was to remain with her six children. Besides fear of death, hunger awaited us. It is then that I proposed to the member of the Jewish committee to send me instead of my father. I succeeded in persuading them – I looked older than a 15 year old. I was certain that I would not fall behind adults since I had more than a year of practice at heavy labor. I was very glad that father remained with the family. Little time remained to say goodbye. At that time, my brother Herzel was not at home. My mother gave me a prayer book and said goodbye with pain in her heart and tears in her eyes. Father blessed me by saying, "God look after you, and take care of yourself." He added "My son, at the first opportunity, run into the forest! Hitler will be conquered; it is just a matter of time. We have no chance for survival with our little ones. Therefore, let at least one of our family survive." I embraced and kissed my younger sisters and brothers, and with a bundle in hand I climbed onto the wagon. On Myadel Street, near the exit of town, my brother Herzel, who was two years younger than I, ran after us. He jumped into the wagon and we said farewell to each other. We looked at one another unable to let go, but promised each other that we will run into the forest at the first opportunity. We knew that in the forest partisans were hiding. Herzel jumped off the wagon outside the town, near the home of the forest ranger. Tears choked us. The dear face of my brother moved farther and farther away, and together with him my whole family, and the whole town...

In the days of Kobylnik's liberation, I experienced time and again lively images from the past which supported and comforted me. Perhaps a few Jews of Kobylnik succeeded in hiding in the forest, similar to those who escaped from Mayadel. Maybe there was also a man like Michael Patashnik (from the town of Hodutishki) who organized the escape of Jews, including women and children, into the forest. Possibly some who experienced difficult situations, succeeded in crossing the front line, and appeared in the rear as happened to me?

I continued to work in the steel fashioning section of the tractor factory, but once, while working on the repair of an electric oven for melting steel, I heard over the loudspeaker that the regional center of Mayadel has been liberated. I was overwhelmed with anticipation and I ran to share the news with my co–workers. Then came the thought of writing home. But something stopped me. My hands were shaking, and I could not collect my thoughts. I was somehow encouraged, seeing what was happening to me. Finally, after several hours, I calmed down and I sat down to write. I addressed my parents, brothers, sisters, relatives and friends, one letter for all. While writing, my uncertainty vanished – they are alive! They will read this letter!

Four months have passed. The front moved and now reached Polish territory. The Soviet Union was liberated. Everyone was happy. I was still waiting for an answer. I did not know how long it takes for a letter to arrive. After all, nobody ever wrote to me in Stalingrad. Every day I passed the list of those fortunate to receive letters, but I looked in vain for my name. Now it was more than a week since I looked at the list. More than previously I was overtaken by doubt and despair. And suddenly a friend runs toward me and informs me that he saw my name on the list. In a state of agitation, I hurried to confirm the finding, but I find on the list not "Swirsky Meyer" but "Swirsky David", the name of my father. That must mean that that my letter was returned... After a couple of days, I gathered all energy and I went to the post office to pick up the letter. I actually saw my father's handwriting! I did not even touch the letter when I lost consciousness. In the ambulance, the first aid nurse read the letter to me, which I remember by heart to this day.

"Our dear Meyer, at this minute there is no limit to our happiness. Today we came out of the forest, and when we returned to town, we received your letter with your greetings. There is nothing more precious than a surviving child! One more Jew survived. We are all alive and healthy. Thirty six Jews from our town have survived. The nicest and best are no longer with us, among them our dear and your lovely brother Herzel. Our town was burned, including our house. But who thinks about that. The survivors: your uncle Yehoshua with sons Israel–Leib, Hertzke and Itzele. Afroike Kravchinsky, Ida

Burgin and her children, Leib Friedman's family, Joseph Blinder's family, Tzifke Harmatz, her sister Sorel and her husband Nathan, Meyer–Shmerl Khodosh, Itzik Chernotzky, Asher Krukoff, Ben–Zion Steingart, Khone and Hershl Dimenstein, Abrasha Khodosh, Khaya–Liba Chernotsky and her brother Feivel. There is hope that several others survived. We were fortunate to survive. God protected us during the most difficult times. Thanks to your mother, who was needed by the Germans because she was a seamstress, we were not destroyed together with the other Jews the day after Yom Kippur 1942. We and several other Jewish families with useful specialists that the Germans needed were transferred to the Ghetto in Mayadel. From there we were freed by the partisans. We stayed in the forest until we were liberated in July 1944. Several people from our town died in the forest. Now is not the time to think about the difficulties we encountered. Thank God that we are alive.

Khana, Mina, Yehoshua and Zundel, who grew up in the forest, send their kisses; and your mother, my dear wife, is too emotional to write to you today. She embraces you and firmly presses you to her heart. In this happy day, we must not forget those who were an integral part of our lives, those who will always remain alive in your heart, and in our hearts. we will never forget them. Also, don't forget our murderers and tormenters – the Nazis and their collaborators. Today we are celebrating your rebirth, simultaneously with our liberation. We are proud of our heroic Kobylnik's partisans: Herzel Gordon, Meyer Khodosh, Khaim–Osher Gilman who together with many other Jews fought with the Germans to avenge spilled Jewish blood. Their fight brings enormous honor for our people. This is a bright page in the history of the awful and dark days which we survived"

We are heartily kissing you

Your father Yosef David–Leib Swirsky Stalingrad, November 1945

After many months of wearisome expectations, I finally received permission to visit my family. Happiness overwhelmed me. After more than three years of separation I will once again see my mother, father, brothers and sisters... my greatest happiness – to see everyone up close with my own eyes.

Yosef David–Leib Swirsky

The train was full of demobilized soldiers. It was impossible to obtain a ticket. But nothing could stop me!... Several days later I was in Moscow. And here by one means or another I was able to push myself into a train destined for Vilno. Time moved very slowly and appeared like endless long hours. Cities and towns flickered by, but I did not notice them, even those that I passed during the difficult trip three years ago when I succeeded in crossing the front line and became a free man. My thoughts were aimed only at one house in the town of Postavy, where my family was living. I wanted to get there as fast as possible.

November 7, 1945

I got off at midnight at the station of Postavy. I virtually ran the two kilometers that separate the station from town. Here I stood on Lenin street, in front of house number 8. Out comes the owner of the house, Mrs. Tsepelovich.

She leads me through the yard to an apartment and opens a door in front of me: "Khava, you have a guest...". After years spent in Russian rear areas I forgot Yiddish and therefore said in Russian "How are you?" and could not make another sound. I lost the ability to move. My legs failed to serve me.

In the house was a holiday atmosphere. Mother, father and a few Jews from our town sat around the covered table. Through the partially closed door of the bedroom one could see sleeping children. As is customary in the Soviet Union in parent's homes the anniversary of the revolution is appropriately noted.

I wore a sweater, warm pants, a hat with ear flaps which slipped over my eyes. Nobody recognized me. The father asked the mother, "What does the guest need?" and added, " Sit him down, give him a shot of vodka, and ask him what brings him to us at such a late hour?" In the meantime, I see that in the bedroom the head of a light haired boy lifts from a pillow (apparently of the 4 year old brother Zundel). The house noises woke him up. One look at me from his bed and he suddenly cried out "Meyer came!" The only person, who could not remember me, recognized me instinctively. Mother removed my hat and finding the mark on my forehead (in my childhood I was injured by a horse) she exclaimed "Meyer!" She threw herself on my neck, and lost consciousness.

A half hour later, washed and properly dressed, I sat at the table with my close relatives and enjoyed my fortunate and happy meeting.

A Short Autobiography

I, Meyer Swirsky, was born in November 1927 in the town of Kobylnik (Narach), located on the picturesque shores of Lake Narach. As a child, I spent the early years in Belarus. My great grandfather Zundel Swirsky was involved in an agricultural enterprise and lived with his family in the village of Yanovichi, located on the way from beyond Narach to Svir. My great grandfather had a daughter and five sons. One of them was my grandfather Meyer. The family of my grandfather lived in Kobylnik. The grandfather died in 1927, six weeks before I was born. I was named Meyer in memory of my grandfather. Our family lived on Postavy Street in the house of my grandmother–Rivka Gordon (based on maternal forefathers).

Near the house were a large garden and an orchard. The latter was known for its plums. My father David sold fish and furs; mother Khava was a seamstress. In the family were six children. The youngest was Zundel, who was born on June 12, 1941, ten days before the outbreak of the war. In Poland (until 1939) I completed 6 years of schooling. (povshekhna) two years (1939–1941) I studied in a Russian school. Although I was quite young when I spent years in Poland – two years under the Soviets, and the years under German occupation – nevertheless it left an indelible mark on me, that affected my subsequent life's path. The experience acquired in my young years affected my life's direction.

I lived under German occupation for 15 months, over that period of time more than half of Kobylnik's population was shot dead. (The last 120 Jews were shot on September 21, 1942.).

At the beginning of the second half of 1942 I was taken into Myadel for construction work (instead of my father, since I was the oldest of the children). There the Jews began planning an escape into the forest. They established a connection with the partisans (freedom fighters). One German of the Myadel military police informed us about the upcoming "action for the destruction of the Jews" of Myadel and Kobylnik. Thanks to this information the majority of Myadel Jews were saved, including me. At night, two days before the planned action, we walked into the forest; I remained there until the middle of November 1942. There were long days and nights. Each passing week included many occurrences and experiences which made time pass very slowly, simulating years. Nevertheless, there was hope for liberation from the fascist's hell.

In November 1942, I crossed the front line together with a unit of partisans that was dispatched to obtain weapons. I was sent to the rear in the Yaroslav region. After a few days spent on the road in a warm part of a train, we stopped on the Yaroslav station, specifically for a train transfer. I was hungry and cold but above all free. The German hell was behind me. At the station in the waiting room, I met unexpectedly my old teacher from Kobylnik – Lev Ivanovich Lvov. He gave me food and proposed that I follow him to Dzerzinsk where he worked as an agriculturist. Unfortunately, I was not allowed to travel with him. Instead I was ordered to travel to the town of Lublin. But for a whole year I corresponded with him, which for me provided a great deal of moral support (I still keep in touch with Lev Ivanovich's son Boris).

In 19,44 I was dispatched from Lublin to Stalingrad to work on the rebuilding of a destroyed tractor factory. This was not an easy time. I did not know anything about my family. I was sure none of them survived. I spent my days at difficult work, in the cold, hungry and in solitude.

Only after our area was liberated did I receive the unexpected message from my family – a letter from my father. My happiness was boundless. I was lucky. My parents and four children were rescued. From my father's letter I learned about the awful Jewish tragedy. My brother Herzel died in Vilno (now renamed Vilnius), as did my uncles and aunts, and my cousins. My father stated in the letter how they succeeded in surviving and how they lived in the forest for almost two years. Only in November 1945 I succeeded in returning for a short visit to Kobylnik. My parents lived in Postavy where our long awaited meeting took place, about which a book can be written. The same November I was sent to Poland. Then through Czechoslovakia and Austria I arrived in Germany where I studied two years via correspondence and obtained a high school diploma.

In 1948 I arrived in Israel and immediately entered the army and participated in the war of liberation. In 1950 I was demobilized and entered Haifa Technical Institute from which I graduated in 1954 as a mechanical engineer. The same year I married Ida. We have two children, son David and daughter Osnat, and seven grandchildren and a great grandchild.

In 1951 my parents and children immigrated to Canada and there my father experienced heart problems. At that time my father's brother and my mother's brother lived in the USA where they immigrated before WW II. Father died in 1954, mother in 1982. Both are buried in Israel. My sister Ann and brother Yehoshua and their families live in the USA, as well as the family of my deceased sister Mina (who died in 1984).

In 1970 my younger brother Zundel (Sheldon) immigrated to Israel from the USA. With all of them I maintain very close and warm relationships.

After completing my studies I worked for six years in an agricultural machine building factory as a project engineer. Subsequently, I opened my own private office where I worked for 20 years in this industrial and agricultural enterprise, dealing with refrigeration assemblies, packaging lines for fruits and vegetables, outfits for impromptu storage facilities and others. Finally, I changed the work profile of our business to the importation of sanitary ware and outfitting of industrial kitchens. The firm became a family business. As our children grew they found an interest in the business. Now the children manage the firm where about 100 people are employed and I function as the president of the enterprise.

In 1990, after 45 years, I visited my distant, dear town of Kobylnik (now renamed Narach). I met old acquaintances from my youth and those who helped Jews during the German occupation. To this day we stay in touch with them and constantly deliver financial aid.

Our Jewish cemetery and brotherly tombstones have been restored in 1992. In Israel exists a society of emigrants from Kobylnik and Narach. I am the chairman of the society. Together we established a fund, which serves to support the Jewish cemeteries and preserves the tombstones in both towns.

At the present time I live in Haifa on the Carmel Mountain, with a unique view of the sea and the unfolding distant spaces.

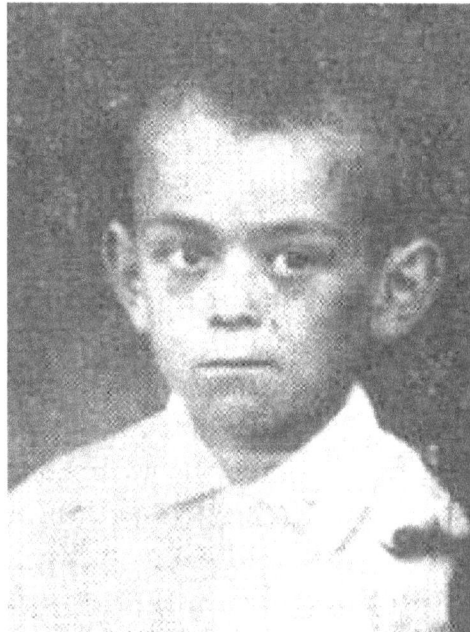

Hertzele Swirsky

[Pages 252-256]

Memories of By-Gone Days
Yitzhak Gordon
Translated by Sarah Mendelson Axelrod z"l

I look for memories long lost and far away.
I look in every corner
and I grovel with my hands.
Maybe my fingers will find a sign in the ruins of the walls.
But time has covered everything with earth
where thistles and weeds now grow on a barren field

So I step lightly in the emptiness
and I wish to see a person
And I ask of every hill of grass
maybe it can tell me
how this could have happened.
I roll over a heap of stones,
silent witnesses which were there
maybe they can tell me
how it all happened
how all is gone and is no more?

Then I go on to the little woods
where grow blueberries
and mushrooms abundantly
where the tall proud trees
surely know all the secrets-
But they also hide them from me.

Then a little wind comes up
and I clench my fists
and my blood seethes
full of pain and anger.
And I shout my pain:
Have you not seen any Jews?

So I was running
and I came to the Market Place

And looked everywhere
as far as my eyes could see -
And here also I saw no one
and found no one.

Then they came into my mind,
Each one with his work and trade.
As though in line,
come first those who deal in leather,
yard goods, iron (hardware)
and all kinds of goods,
And the dealers in eggs
and pig bristles -
Jews who work hard to earn Zlotys.
And after them the workmen,
tailors, shoemakers, blacksmiths, teamsters,
bagel-bakers, butchers,
carpenters, with calloused hands.

Then I go and look in the Shul -
maybe today is Yom Kippur
when everyone is at Kol Nidre
asking forgiveness for their sins.
Or maybe it is Simchas Torah
when Jews drink wine
without fear
and celebrate dancing.

Then I don't think much
and I go to Midler Street
where my father's small house,
roofed with straw
used to be.
But then also I found no one,
neither father
nor mother,
nor my brother,
nor neighbors -

So as though from a fire,
I begin to run away from Kobylnik,

back through Vilner Street,
past the cloisters,
the bridge,
till I come to the tekovic.

And suddenly
from the little woods,
flies a gift -
crows -
toward me -
kra, kra, kra
they call to me.
As though they would say:
Why do you root around here,
have you lost something?
If you really want to know,
Come, we will show you.

Here
nearly in the woods
is the mass grave
covered with cement and iron.
Here lie your brothers,
big and small,
young and old.
They were killed together,
in terror.

Here the Germans,
cannibals,
befell them with guns,
like wild animals,
also Poles and Lithuanians, Letts and Ukraines, Goyim Catholics,
they chased them and tortured them.
Robbers, murderers, hooligans, parasites spilled the blood of
Jews and stole their goods.

Hearing the tragedy,
the trees in the woods near the grave
trembled and the leaves fall.
Also the birds are sad

about what was done to the Jews.
And they surround me
as though they would tell me
about the barbarians
and also the goyim -
how they burned everything:
the Shul, the Holy books, the Torahs.

Exhausted from pain and tears,
the eternal ones wait
through long generations
and through years -
Ash and coal is become of everyone.

Suddenly over me there came
a dark cloud which obscured the sun,
like an eclipse.
I begin to tremble and fear
and I can no longer listen
to the tragic drama
and I get excited
and send up a curse into the air,
to myself and to the moon,
also to the stars -
Let them hear my pain.

I will spit in their faces,
curse them and hate them.
I will shout to the fields the woods,
over the seas.
Let everyone know and remember.
Also the dirt and snow and rain.
Will I never forget the shame.
Forever, I will carry the feeling of revenge.

And Kobylnik,
a small shtetl in White Russia,
your landsleit in Israel
will forever remember you with deep pain.

[Page 257]

Yosef Tunkievich

Asher Krukoff
Translated by E. E. Jaffe

Yosef Tunkievich

In the menacing sea of hatred and persecution there were a few individuals of genuine kindness, honesty and pure compassion. One such extraordinary individual in the dark sea of Jew-hatred and persecution was the simple Kobylnik Christian farmer Yosef Tunkievich, who during the most difficult times under threat of death did not sell his soul to the devil and took a chance with his life to save Jews. Almost all surviving Jews of Kobylnik at one time or another found temporary sanctuary in his home and consequently survived the war. At one time he sheltered a large group of Kobylnik Jews, including Yehudit Friedman with her husband and son, Khone and Hershel Dimenstein, Khia-Liebe and Itzhak Tsernotski, Sholem Yavnovich, and the writer of this article (Asher Krukoff). Tunkievich received us initially and continued to help us when the whole town was occupied by the German military forces.

We had contact with the Vilna ghetto via Yosef Tunkievich. He was supposed to bring Yehudit Todres with her husband and her sister Sheinke. They were already under way, not far from Kobylnik, when they encountered German soldiers and turned back. Only Yehudit's husband made it to Tunkievich's farm.

Several Kobylnik Jews, Shoul Kaplan, Yehudit Todres' husband Itzhak Tsernotski and I - were hidden by Tunkievich in his pig sty for 10 months in a dugout hole measuring three by three meters in size. On top of the dugout grew in summer potatoes and in winter rye. The entrance to the dugout was in the pig sty through a hidden door, covered with garbage. From the door followed a tunnel about two meters long and through another small door made of thin metal designed, in case of a fire, to prevent its spread to the dugout. In midday some light penetrated into the hole, but most of the time we sat in darkness. Only the good food provided by Tunkievich sustained everybody's health.

In spring, Passover time, the dugout was full of water. We were forced to dig another hole and at night remove the water from both holes. That way we were steeped several weeks in wetness causing our deterioration while still staying alive. When Tunkievich would descend into the hideout he cried like a small child and failed to understand how we could survive in this environment.

Yosef Tunkievich was the only ray of hope in the great darkness that surrounded us. His name is mentioned by the survivors with holy trembling of their lips. He served as the only symbol of human dignity and clear consciousness. Kobylnik Jews will forever honor and remember his name.

Before we were able to publish this story which was devoted to the beloved and esteemed Jewish friend Yosef Tunkievich, and his extraordinary relations with Jews during World War ll, at the start of 1967 we received the sad news about his death at an advanced age, in his farm home not far from Kobylnik.

With his demise, the Kobylnik Jews lost a dear friend and human defender whom they will forever appreciate and remember. Let his memory be blessed and his soul be found among the righteous of all nations.*

  * lt is noteworthy that Ann Jaffe has seen to it that the name Yosef Tunkievich
  be properly inscribed in the garden of the righteous gentiles in front of the Bernard
  and Ruth Siegel Community Center in Wilmington, Delaware. His name has also
  been entered in Jerusalem's Yad Vashem, as one of the Righteous Gentiles.

[Page 260]

With the People of Kobylnik in Sorrow and Pain

Leon (Leybl) Solomon, Detroit

Translated by E. E. Jaffe

Edited by Toby Bird

I Become a Kobylniker

My first "acquaintanceship" with the Hitlerite animals took place already in 1939 in Makov Mazovyetsky, 85 kilometres from Warsaw. I lived there with my parents and sisters.

My older brother Boruch ran away as soon as the Germans entered eastern Poland, which at the time was occupied by the Russians. Seeing what he did, we also ran to the Russian side and together with my two sisters, Chava and Rivka, settled in Bialystok, where there were many refugees that were coming from German occupied Western Poland. A little later my brother Boruch found us and brought us to Kobylnik, where he had settled earlier.

In Kobylnik our life was more or less normalized (relative to the times). The Jews of Kobylnik were friendly and welcomed the new refugees in town. We were not the only ones. The children in town laughed at our Polish Yiddish but it didn't take long for us to start speaking the Lithuanian Yiddish dialect, which I speak until today. My brother was the director of the school in Kobylnik, and me and my sisters went there with all the other children in town.

The Outbreak of the German – Soviet War in 1941

In June 1941 war broke out between Russia and Germany. In only a few days we were once again face to face with the German criminals. My brother tried again to run away but there was nowhere to go. The Germans with their troops blocked all the roads and there was nowhere to run; Boruch had to return to town.

Two days later my brother was arrested and, together with 15 other men the local White Russian police identified as communists, was shot.

His former students from the town carried out this horrible verdict on their teacher, who was so loved and talented. The young Jewish scientist, mathematician and educator fell as a martyr in the midst of his blossoming activity.

The Last Slaughter

Orphaned and broken after my brother's death, Shepsl Berger took us in with his family. Together with all the other Jews in town we endured difficult months of slave labour, pain and dejection. Being without parents, perhaps more than others, I was thinking of escaping to the forest where in 1942 Partisans had appeared.

On the eve of Yom Kippur 1942 we received news in town that a few Jews from Myadel together with some Jews from Kobylnik who worked there, escaped to the forest. Everyone in town admired this heroic act. This was the last way out, but no one could imagine how people with small children, women and the elderly could manage to live in the forest throughout the winter with snow and frost. And how would they be nourished when the non–Jewish population hated us so much?

Maybe that is why none of us ran, and like every other day I went to work on Yom Kippur; we already felt the oncoming destruction in the air. And so it was.

Very quickly I found myself with all the other Jews in the middle of the marketplace. From there they brought us under heavy guard to Dam–Ludavi, the Folk –House in town near the church. Here we were confined. In Dam–Ludavi I found my two sisters, who the bandits captured. With tearful eyes we now saw our tragic end. We thought they were going to burn us.

Night fell quickly. In the dark, like herring in a barrel, our hearts were crying and sighing, helpless without a spark of hope to be saved – parting from one another with tears flowing for our sad fate. Everyone puts their hands up toward God and asks, "Why?" Everything is now clear; they are already digging our graves. Some are trying to break the shutters on the windows and jump out; they are immediately shot. The patrol outside is dense.

Together with my 2 sisters and 20 others, we hid under the stage (where we used to perform) hoping they would not look there. In the morning we saw how they were leading everyone out of the building. When it was empty the bandits began to search in all possible places – and they found us! They pulled out my sisters before me. Chava managed to tell me: "See, Leybele, run away. At least one should remain from our family." I, together with Yehoshua Chernatsky, Yitzchak Chernatsky and Reuven Shteyngart (Gedalia's son –in–law), were pulled out last. Two murderers led us to the graves. Yehoshua called out to one of the murderers who was leading us: "Kolya, we grew up together and went to the same school. Let me go. I want to live." His bandit's answer was: "Move forward!" and cursed all the Jews in Russian. Yehoshua managed to escape. The bandit, Kolya, chased after him and shot him.

Remaining with one policeman at the bridge, not far from the church, Chaim and I also tried to run away in the direction of the nobleman's estate. The murderer began to shoot. I ran zig zag and the bullets rang by me. My sister's last words gave me the strength and desire to live, and this is how I managed to escape! Chaim fell wounded and was later shot by the police.

With my last bit of strength I ran to the forest. From the other side of the road I heard the shots. Every shot tore another muscle in my body. This was the murder of the last Jews of our town, including my sisters.

To the Partisans

I wandered in the forest for 2 days. I was hungry, torn cold and wet. Without much choice I entered the village Konstantinova. Luckily I found a few Jews working there and stayed with them for a few days. From there I went to

Svir where there was still a Ghetto. There I met Herzke Gordon who also escaped, like me, from under the gun.

Together with the Jews from Svir, we move to Mikhalishok Ghetto, and from there I was sent to work in Konstantinova. With me was a guy from Kobylnik – Kivke Krivitsky. Working together with a few Jews near the forest we felt hopeful that the time would pass. But after 4–5 months, Spring 1943, we received German orders to go to the Vilna Ghetto where the Germans were gathering all remaining Jews from the surrounding towns that the Germans had liquidated.

But I decided I will not go to another Ghetto! I had nothing more to lose and decided to go to the forest and look for Partisans. I tried to convince others to come with me, but unfortunately they did not want to leave their parents, sisters and brothers. The Jews from the surrounding towns never went to the Vilna Ghetto; they were all murdered in Ponar.

Unfamiliar with the area, I wandered through fields and forests looking for Partisans. From time to time I would receive a piece of bread from a Gentile (at night), risking his life. At the same time, I managed occasionally to spend a night with a farmer under a roof. One night, I came to sleep at a Gentile's home in a small village, and there were Partisans there. I went to them and told them my sad fate. I told them I was Shepsl's son from Kobylnik (It would have been difficult for them to accept I was a Jew from Warsaw.) and I won their trust.

The same night, the Partisans brought me to a small house in the middle of a swamp and told me to wait until someone would come to get me. The Non–Jews who lived there told me to leave the next morning; they were afraid to have a Jew in their home.

Trudging through the mud, I came to another similar small house. The Gentile named Tolayke questioned me and was particularly interested in which Kobylnilk Jews were still alive. He had his doubts, but then took me deep into the swamps to an underground bunker that was hidden between the trees.

When I entered I saw forms that were similar to pre–historic people: hairy dirty faces, glaring eyes which hadn't seen daylight in a long time. It was hard to recognize the Kobylnik Jews among them, my good friends: Leyb Friedman, Yehoshua Gordon, Hirshl Dimentshyn, Feivl Chernatsky and Chamke from Zanarach.

Despite the joy of seeing them, it was clear to me that I could not be a burden to them. Tolayke was a friend to the Jews, but he himself didn't have more than a few peas to eat. It was also very crowded in the bunker. Leybe Friedman said, however, "We will share from our very last," and I remained with them.

At night, I would go through the villages trying to collect a bit of food. I was putting my life in danger, but I wanted, as much as possible to improve our existence and to a certain extent, I was successful.

Once every couple of weeks we would take the risk and bring water from the swamp to warm up food and to wash a bit.

In the same area there were more saved Jews who built underground bunkers and existed like us. At this time, in the area, a Jewish Partisan detachment was founded under the name "Mestitel" (revenge). I immediately joined this detachment as a fighter.

The Big Blockade

Just before the High Holidays in 1943 the forests were under a blockade from a German division that was brought from the eastern front to destroy the Partisans. It was resolved by anti–Semitic Partisan leaders that our Jewish Partisan detachment "Mestitel" should have our weapons taken away. This is how we remained against the Germans empty–handed.

The German divisions surrounded the forest. The chances of tearing away from the blockade were small, especially because we were unarmed. We divided into small groups and went in different directions. I went with the guys from Kobylnik: Sholem Yavnovitch, Yakov Feyve Goldzeger, Motle Gilman, Chemke from Zanarach, and two sisters from Ashmene. We relied on Sholem and Chemke as they were very familiar with the area and knew many of the farmers personally.

We decided to break through the German ring in the direction toward Kobylnik. For a few nights we miraculously evaded the German soldiers. During the day we hid deep in the forest. One morning, after completing our night walk, we found ourselves not far from a village. Suddenly we saw the Germans attacking the village. Farmers were running in our direction, to the forest. We had to run wherever our feet would carry us. At this time, we separated, and decided to meet up in the big forest, not far from where we were.

Yakov Feyve and I ran to that forest, but didn't wait for the others. All the others fell into German hands and were shot. We remained alone, wandering through the forests, not knowing where to go. The Germans continued their hunt. At night we saw the flames of the burning villages. That's how we knew where the Germans were. The non–Jews were now suffering properly, and now had more sympathy toward us, and from time to time would give us a piece of bread.

The blockade ended the eve of Yom Kippur. Many Jews were killed. The survivors emerged from the swamps. I joined a Partisan detachment called "Katuzof" where I remained until liberation in 1944.

In the Red Army

After liberation I fought the Germans in the ranks of the Red Army. In one of the battles I met Chaim Asher Gilman from Kobylnik. We were both consoled that we were taking revenge on our bitter enemy, but, unfortunately Chaim Asher fell in battle in Konigsberg in the ranks of the Red Army.

[Page 267]

Kobylnik to Bergen–Belsen

by Shoshana Pszechodnik (nee Raizel Narotski), Haifa

Translated by Dr. Joe Schuldenrein

Edited by Toby Bird

Yom Kippur eve, 1942. On the heels of large scale escapes to the forest and countryside by many of Mayadel's Jews, among them numerous locally employed Kobylnikers, there was a growing sense of impending doom. My sister and I continued, however, to get up each morning and go to work. I was 15 at the time, my sister Chayka a year younger at 14. We both tended to the courtyard.

The old (gentile) gardener was fond of us. When the word got out that the Jews were being herded to the Mayadel's ghetto, this righteous Christian proceeded to hide myself and Chaya in an attic. My sister Chaya, the olive skinned charmer and beauty, with her shaggy locks, then decided to return to town with everyone else.

Those were gruesome days. Periods of intermittent terror overcame us: that we would be found and that our kin and the entire town would be murderously slaughtered. Subsequently, we learned that a few families were taken to Mayadel, largely tradespeople and artisans whom the murderers found useful.

We worked our way back across the forest and countryside towards Mayadel, hoping, that amongst the tradespeople we'd find surviving family members. Once in town, we ran into Saraleh Toronchik wandering, as it were, away from town with her two children. She told us that there was really no point in staying in Mayadel...we then decided to head directly to the town of Svir....there were still Jews there.

Broken-hearted and physically worn out, we wandered aimlessly, not knowing if we were on the road to Svir at all. Sarahleh's two kids were with us; the trek was hard and strenuous. We thought we'd look around the village, the Goyim making it clear that they were doing us a favor by not turning us over to the Germans.....even in Slutsk, my father's hometown, we found neither sympathy nor support. No one offered as much as a drop of water to drink.

In utter despair, and anticipating death, from hunger, cold, and dampness (if not at the hands of the Germans) our luck suddenly turned when we ran into a Goy, friendly to Jews, who welcomed, fed us, and then pointed us in the direction of Svir. With raw bruises on my feet, I could barely walk. I had been completely bed-ridden for a week and just when I was able to stand on my feet, I took off for Michaliszky, my mother's hometown. This time I was on my own.

I was mid-route when the evening came. And then another stroke of luck, when a Gentile family from a desolate corner of town, allowed me to spend the night. They also let me stay longer in exchange for helping out. This was salvation.

[Page 268]

Good fortune did not last long, however, as the local Gentiles grew suspicious, following me around, shadowing me, essentially insinuating that I was a Jewish kid. Those Good Samaritans, who had come to my aid, were now in some danger and, having no other choice, they led me to the Michaliszky Ghetto. Once there, my mother's uncle Laffuk took me in, passing me off as locally born, which enabled me to stay in Michaliszky for some time. There I encountered other displaced Kobylnik refugees who recounted the events of my family's demise together with that of all the other Jews in town.

Michaliszky was a center for Jewish work transports destined for Vilna; eventually it was my turn to go. I was dispatched to a work-gang on the railway line for an extended period, during which I became overly introspective and spiritually tormented. It was the winter of 1943 and our lot appeared to be completely hopeless.

Jews from the surrounding towns were ostensibly driven to the Kovno ghetto..... Those from the Vilna ghetto elected to go there voluntarily.... No one made it past Ponar.... We already knew that thousands of Vilna's Jews were massacred there.

One sunny morning a round-up was convened in the ghetto for a "special" work detail. Everyone understood that this signaled the trip to Ponar.... Folks immediately took to hiding. A man hunt was ordered by the Germans. They found and rousted us from our hiding places.....Together with other Jews we were loaded up and locked into freight cars. That's where I met up with my old girlfriend Rochelle Yavnovitch[1] with whom I endured all the trials, tribulations and anguish until the liberation.

We were evacuated from Vilna to the work camp of Vaivara in Estonia; the surviving remnants of Vilna's Jewish community and surroundings ended up there. Our lot was to serve the Germans' needs and involved stone splitting and minor construction; but it was our good fortune not to have been massacred.

I remember feeling completely indifferent to fate—not having anything left in this world; the toil, forced labor, hunger, and cold rendered me mentally and physically spent, and all this in early adulthood..... I hadn't the strength to confront this morbid fate, which appeared to me pre-destined.... I no longer felt the need to hide during a camp selection that called out for 100 women. More railroad cars with barbed wire, not knowing where or why. Two girls attempted and successfully escaped---that was unbelievable heroism for the situation in which we found ourselves.

When next evacuated, we re-girded ourselves for death. This time, however, they took us to Kivioli. 350 Jewish men worked in the mines; we women had it a bit easier.

[Page 269]

As we neared the Estonian border, they killed the old and frail.... we, the survivors were remobilized and transported by ship via Port Reval (Tallinn, Estonia), to the hell-hole known as Stutthoff.

That concentration camp should have been the last stop, for us as well as for the thousands of other Jews from all over Europe.

It was only Rochelle who possessed an even minimal will to carry on. The two of us remained so closely bonded, each morally supportive of the other. That bond framed our destiny and enabled us to insulate ourselves from this horrific place. Early on in 1944 we were evacuated again, along with 500 other women, as a forced labor group to Aksenzahl, near Hamburg. We worked there for over a year at a munitions factory. The factory actually depended upon our services and, irrespective of the slave-like conditions, we were able to maintain our sanity.

Hitler's empire was rapidly reaching its end. We, of course, remained only minimally informed of the war's developments, but even the bits of information that filtered our way re-energized us. We began to anticipate living through all of this and witnessing the rout of our bloody tormentors—and we did it!!!

Amazingly, it turns out that the end of the line was liberation at Bergen-Belsen, of all places.

The camp was littered with skin-mantled corpses, some still reflexively moving. Thousands of bodies strewn everywhere, completely still. The murderers exhibited no signs of changing their routines, not even pausing to clean the blood off their hands. They proceeded with business as usual, continuing the bloody processing of Europe's last remaining Jews until the eleventh hour.

We were liberated by the English forces. Our hearts welled with emotion and jubilation, sapping the remaining strength we had left.... Here is where Simcha Pszechodnik, my future husband, was liberated and together we built a new life in the State of Israel.

Footnote

1. Rochelle (Rasza) Yavnovitch is the mother of Anita Frishman Gabbay of Montreal, Canada.

[Page 271]

Reflections of Memory
by Yitzchak Gordon
Translated by Jerrold Landau

As we bring forth the memory of our dear ones of Kobylnik, including their bitter fate, the tribulations, pain, suffering, and death – it is accompanied for some reason by a deep pain in our hearts – an unclear and inexplicable pain, accompanied by a painful question eking at our brains, from which it is difficult to free ourselves: The guiltless blood that was spilled, the great tragedy that took place – who are the guilty ones? Are only the strangers guilty, or do we Jews also bear some guilt, and not just in a roundabout way?

*

The Jewish nation, tried with suffering and tribulations during its long diaspora amongst the nations, generally developed a special sense to discern the time of approaching danger when there was still time to know, shout out, and complain about it. It also knew how to prepare for the disaster. Indeed, thanks to this, entire communities were often saved from the loss and destruction that threatened to annihilate them.

To our great sorrow, this sense was removed from us this time, and did not stand for us at the time of trouble. We lost our understanding. Its sources were sealed off. Means of thought and logic were paralyzed among our people and our leaders. We failed to evaluate the situation appropriately, and did not protect ourselves from the germs of the illness that were carried by the air and were threatening us. Our human nature was not moved, and did not push us out of our complacency to search for means of escape and protection while there was still time, before the fire closed in on us from all around, and when means of salvation and help were still open.

What was the source of this calmness and dissonance, and how was the perplexity and sense of oppression planted, causing us to give up and accept the situation – rather than arising, complaining daily and hourly about the destruction that was crouching at the doors of our houses? Where was the healthy intellect of the nation that had learned from experience? For the wrath did not come upon us suddenly one day. It was preceded by many years of increasing anti–Semitism by the enemy that was known in Europe, and that spilled over to neighboring nations!

Why were we calmed by false hopes, criminally ignoring the dangers that threatened us? From where did we draw the innocence and personal sense of assurance that no harm would befall us? What was the weak staff upon which we rested, and to whom did we ask for help? Was what we endured not yet enough, were the killings and tribulations insufficient?! How did we close our eyes from figuring out what they were preparing to do to us, without investigating at all, and without learning about our unfortunate situation, about the uneven power situation between us and them. And what about our chances of survival? Did we not yet know that they had lost their feelings of mercy toward us? If so, why were we so late in evaluating our situation? Only now, after storm has passed over us with its full fury – only now did it become clear to us that the relationship of the gentiles to us had been "almost self-evident" ...

[Page 272]

Indeed, the entire nation, with its movements and factions with which it was blessed in Eastern Europe, both Zionist and non–Zionist, some aspiring to become the beacons for the social order of our times, and others who prophesied about the end of days and the coming of the Messiah, the great leaders or renown, heads of communities and spiritual leaders – all together were blinded, and did not see what was about to take place.

Our brethren the house of Israel throughout the Diaspora, across seas and continents, upon whom the hand of the enemy did not reach – remained with a quiet conscience, for they were quick in offering help and doing everything to help their brethren during fateful times, when the axe was hoisted over the heads of the Jews of Europe? If there was assistance – was it in appropriate proportion to their ability and to their status of great influence that they gained in the lands in which they settled; or perhaps they too wished to be "proper" Jews, not angering the nations and governments with cries of outrage over our continued existence?

The settlement in the Land, despite its constant battle with the Mandate government and against the White Paper, and despite their significant volunteering through the Jewish Brigade in the fight against the enemy, as well as taking other asks upon their shoulders – did they also do everything possible for European Jewry, upon whose blood they were based? Did they do everything possible for this situation? Or perhaps we too were immersed significantly in the internal struggle, in factions, and in an internecine battle, and did not pay attention at the time as the Jews of Europe were hauled to slaughter?... Why were we late in breaking through the boundaries to offer salvation to the extent that we could?

We here in Israel as individuals – did we not each make peace separately, in the privacy of our hearts, with the bitter fate of the Jews in the lands in which they lived? Did we do enough to bring them to the Land before the inferno? Did we not sin on occasion by the words of our mouth as we slandered the Land, stating that life here is difficult, the work is backbreaking, and the lands consumes its residents?... With this, we perhaps were the cause that many of our brethren tarried, did not make aliya to the Land, and were therefore not saved from the fires of destruction? Indeed, we too were weak in faith. We pushed aside the main thing – and such a high price was paid for our error.

There are many question marks; I have raised many questions – but there is no answer. I did not do this to make it easier from those who are directly guilty for their criminal deeds. I added my thoughts so that we could investigate and understand with full depth the tragedy that took place before our eyes, and in which we were involved...

[Page 273]

Remember That Which the Nazi Amalek Perpetrated Against You

Let us remember with pain and anger the souls of our dear martyrs of Kobylnik, who fell at the hands of the impure murderers who had lost their G–dly image.

Let us remember the human splendor of women, elderly, and children who were murdered by the wild wanton ones; let us remember this forever.

Let us remember and unite with the grief of the mother whose child's head was smashed before her eyes. Let us remember its final quiver before death.

Let us remember and listen attentively to the clicks of the guns and the mist of the pierced bodies of our dear ones as they fell into the pit that was dug. G–d, avenge their blood, and give the perpetrators what they deserve!

Survivors of Kobylnik after the liberation next to the mass grave

[Page 274]

List of the victims from the town of Kobylnik
Translated by Jerrold Landau

Translator's note: The Hebrew and Yiddish introduction each have slightly different nuances, so I translated both. First paragraph is the Hebrew, and second is the Yiddish. The Yiddish version notes that the list contains death date information (yahrzeits).

These are the names of our brethren of the Children of Israel of Kobylnik, the city of murder, in which men, women, and children, were murdered by the enemy troops and their assistants, during the Holocaust of the Second World War. Their memory will never leave us.

The list of Kobylnik martyrs, along with their yahrzeits, who were murdered by the German criminals and their assistants during the great misfortune of the Second World War.

Surname	Given Name	Wife's Name	Children's Names	Details
ALSFIEN	Mendel–Leib	Gissia		Died on Tuesday, Tishrei 11, 5703 (day after Yom Kippur), September 21, 1942, in Kobylnik.
AXELROD	Eliahu		Israel and Yehoshua	Died in Oszmiana, date unknown.
BERGER	Shabtai	Nehama	Moshe, Israel–Benyamin, Hanna and Minna	Shabtai, Nehama, Moshe, and Hanna died on Tuesday, Tishrei 11, 5703 (day after Yom Kippur), September 21, 1942, in Kobylnik. Israel–Benyamin died on Monday, 20 Tammuz 5702, July 6, 1942 in Kobylnik. Mina died in 1943 in Ponar (Vilna).
BOTVINIK	Moshe	Haya	Yosef and unidentified infant son	Died on Sunday, 14 Tishrei 5702 (eve of Sukkot), October 5, 1941 in Kobylnik.
BOURGIN	Hayyim–Mayer			Died in 1942 in the forests of

				Kurenitz
CHERNOTZKY	Fraidel		Ya'aqov and David	Died on Tuesday, 11 Tishrei, 5703 (day after Yom Kippur), September 21, 1942, in Kobylnik.
CHERNOTZKY	Gedaliyahu	Sarah–Rivka	Yocheved	Died on Tuesday, 11 Tishrei, 5703 (day after Yom Kippur), September 21, 1942, in Kobylnik.
CHERNOTZKY	Haya			Died on Tuesday, 11 Tishrei, 5703 (day after Yom Kippur), September 21, 1942.
CHERNOTZKY	Israel	Dina	Esther	Israel and Esther died on Sunday, 28 Adar II, 5703, April 4, 1943, in Ponar (Vilna). Dina died on Tuesday, 11 Tishrei, 5703 (day after Yom Kippur), September 21, 1942, in Kobylnik.
CHERNOTZKY	Yehoshua	Rivka	son	Died on Tuesday, 11 Tishrei, 5703 (day after Yom Kippur), September 21, 1942, in Kobylnik.
COOPERSTOCK	Ze'ev	Shaina		Died on Monday, 27 Elul, 5702, August 10, 1942, in Kurenitz. {Translator's note, the dates do not correspond. 27 Elul 5702 is September 9).
DANISHEVSKY	Barukh Eliahu	Menuha	three children	Died on Tuesday, 11 Tishrei, 5703 (day after Yom Kippur), September 21, 1942, in Kobylnik.
DIMENSHTEIN	Shlomo	Rivka	Beral–Laib and Hava	Died on an unknown date with the Warsaw Ghetto fighters {Translator's note – the second name Laib is not

				included in the text}.
DIMENTSTAIN	Beral–Leib	Nehama		Died on an unknown date in Lithuania.
DIMENTSTAIN	Esther			Died on Monday, 22 Tammuz, 5702, July 6, 1942, in Kobylnik, along with 5 Jewish refugees from Kribichi whose names are unknown.
DIMENTSTAIN	Esther Haya			Died on an unknown date in Ponar (Vilna).
DIMENTSTAIN	Rivka		Esther–Faiga	Died on Tuesday, Tishrei 11, 5703 (day after Yom Kippur), September 21, 1942, in Kobylnik
EINBINDER	Rabbi Yehuda–Leib	Malka		Died on Tuesday, Tishrei 11, 5703 (day after Yom Kippur), September 21, 1942 in Kobylnik
FAIGELMAN	Tuvia	Haya–Sarah	Rahel, Shabtai and Masha	Tuvia died on Monday, Yom Kippur, September 20, 1942, in Kobylnik. Haya–Sarah and Rachel died on Tuesday, 11 Tishrei, 5703 (day after Yom Kippur), September 21, 1942, in Kobylnik. Masha died in 1943 in Estonia.
GANTOVNIK	Baila			Died on an unknown date in Warsaw.
GANTOVNIK	Gittel		And family	Died on an unknown date in the city of Radin.
GANTOVNIK	Hayyim	and family		Died on an unknown date in Warsaw.
GANTOVNIK	Mayer	Gittel	Yehuda	Died on Sunday, 14 Tishrei (eve of Sukkot), October 5,

				1941 in Kobylnik.
GERSHATOR	Moshe	Tamar	Shlomo and Hirschel	Moshe, Tamar, and Shlomo died on Tuesday, 11 Tishrei, 5703 (day after Yom Kippur), September 21, 1942 in Kobylnik. Hirschel died at an unknown place on an unknown date.
GILMAN	Laib	Ida	Lea and Matla (son Hayyim died in service with the Red Army)	Laib, Ida, and Lea died on Tuesday, 11 Tishrei, 5703 (day after Yom Kippur), September 21, 1942 in Kobylnik. Matla died on Wednesday 24 Av, 5703, August 25, 1943 in the forest during the time of the German siege on the partisans. Hayyim died in August 1944 in battle near Koenigsburg while serving in the Red Army
GILMAN	Menashe			Died on Sunday, 14 Tishrei, 5702 (eve of Sukkot), October 5, 1941, in Kobylnik.
GILMAN	Raitza			Died on Sunday, 14 Tishrei, 5702 (eve of Sukkot), October 5, 1941, in Kobylnik.
GLOTT	David		Hirschel–Yona and Yentka	David died on Friday, 3 Av, 5702, July 17, 1942 in Kobylnik. Hirschel–Yona and Yentka died on Av 5702, 1942, in Kobylnik.
GLOTT	Mera–Leeba			Died on Av 5702, 1942 in Kobylnik.

GOL	Ya'aqov (pharmacist)	his wife	Moshe–Aharon, Malka and Sally	Ya'aqov, his wife and daughter Malka died in 1942 in Postavy. Moshe–Aharon and Sally died on an unknown date in the forests near Glubokie. (Translator's note: it seems that Sally is Moshe–Aharon's daughter).
GOLDZEGGER	Avraham (shochet)	Baila	Menahem, Sara, Raizel and Hanna	Avraham died on Friday, 3 Av, 5702, July 17, 1942, in Kobylnik. Baila died on Tuesday, Tishrei 11, 5703 (day after Yom Kippur), September 21, 1942 in Kobylnik. Menachem, Sara, Raizel, and Chana died in Tishrei 5703, 1942 in Myadel.
GORDON	Avraham	Haya–Rivka	Yehuda, Aharon, Shaul–David and Rahel	Avraham, Yehuda, Aharon, Shaul–David, and Rahel died on Saturday, 13 Tishrei 5702, October 4, 1941 in Glubokie Ruchi near Kobylnik. Haya–Rivka died on Wednesday 7 Tammuz 5701, July 2, 1941 in Kobylnik.
GORDON	Avraham–Laib	Haya–Moussia	Eliahu–Moshe	Avraham–Laib and Haya–Moussia died on Tuesday, Tishrei 11, 5703 (day after Yom Kippur), September 21, 1942 in Kobylnik. Eliahu–Moshe died on an unknown date at an unknown place.
GORDON	Eliahu	Baila		Died on Sunday, 28 Adar II, 5703, April 4, 1943 in Ponar (Vilna).

GORDON	Fruma		Malka, Nehama, Devora and Sheina	Fruma and Malka died in 1942 in Pohost. Malka, Nechama, Devora and Sheina died on Tuesday, Tishrei 11, 5703 (day after Yom Kippur), September 21, 1942 in Kobylnik.
				(Translator's note: Malka is mentioned in both lists. One must be an error.)
GORDON	Hava			Died on Sunday, 28 Adar II 5703, April 4, 1943, in Ponar (Vilna).
GORDON	Shaul	Doba	Ya'aqov and Faiga	Died on Sunday, 9 Cheshvan 5704, November 7, 1943 in old Vileyka.
GORDON	Yizhaq–Ya'aqov	Grounia		Died on Saturday, 13 Tishrei 5702, October 4, 1941, in Glubokie–Ruchi near Kobylnik.
GREENBERG	Ya'aqov Bainish	Minna	Laib, Hanna and Esther	Ya'aqov Bainish died on Sunday 14 Tishrei, 5702 (eve of Sukkot), October 5, 1941 in Kobylnik. Minna, Laib, and Hanna died on Tuesday, 11 Tishrei, 5703 (day after Yom Kippur), September 21, 1942, in Kobylnik. Esther died in June 1944 in old Vileyka.
HODOS	Fraidel			Died on Tuesday, 11 Tishrei, 5703 (day after Yom Kippur), September 21, 1942, in Kobylnik.
HODOS	Laib	Assna		Died on Tuesday, 11 Tishrei, 5703 (day after Yom Kippur), in Kobylnik.
HODOS	Minna			Died on Sunday, 14 Tishrei, 5702 (eve of Sukkot),

				October 5, 1941, in Kobylnik.
HODOS	Moshe Zelig	Rivka		Died on Sunday, 14 Tishrei, 5702 (eve of Sukkot), October 5, 1941, in Kobylnik.
HODOS	Rivka		Ya'aqov and Gershon	Died on an unknown date in Kobylnik.
HODOS	Sara			Died in 1942 in Postavy.
HODOS	Yosef	Baila	Haya and Yizhaq	Yosef, Baila, and Haya died on Friday, 3 Av, 5702, July 17, 1942, in Kobylnik. Yizhaq died on an unknown date in Kobylnik.
HODOS	Zippora			Died on Wednesday, 27 Elul, 5702, September 9, 1942, in Kurenitz
HOLFMAN	Shmuel	Hana	Sonia	Died on Tuesday, 11 Tishrei, 5703 (day after Yom Kippur), September 21, 1942, in Kobylnik.
JABLONOVITZ	Azriel	Merl	Zviya and Yosef–Eliahu	Azriel died in 1942. Merl, and Zviya died on Tuesday, 11 Tishrei, 5703 (day after Yom Kippur), September 21, 1942, in Kobylnik. Yosef–Eliahu died on Tuesday, 20 Tammuz, 5702, July 6, 1942, in Kobylnik.
JANOVSKY	Eliahu–Yosef	Reizel	Avraham, another son and Kaila	Died on Tuesday, 11 Tishrei, 5703 (day after Yom Kippur), September 21, 1942, in Kobylnik.
JANOVSKY	Faivel	Sara	Haya–Leeba	Died on Tuesday, 11 Tishrei, 5703 (day after Yom Kippur), September 21, 1942, in Kobylnik.

JANOVSKY	Hayyim–Ya'aqov	Sara–Rivka		Died on Tuesday, 11 Tishrei, 5703 (day after Yom Kippur), September 21, 1942, in Kobylnik.
JANOVSKY	Hirschel	and family		Died on an unknown date in an unknown place.
JANOVSKY	Moshe (son of Avraham–Yizhaq)	Sima	son	Died on an unknown date in Kamelishki.
JANOVSKY	Moshe	Ganasiya	Shmuel, his sister–in–law from Leningrad	Moshe died in 1942 near Postavy. Ganasiya and sister–in–law from Leningrad died on Tuesday, 11 Tishrei 5703 (day after Yom Kippur), September 21, 1942 in Kobylnik. Shmuel died in 1943 in Ponar (Vilna)
JANOVSKY	Pinkhas	Merl	three daughters	Pinkas died in 1943 near Postovy. Merl and three daughters died on Tuesday, 11 Tishrei, 5703 (day after Yom Kippur), September 21, 1942 in Kobylnik.
JANOVSKY	Shlomo Eliezer	Haya–Rivka	Israel, Yizhaq and Esther, along with another daughter	Died on Saturday, 27 Cheshvan, 5703, November 7, 1942, in old Vileyka.
JANOVSKY	Yeshyahu	and his family		Died on an unknown date in an unknown place.
JANOVSKY	Zlata		Gittel, Yehoshua, Devoshka, her husband, and two children	Zlata and Gittel died on Tuesday, 11 Tishrei, 5703 (day after Yom Kippur), September 21, 1942 in Kobylnik. Yehoshua and Devoshka with her husband and two children died on Friday, 26 Cheshvan 5703, November 6, 1942, in old Vileyka.

JANTIS	Haya–Sara			Died on an unknown date in Smorgon.
KAGAN	Laib	Pessia	Yosef and Batya	Died on an unknown date in an unknown place.
KAGANOVICH	Yizhaq	Hana		Yizhaq died in 1944 in old Vileyka. Hana died on an unknown date in Warsaw.
KAPLAN		and family		Died on Sunday, 14 Tishrei, 5702 (eve of Sukkot), October 5, 1941, in Kobylnik.
KAPLAN	Yehudit		Laibel	Died on an unknown date in Vilna.
KIRMILISKY	Baila–Dooba			Died on Tuesday, 11 Tishrei, 5703 (day after Yom Kippur), September 21, 1942, in Kobylnik.
KIRMILISKY	Faivel	and family		Died on an unknown date in an unknown place.
KIRMILISKY	Lieber	and family		Died on an unknown date in Zyrardow.
KLUMEL	Anivta			Died on an unknown date in Vilna.
KLUMEL	Haya–Sarah		Gittel	Died on Tuesday, 11 Tishrei, 5703 (day after Yom Kippur), September 21, 1942, in Kobylnik.
KLUMEL	Yizhaq	Rivka	Avraham, Baila and Shulamit	Died on an unknown date in an unknown place.
KRAVCHENSKY	Yizhaq	Haya–Batya	Sarah–Riezel, Haya–Liba and Nehama	Died on Sunday, 14 Tishrei, 5702 (eve of Sukkot), October 5, 1941, in Kobylnik.
KRIVITZKY	Akiva	Kayla	Benyamin and Yizhaq	Akiva died in 1943 in Komai. Kayla, Benyamin, and Yizhaq died on Tuesday, 11 Tishrei, 5703 (day after Yom Kippur), September 21, 1942, in Kobylnik.

KRIVITZKY	Avraham	Slova	Laib and Baila	Died on an unknown date in Devenishkes.
KRIVITZKY	Gershon	Kayla	Zelig	Died on Friday, 14 Tishrei, 5702 (eve of Sukkot), October 5, 1941, in Myadel.
KRIVITZKY	Hanah–Devosha			Died on Tuesday, 11 Tishrei, 5703 (day after Yom Kippur), September 21, 1942, in Kobylnik.
KRIVITZKY	Yehuda–Laib	Haya	Benyamin and Yizhaq	Died on an unknown date in Glubokie.
KRUKOV	Chyena		Heshel	Chyena died on Sunday, 28 Adar II, 5703, April 4, 1943, in Ponar (Vilna). Heshel died on Saturday, 12 Nisan, April 17, 1943, in the partisan ranks in Smolensk.
KRUKOV	Yisrael	Haya	Arieh	Died on Saturday, 27 Cheshvan, 5703, November 7, 1942, in old Vileyka.
KRUPSKY	Miryam		(added 1999 by M. Svirsky)	Died on an unknown date in an unknown place.
KUBERSKY	Yosef (pharmacist)	Assia	Boris and Raya	Died on Tuesday, 12 Elul, 5703, August 25, 1943, during the German siege on the partisans in the forests of Kurenitz.
KURENIETZKY		and family		Died on an unknown date in an unknown place.
KYEVSKY	Avraham	Haya–Sarah	Yizhaq, Hirschel–Mendel and Taibel	Died on Saturday, 27 Cheshvan, 5703, November 17, 1942, in old Vileyka.
LASKOV	Ya'aqov	Rahel		Died on an unknown date in Smorgon.
LAZAROVITZ	Hayyim	Leiba	Daughter	Died on Tuesday, 11 Tishrei, 5703 (day after Yom Kippur), September 21, 1942, in

				Kobylnik.
LEVCOVITCH	Hillel	Hava	Shimon and Tzyrl	Hilled died in 1941 in Vilna. Hava, Shimon, and Tzyrl died in 1943 in Vilna.
LEVIATAN	Dina			Died on Tuesday, 11 Tishrei, 5703 (day after Yom Kippur), September 21, 1942, in Kobylnik.
LEVIATAN	Yizhaq	Fraida	Israel–Mayer, Avraham and Faiga	Yizhaq died on an unknown date in Glubokie. Fraida, Israel–Mayer, Avraham, and Faiga died on Sunday, 14 Tishrei (eve of Sukkot), October 5, 1941, in Kobylnik.
LIFSHITZ	Ben–Zion	Ginesiya	Raizel and Yeshayahu	Died on an unknown date in Glubokie.
LIFSHITZ	Leiba–Malka		Fraidel	Died on Tuesday, 11 Tishrei, 5703 (day after Yom Kippur), September 21, 1942, in Kobylnik.
LUCHINSKY	Shabtai	Rachel	Shmuel–Hirsch, Yizhaq and Baila	Died on Tuesday, 11 Tishrei, 5703 (day after Yom Kippur), September 21, 1942, in Kobylnik.
MACOVSKY	Rabbi Laib	Laiba	Avraham	Died on Sunday, 14 Tishrei, 5702 (eve of Sukkot), October 5, 1941, in Kobylnik.
MASHEETZ	Yizhaq	Zippora	Shmuel–Hirsch	Died on Tuesday, 11 Tishrei, 5703 (day after Yom Kippur), September 21, 1942, in Kobylnik.
MILCHMAN	Hana		and family	Died on an unknown date in an unknown place.

MILCHMAN	Michael	Mina	David and Yocheved	Died on Tuesday, 11 Tishrei 5703 (day after Yom Kippur), September 21, 1942, in Kobylnik.
NAROTZKY	Arieh Laib	Frieda	Sonia, Raizel, Feiga and Michael	Arieh Laib, Frieda, Sonia, Reizel, and Feiga died on Tuesday, 11 Tishrei, 5703 (day after Yom Kippur), September 21, 1942, in Kobylnik. Michael died on Friday, 26 Cheshvan, 5703, November 6, 1942 in old Vileyka.
NAROTZKY	Hayyim			Died on Tuesday, 11 Tishrei, 5703 (day after Yom Kippur), September 21, 1942, in Kobylnik.
NAROTZKY	Shlomo	Braina–Cherna	Haya and Baila	Died on Tuesday, 11 Tishrei, 5703 (day after Yom Kippur), September 21, 1942, in Kobylnik.
NAROTZKY	Zelig	Kaila	Velvel, Baila, Devora and one more, daughter, name unknown	Died on Sunday, 14 Tishrei, 5702 (eve of Sukkot), October 5, 1941, in Kobylnik.
POTALIK	Rabbi			Died on Sunday, 14 Tishrei, 5702 (eve of Sukkot), October 5, 1941, in Kobylnik.
RAIDER	Hayyim	Ida	Slova and Esther	Hayyim died on Monday, 20 Tammuz 5702, July 6, 1942, in Kobylnik. Ida, Slova and Esther died on Friday, 25 Tammuz, 5702, July 10, 1942, in Kobylnik.
RUDOSHANSKY	Moshe	Shaina	Rivka	Died in 1943 in the Vilna ghetto.
SCHMIDT	Leib	Golda	five children	Died in 1941 in Glubokie.

SCHNIEDEROVITZ	Batya		Yizhaq, Sarah and Haya	Died on Tuesday, 11 Tishrei, 5703 (day after Yom Kippur), September 21, 1942, in Kobylnik.
SHAPIRA	Shraga	his wife	Laibel and Sarah	Died on Sunday, 14 Tishrei, 5702 (eve of Sukkot), October 5, 1941, in Kobylnik.
SHEFTAN	Eliyahu	Gitta		Died on an unknown date in an unknown place.
SHPYTZ	Hayyim	Liba	Sonia and Devoshka	Died on Friday, 27, Cheshvan, 5703, November 6, 1942, in old Vileyka.
SOLOMON	Boris		his sisters Rivka and Hava	Died on Wednesday, 7 Tammuz, 5701, July 2, 1941, in Kobylnik. Rivka and Hava died on Tuesday, 11 Tishrei, 5703 (day after Yom Kippur), September 21, 1942, in Kobylnik.
STEINGARTH	Yosef	Baty	Ya'aqov and Bounya	Died on Saturday, 27 Cheshvan 5703, November 7, 1942, in old Vileyka.
STEINGROB	Reizel			Died on Tuesday, 11 Tishrei, 5703 (day after Yom Kippur), September 21, 1942, in Kobylnik.
STEINGART	Reuven	Monya–Hana	Reizel and Haya	Reuven died on Monday, 20 Tammuz, 5702, July 6, 1942, in Kobylnik. Monya–Hana, Reizel and Haya died on Friday, 25 Tammuz, 5702, July 10, 1942, in Kobylnik.
SVIDLAR	Esther–Leah		Yerahmial, Yosef and Gedalya	Died on 11 Tishrei, 5704, day after Yom Kippur 1943, in Ponar (Vilna).
SVIDLAR	Moshe		and family	Died on an unknown date in Vilna.

SVIDLAR	Yosef	Zippora		Yosef died on Friday, 10 Cheshvan, 5698, October 15, 1938, in Kobylnik. Zippora died on Tuesday, 15 Kislev, 5702, January 14, 1942, in Kobylnik.
SVIRSKY	Herzl			Died on an unknown date in Ponar (Vilna).
TODRES	Itta			Died on Tuesday, 11 Tishrei, 5703 (day after Yom Kippur), September 21, 1942, in Kobylnik.
TORONTZIK	Hirschel	Sara	Luba and Esther	Hirschel died on Tuesday, 11 Tishrei 5703 (day after Yom Kippur), September 21, 1942, in Kobylnik. Sara, Luba, and Esther died on Sunday, 28 Adar II, 5703, April 4, 1943 in Ponar (Vilna).
TRAVSKY	Shmuel	Raizel	Reuven–Menahem	Died on an unknown date in Estonia.
TZOFANAS	Shimon	his wife	son	Shimon died on Wednesday, 7 Tammuz, 5701, July 2, 1941, in Kobylnik. His wife and son died on Sunday, 14 Tishrei, 5702 (eve of Sukkot), October 5, 1941, in Kobylnik.
VAINER	Alter	Faiga	Ya'aqov, Sara–Rivka and an employee Rivka unknown	Died on Sunday, 14 Tishrei, 5702 (eve of Sukkot), October 5, 1941.
WEINER	Israel			Died on Sunday, 14 Tishrei, 5702 (eve of Sukkot), October 5, 1941 in Kobylnik
WEXLER	Shaul	Sheina	children	Died in 1943 in Vilna.

WEXLER	Yeshayahu	Rasia		Yeshayahu died on Wednesday, 7 Tammuz 5701, July 2, 1941 in Kobylnik. Rasia died on Tuesday, 11 Tishrei 5703 (day after Yom Kippur), September 21, 1942, in Kobylnik.
YAVNOVITZ	David	Bouniya	Barukh and Laibel	Died on Friday, November 5, 1942 in old Vileyka.Died on Friday, 26 Cheshvan, 5703, November 6, 1942, in old Vileyka.
YAVNOVITZ	Michael	Matliya		Died on Friday, 26 Cheshvan, 5703, November 6, 1942, in Postavy.
YAVNOVITZ	Shlomo	Raitza	Shalom and Yizhaq	Shlomo died on Sunday, 14 Tishrei, 5702 (eve of Sukkot), October 5, 1941 in Kobylnik. Raitza died on Cheshvan 5702, 1942 in Myadel. Shalom died on Tuesday, 12 Elul 5703, August 25, 1943 in the forest during the German siege of the partisans. Yizhaq died in 1942 next to Lake Narach near Kobylnik.
YAVNOVITZ	Yosef	Rahel		Died in 1942 in Postavy.
			Devora (girl from Baronovitz) unknown	Died on Tuesday, 11 Tishrei, 5703 (day after Yom Kippur), September 21, 1942, in Kobylnik.

[Page 286]

Survivors of Kobylnik, who died after the Holocaust

Yehoshua Gordon (son of Herzl) and his son Yisrael Leib, died in November 1950 in Postavy.

David Leib Swirski died on 11 Av 5714, 1954, in Toronto, Canada Yehudit Friedman died in 1959 in New York, U.S.A.

Avraham Yitzchak Hadash was killed in an automobile accident in 1965 in Kiryat Gat.

Yaakov–Feivel Goldzeger was killed in an automobile accident in 1965 in New York, U.S.A.

May their souls be bound in the bonds of eternal life.

O L–rd, G–d of vengeance; L–rd of vengeance, appear. Raise Yourself up judge of the earth, and give the pride their due. G–d, for how long shall the wicked, for how long shall the wicked triumph?

{Psalm 94}

[Page 287]

Addresses of Kobylnikites in Israel
Translated by Jerrold Landau

Oltoz, Chana	Dov Hoz St. #44, Kfar Saba
Etstein, Naomi	Yerushalayim St. #24, Hadera
Axelrod, Baruch	Brener St. #1, Kfar Saba
Axelrod, Tzipora	Shichun Green #11, Kfar Saba
Burgin, Ida	Kaplan St. #1, Petach Tikva
Blinder, Yosef	Hagiborim St. #25a, Petach Tikva
Bachman, Dvora	Feuerberg St. #7, Neve Shaanan, Haifa
Briker, Tova	Beitar St. #6, Haifa
Gadisewicz, Rina	Shchunat Efraim, Haifa
Gordon, Yitzchak	Sh. Ben–Zion St. #1, Neve Shaanan, Haifa
Gordon, Herzl	Katznelson St. #107, Givatayim
Gentovnik, Chaim	Yerushalayim St. #88, Ramat– Yitzchak
Dimentstein, Chanan	K.K.L. St. #32, Kiryat Motznik
Dimentstein, Tzvi	Trumpeldor St. #13, Neve Shaanan, Haifa
Wexler, Yisrael	Meshek Evron, Doar Nahariya
Zar, Sara	Kfar–Aviv, Doar Na Ashdod
Hadash, Aharon	Shchunat Geula, Petach Tikva
Hadash, Meir	Sderot Rokach #208, Maoz Aviv, Tel Aviv
Hadash, Menashe	Derech Elnavi #112, Kiryat Eliezer, Haifa
Hadash, Shraga	Moria St. #53, Haifa
Chermatz, Tzila	Kfar–Aviv, Doar Na Ashdod
Yavnai, Chaim	Gedalyahu St. 27/18, Neve Shaanan, Haifa
Yavnai, Meir	Miriam Hachashmonait St. #26, Tel Aviv
Katz, Batya	Yitzchak Sadeh St. #12, Petach Tikva
Lipshitz, Chana	Beilinson St. #9, Kfar Saba
Narochki, Baruch	Ben–Dor #150, Haifa
Swirski, Meir	Ayalon St. #24, Kiryat–Bialik

Platzer, Ida	Meshek Ein–Charod, Haichud
Parchov, yafa	Ein Karmel, Doar Na Chof Karmel
Pashchodnik, Shoshana	Mem Chet St. #23, Kiryat–Chaim
Chernochki, Yitzchak	Kfar–Aviv, Doar Na Ashdod
Kochvichki, Binyamin	Hayeladim St. #6, Kiryat Motzkin
Krebchinski, Ephraim	Shapira St. #17, Petach Tikva
Krokov, Asher	Mem Vav St. #5, Kiryat–Chaim
Kariv, Pinchas	Nehelal
Steingort, Ben–Zion	Kiryat–Nazareth, Block 14/303
Schmidt, Sarah	Hagefen St. #30, haifa

[Page 288]

Kobylnik natives in Israel, 1967

[Page 296]

A Memorial to our Hometown

It is with a feeling of great awe and trepidation and humility that we undertook this holy task of editing and publishing the book Kobylnik. We undertook this task despite our feeling of unworthiness and inefficiency to give expression to the vast catastrophe that has befallen our dear brethren of Kobylnik. No human language is rich and eloquent enough to describe the shocking disaster perpetrated by the Nazi Satan against our unforgettable near and dear ones.

Stunned and bewildered do we stand at the graves of the innocent victims.

Though we ourselves counted the number of the fallen, we feel that we are unequal for the task of evaluating the immense spiritual and moral treasures that disappeared with their untimely death.

25 years have passed since the immense and indescribable tragedy happened and the only thing we can do for the perpetuation of those innocent and holy souls is to collect the few data for publication.

Very few members of this extinguished and glorious community remained alive and these are scattered all over the globe thus making it impossible to make all of them part take in this difficult and formidable work.

Whilst turning the pages of this book, we will see with our mind's eye the life of the community of Kobylnik that has gone forever.

In this book we will see their daily life with its lights and shadows, with its joys and sorrows, struggles and victories, pleasures and sufferings, bitter realities and unrealized dreams.

Let these pages remind us of the "Shma-Israel" utterances of the upright and pure, unstained characters, while bravely facing their fate at the brinks of their own graves.

[Page 295]

The number of those Kobylnikites who escaped death and who could help us in recovering the calamitous events are very small and the "Pincas", the protocols and minutes of the sessions of the community which were usually kept in the synagogue, were burnt and destroyed thus making the undertaking of the editors more difficult.

It is only the keens and zeal of the publishing boards that has enabled us to accomplish this arduous project. While we do not claim that our enormous efforts to enrol the participation of all those capable of contributing to this book were successful, and that this publication is free of faults and flaws, we feel that the most important facts and data available are well recorded here.

We have endeavoured to ensure the cooperation of the maximum quantity members of the Kobylnik community who survived the calamities, part of whom live in Israel and who helped us in giving an authentic and chronologic account of events during the Nazi occupation of Kobylnik, beginning from 1941 and ending with the liberation in 1944.

The reader will find in this book articles and material from the pens of those who, in our opinion, were qualified to express, in a fitting manner, their personal impressions of the life of some heroes of the community during the mentioned period.

Our work would not be complete if we, in conclusion, would not mention with gratitude the monetary contribution of our "Landlite" in Israel and the U.S.A. which made this publication possible.

Our sincerest thanks to the chief editor of the book, Mr. Itzchak Ziegelman as well as Mr. Itzchak Gordon, the secretary of the Kobylnik society, who headed this venture.

Editorial Board

INDEX

A

B

C

D

Myadel, Belarus Addendum

Contributors: John Alper, Shmuel Biran (Bernstein), Yosef Chadash, Arye Geskin, Nancy Collier Holden, Luba Bernstein Katzman, Chaya Lupinsky, Meir Svirsky z'l, Dvora Kosczevsky Tennenboim

Introduction

Myadel first mentioned in the year 1434, has historically been divided between Stary (Old) Miadel and Nowy (New) Miadel. The spelling and pronunciation of the name of these two towns has varied with each the ruling nation.

Prior to the First Partition of Poland, all records and documents were written in Polish (thus, Miadziol or Miadziel) The Grand Duchy of Lithuania Records of 1784 were written in Polish but records after that date were written in Russian (thus in the Revision Lists of 1811 the spellings were Miadel and Miadelai). In Yiddish one hears Mah-del. In the Myadel area many languages formed the base of understanding: Lithuanian, Polish, Hebrew, Yiddish, Belarusian and Russian. Although for residents of Myadel, Belarusian is currently the native language, the current, and only legal language, in Myadel is Russian.

Modern day Myadel is a sprawling urban settlement whose population in 1989 was 6700 but today is closer to 20,000. The two Myadels seem to rise together through the trees and clouds. Soviet buildings and tall resident-owned apartments have replaced the small, dark, Jewish houses and brightly painted, peasant ones of the past. Fertile soil, trees and lakes in the area provide the main industries (farming, fisheries and sawn timber) past and present. Today, the accepted proper spelling is Myadel.

The Myadel Region

REGION OF CALM AND DREAMING LAKES

RABBI ELIJAH GORDON
HIS LIFE AND WORKS
By
Hirsch Loeb Gordon

copyright 1926 by Rabbi Elijah Gordon

Part I

The northeastern part of the government of Vilna, (formerly) Russia, is covered by vast and impenetrable forests, impassable marshes and thickets, numerous lakes and swampy meadows, with cleared and dry spaces occupied here and there by manors, villages and small towns. The moisture of the soil feeds the four rivers Disna, Dvina, Vilyia and Nieman and forms many larger lakes like those of Svir, Vishniev, Shvacksenta, Miastra, Narotah and Myadsiol. The country people consist mainly of White Russians Byelorussia, whose Russian vernacular has been greatly Polonized, and in whose veins flows much of Lithuanian blood. These peasants are uncouth, ignorant and superstitious rustics but, like the average Russian *Mouzhik* simple, god-fearing and amiable. While some of them are engaged in agriculture, their main occupation is fishing, for the swarming lakes provide them with abundant supplies, which they carry to the cities of Vilna and Minsk for further distribution.

ENTENTE CORDIAL

The villages are grouped around the small towns or *Myestetchkos*, populated mostly by Jews, whom cruel Czarist laws forbade to own land in the open country, even within the few governments, where their sojourn was tolerated. The peasants flocked to the Myestetchko on Sundays to attend the services at the *Tserkov* (church) and to the weekly *Rynock*(Fair) held on Wednesdays, when they could sell the products of their net, stable and plough and in turn buy imported wares and implements in the Jewish stores. The *Myestetchko*, or more exactly, its Jewish inhabitants, were on a higher plane of civilization. Peasants visited it daily. One ordered a holiday suit from the Jewish tailor, another-a pair of fancy *sapogi* (high boots) of the Jewish shoe-maker, and a third had his horse shoed or his cartwheels rimmed in the ever-busy Jewish smithy. It was from the Jewish traveling merchant or newspaper reader that the peasants learned of what was going on in their country and in the wide world. The Jewish *tsirulnick* (barber. surgeon) or *feldsher* (quack) relieved him of his pain by letting his blood, extracting his aching teeth or pacifying his colic with vials of cubeb and licorice. It is a region of calm, the calm of dreaming lakes never disturbed by marked changes. Life flows unruffled, still. The marshes and extensive forests did not encourage much rambling and journeying, and peasants, living villages a dozen miles apart, saw each other only on the *Yarmarki.* (Annual fairs). Tolerance towards alien creeds peacefulness of mind, resignation to fate and to allotted position, typify their character and life.

HOW MYADSIOL ADOPTED FAMILY NAMES

Part II

One of the *Myestetchkos* in that region is that of Myadsiol. Its history goes back more than eight centuries and is quite prominent on mediaeval geographical maps. Local legends ascribe to it great prominence in the period of the ancient Lithuanian monarchy. Its Jewish community, numbering about 200 souls, is also of very remote beginnings. Most of them bear the family name Gordon, while the remainder of the surnames are Hodosh. Gordon and Hodosh are still predominating names in the membership list of the Myadsiol Benevolent Association of New York City, the president of which is Mr. L. Gordon, a brother of Rabbi E. Gordon. According to local tradition the surname Gordon was suggested for adoption by one of the Jewish burghers of Myadsiol, a business woman, who on her travels met venerable merchants by that name. But, as a matter of fact, the Gordons seem to be related to the reputed Gordons of Bialystock. The surname Hodosh is said to have been bestowed upon the latter settlers of Myadsiol to denote their recency; Hodosh, meaning "new" in Hebrew.

ELIAHU'S PARENTS AND CHILDHOOD

One of the most esteemed citizens of Myadsiol was David Zeeb Gordon (d. Oct. 24, 1913),*(all dates are according to the Gregorian Calendar) who with his wife Esther Hayah (d. April 12, 1917) represented the ideal type of Lithuanian Jewry. Well versed in the Bible and Rabbinical lore, virtuous and upright above all praise, with almost saintly piety and meekness and with the ever hopeful endurance that sweetened and gladdened their toilful life, they were living examples of the righteous and pious eulogized in the Psalms. On February 27th, 1865, Esther Hayah gave birth to her first child, Elijah, who was immediately consecrated to a divine life. Elijah entered one of the local *Heders* at the age of five and his unusual intelligence very shortly won for him the fame of a prodigy. The facility with which he acquired the difficult parts of the Hebrew Bible and the keen *pilpul* (casuistry) of the Talmud, was above any precedent in his birthplace and in the neighboring Jewish towns. After he had been transferred from one *Melamed* (teacher) to the other, they finally decided that he exhausted their erudition and by their advice he was sent to the Rabbinical school of Smorgoni, about 60 viersts north of Myadsiol, under the presidency of Rabbi Loew Lichtmacher, His preciosity amazed his new masters and when he reached the age of thirteen he was transferred to the Mayleh Yeshiva of Vilna, founded in 1832.

JEWS and LITHUANIANS

Part III

The Jews and Lithuanians lived in peace and in harmony. They are both very ancient nations, both in numerical minorities among their neighbors and both oppressed for centuries. The Lithuanian language, which is, according to I. Taylor and W. Dwight, the primitive Aryan tongue, challenges the archaity of the Hebrew. Many scholars claim that the Lithuanians are descendants of the Biblical Hittites, who, together with the Pelasgians, gave birth to Hellenic culture. The evidence submitted is very plausible. The friendship between the Lithuanians and the Jews is four thousand years old, for it was Abraham who was a sojourner in the land of the Hittites and it was in their ancient city Hebron that he bought a burying place for his family.

The *mystetchko* of Komai, in the government of Kovno, can be taken as the typical Lithuanian town. The Jew and the Lithuanian were *brolai* (brothers) to each other. They shared their *liudimas* (sorrow) and *dziaugsmas* (joy). In the weekly *turviete* (market) days the farmer visited his Jewish *draugas* (friend) to discuss business and family affairs at a glass of hot arbata (tea) or cold *alus* (beer). The Jewish *daktaras* of Komai cured their ailments, the Jewish *skrybelius* (hatter), *kurpius* (shoe-maker) and *kraucis* (tailor) furnished them with their holiday attire. The old *kalvis* (smith) was kept continuously busy with a gentile clientele. When *Simhat Torah* came many a Lithuanian *jaunikaitis* (boy) and *mergina* (girl) filled up the side benches of the old synagogue, gleefully and in astonishment watching the *Hakafot*, the songs and the fantastic candelabra with their self-propelling parchment-hoods.

Rabbi E. Gordon was especially esteemed by the Lithuanian rustics and townsmen, as if he were their own *Kinufas* (priest). They submitted their grievances to him sought his counsel and asked his benediction. Twice a year, before Passover and before Sukkot (Feast of the Tabernacles) they emptied many carloads of potatoes in his yard and other products of field and garden to be distributed free among the poor Jews of Komai.

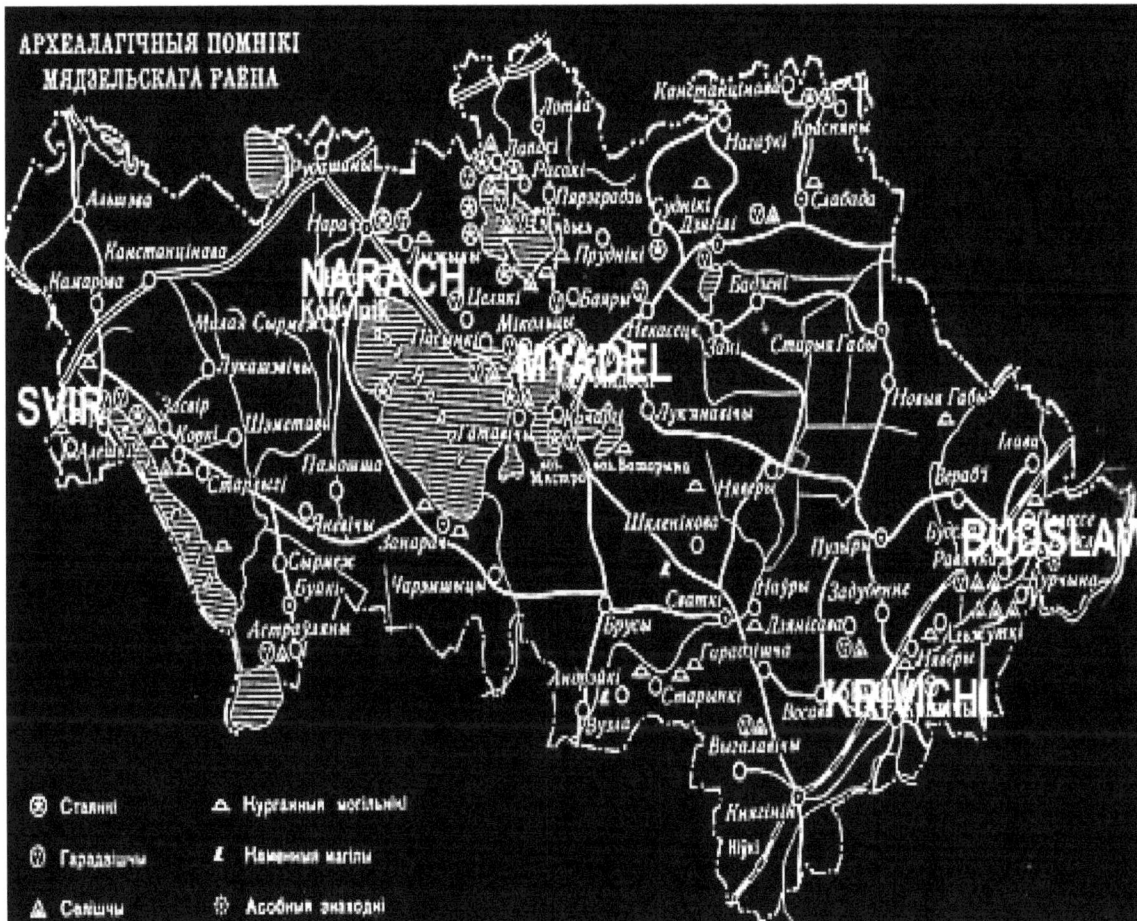

THE JEWS OF MYADEL

Surnames in Myadel

Householder Surnames in Myadel Revision Lists 1811 - 1850

H=Households or Family Groups
h=Male head of family

1811	1816/1818		1834	1850	
Gordon	4H	4H/19h	8H/9h	9H/22h	12H/28h
Chodash	20H	21H/26h	23H/39h	30H/95h	33H/95h
Svirdler	2H	2H/5h	6H	5H/10h	5H/11h
Smytski	2H	2H/3h	2H	2H/5h	2H/2h
Kopelevich	3H	3H/4h	2H/3h	1H/16h	7H/8h
Maleschevich	3H	3H	2H	1H/3h	4H/4h
Svirsky				1H/	2H/
Taits		1H		1H/	2H/2h
Sheven				1h	

1923 Myadel Business Directory

Description: Miasteczko, gmina Miadziol, powiat Postawy, s[1]d pok. Miadziol,s[1]d okr. Wilno, 635 mieszk. B (18km) •i3r Kobylnik ^ 9. Miadziol,l 01 kat. Garbarnia. Hodowla ryb.

Translation: Petite yille, commune de Miadziol, district de Postawy, just. do paix Miadziol, trib. d'arr-t Wilno, B35 h.ibil. S (18 km) Kobylnik
Miadziol, catholic church. Tanneries. Pisciculture.
Straz ogniowa ochot n.Komendant (Corps duœ pompiers volont. Commandant): Kaz,Horodniczy.

The Business and Business Proprietors
1. **Lêkarze** (medecins): Pietlicki K
2. **Akuszerki** (sagesfemmes): Donilo A.
3. **Apteczne sklady** (drogueries): Chodas L.
4. **Apteki (**pharmacies**)**: Lenczewski M.
5. **Stawa[3]y (**tissus): Cejtlin J.;Estryn Ch.;Gordon O.; Mindlin I.;Szwindler R.
6. **Ciesle** ( ) Chocianowicz
7. **Ciapnicu** (fabricants de casquettes): Zajdêl B.
8. **Falczerzy** (barbiers-chirurgiens):Maiko M.
9. **Fotograrficzne zaklady (photographes)**: Davidowicz J.
10. **Garbarnie (tanneries)**: Adamowicz.
11. **Herbaciarnie (debits de-the)**: Perkowski, J.
12. **Kolonjaine artykuly (spiciers)**: Alperowicz E.; Alperowicz S.; Chodes J.
13. **Kooperatywy (cooperat.)**; x„Plug" Siow. Spo¿.
14. **Kowale (fogerons)**:Afranowicz J.; Buniuszku W.; Burdecki J.;Stabkowicz M.
15. **Krawcy (tailleurs)**: Bzszkiewicz, F.; Burdecki, W.; Podhajski P.
16. **Lasy — eksploatacja (exploitations forestiers)**: Kaw W.
17. **Mlyny {moulins)**: Obolewicz J. (par)
18. **Piekarse (boulangers)**: Berensztejn, S.; XTarañczuk H.; Zekowski J.
19. **Piwiarnie (brassiers-debit)**: Horodnicz M.; Sawicz A.; Sidorowicz T.
20. **Restauracje (restaurants)**: Zdanowicz A.
21. **Rozne towary (articles divers)**:
    Achramiowicz J.; Alperowicz B.; Alperowicz L.
    A'perowirz M. Chodes Jank.; Chodes Joch.; Chodes S.; Chodes T.; Chodes, Z.;
    Geler E.; Gordon M., Gordon N; Istra, S.; Rzeczycki,J.; Swirska T.
22. **Ryby (poissons)**: Chodes A.; Siemienowicz B.
23. **Rzeznicy (bouchers)**: Chodes L.
24. **Skóry (cuirs)**: Alperowicz J.; Narocki J.; Narocki S.; Swirski J.;
    Zajdel B. Menkis Z.
25. **Spirytualia (spiritueux)**: Hoppen B.
26. **Spozywcze artykuly (comestibles)**: Chodos B.
27. **Stolarze (menuisiers)**: Chocianowicz S.
28. **Szewcy (cordonniers)**: Chodes N.; Chorodniczy K.; Sawicz H.; Wyrwicz J.
29. **Terpentyniarnie (fabr. de terpenthine)**: Budny E.
30. **Tytoniowe wyroby (tabacs)**: Horodnirzy N.; Zienkiewicz J.
31. **Wiatraki (mouiins a vent)**:

Page intentional left blank

Page intentional left blank

Page intentional left blank

Leaving Myadel

Passenger Name	Town Name (index)	Date of Arrival	Age	Ship's Name	Going to
Alperowitz, Elia	Mjadel	June 21, 1903	35	Rotterdam	Sister 123 Blue Island Av Chicago IL
Alperowitz, Schloime	Miadel	April 3, 1906	18	Potsdam	Uncle J. Gordon 38-35 Canal St. NYC
Baszykerciz, Chana	S. Midal	March 14, 1908	19	Graf Waldersee	Cousin Leser Lechengold
Belkin, Michal	Miadla	July 15, 1914	31	Imperator	No Image Available
Berhenholtz, Chajhe,	Miadlo	August 7, 1909	7	Campania	Father H.D. Silva Newport RI
Berhenholtz, Ester	Miadlo	August 7, 1909	10	Campania	Father H.D. Silva Newport RI
Berhenholtz ,Scheil	Miadlo	August 7, 1909	5	Campania	Father H.D. Silva Newport RI
Berhenholtz, Scheine	Miadlo	August 7, 1909	32	Campania	Father H.D. Silva Newport RI
Berkenholz, Jankel	Miadel	1911	30		
Berton, Scheins	Miadol	June 26, 1906	20	Nieuw Amsterdam	No Image Available
Bresum, Slawe	Meddel	June 6, 1910	18	Nieuw Amsterdam	Uncle B. Harwitz 2151-53 Grand St. NY
Bromberg, Chane	Meatyle	May 9, 1907	17	Rijndam	brother-in-law E. Cohen 90 Suffolk St. NY
Chadash, Itzhok	Miadle	January21, 1914	18	Vaderland	Brother-in-law L. Aras 26 Rutgers St. NY
Chodas, Minka	Mjadel	November 30, 1907	4	Smolensk	Father A. Chodas Orange St. Syracuse NY
Chodas, Ziwje	Mjadel	November 30, 1907	26	Smolensk	Husband A. Chodas Orange St. Syracuse NY
Chodash, Livie	Miadly,	March 18, 1913	19	Zeeland	Uncle Aron Chodash 393 Main ?, CT.
Chodes, Alter	Miadly,	June 4, 1909	20	President Lincoln	Father Rubin Chadash 1036 Montague St. Syracuse NY
Chodes, Chane Bosche*	Miadal	December 13, 1898	20	Italia	Brother in law Shlome Reback NY

Chodis, David	Niatel	January 7, 1908	28	Blucher	Brother in law Elie Rorinciki (?) Chelsea MA
Chodis, Miry	Miodel	June 4, 1907	21	Noordam	Brother in law C. Damschewsky 56 Monroe St. NY
Chodos, Abram	Mjadel	September 22, 1911	15	Kursk	No Image Available
Chodos, Chazkel	Miadel	November 22, 1911	35	Oceanic	Sister J. Solowitz 215 3 121st St. NY
Chodos, Elie	Miadel	September 20, 1911	17	Coronia	Brother David Chodis 130 Asylum St. NY
Chodos, Freide	Mjatly	November 30, 1907	22y	Smolensk	Brother Leib Kurtz 1603 Bergan St. NYC
Chodos,Josse	Mjatly	November 30, 1907	16	Smolensk	Brother Sam Chodash 530 Harrison St. Syracuse NY
Chodos, Lea	Mjadel	March 14, 1914	19	Kursk	Uncle Jacob Ho?isk 928 1/2 grape St. Syracuse NY
Chodos, Rachmiel	Mjadel	September 22, 1911	17	Kursk	No Image Available
Chodos,Riwa	Mjadel	September 22, 1911	20	Kursk	No Image Available
Chodos, Sara	Mjatly	November 30, 1907	27	Smolensk	Uncle M. Sheffer
Chodos, Sora	Mjade	September 22, 1911	63	Kursk	No Image Available
Chodosch,...oschke	Mjadel	August 20, 1906	4	Rijndam	Father Ish Hordes 11 monroe St. NYC % N. Fine
Chodosch, Basche	Mjadel	August 20, 1906	3	Rijndam	Father Ish Hordes 11 monroe St. NYC % N. Fine
Chodosch, Chaie	Mjadel	August 20, 1906	44	Rijndam	Husband Ish Hordes 11 monroe St. NYC % N. Fine
Chodosch, Chaie	Mjadel	February 16, 1909	17	Korea	Brother Abraham Chodosh 700 Orange St. Syracuse
Chodosch, Hinde	Njade	April 3,1911	28	Prinz Fredrich Wilhelm	Brother Jacob Chodos 99 E. Broadway NY
Chodosch, Leiser	Mjadel	June 6, 1905	21	Rijndam	Uncle Sam Weinstein 16 Rutgers St. NYC
Chodosch, Rachmiel	Miadlo	August 12, 1910	18	Graf Waldersee	Brother Leibe Chodash 412 Springfield Av Summit NY

Chodosh, Chainw	Mjadel	February 16, 1909	7	Korea	Brother Abe Chodash 700 Orange Av Syracuse NY
Choldes,Schmer	lMiadel	February 27, 1909	20	Main	Brother David Chodes 491 Oak St. New Haven CT
Cleodes, Arme	Myad	July 20, 1910	20	Kroonland	Sister N. S..?
Dimenstein, Ester	Medel,	1910	17		
Goldstein,Soba	Medille	1903	18		
Gordin, Kalmen	Medel	1913	22		
Gordon, Abram	Miadel	July 12, 1904	27	Potsdam	Uncle A. Berson 252 Clinton St. NYC
Gordon, Chaike	Miadel	August 20, 1906		Rijndam	Brother in law Sklarsky 62 Montgomery St NYC
Gordon, Dawid	Niadly	September 2, 1909	9	Lusitania	Father Shmuel Gordon 106 Henry St NYC
Gordon, Frume	Niadly	September 2, 1909	40	Lusitania	Husband Shmuel Gordon 106 Henry St NYC
Gordon, Itzig	Miatla	February 5, 1904	27	Blucher	No Image Available
Gordon, Jeze Ber	Miadel	January 13, 1905	24	Breslau	Cousin A. Berson 252 Clinton St NYC
Gordon, Jose	lMidyl	December 18, 1905	9m	Pretoria	Father Moische Gordon Trenton NJ
Gordon, Jossel	Niadly	September 2, 1909	7	Lusitania	Father Shmuel Gordon 106 Henry St NYC
Gordon, Kalmen	Miadel	December 6, 1911	18	Zeeland	Uncle F. Gordon 332-4 L?endekir Av Brooklyn NY
Gordon, May	Miad	November 28, 1907	22	Merion	Brother Abe Gordon 186-88 ? St. NYC
Gordon, Minna	Niadly	September 2, 1909	11	Lusitania	Father Shmuel Gordon 106 Henry St NYC
Gordon, Morduch	Miadel	July 12, 1904	30	Potsdam	No Image Available
Gordon, Mowsche	Niadly	September 2, 1909	15	Lusitania	Father Shmuel Gordon 106 Henry St NYC
Gordon, Nechame	Midyl	February 5, 1905	3	Blucher	Father Moische Gordon Trenton NJ
Gordon, Reise	Niadly	September 2, 1909	18	Lusitania	Father Shmuel Gordon 106 Henry St NYC
Gordon, Sore	Midyl	February 5, 1905	24	Blucher	Husband Moische Gordon Trenton NJ

Gordow, Beinesch	Miadel	June 21, 1899	50	Albano	Son in law Shmuel NYC
Gordow, Chanze	Miadel	June 21, 1899	10	Albano	Shmuel NYC
Hurmancz, Jankow	Miadela	July 17, 1904	25	Graf Waldersee	Wrong Image
Katz, Feigel	Miadl	September 18, 1911	18	Finland	No Image Available
Kissen, Beile	Miadel	March 28, 1911	18	Vaderland	Brother J. Kissen 206 ? NYC
Kopelowitz, Wulf	Mjadila	December 27, 1906	26	Petersburg	Brother Max Kopelowitz Canal St. Fulton OH
Leitlin, Israel	Miadel	March 16, 1906	17		Cousin Israel Bass 165 Stanton St. NYC
Lewin, Berko	Mjadel	September 4, 1907	39	Saratov	Cousin L. Breslaw 739 Albany Av Schenectady NY
Lewin, Ester	Njatel	September 26, 1910	41	Grosser Kurfurst	husband Ber Lewin 16 Miller St. Westfield MA
Lewin, Feige	Njatel	September 26, 1910	14	Grosser Kurfurst	Father Ber Lewin Miller St. Westfield MA
Lewin, Hirsch	Njatel	September 26, 1910	9	Grosser Kurfurst	Father Ber Lewin 16 Miller St. Westfield MA
Lewin, Israel	Njatel	September 26, 1910	5	Grosser Kurfurst	Father Ber Lewin 16 Miller St. Westfield MA
Lewin, Kusiel	Mjatel,	August 29, 1909	16	George Washington	Father Ber Lewin 16 Miller St. Westfield MA
Lewin, Kussiel	Mjadel	September 4, 1907	17	Saratov	Father Ber Lewin 16 Miller St. Westfield MA
Lewin, Sonja	Njatel	September 26, 1910	7	Grosser Kurfurst	Father Ber Lewin 16 Miller St. Westfield MA
Lewin, Teige	Mjadel	September 4, 1907	20	Saratov	Father Ber Lewin 16 Miller St. Westfield MA
Maloskowitz, Abram	Myadel	January 25, 1912	19	Kroonland	(Father in Miadel David) Brother M. Miller 924 grape St. Syracuse NY
Maloskowitz, Kopel	Myadel	January 25, 1912	19	Kroonland	(Father in Miadel David) Brother M. Miller 924 grape St. Syracuse NY
Malischkewicz	GMiadel	August 3, 1902		Potsdam	brother L. Malishkewitz 16 Rutgers Pl NY NY
Menkes, Itti	Miadle	December 16,	18	Pennsylvania	Brother-in-law Jankel Disent

Rochel		1912			202 Prince St. NYC
Menkes, Joel	Miadle	December 16, 1912	20	Pennsylvania	Brother-in-law Jankel Disent 202 Prince St. NYC
Norodski, Alte	Miadel	December 7, 1905	28	Zeeland	Husband 7 Rose St. New Haven CT
Norodski, Liebe	Miadel	December 7, 1905	3	Zeeland	Father 7 Rose St. New Haven CT
Norodski, Meite	Miadel	December 7, 1905	5	Zeeland	Father 7 Rose St. New Haven CT
Reichel, Sch...	Mjadel	June 8, 1903	18	Batavia	Brother Leibe Reichel 76 Suffolk St NYC
Slawin, Boruch	Miadel	September 18, 1911	18	Potsdam	No Image Available
Slawin, Mendel	Maidel	May 3, 1912	40	Potsdam	Brother-in-law Louis Hordes 206 Broadway NYC
Suzkenes, Efraim	Mjatly	November 30, 1907	42	Smolensk	Uncle M Stelpa 155 Division St. Detroit MI
Sweidler, Rochel	Mjadel	July 30, 1907	17	Potsdam	Cousin Joseph Sweedler 158 monroe St. NYC
Swiroski, Esterimia	Miadel	June 19, 1904	15	Blucher	Uncle Bernie Svirski New Haven CT
Swirski, Chame	Madel	May 2, 1906	15	Bulgaria	No Image Available
Zuckerman, Abram Jude	Miadel	September 27, 1909	10	Birma	Father Moische Zuckerman Brooklyn NYC
Zukerman, Lore	Miadel	September 27, 1909	11	Birma	Father Moische Zuckerman Brooklyn NYC
Zuckerman, Riwe	Miadel	September 27, 1909	33	Birma	Husband Moische Zuckerman Brooklyn NYC

JEWISH LIFE IN MYADEL

The Myadel Jewish Community
By Arye Geskin

According to historical findings the shtetl Myadel in Belorussia was established in 1324. A monument at the south entrance of Myadel points out this fact. Myadel lies between two lakes the Miastro and the Batorino. History relates that Napoleon' s army drowned in Lake Batorino as the ice which covered the waters was not strong enough to support the weight of the soldiers. Another lake called Naroch lies in the vicinity of the town. All these lakes teemed with bountiful fish and supplied the fishermen, the Jewish merchants and the population with essential nutrition. The forests surrounding the town provided the materials for the buildings as well as for heating the homes. The woods also had an abundance of berries, mushrooms and other forest growth.

The Town
Sixty-five Jewish families lived in Myadel Nowy and seven families in Myadel Stary before the second World War. In the center of Myadel Nowy was a cobble-stoned square bordered on one side by the Jewish Street. Almost all Jewish stores were to be found in that square. These stores were owned by Jewish merchants as well as Jewish craftsmen: tailors, shoemakers and carpenters. The synagogue was located on the Jewish street. On Thursdays, market- day in Myadel, the farmers from farms that surrounded the town displayed their produce for sale to the public. They sold cereals, fruits, vegetables and chickens, while the Jews sold clothing, cloth, shoes and sundries. On the edge of Myadel, there was also a cattle market which sold, aside from cattle, goats and sheep and horses. Mostly Gypsies and a few Jews traded at this market.

Education
There was an elementary school in Myadel Nowy which all the children attended. The language used in the school was Polish. All the Jewish boys were obliged to attend the **'cheder'** ("classrooms" in Yiddish and in Hebrew) one or two years before starting their obligatory studies.
 In Myadel, for a year or two (between the ages of five and seven) the boys went to study in the public elementary school, they studied Tphilot (prayers) and Chumash (Torah) in the Cheder with the Melamed (teacher). When they reached elementary school age (seven) they studied with all the children in the public school but, in addition, in the afternoon after school, they went to the cheder to study with the meladed for another three hours. They studied Haftora and began preparation for their Bar Mitzva, reading from the Pentateuch in the Synagogue, Gmara (Talmud), Tanach(the holy Scriptures) and continued the study of Hebrew grammar.
In Myadel (Stary Myadel and Nowy Myadel) there was a cheder in each synagogue and in private houses too. The Melameds were:
   * David Pliskin from Glubokje - Melamed in the cheder of the synagogue in old Myadel.

- Yeruchem (his surname now forgotten) from Dolhinov -
Melamed in the cheder of the synagogue in Nowy Myadel.
  - Chaim Sholem Estrin - Melamed in his own house.
  - Reb Salitan (his personal name now forgotten) - Melamed in the cheder of Zalman Chadash.

There was also a small branch of Hashomer Hazair (a leftish inclined Zionist movement) that prepared young people who wished to reach the shores of the Holy land. by sending them to Hachschara (training camps for the emigration to Palestine)

Religious Life

There was a synagogue in Myadel Nowy and in Myadel Stary. In the synagogues, and in several private homes, was a 'cheder' (classroom) where the sons of Myadel families studied the Jewish themes that were taught by the Melamed (teacher). Some young scholars went to study in Yeshivas outside of Myadel. Myadel's Jewish community life centered around the synagogue in the Jewish street in Myadel Nowy. The synagogue was a two storied building, the lower story was for men and the upper story for women (Ezrat Nashim). The synagogue had a yard where the children played, a wall and a gate. There was an inscription on the external wall of the synagogue which read : "ki baiti bait tphila ikare lechol haamim" ("For my house shall be called a house of prayer for all people") Jesaias 56;7. The synagogue was always crowded with people, especially on Jewish holidays with Rabbi Kosczevsky attending and presiding over the service. He was the spiritual leader of the Jewish congregation. On Shabat morning the Rabbi rendered his usual drasha . His sermons struck a chord in the hearts of the members of the community. With the occupation by the Russian army on the 17th of September 1939, all the religious life ended, and by the end of the war, the synagogue no longer stood, having been burned.

The German Occupation

The danger to the Jews in Myadel began with the German occupation on 22nd of June 1941. Only ten young persons managed to escape east to Russia. All Jews were made to wear a yellow Star of David on their chests, there was compulsory work, murder of individual Jews and in stages, the decimation of the Jews began. First, the torture and murder of twenty-one Myadel Jews at the bridge (among them the Rabbi Avram Shmuel Kosczevsky and the Shochet Israel Shoag) on 30 August 1941 by the local Poles and by German soldiers. After two weeks they were buried in the old cemetery in Myadel Stary. A partisan movement arose in Belarus and the Judenrat of Myadel established contact with the partisan Yacov Segalchik from Dolhinov-Myadel, and with his help one hundred and forty-four (144) Jews managed to escape, on the evening of Yom Kipurim the 21st of September 1942, and to reach the safety of the woods. The next day the Germans took the rest of the Jews and enclosed them in the Ghetto inside a building over night. The next morning, the 23rd of September 1942, they were led handcuffed to the forest south of Myadel by the Lake Batorino. They were brought fifty meters from a ditch which other Jews had been forced to dig. Then, they were taken , couple by couple, to stand at the edge of the ditch and shot by the Germans. Sixty-five people were murdered...whole families, men ,women and children, including infants .

Rescue

My parents Itze and Taibl Geskin were among those led to the forest. My sister and I were fortunate to have been saved at the very last moment. We were part of the death-march and the shots killing the Jews were clearly heard. The German commander suddenly remembered that my sister had not finished a sweater she had been knitting for him. He ordered my sister to be released in order to finish his sweater. She asked the commander to release me as well. He agreed, and my sister and I were taken out of the ranks and returned to the Ghetto where we stayed. In the Ghetto, craftsmen from Myadel, Kobylnik and Oshmany were retained by the Germans because they were needed as workers.

The Forests

On the 1st of November 1942 , the Partisans attacked the garrison in Myadel . The leader of the Jewish partisans, Yacov Segalchik broke the Ghetto fence and eighty-six Jews escaped, together with the Partisans, to the woods. I was among those who managed to escape and, by the grace of God, I am relating the tragic story of the Jewish community of our Shtetl Myadel.

Rabbi Avraham Shmuel Kosczevsky
By Dvora Kosczevsky Tennenboim

My father, Rabbi Avraham Shmuel Kosczevsky, was born in 1887 to Arye Leib and Malka in Zambrow (Zambrove) nearby Lomza, Poland. In his youth, he studied in Lomza's Yeshiva and in Slovodka's Yeshiva in Kovno, Lithuania. At the age of 20, he married Beila Raichman (parents: Moshe and Chana Shifra) from Zaremby Kosczelne.

After his studies, he was sent to be a "Magid Shir" (teacher) in Eisiske's Yeshiva. The occupation period by the German army in the first World War was a time of severe conditions which caused hunger in the population, so the Rabbi sent his wife and children to her parents. Soon after, the border was closed and the Rabbi was separated from his family for four years. After the war he returned to his family in Zaremby Kosczelne. He had no employment there, so he came to Vilnius to seek advice from the Rabbi 'Posek' Chaim Ozer Grodzansky who advised him to accept the first offer that came to him. In 1922, he became the Rabbi of Podberezy and, in 1932, he became the Rabbi of Myadel.

He replaced Rabbi Zipkevich who was known to be the Shochet, Shoag Israel's brother-in-law . The Shochet, who came to Myadel from Vilnius, became the Rabbi's son-in-law. The Rabbi, the Shochet and nineteen men of Myadel they were tortured and murdered by the Nazis and their helpers and died 30 September 1941(gimel Elul, taf shin alef)

The Rabbi and his wife lived in Myadel from 1932-1941/2. They had six children :(1 son and 5 daughters)

1.Rabbi Reuven Zalman Shlomo - b.1910, married Fiegl (Rabbi Ben Zion Mitvavky's daughter from Lebedova nearby Molodecno) and was the Rabbi of Lipnishak (Lipniski).He perished in the holocaust.

2. Yudit- b.1911.She married Myadel's 'Shochet' Shoag Israel in 1932 .She and her two children Yehoshua and & Malka were murdered in the massgrave on 23.09.1942.

3.Gittle- She married Rabbi Arye-Leib Lis in 1937 and they lived in Ostrovietz nearby Vilnius. After her husband was murdered, she returned to Myadel (the end of 41) with her two sons. One of the boys she lost in the woods, the second one is Rabbi in Israel .Gittle remarried Rabbi Chaim Zaiczik.

4.Sara- she married, Rabbi Nachum Lebovich scholar of Kaminetz Yeshiva, in 1946 .He was the nephew of the Rosh Yeshiva Rabbi Baruch Ber Lebovich. They have 4 daughters all married in USA.

5.Dvora- b. 1922, married Rabbi Arye Leib Zilberstein scholar of Radun Yeshiva (Hachafez Chaim) in 1946. She has four children ,three of them in the USA and a daughter in Israel. She remarried to Rabbi Tennenboim.Dvora Lives in Jerusalem.

6.Perke (Perel) – the youngest daughter was married to Abram Yakov Rotkin . They have 5 children In USA."

In Memory of the Jews in Myadel murdered 1941-1945

In 2003, two tombstones were built to commemorate the Jews of Myadel who were not identified on the two memorial plaques on the mass graves. The 65 and 21 Jews who were murdered by the Nazis in Myadel and its surroundings, in the forests near Kaminka and Usaci, on the battle front, and with the partisans.

In memory of the Jews of Myadel murdered by German Nazis and their collaborators 1941-1945.

Istrin, Sore and her son Leibe
her son Zelig and his children Grunye Golde Libe and Noach
Istrin, Sore- Freide bat Avraham
Alperovich, Shlomo and his children Simke and Zalman
Alperovich, Meir- Arzik his wife Leshke and their 3 children
Estrin, Chaya- Raizl and her daughter Pesya
her daughter Sara Estrin and gdaughter Shulamit
Bampi, Rachel- Leah and her children Ester- Libe and Molale
Bernstein, Chaya-Keile bat Shimon
her son Shimon his wife Asne and their daughter Mirale
her son Azriel and his wife Chyena
her son Zalman his wife Itke and their son Moshele
her daughter Roche-Mirke Rubin and her children Leah Masha & Maishe Gotkin Sara and
her daughter Dina
her daughter Dvairke Chadash and her son
Goldman, Nachum his wife Teibl and their daughters Yente and Ester-Libe
Gordon, Noach his wife Itl and their daughter Chaya-Sore
Gordon, Asher his wife Ester and their son Heshl
Geller, Elczik his wife Raizl and their daughter Nechama
His daughter Malka bat Nechama
Dimenstein, Shimon his wife Ester-Leah and their daughter Chaya-Dvora
Zaidel, Bella and her sons Chaim and Fidni
Chadash, Benes Yankl Hirshl and Dvora the children of Avram Leib& Freide
Chadash, Shalom and David the children of Yankl and Shifra
Chadash, Leibe and his wife Asne
Chadash, Berl and his wife Keile
Chadash, Zelda bat Chaim-Velvl and Sore - Freide
Chadash, Sore- Rivka bat Motke and Soshe
Chadash, Bunye and her daughter Merke
Chadash, Dovid- Leib and his wife Itke
Chadash, Bailke and Yequtiel the children of Itzchak and Chaya - Sore

Chadash, Rivka bat Fishl and Dvora
Her son Tuvya his wife Chana-Rochl and their daughter Shulamit
Katz, Shlaimke and his daughter Gutke
Menkis, Chaim his wife Tirza and their daughters Braine and Rashke
Narotzky, Yoseph his wife Tzila and their sons ChaimYacov Shlomo Shmuel
Furman, Chyena & her children Genya Chana-Gita Favish Batya Shalom
Perlman, Sara bat Benes and Tzipe-Maire
Zeitlin, Idl his wife Asne and their sons Michael and Chaim
Kutzer, Benye his daughter Hinde, his son Shimon and gson Eli - David
Klorin, Avram his wife Shula and their daughter
Radoshkovich, Shainke bat Berl Alperovich and her children
Rubin, Chanke bat Ber Alperovich and her son
Rubin, Natan his daughter Yente
Raichl, Chaim Yoshe ben Israel and his son Yechezkel
Shvimer, Motle his wife Chana and their grandchildren Leilale and Mina
Shulman, Tzivya bat Yudke & Bat Sheva

The Twenty-One killed in Myadel 25th of August, 1941

Irgun yozai Myadel 1993
Tombstone in the Myadel Cemetery

1. Rabbi Kostzevsky
   Avraham Shmuel
2. Shoag Israel ('shochet')
3. Alperovich Bunke
4. Alperovich Berl
5. Astrin Chaim-Sholem
6. Bampi Hilel
7. Gordon Michel
8. Gordon Lipke
9. Chadash Avraham Leib
10. Chadash Zalman
11. Chadash Motke son of Berl.
12. Chadash Motke son of Leib
13. Chadash Moshe Yoshke
14. Chadash Ruvke
15. Yanovsky Yoshe Leib
16. Narotzky Zelig
17. Finkelstein Gershon
18. Kugel Zalman
19. Kupelevich Yoshe
20. Shulman Yudke
21. Shkolnik Meir

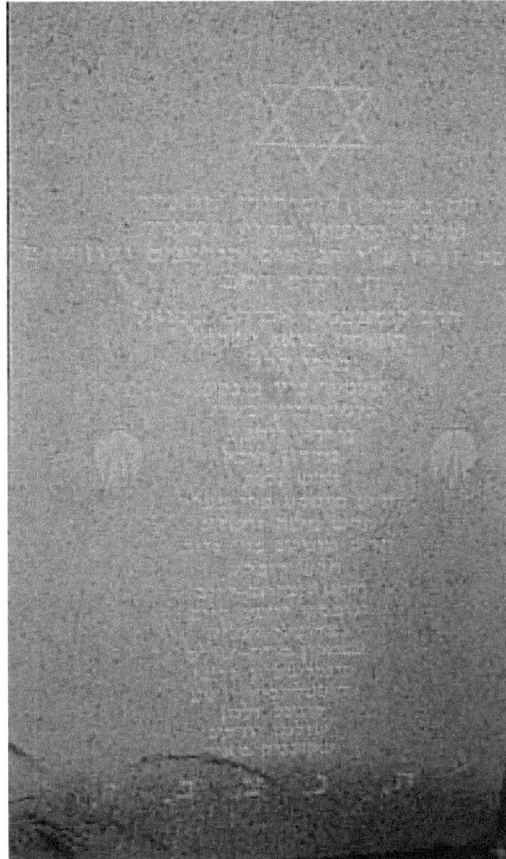

Thus says the Lord God: O my people, I will open your graves and have you rise from them, and bring you back to the land of Israel. Then you shall know that I am the Lord, when I open your graves and have you rise from them, O my people! I will put **my spirit in you** that you may live, and I will settle you upon your land; thus you shall know that I am the Lord. I have promised, and I will do it, says the Lord."
Ezekiel 37: 12-14 (34)
To the memory of the Myadel People whose place of rest is unknown.

Rabbi Avraham Shmuel Kostzevsky and twenty other Myadel Jews are buried in four mass graves in the cemetery in old Myadel and their names are etched on the tombstone that was put into position in 1993. These Jews were tortured and murdered on the 25th of August, 1941 by the Germans and their local associates, may their name be erased. They were murdered near the bridge just outside the shtetl in the swamp area. Before they were murdered, they were forced to dig their own graves. After two weeks they were buried at the cemetery with the help of some Gentiles that had the grace to help and retrieve the bodies from the boggy mud. Among those that brought the bodies for burial to the four mass graves in the cemetery were the late Yerachmiel Chadash (whose father was among the ones murdered) and Mr. Arie Geskin, may he live long! -*Chaya Lupinsky*

Memorial 1993

"The last of the Myadel Jews men, women, old and young, who were murdered and buried here on the 21st of September of 1942 the day after Yom haKipurrim by the German Nazis. May G'd revenge their death"

(left) Arye Gaskin standing in front of the mass grave of the sixty-five people murdered on the 21st of September 1942 in 1993.

Donors for renovation of the cemetery, the mass grave and the memorials in Myadel:

John Alper - Canada , main donor
Rabbi Kosczevsky's family - USA, Israel
The Rubin brothers - USA
Harold Svidler - USA
Ben Gordon - Canada
Efraim Chadash - USA

(above) the massgrave 1942-1992

To my dear friends Miadler (An open letter from Sarah and John Alper of Canada)

To my dear friends Miadler

From the depths of my heart, do I wish to express my best and warmest thanks to you, Leibke (Arye Geskin) and to you Yosef Chadash, and to all who helped in the monuments and that the memorial should come about.

In the beginning, I had doubts if this was the best, and practical undertaking, to perpetuate in everlasting memory the names of our near and dear ones. But after a while, I came to the conclusion that you are right. Firstly, seeing your devotion and your strong conviction, gave me the enthusiasm and convinced me to add my hand, and assure the financial responsibility to such a worthy undertaking. I could not leave this project, which would mean that I have no responsibility in such a holy obligation to our dear ones. It was impossible for me to stand from afar. It is very sad to thin, when it comes to mind, where we are, and where "they" are. Therefore, how can we forget them? Would they not have done for us what we are doing for them?

Each name, that is chiseled on the monument, not withstanding how long it will last, is a proof that a man existed and that there have survived people who did not forget that man. There is no price, no matter how high, for the person (man) who was fortunate not to have seen these monstrous and unrecordable tragedies that they were forced to live through. I always had the question, how did this happen? That this one or the other one perished, and I and others remained alive?

They were not more foolish than us. And we were not smarter than they. We can only answer this question with the word 'mazel'. This remains for us once again "a saving". Our small city., implanted in us, the warm feeling of one for another. The pain of one was the suffering of all. They truly took me out of Miadel but they never removed Meidel from me.

There stands in front of my eyes the faces, from the names etched on the monument. As well as the faces of the people from our city, in front of my eyes, I see the 'cheder' with the teachers as Chaim Shalom, Yeruchem from Dolhinov. As well as Felix and others, who helped to teach and raise a generation of self respecting youth. As well as with the help of the small library that was in Meidel. To our great sorrow and despair the youth had no future.

When I look at our children, the second generation, and I see how they established themselves in life, Many are doctors, engineers, and other in the free professions. This causes so much 'noches' (joy) for their parents and humanity at large. We have to realize how much more would the victims who perished in the holocaust, and their children, have contributed to this humane purpose. To our sorrow, our dear ones were killed, and did not live to see succeeding generations.

Our children, born in America, Canada have often times asked, how is it possible that you have no brothers, no sisters, no grandfathers, no grandmothers, no uncles, no aunts - from where do you originate - who are your antecedents?

Therefore, I believe, that perhaps the monument that was erected in Meidel will answer this question. The one who will visit Meidel will know that tragedy occurred and where are all of our relatives. When we say 'yizkor' in shul and we mention the victims and undertake to give charity to perpetrate their memory - I believe that the erecting of this monument and inscribing their names for everlasting memory is of a higher state "מדרבה".

I received from Feivel's son, Dr. Shapiro, a cassette with the complete description of the monument. It is a wonder, how everything is so well arranged, and so well planned. I am lacking words to describe my feelings, when I saw the opening of this important assembly. It was very moving to hear how you, Leibke, presented your thoughts, and expressed, "all that was in our hearts with the 'kadish' and 'Hazkara' that you recited, you fulfilled our responsibility, our debts and our feelings.

Meidel has, for the first time after 50 years, heard the cry of the hearts expressed in the 'kaddish'. The stone monument that you have erected will remain as a memorial and an answer for all those questions - what did take place? And the answer will be, that here (in Meidel) lived for hundreds of years, Jews, upright, honest people, good working Jews, who never hurt or caused harm to anyone.

In 1941, the worst storm of wild animals in human form, befell the Jewish world. The Nazis have destroyed and murdered young and old - all inhabitants in our cities in the most barbaric manner. Therefore, the world, and all those who will visit the monument, will forever remember, and never forget that which happened to the Jews of Meidel.

Sarah and John Alper
August 16 1996

ALPER, John ז״ל
A Holocaust Survivor

Peacefully, at home in Montreal, on Saturday morning, February 23, 2019, in his ninety-eighth year. Beloved husband of the late Sara Ehrenfeld. Survived by his treasured and devoted daughters, Hannah Alper and Sheila Alper Kleiman, and by his son-in-law, Dan Kleiman. Adored Zaidie of Kolby Kleiman, Brittany Kleiman Swisa and Michael Swisa. Proud great-grandfather of Jacob Nisim Swisa. Predeceased by his siblings, Benyomin, Zalman and Sima. Born on July 15, 1921, in Myadzel, a small Jewish village in Belarus, John was educated at The Chofetz Chaim Yeshiva in Radun, Poland, and graduated with a degree in Accounting from an esteemed University in Russia. He served in the Russian Army and immigrated to Canada in 1951, after living in Sweden where he met his beloved wife, Sara. John was co-founder of Toulon Development Corp., and a developer of multiple national and international properties. He was a generous philanthropist of the State of Israel, Jewish Community, and various Canadian and international non-profit organizations. He was an avid fisherman and hunter. He was a remarkable man who touched the lives of many and will be dearly missed. The family would like to express their gratitude to his doctors and to his compassionate caregivers.

Obituary of John Alper

Memorial and names from the murder site, September 21 1942

Alperovich, Shmuel Mulye Alperovich, Leah (nee Danishevsky) Shmuel's wife Alperovich, Yehiel - their son Alperovich, Itke - their daughter Alperovich, Freide - Shmuel's sister Alperovich, Leike - Shmuel's sister Alperovich, Mirke Alperovich, Mirke's daughter Alperovich, Mirke's daughter Alperovich, Masha	Bernstein, Joseph Bernstein, Rivka - Joseph's wife Bernstein, Avraham Itze -their son
Chadash, Beilke (nee Astrin) Chadash, Zalman - her son Chadash, Yoshke Chadash, Rochke (nee Katz) Chadash, Mira - their daughter Chadash, Leah - their daughter Chadash, Dveirke Chadash, Dveirke's son Chadash, Sarah Freide Chadash, Shaye Chadash, Pesya Liebe - Shaye's wife Chadash, Freide Chadash, Artzik - Freide's son Chadash, Itke - Friede's daughter Chadash, Zelda Chadash Leibe Chadash, Lisa - Pharmacist	Gaskin, Itze Gaskin, Teibl (nee Chadash) Geller, David Geller, Meir Geller, Rachel Geller, Malka Katz, Shimon Katz, Elka - Shimon's wife Katz, Leike - their daughter Katz, Sarah Rivka - their daughter Katz, Gutke - their daughter Mindlin, Itze Mindlin, Chaya-Geishe - Itze's daughter Narotzky, Keyle Narotzky, Mones Mones's daughter Narotzky, Chaim Velvel
Pearlman, Mordechai Raichl, Bashke Rotzaisky, Chana Leah Rotzaisky, Sarah Rivka - Chana's daughter Shulman ,Bat-Sheva Shulman, Malka - Bat-Sheva's daughter Shvag, Yehudit (nee Kostzevsky) Shvag, Yehoshua - their son Svirsky, Chana Svirsky, Esther Leah - Chana's daughter	Vitkin, Bluma - theirchild (adopted) Vitkin, Hirsch -their child (adopted) Zeitlin,Idl 63 - 65. Unknown.

(Left) Monument to the sixty-five people murdered by the Nazis on September 22, 1942
(Above) Position on the road: 150 meters from mass grave

ПАБЛІЗУ ГЭТАГА МЕСЦА 21 ВЕРАСНЯ 1942 ГОДА НЯМЕЦКА-ФАШЫСТКІМІ ЗАХОПНІКАМІ РАСТРАЛЯНЫ 60 МІРНЫХ ЖЫХАРОЎ СТАРЫКОЎ ЖАНЧЫН І ДЗЯЦЕЙ ЯЎРЭЙСКАЙ НАЦЫЯНАЛЬНАСЦІ З ГАРАДСКОГА ПАСЕЛКА МЯДЗЕЛ

Deaths in Myadel 1941 – 1944

Chaya Lupinsky has conducted exhaustive research creating this list with cooperation of the survivors of Myadel. This small community in Israel, Canada and the United States meets yearly in October. For further information contact Chaya or Meyer Svirsky.

(Among the first killed) - the people who were killed before September 30 1941
* killed at the bridge 25 August 1941 (memorial in Myadel Cemetery)
**the sixty-five killed in the woods at the site of the Mass Grave 22 September 1942, a day after Yom Kippur.
***the murder in the woods at Kaminka near Dolhinov 27 October 1942
****May 1944 "in the woods" exact location: Oshatzski Region. When the German Army was retreating, they killed many people who had been hiding with the partisans in the woods.

Chaya Lupinsky is in the process of verifying all the information in this list. There are some corrections that may still need to be made. Survivors have been contacted to verify this information.

House # according to chart of Householders in about 1937

- Alperovich, Berl ben Yecheil* 1906 - 30 August 1941 - House # 15
- Alperovich, his wife Ester Mirke bat Hershel Yanovsky** 1906 - 23 September 1942 - House # 15
- Alperovich, his daughter Judit ** 1931 - 23 September 1942 - House # 15
- Alperovich, his son Ezra** 1934 - 23 September 1942 - House # 15
- Alperovich, his son Yechiel** 1936 - 23 September 1942 - House # 15
- Alperovich, Shmuel ben Yecheil** 1904 - 23 September 1942 - House # 60
- Alperovich, his wife Leah bat Baruch Danishevsky** 1906 - 23 September 1942 - House # 60
- Alperovich, his son Yechiel** 1934 - 23 September 1942 * - House # 60
- Alperovich, his daughter Itke** 1942 - 23 September 1942 * - House # 60
- Alperovich, his sister Freide bat Yechiel** 1901- 23 September 1942 - House # 59
- Alperovich, his sister Leah bat Yechiel** 1903 - 23 September 1942 - House # 59
- Alperovich, Shlomo ben Itzhak 1894 - 1941 (Among the first killed) - - House # 66
- Alperovich, Benjamin ben Shlomo 1925 - 30 August 1941 (Among the first killed) - - House # 66
- Alperovich, his daughter Simke - Russia - - House # 66
- Alperovich, his son Zalman 1926 - Partisan - - House # 66
- Alperovich, Meir Arzik - 1941 Partisans - - House # 52
- Alperovich, his wife (Leshke?)Geller, sister of Raizel Geller 1941 Pasinki - - House # 52
- Alperovich, his son - 1941 Pasinki - - House # 52
- Alperovich, his daughter - Pasinki - - House # 52

- Bampi, Hillel ben Chrone* 1900 - 30 August 1941 (Among the first killed) - House # 54
- Bampi, Rachel Leah bat Yoshe Hirsh Svirsky 1909 - 22 September 22 1942

- Bampi, his son Mota 1932 - 22 September 1942
- Bampi, his daughter Ester Liba 1935 - 22 September 1942
- Bernstein, Chaya Keile bat Shimon - 1942 Dolhinov
- Bernstein, Shimon Maishe Mordechai 1901 - 18 May 1944 - House # 22
- Bernstein, Asne bat Shlomo Istrin 1907 - 4 May 1944 - House # 22
- Bernstein, his daughter Mira'le 1939 - 30 March 1942 - House # 22
- Bernstein, Joseph ben Maishe Mordechai** 1903 - 23 September 1942 * - House # 67
- Bernstein, his wife Rivke** 1906 - 23 September 1942 - House # 67
- Bernstein, his son Avram Itze** 1929 - 23 September 1942 * - House # 67
- Bernstein, Azriel ben Maishe Mordechai 1905 - 1942 - House # 17
- Bernstein, his wife Cheyna - 1942 - House # 17
- Bernstein, Zalman ben Maishe Mordechai 1910 - Dunilovichi
- Bernstein, his wife Itke 1912 - Dunilovichi
- Bernstein, his son Moshe'le 1940 - Dunilovichi

- Chadash, Avram Leib ben Yankel* 1884 - 30 August 1941 (Among the first killed) - House # 64
- Chadash, his wife Freide bat Benes Chadash** 1894 - 23 September 1942
- Chadash, his daughter Etke** 1930 - 23 September 1942
- Chadash, his son Aron** 1926 - 23 September 1942
- Chadash, his son Benes - 1941 Russia
- Chadash, his daughter Dvora 1919 - 1941 (Among the first killed)
- Chadash, his son Yankel - killed at the front
- Chadash, his son Hershel - killed at the front
- Chadash, Ruvke ben Yankel* 1924 - killed at the bridge - 30 August 1941 (Among the first killed)
- Chadash, his brother David ben Yankel - killed at the front
- Chadash, his brother Shalom ben Yankel - killed at the front
- Chadash, Leibe ben Chaim Velvel (the butcher) 1874 - 21 September 1941 Kobylnik - House # 69
- Chadash, his second wife Asne** 1868 - 21 September 1942

- Chadash, Motke's wife Beile bat Shlomo Istrin** 1900 - 23 September 1942 - House # 51
- Chadash, their son Zalman** 1927 - 23 September 1942 - House # 51
- Chadash, Berl (Chaim) Velvel (the butcher) - killed in the woods date unknown - House # 16
- Chadash, his second wife Keile bat Efraim Matzkevich -1941 - House # 16
- Chadash, their son Maishe Yoshke* - 30 August 1941 (Among the first killed) - House # 16
- Chadash, his son Motke* 1896 - 30 August 1941 (Among the first killed) - House # 62
- Chadash, his wife Soshya Chadash (no information as yet) Her sister Sore Chadash (see Pearlman) - House # 62
- Chadash, his daughter Sore Rivka 1929 - killed in the woods, date unknown

- Chadash, his daughter Adle (see Zelig Istrin below)
- Chadash, second wife of Chaim Velvel Sore Freida** 1880 - 23 September 1942
- Chadash, their daughter Zelda bat Chaim Velvel** - 23 September 1942 - House # 14
- Chadash, their son Yoshke ben Chaim Velvel** 1905 - 23 September 1942 - House # 14
- Chadash, his wife Roche bat Shlomo Katz** 1913 - 23 September 1942 - House # 14
- Chadash, his daughter Leah** 1939 - 23 September 1942 - House # 14
- Chadash, his daughter Mira** 1941 - 23 September 1942
- Chadash, his sister-in-law Dveirre** bat Yankel** wife of Yudel David 23 September 1942 (see note at end)
     -    House # 13
- Chadash, Dveirre's son Yudel Dovid ** - 23 September 1942 - House # 13
- Chadash, Zalman ben Ephraim* 1890 - 30 August 1941 - House # 57
- Chadash, his wife Henya bat Avram 1895** - 23 September 1942 - House # 57
- Chadash, Bunye*** - 27 October 1942 - Kaminka House # 24
- Chadash, his daughter Merke*** 27 October 1942 - House # 24
- Chadash, Dovid Leib ben Noach*** 1890 - 27 October 1942 - House # 7
- Chadash, his wife Itke bat Chone Menkis 1892 - killed in the woods in Oszensk - May 1944 - House # 7
- Chadash, Tuvya ben Israel 1896 - killed in the woods in Oszensk - May 4 1944 - House # 48
- Chadash, his wife Chana Rochel bat Chaim Shlomo Estrin *** 1904 - 27 October 1942 - House # 48
- Chadash, his daughter Shulamit*** 1936 - 27 October 1942 - House # 48
- Chadash, his mother Rivke - 1942 House # 48
- Chadash, Liza bat Israel 1894** - 23 September 1942
- Chadash, Shaye ben Gershon** - 23 September 1942 - House # 20
- Chadash, Pesya Libe bat Hirsh Rygorovich** 1918 - 23 September 1942 - House # 20
- (see Vitkin below their adopted children) - 23 September 1942 - House # 20

- Dimenstein, Shimon ben Avram 1885 - December 1941 - House # 2
- Dimenstein, his wife Ester Leah bat Israel 1890 - December 1941 - House # 2
- Dimenstein, his daughter Chaya Dvora - December 1941 - House # 2

- Estrin, Chaim-Sholem* - killed at the bridge - 30 August 1941 (Among the first killed) - House # 33
- Estrin, his daughter Pesia 27 October 1942 - House # 33
- Estrin, his daughter Sore - 27 October 1941 - House # 33
- Estrin, his grand daughter Shulamit bat Eliezer Estrin *** - 27 October 1942 - House # 33

- Finkelstein, Gershon ben Ure and Basia Chadash* 1921 - killed at the bridge 30 August 1941 (Among the first killed) -   House # 32
- Freedman, Ester bat Itzchak Zeev Alperovich** - 23 September 1942

- Furman, Chyena bat Leib Chadashevich*** 1903 - 27 October 1942 Kaminka - House #34
- Furman, her daughter Genya bat Joel*** 1931 - 27 October 1942 - House # 34
- Furman, her daughter Chana Gita bat Joel*** 1933 - 27 October 1942 - House # 34
- Furman, her son Favish ben Joel*** 1935 - 27 October 1942 - House # 34
- Furman, her daughter Basia bat Joel*** 1937 - 27 October 1942 - House # 34
- Furman, her son Sholom ben Joel*** 1939 - 27 October 1942 - House # 34

- Geller, Ela - 1941 Pasinki - House # 18
- Geller, his second wife Reizel - 1941 Pasinki - House # 18
- Geller, their daughter Nechama 1941 - 1941 Pasinki - House # 18
- Geller, his daughter Malka** 1927 - 23 September 1942 - House # 18
- Geller, his daughter Rochke** 1929 - 23 September 1942 - House # 18
- Geller, his son David** 1928 - 23 September 1942 - House # 18
- Geller, his son Meir** 1932 - 23 September 1942 - House # 18
- Geskin, Itze ben Leib** 1890 - 23 September 1942 - House # 10
- Geskin, his wife Teibel bat Noach Chadash** 1893- 23 September 1942 - House # 10
- Goldman, Nachum ben Chaim 1910 - Dunilovichi
- Goldman, his wife Teibel bat Yoshe Hirsh 1912 - Dunilovichi
- Goldman, his daughter Yente 1935 - Dunilovichi
- Goldman, his daughter Ester Libe bat Nachum 1939 - Dunilovichi
- Gordon, Gershon ben Menachem Mendel 1896 - killed in the woods May 1942 in Oszensk - House # 49
- Gordon, his wife Cheyna bat Jacov Mendel*** 1903 - 27 October 1942 - House # 49
- Gordon, his son Akiva*** 1934 - 27 October 1942 Kaminka - House # 49
- Gordon, Michel ben Menachem Mendel* 1894 - killed at the bridge 30 August1941 (Among the first killed) - House # 68
- Gordon, his wife Chana Breina bat Noach***1904 - 27 October 1942 Kaminka - House#68
- Gordon, his son Chaim*** 1929- 27 October 1942 Kaminka - House # 68
- Gordon, Noach ben Israel Moshe 1894*** - 27 October 1942 Kaminka - House # 45
- Gordon, his wife Itke bat Taitz*** - 27 October 1942 - House # 45
- Gordon, his daughter Chaya Sore*** 1923 - 27 October 1942 Kaminka - House # 45
- Gordon, his son Lipke* 1924 - killed at the bridge 30 August 1941 - House # 45
- Gordon, Asher ben Israel Moshe 1898 - 28 April 1942 - Krivichi - House # 40
- Gordon, his wife Esther bat Chone 1902 - 28 April 1942 - Krivichi - House # 40
- Gordon, his son Heschel 1923 - 28 April 1942 - Krivichi - House # 40
- Gordon, Moshe ben Menachem Mendel 1890 -memorial in Myadel Cemetery
- Gotkin Sara -wife of Yankel - (She was Chana-Ester or Motl Shvimer's sister)
- Gotkin Dina - her daughter
- Her daughter Chadash, Dvierke (ne Gotkin) and son **23 September 1942

- Istrin, Zelig ben Moshe 1905 - May 1944 - House # 3
- Istrin, Adle Chadash (no information as yet) - House # 3

- Istrin, his daughter Grunya 1929 - May 1944 - House # 3
- Istrin, his daughter Golde 1931 - May 1944 - House # 3
- Istrin, his daughter Liba 1933 - May 1944 - House # 3
- Istrin, his son Noach*** 1935 - 27 October 1942 - House # 3
- Istrin, his mother Sore*** 1880 - 27 October 1942 - House # 1
- Istrin, his aunt Sore Freide*** 1875 - 27 October 1942 - House # 1
- Istrin, his brother Leibe ben Moshe*** - 27 October 1942 - House # 1

- Katz, Shlomo ben Avraham 1884 - 1941 (Among the first killed)
- Katz, his wife Elka bat Mendel** 1890 - 23 September 1942
- Katz, his daughter Gutke** 1914 - 23 September 1942
- Katz, his daughter Leike** 1920 - 23 September 1942
- Katz, his son Shimon** 1927 - 23 September 1942
- Katz, his daughter Sore Riva** 1929 - 23 September 1942
- Klorin, Avraham - Dolhinov - House # 36
- Klorin, his wife - Dolhinov - House # 36
- Klorin, his daughter - Dolhinov - House # 36
- Kopelevich (Rabinowitz), Yoshe* killed at the bridge 30 August 1941 (Among the first killed)
- Kopelevich (Rabinowitz), his wife Masha bat Raphael** - 23 September 1942 - House# 55
- Kosczevsky, Avram Shmuel ben Arye Leib Rabbi* killed at the bridge 1887 - 30 August 1941 (Among the first killed) - House # 55
- Kugel, Zalman ben Itzhak* 1912 - killed at the bridge 30 August 1941 (Among the first killed) - House # 26
- Kutzer, Benye 1862 - June 1942 Azarki - House # 39
- Kutzer, his daughter Hinde 1900 -15 June 1942 Azarki
- Kutzer, his son Shimon - June 1942 Azarki - House # 39
- Kutzer, his grandson son David ben Shimon - June 1942 Azarki - House # 39
- Kutzer. his grandson Eli ben Shimon - June 1942 Azarki - House # 39

- Menkis, Chaim ben Chrone 1895 - 18 November 1941 - House # 9
- Menkis, his wife Tirtza bat Shlomo*** 1900 - 27 October 1942 Kaminka - House # 9
- Menkis, his daughter Braine bat Chaim*** 1926 - 27 October 1942 Kaminka - House # 9
- Menkis, his daughter Rashke bat Chaim*** 1928 - 4 May 1944 "in the woods" Oshatski Region Kaminka - House # 9
- Mindlin, Itzhak ben Zalman ** 1896 - 23 September 1942 - House # 56
- Mindlin, his daughter Chaya-Geishe** 1925 - 23 September 1942 - House # 56

- Narotzky, Joseph ben Shlomo 1882 - May 1941 (Among the first killed) - House # 4
- Narotzky, Tzila bat Avraham Narotzky 1908*** - 27 October 1942 - House # 4
- Narotzky, his son Chaim ben Joseph*** 1929- 27 October 1942 - House # 4
- Narotzky, his son Yacov ben Joseph*** 1931 - 27 October 1942 - House # 4
- Natotzky, his son Shmuel ben Joseph*** 1934 - 27 October 1942 - House # 4

- Narotzky, his son Shlomo ben Joseph*** 1939 - 27 October 1942 - House # 4
- Narotzky, Zelig ben Leizer* 1905 - killed at the bridge 30 August 1941 (Among the first killed)
- Narotzky, his wife Keile bat Chaim Velvel Chadash*** 1909 - 27 October 1942
- Narotzky, his son Chaim Velvel** 1932 - 23 September 1942
- Narotzky, his daughter Beile Dvierke** 1934 - 23 September 1942
- Narotzky, his son Mones ben Zelik** 1934 - 23 September 1942

- Pearlman, Mordechai ben Benas** 1872 - 23 September 1942 - House # 63
- Pearlman, his second wife Sore bat Benes Chadash died 1945 - House # 63

- Raichel, Chaim Yoshe ben Israel 1884 - 1941 (Among the first killed) - House # 31
- Raichel, his second wife's daughter Bashke bat Itzchak and Ester Katz** 1922 - 23 September 1942 - House # 31
- Raichel, his second wife's son Yechezkel ben Itzhak - House # 31
- Roczaisky, Chana Leah bat Chaim Velvel Chadash** 1894 - 23 September 1942 - House # 25
- Roczaisky, her daughter Sore Rivke bat Motke** 1924 - 23 September 1942 - House # 25
- Rubin, Natan*** - 27 October 1942 - House # 65
- Rubin, his daughter Yente*** - 27 October 1942 - House # 65
- Rubin, his daughter-in-law Chanke bat Berl Alperovich - Krivichi - House # 65
- Rubin, his granddaughter bat Berl Rubin- Krivichi - House # 65
- Rubin, Roche Mirke bat Maishe Mordechai - 1907 - 1942 Dolhinov
- Rubin, her daughter Leah bat Gershon 1930 - Dolhinov
- Rubin, her daughter Masha bat Gershon 1932 - Dolhinov
- Rubin, her son Moshe ben Gershon 1934 - Dolhinov

- Shkolnik, Meir** (husband of Musya)- 30 July 1941 (Among the first killed) - House # 43
- Shoag, Israel ben Itzhak ('shochet')* 1905 - 30 August 1941 (Among the first killed) - House # 50
- Shoag, his wife Yehudit bat Avram Shmuel Kosczevsky** 1914 - 23 September 1942 - House # 50
- Shoag, his son Yehoshua** 1934 - 23 September 1942 - House # 50
- Shoag, his daughter Malka** 1939 - 23 September 1942 - House # 50
- Shulman, Yudke* 1886 - 30 August 1941 (Among the first killed) - House # 21
- Shulman, his wife Bat-Sheva** 1876 - 23 September 1942 - House # 21
- Shulman, his daughter Malka** - 23 September 1942 - House # 21
- Shulman, his daughter Tzivya 1928 - 23 September 1942 - House # 21
- Shvimer, Motle - 27 October 1942
- Shvimer, his wife Chana Ester - 27 October 1942
- Svirsky, Chana bat Avraham 1884 - 22 September 1942

- Vitkin (see Leibe Chadash-the butcher) Bluma - their child (adopted)** - 23 September 1942
- Vitkin (See Leibe Chadash-the butcher) Hirsch -their child (adopted)** - 23 September 1942

- Yanovsky, Yoshe Leib ben Hershel* - 30 August 1941 (Among the first killed)- House # 27

- Zeitlin, Idl ben Avraham** 1904 - 23 September 1942 - House # 45
- Zeitlin, his wife Ashe bat Israel Moshe*** 1896 - 27 October 1942 Kaminka - House # 45
- Zeitlin, his son Michel*** 1929 - 27 October 1942 Kaminka - House # 45
- Zeitlin, his son Chaim*** 1934 - 27 October 1942 Kaminka - House # 45

Notes:
Yerachmeil ben Motka Chadash survived the war and died 1998 Lepel, Belarus.
Yudl Dovid ben Leibe (Chaim Velvel) 1897-1994

Eternal Testament: Memoirs of a Partisan by Yakov Segalchick. Translated and transliterated by Eilat Gordon

Invasion of Amalek

On June 22, 1941, Nazi Germany's attack on the Soviet Union took us by surprise. At the time, I was living in Myadel, a shtetl situated on the shore of the Narutz Lake, where I had moved the previous year after marrying a native girl. The next morning, I left the area with 9 other youths from Myadel in an attempt to escape the rapidly approaching Nazi Army. With great rapidity we walked all the way to the Kanhanina train station, and in the last moment managed to push our way into the very last train car. As it turned out, the train was to be the last Soviet train to leave the area for some years.

The train was full of soldiers and officers of the Red Army, as well as some local civil servants for the USSR. There were also some prisoners of the Soviets who were taken from Vilejka's (aka Vileyka) jail. Also, some locals (mostly Communists and Jews) who wanted to flee the Nazi occupation had crowded the train. The young people who came with me from Myadel were Moshe Hadash, Hirsch Hadash, Yitzhak Alperovicz, Yoshue Leib Yanovsky, Yitzhak Keller, Shimon Kotzer, Yosef Rubin, Zalman Kaplan, and Nahum Perelman from Dokshitz. We barely found a spot to stand as the train departed. The

ride was very peaceful until we reached Karlovisziczina, where about a dozen Luftwaffe Foch-Wulfes appeared. There were no Soviet forces in the area to repel them, so they rained their gifts down freely upon us. One of their huge bombs exploded right by the train and derailed the last three cars of the train, including the one we were on.

To our great fortune, we were not physically hurt, but we were very anxious since we could not continue on our journey. When we got out of our car we realized that the rest of the train was long gone. After a moment to gather ourselves, we decided to walk to Dokshitz, a place where we thought we would have easier access to cross the border of Poland and the Soviet Union (the pre-partition border from 1939).

Dokshitz was situated on the outskirts of the border. After arriving at Dokshitz, we found hundreds and I might not be exaggerating if I said thousands of refugees by the side of the road. Some came by horse and buggy, some by foot. They were running back and forth, looking for a place to cross to the other side and save themselves from the disaster to come. However, Soviet guards stood with weapons ready at every crossing point. They demanded that everyone go back, saying that we were all causing unnecessary panic, and that we must return to our proper places.

We had no choice but to return to our homes, but first I decided to visit Dolhinov (aka Dolginovo), the place where I was born and raised. My mother and my married sister with her children lived there, and I wanted to help them. As it turned out, although I was able to help out many and save their lives from the hands of murderers, I was unable to save my mother, my sister, or her children. My sister on the other hand, saved my life from a certain torturous death at the hands of the Gestapo, as I will tell you later.

Back to my visit to Dolhinov. Shortly after I arrived, on Saturday the 28th of June 1941, the first German scouts entered the town. They didn't hurt anyone at first, they just shot at a few farmers. We then decided that it was time to go back to Myadel, where our wives and children were.

Four young people from Dolhinov walked with me to Myadel. On the way we didn't see any Germans. We avoided the main roads, sticking to more out-of-the-way routes and we safely arrived at the village Nyavia, a few kilometers from Myadel. Here we had to cross the river using a boat since German planes had demolished the bridge. We saw a few farmers taking out the bridge debris from the river. After begging, pleading and bribing, we were able to convince one of them to take us with his boat across the river for a large amount of money.

At home, my wife and father-in-law received me with great delight. "The husband and son-in-law has returned," they said. However, after a few moments of discussion of the situation of the Jews, I realized, "What did I really achieve? Why did I leave and then come back?"

Forthwith I was told that there was already carnage in town, and blood was flowing like a river here. As soon as the German troops arrived, they appointed some local collaborators to take charge of the police department. Most of the youths in the police force were local Polish people, amongst them about 20 hooligans and thugs who were full of animosity toward the Soviets, and showed even greater repugnance towards the Jews. They declared, "All the Jews were Communists." That statement launched the first event in a series of tragedies and tortures that I would experience. Immediately I realized that we must organize young people to fight the enemy, though the road to achieving that goal was very long and there were many twists and turns on the way to accomplishing that lofty idea.

At the head of the local police in Myadel, there were two corrupt, cruel and bloodthirsty goons. The head of the police was Baginisky, and Koprevicz was his assistant. As soon as the Nazis appointed them to the job, together with the gendarme of Vilejka they started torturing the Jewish community, which was totally without defense and had never committed any crime. In some ways, the local assistants were many times crueler than their German   bosses.

The First Massacre and Its Victims

One Sunday, in the first weeks of the occupation, two bodies of prisoners from the Vileyka jail were brought to Myadel. When the Soviets started retreating from Vileyka, they killed a few political prisoners that they thought were too dangerous to be taken to the Soviet Union. Those executions of those sentenced to death were done near the village Ravoni, which was in the vicinity of the jail. When later the bodies were found, one of the thugs who found them was from Myadel, and he recognized two of the bodies as of natives of Myadel.

The locals said, "Who is guilty? The Jews. They were the cause of these people's imprisonment, and now they were the cause of their death." They soon organized a majestic burial ceremony that paid great homage to the deceased in which they made fiery speeches laden with malevolence called for retribution on the Jews. They also invited some Germans from the engineering troops that were rebuilding the local infrastructure to take part in the ceremony.

The Germans who were responsible for the improvement of the infrastructure decided to exploit the Jews to do the hard labor as slaves. They started kidnapping Jews and forced them to build the roads. One day for no clear reason they gathered 22 young Jews from Myadel and ordered them to walk. At the head of the procession they put the Rabbi and kosher slaughterer (shochet). Soon after, they started tormenting them and moments later they begun torturing them. The tortures were executed methodically and brutally. They used clubs and attack dogs that tore at their victims' limbs and flesh. I saw everything with my own eyes, since in all the panic around I was able to escape and hide in a house not far from this tragic event. I saw an agitated German officer holding a ferocious dog ordering it to attack the rabbi, who was already too weak to stand on his feet. The dog pushed him on the ground and started eating his flesh, which was bleeding profusely.

The killers ordered the other victims to put the rabbi's body, which was still twitching, on a wheelbarrow and to take him outside of the town. Others were also tortured mercilessly, and at the end, they ordered the few survivors who were still able to walk to take shovels and to start marching. Soon after, they were told to dig holes. When they had finished digging, they were shot on the spot and buried in the holes that they had just dug. In outrage, I escaped from my hiding place and took with me Berl Hadash, my father-in-law, who was also hiding out there.

Days of preparation

I decided that the family must leave Myadel but at that point I was determined not to take them with me. First, I must go to prepare a safe place for them in Dolhinov, then I would return for them.

Three people left with me: Hendel Swardlov, Chaia Dimmenstein, and Sara whose last name I don't remember. When we arrived in Dolhinov, life seemed very different here. There were Germans and also local police, and a Polish mayor by the name of Zygmund Volk. He was a local resident who used to be in business. He treated the Jewish people decently until their bitter end. Also, the head of the police, Anton Krosovsky, was a decent Christian man. For a little bit of alcohol you could gain his favor and he would do anything for you. Here also the Germans ordered the institution of a Judenrat, but during the first months in Dolhinov you hardly experienced the troubles that the Jews of Myadel experienced. The Jews of Dolhinov went to work for the Germans everyday, and in general, at that point of time they were not treated badly.

In September of 1941 we started hearing horrible rumors about the annihilation of the Jewish communities. Around Rosh Hashanah of 1941 we heard about the annihilation of the Jews of Zambin, near Borisov. A few days later we heard of the annihilation of the Jews in Kriyesk and Lagoysk. Early in October, sometime before dawn, we heard a knock on our door, and when we opened it, we saw our Aunt Rachel and her daughter Lyuba. They said that yesterday, in the middle of Yom Kippur, all the Jews of Plashensitz were taken to the forest of Borisov to be killed. On the third week of October 1941, we heard that during Simhat Torah, they killed 54 Jews in Kurenitz, which was located 37 kilometers from Dolhinov.

Searching for a way out

Amongst the refugees who arrived after the Plashensitz massacre was a Jew who was born in Minsk by the name of Leib Mindel. By this time Leib had survived three German massacres. He came to us for assistance and we provided him with food and shelter. We had a good reserve of food at that point and we were always able to find a way to get some more supplies during the weekly market days.

It wasn't a dilemma for us to allow refugees to reside with us. Almost all the Jews of Dolhinov helped their Jewish brothers with shelters. Sometimes we had refugees who stayed with us for weeks. Very quickly Leib Mindel and I became good friends and this friendship proved itself time and again during the horrible days to come and later. Leib was a man full of energy and he had a "take charge" quality, and I felt that I could always rely on him. We had many conversations in those days and we realized that it was just a matter of time before catastrophe came to our town. We decided that, first and foremost, we must find a shelter for the women and children.

We recognized that as soon as the horrors came, women and children would be the primary victims, so we had to find a good hiding place for our family. We secretly started constructing two hiding places; the first was under the land in the barn of our neighbor

Yosef Kremer. We dug a very deep hole in the soil. It was four by four meters and we made all the walls strong by using large and sturdy wood posts. We camouflaged the hideout and we were sure that no one would ever realize that there was a hiding place in this vicinity. The second hideout we built was inside our cow shed. We used double walls to camouflage the hideout. In these two hideouts, many people hid during the first and second massacres.

Our second plan was to escape to the forest, though we had to delay the escape a few times since the winter that year was extremely cold and everything was frozen around, so we decided to wait until there was a break in the frost. This break never occurred.

The atmosphere became more and more ominous. Every day brought another terrible tale of destruction in the towns around us. On Wednesday, the 12th of March 1942, a few survivors escaped from Ilya and told us about the harrowing annihilation of their town. About 100 killers came by car during the night. Early in the morning, all of the Jews were forcibly taken from their houses into the market. From there they were ordered to walk outside of town and then they were placed in a stable and were shot inside it.

Now it was clear to all of us that very soon our town would be annihilated. We decided to organize two dozen young people to escape to the forest. Since we were overseeing this mission, we gathered about 20 young men to decide what to do. A decision was made on the 14th of March 1942. Leib Mindel and I would go to the forest to try to connect with a Christian villager by the name of Bronka Klaga. He lived in the Kalich forest, which was situated between Dolhinov and Dokshitz. I knew Bronka as a very honest man, civil minded, and very capable. I was hoping that if I could get in touch with him he would connect us with partisans.

The next day we started walking to the forest. We made a huge strategic mistake: instead of going early in the morning when it was still dark, we left during the later morning hours. Seeing Jews walking freely made the Germans and their local aides very suspicious. We did have in our hands a letter signed by the mayor permitting us to leave. The letter stated that we were going to the forest to cut trees for the municipal building. We also carried axes and saws, so we would not raise suspicion, however, we were only able to walk one kilometer away from town when we heard loud sounds of horses following us.

We looked back and we saw that they were chasing us. At the head was the head of the police, who was not Anton Kosovsky anymore but a thug who came from Kriviczi. Sitting next to him on the sled was a German officer. Beside the horses and sled there were also some policemen on bicycles.

As they came near us they ordered us in Polish, "Stop and put your hands up!" When they reached us they started beating us. One of the policemen used his rifle to hit Leib Mindel on his head. He momentarily lost his consciousness and fell to the ground, and shortly after there was a puddle of blood encompassing him. All of them turned to me now and started hitting me with their rifle butts, all over my body, to every place they could reach. I was lucky that they didn't get my head. Maybe they didn't want me to lose consciousness as Leib had, so they kept hitting me on my shoulders, back, and waist. They kept doing it until one of the rifles broke. We later on took that rifle, during the first attack on the Dolhinov when I was with the Russian partisans.

Momentarily they stopped the tortures and had a discussion between the head of the police and the German who came with them about what to do with us. They decided to tie us to the sled. They turned the horses back toward the town and sat back in the sled. We were tied to the back of the sled and as long as the horses walked slowly, we could run behind. But when they started hitting the horses, urging them to go faster, we fell down on the ground and we were pulled along. Hence half-fainted, we arrived at town followed with the rest of the policemen on bicycle.

The Jews in town panicked when they saw us in such a state. As we reached the town they put us next to the well and the policemen kept taking water from the well using a bucket and drenched us from the top of our heads to the tip of our toes. Since the weather was very cold, we started shaking feverishly. In this state we were taken to the police station, where two German officers were waiting for us. These two Germans worked in the communications unit, building telephone lines. They were infamous for beating up Jews who they caught walking on the sidewalk (which was forbidden to the Jews), or who failed to give the proper salute of taking off their hats when they saw them.

As soon as we entered, the two Germans along with the head of the police started interrogating us, beating us continuously. They kept asking us questions about our contacts with partisans and any secret meetings that we had with them. We denied all connections with the partisans and said we knew nothing. The more we protested we knew nothing, the more they beat us.

Mindel lost his consciousness again and was covered by blood. I was barely conscious, lying on the ground and praying to God that He would bestow on me a swift death so I could be saved from this unbearable torture.

While I was on the ground I heard a phone conversation of one of the Germans with the Gestapo in Dokshitz. He let them know that they had arrested two Jewish partisans. I couldn't hear the response, but I understood that we were to be put in the prison to wait for the next day.

By the time they deposited us in the prison cell it was already dark. The cell was three by three meters and there were two big, open windows that had no glass but had bars. This night in March was extremely cold. There was a storm and since the Windows were uncovered we were shaking mercilessly. Our clothes were drenched and we were twitching like we had pneumonia. Since our situation was so bad, they locked us there but they didn't put any guards to watch us, they must have been thinking that we would never be able to escape. All they did was to lock the door of the cell from the outside.

The cell had only one place to sit. The floor was much too cold to lie down on. All night we couldn't rest. We hardly had a place to sit, so we kept changing from sitting to standing positions until it was about midnight. There was silence everywhere, and all of a sudden we heard steps that sounded unsure, they clearly came from the outside of our window. I looked out the window and I recognized my oldest sister, Peshia Riva.

She came near us and asked if we were still alive and if there was anything she could do. She couldn't stop crying. I comforted her by saying, "You have no time to cry now, you must do everything possible to get us out of here. Run home and bring an axe. It would be better if your husband Yerochmiel (Katz) came to help us."

She ran to the house and after half an hour, my brother in law Yerochmiel Katz came with an axe hidden in his jacket. He tried to break the bars but was unsuccessful. He was able to push the axe inside the cell. We took the small chair and stood by the window. We realized that we were very lucky. The bars were attached to the wall by heavy nails. So we started disconnecting the bars one by one, and after a quarter of an hour, we opened a big enough space to get out.

Immediately we ran to the hideout that we had built in Yosef Kremer's barn. We entered the hideout and changed our wet clothes. We tied a wet towel around the head of my friend Leib Mindel, then we lay down on a haystack and fell into deep sleep. As much as they wished to see us, our household members restrained themselves from entering the hideout, fearing that someone would see them. A day passed and only then did Yosha Kremer and my sister Peshia Riva enter, visiting us the next day during dusk. They told us that at nine in the morning a Gestapo troop from Dokshitz had entered town to continue our interrogation. There must have been some turmoil when they found out that the "partisans" had escaped, since immediately the Judenrat head was called and told that if the two Jews did not return instantaneously, they would annihilate the entire Jewish community.

The members of the Judenrat immediately went to look for us but they couldn't find us since only my family and the Kremer family knew of our hiding place. The Saturday passed on the Jews of the town with extreme panic. The Gestapo was in town the entire day, and during the evening they left. For the time being, nothing happened.

On the 28th of March 1942, the Germans did what they promised. The first massacre in Dolhinov occurred on that day. Would they have not done it if my friend and I had sacrificed ourselves? Looking at other towns' experiences, it doesn't seem like it would have made a difference.

I'm not going to write much about the massacre since I was not a witness to it, and others who witnessed it can write much more about it. I only want to say that one fact that must be cleared: the head of this action was a Brigadier Weiss who came specially from Vilna per the instructions of General Koba, the head commissar for Belarussia, from his headquarters in Minsk. A few local Christian thugs joined them.
During the entire day of the massacre, we sat in the hideout in the barn of Yosef Kremer. With us sat my mother Leiba Haya, my sister Peshia Riva, her husband Yerochmiel Katz, and their three children. (8 people? But he says 18 people were hiding with them? Also Yosef Kremer's family?)

We didn't know anything of what was happening in town, but we could hear horrible sounds. We heard the barking of the Germans' orders and the horrified sounds coming from the people they caught. We heard the steps taken by Jews who were forcibly snatched to be killed and we heard the shots. Through the entire day until the evening we heard the shots. At one point we started smelling burning flesh and burning clothes. Only afterwards did we find out the details of the killing machine.

When we finally left the hideout, after everything was quiet, we saw from afar the flames from burning barns. We could also smell burning fuel mixed with the smell of burning human flesh and clothing everywhere we went. At ten in the evening we escaped the town on our way to the forest. There was a ghastly quiet on all the streets of the town, and we trudged amidst this deathly silence. Among us were Yosef Kremer, my brother in law Yerochmiel Katz, Leib Mindel and I.

We walked in the direction of the forest Shimkitzetzni. We trudged through deep snow. Some of the roads we were forced to take were in open fields. We were successful in not being seen, and around midnight we found ourselves in the forest. The freezing weather and the deep snow beneath our feet made our walk very difficult, while the sky was above us looked as if it...

We were too afraid to put up a fire, so we kept walking around like caged foxes. We were too afraid to sit in one place, fearing that we would freeze to death, so we walked like that the entire night and the next day. We were hungry and tired but didn't know what else to do but keep walking. We couldn't wait until the night hours came so we could return from the forest in darkness. We were arguing about what to do.
Finally we arrived into a little farmhouse at the edge of the forest. We could see that there was a little candlelight in the window. We knocked on the door and the farmer opened it, letting us in. He invited us to sit down. He pulled down the heavy drapes so no one would see us.

He told us that he visited Dolhinov and the Jews who survived were now walking around and no one was disturbing them at this point. So once again we discussed what we should do and how we could survive in this freezing forest with a man who was sick, his head crushed and bleeding. He didn't get any medical care and he was becoming more and more feverish. We knew he couldn't survive in this weather, so we decided that we must return to town for a few days. Once he healed and the weather improved, we would try again to contact the partisans.

When we returned to town, my mother opened the door and let us in. She told us the horrible story of what had happened and we decided to hide in the house and to not be seen since we were "unkosher" for both Christians and Jews. People kept complaining, "If it weren't for Segalchik and Mindel trying to join the partisans there would have been no disaster." Others complained that we had made it come sooner, although we knew it was only an illusion that the massacre could have been prevented.
We decided to hide in the barn. Ten days passed and there was an order that all of the Jews must move to a ghetto that was situated around our street, Borisov Street. There were

explicit instructions about the location of the ghetto. Immediately they built a fence around it with a gate. Policemen from the Judenrat patrolled inside, and the local policemen patrolled outside.

One evening, about 20 young people came to our house to decide how to escape to the forest. I don't remember exactly who was there, but I remember Avraham Friedman and his nephew Mitzia Friedman from Postov, both of them later on were involved in extremely important missions, but we'll return to that later. Leib Mindel and I said that we should take two other people and leave the ghetto and the rest would wait to hear from us. When I asked who would go with us, all of them said they wanted to go.

We had a big problem. How could we go in such a big group? For such a big group, we needed to prepare supplies, and how would we do that? Finally a decision was made that Leib Mindel, Moshe Forman and I would go to a farmer, a friend of Moshe's, for a few days. We would try to connect with sympathetic people in the area and the weather meanwhile would most likely improve and the floods caused by the melting snow would subside. When that happened it would be a better time to take the rest of them, but during the waiting period they would have to store some supplies, gathering up anything they could get their hands on.

We left the town on a dark and rainy night. During an early morning hour we knocked on the door of the farmer, Anatosh, who let us in. He was very gracious and friendly. He suggested that we stay in the village bathhouse, which was 300 meters from his house. He gave us a huge loaf of bread, a stick of butter, and a jug of milk. At ten in the morning, he came again and told us that we could stay there longer since at that point no cars could get to the area as a result of the floods and mud. No sort of transportation was possible here. So long as the snow was melting we could stay there, and once the situation changed he would find a new place to hide us.

We immediately told him that we didn't want him to think that it was just the three of us who needed a shelter. We told him that we had left a group of young men in the ghetto that wanted to get out. He said he wouldn't be able to take care of such a big group at that point, but he promised to go to Dolhinov the next day and bring a note from us to our friends. The note said that on Sunday night, five additional people should join us with food supplies and that we would take them to the bath house.

The next day, when it turned dark we went near the fence of the ghetto. Everywhere we walked we saw a fence made of wood and around it was barbed wire. For a long time we walked around, looking for any place where we could enter. Finally we found a place that we could enter. Since we had to hide, we climbed to the attic in our house so no one would see us. During a later night hour, we went down to send a messenger to tell our friends to come. We told them of the situation and we decided to take the five people with us along with food supplies, and in a few days we decided that some of us would return to the ghetto to get the rest of them, 22 people altogether. The people who went with us that night were Israel Ruderman, Ruben Kremer, Yosef Baksht, Eliau Maisel, and Efraim Friedman (?). We walked through the night, through puddles and little lakes, but fearless since we knew no Germans would attempt to walk outdoors on such a night.

Once we arrived, we started preparing the place for the rest of the group. Three days later, on a Wednesday, Anatosh arrived in the early morning hours and with great excitement he told us that he had heard from a very reliable sources that last night a troop of partisans, wearing Red Army uniforms, had arrived in the village Kamyin. They confiscated large amounts of meat, bread, salt, and grains from the farmers and disappeared to the other side of the river. He said, "It's very clear that there is a partisan troop in the nearby area."

We felt as if a fresh flesh and skin coated our bodies. It was as if we were newborns! We begged Anatosh Zutzman to go and look for the partisans. We asked him to find a way for us to cross the river Vilja and that maybe he could find a boat for us. We told him that as soon as we knew the information, we would be able to leave the hiding place.

We didn't need to beg him for long. He left and the next day, and at two in the afternoon, he returned, brimming of merriment. Everything he heard was the honest truth, he said. Every night, the partisans crossed the river armed with automatic weapons and grenades, and there is already a large number of them in the area.

In the evening we walked to the ghetto to let the rest of our friends know the wonderful news. We asked that they all come. The next evening, only Mitzia Friedman and Eliyau Maysel came with us, but we arranged with them that at midnight we would get the rest of them out of the ghetto from behind the barn of Haya Heshka. We would break two or three pieces of wood there and from there the rest could come. We would all meet in the Russian cemetery. Everything was planned, but the plans didn't quite work out as we wished.

On the same day of April after we returned to the ghetto, a large number of cars of the Gestapo arrived at the police station in Dolhinov. Only moments after deciding on a plan we were told that police and Gestapo surrounded the ghetto, making it necessary for us to go to a hideout. I decided differently. I said that we must find a way to get them out. We must look for an escape route. I left to look for such a place and encountered three friends, Yehuda Ginsburg, Mikhail Lankin, and Avraham Friedman. Avraham told me that he had made an agreement with two of the local police, Meltzko and Zakhovicz, who were now guarding the ghetto, where they would let him escape as soon as the Gestapo people left. He showed me a break in the fence that he had prepared for his escape. While we were talking I saw in the darkness two people approaching, and I heard someone saying in Yiddish, "Avramil, itz geits arous."

I was very surprised but immediately I jumped after them. We started running and we went for about a hundred meters, when all of a sudden I said to myself, "What did I do?" I had left my friend Leib Mindel. For some reason, I didn't think of Moshe Forman or my mother or my sister. All I thought of was Leib who had gone through so many troubles with me. I stopped and told my friends that I had to return to the ghetto to get Leib Mindel out. Avraham said that this was crazy, but I didn't listen. I returned and waited for the police to pass the opening in the fence, and then entered the ghetto.

I walked quickly through backyards and houses, but no one was to be seen anywhere. I entered the hideout and yelled, "Get out Leib! I found a way out!"

Immediately 12 people left. Leib, Moshe Forman, Reuven Rubin, Arie Liebske, Abba Gitlitz, and Kelman Alperovicz, Yosef Baksht, Molke Ruderman, Eliau Mindel, my brother in law Yerochmiel Katz, Mitzia Friedman from Potsov, and Yehuda Mindel from Plashensitz.

We quickly passed through the backyard into the tract where there was an opening. We couldn't wait for the police to pass the area, and immediately we left the ghetto.

We walked toward the bathhouse of Anatosh Zutzman from the village Falian. We didn't have any food supplies because we had to run fast and we had to leave behind everything we had prepared. And like this we arrived at the new hiding place.

Early in the morning we heard loud sounds of gunfire. We understood perfectly that something awful was happening in town. For three days they annihilated one thousand two hundred men, women, elderly, and babies. The hideout that we prepared under Yosef Kremer's barn was discovered and everyone that was hiding there was shot. Amongst them were my sister and her children. My mother was saved once more; the killers and their helpers did not discover the hideout that we made in the double wall in our cowshed. With my mother there were another 14 people who survived for the time being.

After we found out what the killers did, we were even more resolute about joining the partisans. We walked to the village Kamyin to continue our search for contacts with the partisans. Now we knew very clearly that they were in the area. We entered one of the homes and asked that they connect us with someone with a boat so that we could cross the river. They told us where we could find such person and we went to his house and demanded that he help us cross the river. Since at that point they were already respectful and fearful of the partisans, he accepted our demands. We had fourteen people with us; almost all the people who had left the ghetto with us came. He could only take three or four of us across at a time, so he had to go back and forth to take us all. The river was about 1 kilometer wide and the waters were rough and overflowing that day, making the ride rough.

All night we crossed the river, three at a time. Finally we were all on the other side. Here we felt much safer and with great anticipation we waited for the meeting with the partisans. One day, when we searched the Malinkowa Forest for them, a partisan unit stopped us. They yelled in Russian, "Stop! Who's coming?" It was clear to us who they were, so we said "We are friends, we are Jews from Dolhinov."
We were ordered to wait and not to move until the unit commander arrived. We waited with eager hearts. The commander arrived and was informed that there was a group of Jews there. He said,
"So you are from Dolhinov? Do any of you know Ivan Matyovich Timczok?"
"I know him very very well," I answered with great confidence. "And just like I know him, everyone else here knows him because he was our employer in the sobkhoz."
"Soon you will meet him," the officer told us, and he went about his business. With our hearts racing, we waited for the exciting meeting. I knew Timczok as a very warm and

loving person. All through the time when Moshe Forman and I worked in Zviyara sobkhoz, a ranch used to raise silver fox, I worked as a supplier of feed for the foxes and Moshe was the accountant. Timczok was not just our manager but he was a true friend. And now they were asking if we knew him? Tears came to my eyes and when I looked at Moshe, I saw that he was practically crying from happiness and excitement.

We waited for a few long hours and around six in the evening we saw three people dressed in green uniforms, coming from afar. As they came closer we could see that they had Mauser pistols that they wore on their hips in holsters made of wood. Two of them were looking through binoculars and then all three came in our direction. When they came about twenty meters from us, we stood at attention and our hearts were shaking with excitement. Moshe and I immediately recognized him. He came towards us and shook our hands and kissed us. I could see that he was extremely excited and he had tears in his eyes. He was a man with a very warm soul. He was a friend and lover of all people. Many will tell about all his deeds and forever people of our town will talk about him, and not only our town's people, but people from the entire area. With his help, hundreds of Jews were saved from certain annihilation in the shtetls and the ghettos. Timczok couldn't stop asking about every minute and vital detail. How were we saved? Which of the people he knew were saved? Who was annihilated and missing? He was particularly saddened at hearing of the loss of Mikhail Lankin and his brother in law Chonka. "Takya raviata inimogli spastasa," meaning such great guys and they couldn't save themselves? It is true that these two guys were strong and fearless guys but they were not lucky guys. They perished.

For a while we continued the conversation and he asked how many of us were here. 14 men I said. "Very well," he said. "For now you will be nearby along with another group of 22 Jews from Dolhinov. We will bring you there soon. Rest for a day or two, then we will see what we can do with you. It's very bad that you don't have any weapons, but we will see. For now we must part, but we will see you later."
He called the unit commander and told him to take us to the other Jews in the forest. The commander took us through a path in the forest and finally we arrived at a place where there were two tents camouflaged with tree branches and leaves. Near the tent there were two barrels tied to tree trunks and under them was fire. They were cooking food there. As we came near we recognized Chana Leib Bronstein, who was stirring the food, and Eliau Maisel was standing as a guard. I cannot describe our extreme excitement at realizing that there were other survivors from our town. As I found out that the same night we left, with Anatoz Tutzman, there was a group of 15 people lead by Eliau Maisel who escaped the ghetto using the darkness of the night. On the way to the forest they met with Avraham Friedman and a few other guys, and together they were 22 people. As we were talking, the food was ready to eat. About 15 people ate from each barrel.

Not everyone had utensils to eat, so we made some utensils from sharpened pieces of wood and we stuck them in pieces of cooked meat. The atriad commissar (political officer) distributed the meat to us. This was our first partisan meal, under the sky in the heart of the woods. It was a true "picnic" in the midst of nature. The people who we met were Avraham Friedman, Mitzia Friedman, Eli Maisel, Chana and Raia Brunstein, Mulke Koritzky, Haya Shulkin, David and his brother Avraham Itzhak Shuster,

Yosef Kremer, Shmeryl Friedman, Hirschel Katz, Goodman and Rubin, Gershon Gordon, Elka Gordon, Velvel Zaev Minkel, Minka Chana Mindel, Etka and Razel Mindel, and Epelbeim, a refugree from Warsaw. At night we slept next to them and we stayed there for a few days.

AMONGST THE PARTISANS

Two days later, in the afternoon, a runner came with an order that Eliau Maisel and I must immediately report to the atriad's headquarters. We followed his order and came running. At the headquarters we met the head of the Nardony Mastitya (the Revenger of the People, the partisan group's name), "Uncle Vasya" met us. With him were Timczok, the political commissar of the brigade, and the head of (something else?) Major Sirugin, a very pleasant and talented person. We were asked to choose among our group 10 people who knew the area very well. They said that a unit would go into Dolhinov that night to take control of it, and they had to have people who knew every corner of the town.

Then ten people would be divided amongst the different units. They would send five units of partisans, and we would be their guides to take them to their targets. Moshe Forman and I were going to guide Unit One of Troop B, which was headed by a Paponov with thirty fighters. The entire atriad contained one hundred and sixty people.

The five units arrived at the meeting point one kilometer from Dolhinov and were ordered to wait until 11 o'clock, and at that time they were to disconnect all the phone lines. All the units were supplied with axes and saws to cut down the telephone poles and to disconnect the lines. Each one had an exact destination. One at the entrance of Kriviczi Street, another on Vilejka Street, one in Dokshitz Street, one in Vilija Street, and one in Budslav Street. The sawing and the disconnecting of telephone lines made a lot of noise, which made the Germans realize that something was happening. They immediately organized themselves in defensive positions, so we lost the element of surprise and the enemy was prepared.

When Moshe Forman and I arrived at the police station with our units, we found it empty. After we threw a grenade, we broke in and found the place clear of any people. We put up lights and started looking. We could see that the members of the police had escaped hastily. We found hats on one of the beds, and we also found clothing and shoes and so on. Near the entrance to the 2nd room of the police station, we found 14 German rifles, amongst them the German rifle that was broken after they clobbered me with it when I was arrested with Leib during our first attempt to escape to the forest.

I cannot describe how happy we were to see this treasure of rifles there. The atriad was very needy of weapons, of which we had a very limited supply. All of us, the Jews, had no weapons other than my pistol so you can comprehend how happy we were to have not only rifles, but German ones. When we got out of the police station, we could hear constant, powerful gunfire from many directions. One came from the direction of Dr. Sadolsky's house, the place where a German communications unit was living. There were 11 soldiers, and at their head were a sergeant and an officer. As we found out, they were able to gather all the policemen from the station, about 15 people. All the Germans carried automatic weapons and they were able to defend the building. When the unit came near the house, they lit up the area with rockets and they fired on us constantly. In spite of it, a few units tried to approach the house, but they were not very successful. The other units decided to retreat and our units also took some losses. Right under my feet, the politruk fell dead, and another partisan was gravely wounded. I was only able to shoot a few rounds. First, I didn't have much ammunition, and second I was ordered to take one of the wounded away from the battlefield. So ended my first combat under fire, and soon after the operation ended for the rest of them.

The atriad Nardony Mastitya had lost five of its troops. The wounded were taken care of except for one gravely wounded man who we were not able to reach. This operation taught us that it is hard to have great successes if the enemy is prepared. Also, most of us were not really experienced and had little ammunition, but in spite of it all it was very successful because now we had 14 rifles and much ammunition. For us, the Jews from Dolhinov, it was extremely successful since those rifles were given to those without weapons. So now Avraham Friedman and I received two excellent rifles. Still, because the operation didn't achieve all it had set out to achieve, we had to retreat with the entire Mastitya since we knew there would be an immense German brigade coming to the area to destroy the partisans. There was no sense in staying nearby so all the units, including our group, were ordered to get out of the "Yellow Beach" (zashlati bjerg?) in the forest of Malinkowa and to go east. The retreat took place the day after operation, starting at dusk. All night, the troop of Mastitya jumped like rabbits, we jumped in weaving paths so that the Germans would not be able to recognize where we were going. I must tell you that just before the retreat, a few hours prior to the departure, all the Jews who came with us were accepted to the partisan brigade and were divided among different units.

So now we became full-fledged partisans and we started getting accustomed to the new units. After three days there were rumors spreading all over the atriad. People whispered that here in the meadow there would be gifts from Moscow dropped by parachute. Real treasures: supplies for the unit. To tell you the truth I did not really believe it. I saw it as the imaginations of dreamers. However, I was very surprised when two days later I was ordered to go with the radio operator to help him carry the radio's power supply. We went farther into the thickest of the woods. He took off his load, quickly put an antenna at the top of a tree and then searched for the proper channel to connect with Moscow. He received a message that this evening a plane would arrive by the meadow between Kriyesk and Lagozina and drop presents for Nardony Mastitya.

At midnight we could clearly hear the sounds of a rapidly approaching plane. After a short time it passed by our forest. It went around the area where we stood, circling a few times and then it turned back east. Shortly after, the special unit came from the meadow. As they came near we could see that many of the partisans were holding heavy containers on their backs. We were rewarded with ten automatic rifles, two machine guns, and a large number of (ask brother about this? What kind of equipment?) bullets for Russian and German rifles. I myself got a little bone: ten new bullets that were shining like gold. So now I had a rifle and a large supply of ammunition.

That morning, the atriad's scouts announced that a large force of Germans had arrived at Lagozina and Kriesk. Immediately we got an order to move. It took a few minutes for everyone to get prepared. Before we left, Uncle Vasya made a short speech.

"The agents of the enemy announced to all the headquarters in the area that tonight we received weapons from Moscow and maybe also extra units. It seems like the Germans are going to launch an offensive against us. We must immediately disappear in spite of the inconvenience and the danger. We are not yet ready for frontal battles with the enemy, but if we do encounter them, we must listen to the officers and not retreat in panic. I am sure that we will all move together as one brave unit, fighting alongside one another, shoulder to shoulder, until the last bullet."

Immediately afterward, the entire atriad left, one by one, in one long line through the forest. Obviously the scouts at the head of the line were armed, as were those at the tail. All day long we walked through the forest and we hardly used any paths through open fields. At dusk, around six o'clock, we arrived at Paranalina, in the area near Lagyosk and Plashensitz. We did as the general ordered when we get to a new base. We settled with each of the different units. Here the entire troop of Mastitya felt at home. There was much more safety since we were farther east, closer to the protection of the powerful Red Army.

The night passed quietly and no one disturbed us, so we could rest from the long walk. The next day, a small detachment headed by the officer Mayelnikov, went for non-military operations, meaning they appropriated food from the peasants for the atriad. We came to the ranch of Borosky in Sharkovichzina near the town Hatzinzin. As we arrived there we were treated with great respect. This was the first time where we felt like we were the bosses. We confiscated many supplies; cheese and other dairy products, flour, grains, all in large amounts. We harnessed two horses to wagons and filled them with supplies. We also took five cows and a huge bull, and like that we returned to the base. We were all in a good mood and we ate as much as our hearts desired. Not only did we bring back a large amount of supplies, but we started feeling that we had gotten some revenge over an anti-Semitic landowner. We felt our self-respect coming back. Here people respected us and treated us like equals. They gave us important missions. We felt pride as Jews for the first time since the Germans had arrived.

After three days of rest, the politruk Timczok addressed the entire a triad. We sat in a circle on the ground in the middle of the forest and listened to him. "We are nearing an important day, the Day of the Workers [May 1], the day of the Proletariat, the day of the International Brotherhood of the Working Class. In every place, everywhere in the world, it is a celebration. This celebration must pass for us with victories and military achievement against the invading enemy. We didn't come to the forest to hide from the enemy and to be parasites on the account of the working farmers, or even the few large ranch owners who recently returned to the area under the wings of the enemy. We must attack the Germans and the collaborators in every place that our hands can reach. We must attack the traitorous policemen and the municipal leaders who are enemies of the people."

At 8 in the morning the next day, I was added to a nit of 12 people, headed by Vlodia Kavilin, a partisan who was fearless and extremely energetic. Surprisingly he was an alcoholic but in spite of it, a staunch and brave fighter. He was once an officer in the Red Army. After the war started, he became a POW of the Germans near Molodechno. He escaped from the POW camp and Jews helped him when he arrived at Ilia, especially by Shrage Dagan Solominsky. You can read about it in the Yizkor Book for Ilia. All the people in the towns around us can tell about his bravery and all his deeds.

As soon as he received the order to head the new unit, he arranged us in a line and checked each one of us and our weapons. A sniper by the name of Kozantzov, who was the best sniper in the entire atriad, was added to our unit (along with his special rifle that he had received from the supplies from Moscow). I was designated as his assistant, and I received a backpack with six packages of ammunition. We walked for about two hours, stopping fifteen kilometers from our base to sit down for a meal. Our aim was to arrive at a village Toltaki, between Doshkovitz and Lagyoz, about 40 km from Minsk. In this village there was a huge lumber mill. Originally it was a Soviet mill, but now it was working for the Germans, and big trucks went back and forth to supply the Germans with wood. We arrived there hoping to surprise them and give them a present for the holiday. Our officer Kavilin checked out the place and decided that we would surprise them on a small hill where we could hide and not be seen.

We waited for about two hours and my hands were burning from holding the weapon tight. The hour of revenge was coming. Finally, at around 8, we heard the sound of heavy trucks coming. After 15 minutes we saw two big trucks loaded with boards. Above the boards there was a troop of Germans sitting on each. The trucks came near, Kavilin gave the order and we started firing. In a few minutes we were able to kill all the people in the first truck. They didn't even have time to protect themselves. Now we waited for the second truck, which was about 200 m away. Since there were a lot of supplies loaded on it, the truck moved very slowly and they must not have heard the sounds of shooting.

They stopped when they saw the other truck, but by then it was too late. They just had time to jump. There were about seven Germans and a driver, and we were able to get them. Now Kavilin told us to take clothes and everything we could find from the dead Germans. We took all the weapons and boots and uniforms. Inside the trucks we found many supplies, as well as food that had been stolen from the farmers. After fifteen minutes we left with all the supplies. Before we left, Kavilin shot into the gas tanks and lit them on fire.

Each one of us carried at least 30 kilos of supplies, but we were very happy and excited. We passed through three villages on our way back and we proudly showed the residents the "trophies" that we had taken from the Germans. Since we were wearing German uniforms, a guard unit of the partisans saw us and mistakenly thought we were Germans. He immediately announced a small unit of Germans coming near the base. Lucky for us, the head of the unit that was sent to attack us looked in his binoculars and recognized us. When we arrived, Kavilin jumped to a saluting position and said, "Commander, your order was carried out. We burned two big trucks full of supplies and we killed nine Germans. We took

15 rifles with us, 10 pistols, 940 bullets, 15 pairs of boots, and 19 backpacks full of other supplies."

Three days later, at dusk, there was a siren in all the atriad. The scouts had discovered a large number of Germans driving towards the village Kramnitz. Uncle Vasya ordered us to be ready for action. When night came we started walking through the fields and forests, and took a defensive position in a semi-circular formation from west to northeast, and hid behind the forest. We didn't have to wait long. At six in the morning we saw clear signs of the enemy moving toward us. Soon we saw about 20 cars, each of them carrying German troops, about 300 all together. They seemed to be very confident, thinking that there were no partisans waiting for them in the area. At the head of them was a villager from Maslitza. The traitor. He was their scout. Following him, they walked in groups and arrived at about 50 meters from us when we heard the loud, confident order of our commander, "Ogon!" (Fire).

Gunfire came at them from three directions. They didn't have time to get ready, and they began to fall like stalks of wheat before a reaper. It took fifteen minutes and the entire area was filled with the bodies of the gray-uniformed killers. Very few managed to escape by hiding under the bodies of their friends. But our job was not done yet. As we were ready to pounce on them, another large unit arrived with heavy fire. After half an hour we started retreating, with each unit covering the other. The retreat was done efficiently and quickly, and there was not one man left behind on the field with the enemy victims. During the retreat we had only one loss, which was very dear to me. It was my cousin Mulke Koritzky, a native of Donilovich, the youngest son of my aunt Frieda. He fell victim to the enemy during the retreat. Honor to the memory of a young, brave fighter. After we found his body, we buried him nearby and put a plaque with his name on it to commemorate a lost partisan.

The farmers from the village later told us that the Germans brought 17 trucks filled with bodies to the school, and they called a special medic to come and take care of the wounded, but they were not successful. Being very angry, they caught a few farmers and shot them. Later that night they left the area and went to Minsk.

Logistics and safety issues made the Revenge of the People leave the area for other locations. First the atriad had hardly any ammunition left after the battle, and it became so renowned in the area that we knew that the Germans would try to get their revenge. So we all left for the east, for the marshes and everglades around Borisov, Lapal, and Poloczik. On the one hand, we felt absolutely safe there, but on the other hand, the food supply was very limited. There was already a huge brigade of partisans in the area by the name of Staika, and there were members of that brigade from our area. Amongst others we met our Aharon, Herzl Zuckerman from Kriviczi, the very brave Riva Melamed and her sister-in-law Ester Sussman from Dokshitz. They all had tales of days of starvation and the impossibility of finding food in the area. I decided that staying hungry in the area, I should attempt to check if my wife and baby girl were still alive in the Myadel ghetto So I asked Timczok if I could go west, saying that other than bringing my wife and daughter I would also bring food supplies. Timczok, who was always worried about our safety, was reluctant, but when he realized that no tales of danger would prevent me from going, he offered to let me choose any three men to accompany me and emphasized that I must take every caution in this mission. So I chose Mitzia Friedman and Yuzik Blachman who was known as the Estonczik (a native of Estonia, whom many others wrote about), and also a non-Jewish farmer by the name of Kolke Voroshniko. Our rifles were taken from us and were replaced by personal weapons. We received three pistols from the Nagan (Nagan pistols?). One was from Pistolet, and also we received four hand grenades. We started walking west. After we walked for about 20 km, it was easier to get food supplies and our morale rose.

After three days we arrived at the old Russian-Polish border near Dolhinov and we rested in the village Bakunik. From there I sent the (non-Jewish) farmer Jozef Zraba to Myadel so he could find out the fate of my wife, my daughter, and my in-laws. He returned after two days to tell me that my in-laws, wife, and daughter were alive. That evening, we left Bakunik. We arrived in the farmhouses near Zari and the farmers told us that there were a bunch of thieves who walked around the area and stole and confiscated supplies from the local population, pretending to be partisans. We continued towards the Malishka forest, when all of a sudden we encountered two men. They didn't see us since we walked like partisans, in a line with our weapons drawn.

When we arrived about five meters from them, we ordered them to stop and put their hands up. I asked if they had any weapons and they denied it. I asked Mitzia to check them, and we heard something falling. We looked and it was a small pistol. Mitzia kept searching them but found nothing else. When we asked who they were and what they were doing in the middle of the forest, they said they were looking for a way to join the partisans. We asked for their names, and one said he was Mleczko from Dolhinov. I looked at him closer and realized that he was a known killer and a real bad character who took part in all the actions against the Jews.

We went back to the first farmhouse that had told us of the "partisans" who had demanded gold and money from the farmers, while threatening they would burn the houses and kill the people. Although it was 2 in the morning, we woke the farmer and asked him to identify the men. He said that only yesterday these men had threatened him, and he recognized the gun we had found on them.

We took them out and discussed what we should do with them. As partisans we wrote down the testimony of the farmer and his household and decided to give the men death sentences. We took them to the forest and shot them, and put our reports on their bodies, and started walking toward Myadel via Kriviczi. We asked around about how we could go inside the ghetto of Myadel, and what was going on in town. After a short time we decided that in the evening, Friedman and Dolshenko should go to Postov, and I with the Estonczik should go to Myadel. I sent the wife of Stalyuk with a note for my wife that in the evening time I would wait for them near the Nivisolki cemetery on the outskirts of town. I gave her instructions that she and her parents and our daughter and some other relatives should escape from the area and come to a place where we would wait for them.

After a few hours, the woman returned and told me that that evening, my wife and her friend Golda Yanovsky would come along. Our baby was sick and my father-in-law refused to take her in such a condition, and that he would stay with her. I also learned that my mother-in-law had passed away a few weeks ago. I was very sorry that my child could not come, but I was hoping that in another occasion I would be able to get her out along with my father-in-law.

Around 8 in the evening we waited near the road to Myadel, when all of a sudden I saw two shadows walking toward our direction. I couldn't wait and I yelled, "Batya!" For one minute they seemed to be scared, then they recovered and ran toward us. I hugged and kissed my wife, and immediately we turned to Niviriyeh. We waited a few days for the return of Mitzia Friedman and Kolke Dolshenko, and when they returned they had 13 people who they got out of the Postov Ghetto, among them the sister and brother-in-law of Mitzia, his brother Hanoch and two other brothers; all together 13. Almost everyone survived to this day, except for Mitzia and his brother Hanoch. They were killed in battle in March of 1944. Immediately we left for the east to rejoin our atriad.

Shortly after our return, they organized a big group of Jews who were designated non-combatants, women, and children, to take them past the front and deep into the Soviet Union. The group consisted of sick and wounded partisans, women, old people, etc. Among them was my wife Batya. On September 12, 1942, they left from Biarozvyamast. About 70 people were in this group which was led by Captain Latishyev. Amongst the people who left from Dolhinov were Motel Friedman, David and Avraham Yitzhak Shuster, Yossel Baksht, Reuven Kremer, Leah and Moshe Friedman from Postov, and other Jews from the area. It was not easy to convince my wife Batya to leave. She wanted to wait for her father and daughter, and to stay with me, but I promised her that I would soon take my daughter and her father out of the ghetto.

So the group left. They had to go 1500 km past enemy lines, in freezing conditions, and with the possibility of starvation, in areas that still had some fighting, but they made it. I did as I promised to my wife. After three weeks I went with three other people to Myadel. It was easy to get permission at this time. Again I stayed with my friend Stalyuk and sent a letter with his wife to my father-in-law, telling him to give my baby to her to be taken out. At nighttime they must organize all the Jews in the ghetto and escape to Kunica.

On the road from Myadel to Niviyeri

Stalyuk's wife returned home riding on a black horse, carrying two girls dressed in farmers' clothing. It was my daughter, who was now 18 months old, and the daughter of my brother-in-law, Natashka Istrin, who was five years old. I couldn't wait to take my daughter in my arms and hug her. When we went in the house she told me how lucky she was to be able to take the girls and not be seen. She also gave me a letter from my brother-in-law, Zelig Istrin, that at 10 p.m. he would bring out all the Jews of Old Myadel.

At 10 pm I left with Mitzia Friedman to welcome the escapees. It was a dark and rainy night, and there was a non-stop storm. After getting halfway, we heard loud sounds of people walking and yelled out the name of my brother-in-law Zelig, who I knew would be at the front of the line. Immediately the line stopped and once again I yelled, and when he recognized my voice he ran to me with the rest of them behind him. I hugged my brother-in-law and then we took the entire procession to Niviyeri. Shortly we were in the village, and only now do I realize what a huge mission I took upon myself. All together we had 144 people, mostly old and children. The young men and women didn't survive. I divided them into three groups, one group of 50 I would take east with me immediately. I would temporarily leave the second group in the marshlands between Nayivery and Dumosalvia, in granaries. The rest of the people would be divided for a few days among the loyal farmers, and then the Estonczik would take them east later on.

At a late night hour I left with my group toward the forest of Malinovka and Hodaki. Two days after, all the groups who came with me were added to a group of 150 people that the partisans were taking east, past the front and into Soviet territory. I decided to leave my little girl with me, and I gave her to a farmer by the name of Olga Samonik, from the village Bobrova. The group that left with the Estonczik faced a terrible tragedy. I don't know exactly what happened. Was it a bad judgment by the partisans who took them? But after two days of walking, the procession crossed the river Vilya near the villages Kamyin and Bakonik and decided to rest during daytime, without posting a lookout. Near them was a Polish shepherd with his flock by the name of Jan Ruzayetski, from the village Kamyin. When he realized who they were, he immediately went on his horse to Dolhinov and brought with him the Germans and the police. After a short time, they arrived while the group was sleeping. They opened fire, and only a small number from that group survived. Many old people and children perished.

A few days passed and I found out that the atriad was organizing demolition teams for sabotage missions in the area. I demanded to be a part of it. The commissar smiled when he heard me and immediately agreed to let me take part. Once again he asked me to choose three other fighters, so I took the Estonczik, Kolke Doroshniko, and Mikhail Yitzhak Friedman. On the evening of October 17, 1942, we arrived by the train tracks between Parafianow and Krolevshtchizna, near the village Paraplishtz. At ten, Doroshniko and I approached the train tracks. In minutes we placed a large amount of explosives on the right side of the track. We returned to our position 50 meters away, with the detonator and waited for the train. We heard it coming. When it came near we saw the little light from the first car, and immediately we pulled on the rope (?) and ran. We heard a huge explosion. We ran for 5 km, running until we arrived at a village where we went to sleep. We couldn't wait to hear what had happened. We sent one of the villagers to see the results of our work, and he came back to tell us that there had been a huge amount of destruction and that many Germans were killed and wounded. The effect, it seems, was tremendous: not only had we killed many Germans and damaged or destroyed much equipment, but railway traffic had also stopped for fourteen hours.

The twenty-eighth of October was a happy day. Our atriad moved from the Roskovsky forest to near Niviyeri. We put our base near Karikriznovka, on an island that was known by the villagers as Viyaski Ostrov. I, with my three friends, along with a group who came from Groboki, settled in the marsh area into granaries. There were about 10 others from Dolhinov, others went east, but I was very happy to meet with them.

On the evening of October 31st, 1942, I was called to the headquarters of the atriad when I arrived I found all the commanding officers there. I was asked to sit. Sokholov let me know that a decision was made that part of the atriad would become a national unit that would consist entirely of Jews, and that I would head that unit. We were given ten rifles. We already had five at that point, and also three that needed repairs that had come from Globok. From this point I walked very fast, as if I had extra energy from somewhere. Immediately I made a list and gathered eighteen people and marched them over to headquarters. The commanding officers called the names of each one of the troops and immediately they stood at attention and received their rifles. They added ten other veteran fighters. All of us were extremely excited and I swore to myself that my unit would be a symbol and example of loyal fighters for all Soviet partisans.

I returned to the headquarters and Sokholov, the commander of Nardony Mastitya, let us know about a big operation that the entire atriad, with the addition of the new atriad which was headed by Markov, who was still inexperienced but had a large amount of ammunition and troops. We were told that the next day, on November 1 at four in the morning, the entire atriad would attack the Germans near Myadel. Troop A, headed by Sashka from Rozkov, and guided by me, would enter Myadel secretly through the Niviolsky Cemetery. We were to quietly capture the German bunker there and incapacitate the Germans there. From there we had to go to the gendarme and police station in a two story house, and there secretly and without having anyone discover us, we must wait for Troop B, which would open fire on the Lithuanian troops who were located in the two-story home of Alperovicz.

The first part of my mission was to transport the three Troops of Company A inside the town and try to control the guards without making any sounds. The town was very quiet, as if everyone was asleep. We didn't even hear a dog. Our forces went to the locations, we yelled at the gendarmes and the policemen, "You are surrounded, fascists! Give up!" Immediately they started shooting with every weapon they had. I saw an armed German coming toward us, then Dantzov and I shot him. We kept waiting, but others didn't come. All of a sudden, a messenger came and told us that the commandant of the atriad said that the third troop must temporarily leave the area. We must take anything that could be used for burning and go immediately to the house where the police and the gendarmes were staying, while the other two units covered us. We were to ignite all the houses in the surrounding area, which would then force the Germans to get out of there.

I made a quick decision that we didn't need the entire troop for this mission. I sent Mikhail Yitzhak Friedman and a few men to a nearby field where they could find bales of hale to transfer to the area around the house, and then burn all the nearby houses. It took only 15 minutes and the houses started burning. All of a sudden, I saw that at the top of the church, the Germans were shooting at the people who were collecting the hay. I commanded my unit to open fire on the church tower. I then took Biyanish Kuzinich and another three fighters to put some bales of hay by the church tower to burn it. Then we entered the outpatient clinic of the municipal hospital that was used only by the Germans. We took a large supply of medicine, first aid supplies and dentistry supplies, and then we lit the place on fire.
All the houses around the police station were now on fire, as well as the church and its tower. All of the units now set up positions surrounding the enemy, waiting for them to escape the burning area. Shortly they started running out and we shot them.

Still, the mission was not a complete success. We couldn't come near the Gestapo's Lithuanian and Latvian volunteers since there was constant, heavy fire in their area. Their situation made it more difficult to get to them, for they were in a building that was built out of cinder blocks and the roof was made out of tile. The building contained 125 killers that had the best weapons. They shot at us from every window, and even from the basement. There was one attempt by Company B to get near the house and throw grenades, but it was a failure and immediately three partisans died from enemy fire. For two hours we tried, but we couldn't do it any longer since they were able to notify a unit in Postov that had armored vehicles. At around ten in the morning we could hear the sounds of their vehicles.

Markov's atriad was waiting for the enemy 10 km from Myadel, so the first tank was destroyed by the atriad, but the force was too big, and we knew we must leave immediately. Sokholov announced a retreat of all our forces, but without panic. Although we had to leave five of our troops who were killed since there was no time to take them off the battlefield. The minute I heard the order to pull back, I asked Mikhail Yitzhak Friedman what would happen to the Jews who were still left in the ghetto. He said from what he knew there were still about 86 people, 15 or 16 families, whom the Germans used as specialists. They were made to work for them in jobs like feeding the chickens, cleaning the horses, and other jobs. I knew that they had a death sentence hanging over them. Amongst them was my sister-in-law Shosha Hadash and her five children, whose husband was killed among the 22 young people killed in the first month of the war. I decided to try to save them. I didn't ask for anyone's permission, but I took my two friends, Mitzia and Bianish Kuzinitz, and immediately we ran to the ghetto.

When we arrived we realized that the barbed wire surrounding the ghetto and the fence was not cut, so we knew there must still be some Jews in the area. We broke the barbed wire and the fences with our rifles and jumped inside. Immediately I ran to the window that was covered with sheets, and with my rifle I knocked it in and yelled, "What are you standing here for? Do you wish to die without trying to save yourself? Pretty soon they'll come here and slaughter you like sheep!"

I looked inside and saw on the floor many people were lying down. Some were known to me, some were unknown. "Get up! Run for your lives!" I yelled. "Immediately run to the marshes of Yarmuling, to the Cemetery of Nivisolaiki."

When they heard my shout they started running and escaping. The same as I did, some others did at homes nearby. So this is the way the battle ended. From our side there were five dead from Company B. Amongst them was one Jew from Minsk by the name of Kissel. We also had 13 wounded. The enemy had 33 killed and many wounded. Also there were many (an unknown number) who were killed among the Germans coming from Postov. I felt particularly happy about the 90 Jews that we had gotten out of the ghetto. I was sure that if we hadn't gotten them out they would have all been killed. Some of these Jews could join the partisans too.

During the retreat I passed by a house where a woman who we called Litovka lived. She was half Polish, half Lithuanian. This house was home to one of the cruelest families. The day the

22 young men were killed, she ran all over the streets yelling, "Now the day of revenge on the Jews has come! Let's kill them all so they won't contaminate the town!" I couldn't let it go. I turned back to her house, feeling waves of anger invading my body, preventing me from following the order to immediately retreat. I yelled to open the door and she opened it. I shot her immediately. She fell at the entrance of the house, dropping in a huge puddle of blood. But she was a lucky bitch and she survived. She was respected and adored by the Germans: they took her on an ambulance to Vilna where she had an operation to take the bullet out of her limbs.

The next day, all the officers gathered. Koznitzov, the commissar of the atriad (the politruk), read the order of the day which expressed the deep thanks to all the fighters that did such a great job during the battle. Among the first to get special respect was my troop, and I received a medal, The Red Banner (Flag?) medal. After the war I received it, signed by the head of the Russian Partisans, A. Golky. On the fourth of March, 1942, #982516.

The need to get revenge on all the killers without uniforms who were running free, people who were our neighbors in yesteryear then who later became our killers, could not let go of me. So I used every free day I had to get revenge. First, I asked the commissar to let me find the killers in the village Kamyin. The commissar said, "If we will spend this time taking revenge, we will have to punish about 90% of the population for collaborating with the enemy on the killings. You can go to Kamyin and bring Jan Ruzietski here, but you must not kill him. All I will allow you to do is to beat them up so they will remember that they must respect human beings." I understood his message.

I took with me ten fighters, and we arrived at Kamyin around midnight, but when we knocked on the door of Ruzietski's house, only an old woman was there. I found out that now he was not sleeping here, that he usually slept in Dolhinov. So instead we went to the Novtisky families. They were the people who took the clothes off the dead people they found in Myadel. When they opened the door we ordered them to put lights on and to return everything that they took off the dead Jewish bodies. At first they denied everything, but after we beat them, they started returning things. They brought from the storage place behind the oven clothes that were stained with blood, boots of little children, dresses of women. So we started beating them harder and harder. Three of them we found out later died from the wounds.

A few weeks later, we got revenge on the killer in the village of Dubricka by the name Ignolia. His crime was that in the summer of 1942 he encountered a young Jewish woman from Dolhinov by the name of Reza Musia Schmerkovicz. She had escaped from the ghetto, and when he caught her he beat her up, stole her money, tied her up and tortured her. Then he took her to Dolhinov and gave her to the Germans and the policemen who continued torturing her until she died. We knew also that his daughter had taken part in the robbery and the transfer of the Jews to killers. In February of 1943 we knocked on the door of the killer and again an old woman opened the door and told us that he was sick. I told her that we had a doctor with us who would cure any illness, and showed her David Glasser, who looked like a Red Army commissar. Ignolia was leaning on the oven with his head covered by a wet towel. I ordered him to get up, but he said he was sick with typhus and could not get up. Menashe Kaye and I pulled him by his hair and David Glasser started counting while we beat him with rubber bats while I explained to him why were giving to him this punishment. The next day we found out that 25 policemen in seven cars came and took the killer and his daughter to the hospital in Dolhinov but Ignolia died a day later.

In the middle of March, 1943, I was appointed as the commander of the medical unit, not far from the village Lishinski. In a large house there they had established a sort of hospital to take care of the wounded and sick people from the brigade. Dr. Sigelov, a Jew from Minsk, was the medical director and his helper was Kotler, a Jew who had been able to escape from Dolhinov. I was given 12 partisans with weapons and we had to take care of every need of the wounded, from clothes to food to medical supplies.

Everything went fine until May 15, 1943. On that day, we found out that a large force of the enemy was concentrating in Dolhinov and Kriviczi. All day long new forces arrived in the area. Amongst them were also Ukrainian traitors and Vlassoviches (troops headed by General Vlassov, who betrayed the Soviet Union and took all his troops in the first month of the war in 1942 and joined the Germans). This entire huge army was sent to take care of the partisans. So on the 19th of May, 1943, the fight against the partisans from Minsk to Smolensk to Vilejka, Dolhinov, Kriviczi and Disna and other places began. We fought fearlessly but finally had to retreat to the marsh area between Bihimvol and Borisov and Poloczek. So now there were 16 partisan brigades in the area of Palik and Domzherevicz until June of 1943. Once again we had a problem of collecting supplies for such a big force.

Before the retreat, on the 21st of May, 1943, we started pulling back with the hospital from the forest of Lishinski to the area of Palik. Every day new wounded troops were added. Our brigade, Nardony Mastitya, took defensive positions on the 31st of May on the left bank of the river Brazina. The hospital unit with all the wounded was situated on an island surrounded by the marsh. This was a very convenient place since it was almost impossible to get here, but once again there was a problem of food. We had a very small supply, only about 30 kilos of beans and about 20 kilos of dry bread.

On the evening of June 1, 1943, we knew that we had to leave. The Germans were coming closer and we couldn't stop them. We decided to divide the wounded and the watchers into three groups. The severely wounded had to be left in the area, underground with Dr. Sigolov. The second group of lightly wounded were taken to another island with Dr. Kotler taking care of them. The third group consisted of the very lightly wounded men who could still walk, and the rest of the troop that was watching them, went with me to the deepest of the marshlands. So with me I had ten wounded people who could walk, and a few others, non-combatant partisans, amongst them my friend Mindel, Leib Schreibman, and Leib and Israel Rodoshkovicz, and the niece Nehama, a refugee from Sharko Lish Sitzna. Also coming with us were the two women who worked in the kitchen, Dora Sussman and Sila Solovyechik. We took with us some of the beans and dry bread and went on our way.

After a short time we didn't know exactly where we were. We went inside the marsh without a compass or a map, and with barely enough food. The enemy shot from all directions, and we were standing deep in water. We walked to one direction and if we heard shots from there we went in another direction. We heard shooting in every diretion, and like this we walked for 19 days.

By the fourth day we were practically starving. On the fifth day we came to an island where there was a lot of grass. So we devoured the grass (which was very bitter) but it still it didn't stop the hunger. We forced ourselves to continue walking. Finally, on the 19th of June, 1943, all the shooting stopped and with help I climbed on a tree to see if we could see any signs of human life, maybe some smoke. However, I was so weak that I fell on the ground. Minutes later I said to everyone, "We must continue. Although we don't know where we should go, if we stay still we will die of starvation."

I took a stick to lean on and with all my might I started walking, and everyone followed behind me. I decided to go where I thought was southeast. I knew from memory that the river Berzinov was nearby. We passed the entire day of June 20 like that, and we still didn't find the river. There was a total quietness in the swamp. It was as if it was a huge, never-ending cemetery. In the evening we arrived at a very muddy forest, and I thought it must be near the Berezino River. We sat on the ground and lit a fire and took some dirty water, boiled it, drank it, and then slept.

Finally, on June 25th, 1943, we came to the area between Lashniki and Kraznow to the base. We found out that our old hospital in the forest had been burned by the Germans along with all of the atriad's other buildings. So now we started building everything anew and gathering all the wounded. We found that everyone had survived in spite of the starvation. Everyone in the units of Dr. Sigelov and Dr. Kotler were fine, a few even recovered and went back to fighting. Now I was busy with taking care of the wounded. The entire brigade suffered few losses during that bitter battle in the area of Palik. When they came back I found out that on June 4, 1943, on the third day of the blockade they managed to break out of the ring of surrounding Germans and they only suffered a few wounded who were sent to me.

Now that I was the head of the hospital unit, I was pretty much in control and I could do whatever I wished, so I decided to take revenge on more of the killers. First on my mind was once again Jan Ruzetski in the village Kamyin. We found out from the villagers that he could usually be found in his aunt's house in Kamyunka. Early in the morning we found him at home. When we got to the house his aunt was awake and there was a young man, about 20 years old, who was sleeping. I asked the woman who he was, and she said it was her son. I told her that if that was her son, she would be punished too. She started crying and said that he was not her son, that he was the nephew of her husband. She said that he was afraid to stay in his village so he slept in her house. I took a rope and tied his hands behind his back and took him to a villager in Bakunin and asked him if he knew if this was the guy who called the Germans from Dolhinov. He and everyone else in the area said that this was the one, so now that we had no doubt, I said to him, "You can choose your death. If you will confess immediately we will shoot you. If not, we will cut your flesh off." He kept quiet, so we took him to the river, to the place where the Myadel survivors were killed. I gave an order to tie his legs and open his hands which were blackened by the rope. We threw the other side of the rope on the top of a pine tree and pulled it up. So now he was tied to the tree upside down. We collected some of the torn pieces of clothing taken from the Jews killed because of him that we were still able to find in the area. We gathered some dry sticks lit them on fire. In a few minutes, he turned into a flaming torch. He was burned next to his victims' graveyard. We stuck a document to the burnt pine tree that said, "Revenge of the People."

A few days later we visited the village Parodnik near Kriviczi. This was the first visit of partisans in the area. Until then, all partisans had avoided the area because Kriviczi, which was only 1 km away, had a big force of Germans and their helpers. After they killed all the Jews in the shtetl, they used the village as a road to get to the train station at Kanihanin.

Despite the danger we decided we must take care of the killers, the brothers Mamek Skorot (or Mamek and Skorot?). Avraham Friedman, Bianish Kuzenitz. Zanka Muhammad, and Dinka Treykovski went with me. We came to the first house of the village, "Auf machen!" (?) I yelled. Immediately the door opened and they turned on the light. We ordered them to close the drapes. First we demanded that he return the gold teeth of Hana Katzowitz, which we knew he took out of her body with pliers. They tried to deny it, but we kept beating them. We only beat the two men; the women and children we left alone.

The killers opened graves, amongst them Hana's, the widow of Ishaiau Katzowitz and also the sister-in-law of Rabbi Malkiel Paretzi (the last rabbi of Kriviczi) who was annihilated with the rest of the community in 1942. The brothers opened the graves of her and her children. We received this information from Herzl Rodoshkovicz and Aron Shulman from Kriviczi who were also partisans with the brigade of Kirov.

Now we had to find the killers of the Jews of Dolhinov: Mikhail Proclowicz and the evil brothers Tarahovitz; men who showed no mercy, not even to children. We first had to do some investigating about how we could go to Dolhinov and when and where we could find the killers. Varovka, a villager who hated those killers, found out that Proclowicz had returned to his ranch in Dolhinov. Originally he was too scared to stay there, but after a year had passed and no one had come to repay his evil deeds, he assumed that even the Jewish partisans had forgotten him. Since neither his house nor his family members suffered any consequences, he returned to his home after a year of wandering.

One clear and cold night in December of 1943, Gershon Yafeh and Biyanish Kuzinitz and Dimka Traikovsky went with me on a sled. As we knocked on his window he opened his door dressed in a fur coat and boots. Immediately we ordered him to go inside with his hands up. We turned on lights, and when he recognized us he started shaking. He begged us not to shoot him, but he saw that his death was coming. I asked him how many Jews had he killed and where were all the possessions that he had stolen from his victims. I ordered him to return everything, saying, "If you will return all that we want, we won't kill you. We'll just beat you up."

He called his wife and told her to return all the possessions from the hideout, which he'd buried in a deep hole in the ground, which was covered with snow. We sent one of our men with her to check on it, and we found a large amount of robbed possessions about a hundred meters from the house. I became furious. I yelled, "Confess and tell us how many Jews you killed! How many mothers asked for mercy for their babies?" I started cursing at him violently and uncontrollably. I was crazed. "You must take responsibility and die the death due to an evil and wretched person." I shot him in his head and he dropped dead.

Now it came to the most important mission, the hunt for the biggest murderers, the brothers Tarhovitz. I had a personal vendetta against them. The blood of my mother was on their hands. They took part in her killing and this is how it happened: the day after we raided Dolhinov in 1942, my mother with the two daughters of Katzowitz, Gashka and Nyakha, escaped from the Ghetto and walked in the direction Pogost to the forest where we had our base. The two brothers, together with the head of the police, found out and chased them on bicycles and were able to find them. They returned them to town while beating them and torturing them along the way. After hours of this torture, they were taken near the Jewish cemetery and were shot.

That was not the only murder that they committed with their own hands. They killed many before and after this incident. I saw with my own eyes how they chased the family of Shimshel, the family of Shalom Dukshitzi, and Nehama Leviczi's with her children and other relatives. They were tortured and beaten and I will never forget it. But how could we reach them? They lived at the very edge of Dolhinov and to reach them you had to go through the entire town, next to an old stone fortress that was garrisoned by German troops. Like an angry dragon it spit out fire at all who came near it, and we did our best to avoid it.
Finally I found an opportunity. In the middle of February of 1944 I was called to headquarters. Yoskov, an officer at headquarters asked me to get food and other supplies to the headquarters since they were waiting for very important people to arrive and they had nothing to feed them. It was a difficult time at that point to achieve such things, but after thinking for a minute I said to Yoskov, "There's only one complicated way I can think of for achieving this mission. Since there is no food in such amounts near our base, we cannot do it in one night, but we what we can do is go to Dolhinov and we can surely find food there. But I must have a group of fourteen to sixteen fighters. I can take four from my hospital unit, so I'll need ten to twelve fighters from headquarters. With such a force we can overwhelm them and bring back a large amount of supplies."

The idea pleased him so he gave me permission. He assigned 12 well-armed men headed by Major Tzonkov to go along with me and four from my unit, and left for Dolhinov at six that evening with four sleds harnessed to fast horses. Around 10 in the evening we arrived in the outskirts of Dolhinov. After a short visit with Varovka to gather infomation about the town, we left. At 11 at night we arrived near the large home of the Taharovitz brothers. We put two snipers facing the center of the town to cover us, and immediately we went to work. We ordered them to open up the door, turn on the lights, and to pull down the drapes. Then we made them open up the cowshed and horse stables, which were tightly shut with heavy iron bars. I ordered six of the troops with me to take all the livestock out of the cowshed and stable and to herd them in the direction of the forest. Four men took on the sled all the possessions in the house. It took us half an hour to complete the job, which included four cows and six first-class horses. In the sled we gathered bread, lard, flour, salt, kidneys, beans, and also pillows, blankets, sheets, which had all been robbed from Jewish homes. Before we left, I ordered the Taharovicz brothers to go outside. They were dressed only in their underwear and barefoot, and just as they ordered their victims during the slaughter to run, I made them run in the freezing winter night.

After we left, about half a kilometer from town, a steady stream of fire from the fortress came upon us. They shot at us with automatic weapons, but it was harmless fire. It couldn't reach us since they had no idea where we were headed. They only heard from the wives of the killers that we were most likely heading to Pogost. So without much thinking, I ordered everyone to go on a side road. Immediately we shot the two killers dead. We sat in our sleds and after shooting in the direction of the enemy, we ran away to headquarters. So like this I revenged the blood of my mother and many other Jews who were killed by those evil and cruel men.

When we returned to headquarters, they were very happy to see the food and the supplies and I was assuming that all was well and like that I returned to the hospital. However, the next day early in the morning I was ordered to come to the headquarters of the brigade. When I entered the ComBrig, the head of the brigade, Pokrovski, and Misonov, commander of another brigade that was responsible for the area around Kriviczi and Dolhinov was also there. Immediately I saw they were looking at me in a way very different way than they had yesterday, and I realized that Misonov came here only for me. I jumped to stand at attention and saluted, and announced that the commander of the hospital unit was present as ordered.

"Who gave you the permission to shoot two citizens, peaceful residents?" Asked the leader of Nardony Mastitya.
"No one gave me permission," I said. Then, after thinking for a while I added, "My conscience and my need for revenge gave me liberty to do that. I only did what was my duty, which was to get revenge for my murdered mother and my people who fell at the hands of those two cruel, evil murderers who you called peaceful citizens. They killed my mother, my sister and Jewish brothers. They were wading elbow-deep in the blood of Jews. I had to do it, and I did it as a loyal son to my mother and my nation."
He called his assistant, Kanzow and ordered him to take my weapon and put me in a prison cell until the investigation ended. Stoically, I gave my pistol and under guard I was taken to a prison cell. In the dark mud house, where three other partisans were held prisoner, my heart was aching, but I felt complete with all that I had done. I thought to myself, "Even if they decide to put me under partisan trial, I shouldn't be panicked. I have many, many good friends among the leaders and I have a large amount of achievements with the atriad and the entire brigade. Even in the worst case, if for political reasons or to make an example of me they decide to sacrifice my head and spill my blood, even then, I fulfilled my duty to my mother and my people. I will not be afraid. I will look them straight in their eyes before my death."
While pondering that, after a few hours they opened the locks of my cell and I was called to see the head of the Special Unit, Grishenko, my friend and comrade since he had been one of the wounded in the hospital of the brigade. The same as I was liked and looked up to by all the wounded and sick who we took care of, I was loved and cared for by him, since immediately I took care of all the capricious needs that the patients had. We smiled, always wishing to aid them and to lessen their pain. Even before I talked to him, I felt strongly that

he didn't wish me ill and that he would emphasize my achievements, my service to the people, and my kind regard to the wounded. I knew that my connections would be my shield and my deeds would be my armor against the charges. He asked me for every detail and wrote it down in his file. But before he took me back, he said , "Don't be scared, Segalchik. You must not be worried. Everything will turn out ok."

Once again the doors were opened and I as taken to the office of the ComBrig. Here there were about ten of the top leaders of the brigade. Everyone came to decide what to do with me. Immediately as I entered, a commissar of the brigade by the name of Propieczko, who was formerly in the Red Army and was now sent to us from Moscow, started lecturing me about my crime. "Your crime was very severe as far as the political managing and morals accepted by us. Even if those men deserved a capital punishment, you were forbidden from doing it in such a way. The way you did it vilified the image of our cause and its struggles in the eyes of the population, which is being oppressed by an invading force. I have no doubt that you deserve the most severe punishment. Talking truthfully we must put you through a quick trial here in the field, and I have the authority to give you a summary execution. But when I look at your past, which is clear of all crimes and I take into account all your great deeds and achievements in the fight of our Soviet Union, and consider your service to the brigade of partisans that you belong to, we have decided to forgive your huge crime with a warning that you must never in the future do what you have done." Immediately my pistol and the rest of my ammunition were returned to me.

I returned to the base of the hospital and the heavy shadow of this trial (field trial?) was behind me. I had completed all my personal revenges against the killers of my people, but I still made a vow that I must never forget, and that I should think about every move that I made. From now on I would take care of the wounded, and this is what I did until the happy day of liberation on the 26th of June, 1944. The day we united with the Red Army in the forest of Palik.

In returned to my hometown of Dolhinov, which was now "Free of Jews", together with a few of my fighting comrades. Most of the town had been burned and there was not one Jew left. In spite of it all, we felt honored and proud to be there. Everyone's heart was crying to see the devastation of a town that shortly before had been lively and full of vitality. It had once excited our hearts with its colorful character, giving us once-youthful dreamers hopes a better future, but now it lay under my feet, burnt and silent.
Alone, I walked along the ruins. Nothing was left of my mother's house except for a few blocks. Like this we walked around, a small number of Jews, members of the partisans. The Jews who immediately returned to town were Leib Shreibman, Leibl Flant, Avraham Friedman, Gershon Lankin, and David Mirman. A few days later arrived Yitzhak Radoshkovicz and David Kazdan from Plashensitz, followed by others. Already in the first days we organized a Battalion of Punishment. I was head of it and we looked for the Nazis and their collaborators. Now it was their turn to run and hide. Leibl Flant was appointed as head of the police. Many from the gendarme and the collaborators and Gestapo people were now hiding in the forests. Originally when we recognized Gestapo people we shot them, but soon the authorities ordered us not to shoot them, telling us that we would pay dearly for such things. Now everyone had to be put through a trial, so we changed the system. In

Kriviczi there was a prosecutor from the NKVD so we followed the new orders and brought the criminals and killers to trials. We had good communication with the NKVD prosecutor, which made our job easy.

So like this we stood, a few Jews, lonely and mourning, but also full of anger at our people's killers and the collaborators who would inform on the Jews and incite the killings. We remember and we will remember until our dying moment, every Dolhinov and local area youth that helped to fight the enemy and fell in the battle. Amongst them, Mulke Koritzky, Haya Shulkin, Hyena Shulman, Zalman Friedman, Mordechai Gitlitz, Mordechai and Mina Hadash, Shimon Gordon, Matityua Shimhovitz from Horodok, Shimon Kiednov from Kriviczi, Shimon Meirson, Gershon Meirson ,Mashka Dimmenstein, Avraham Itzhak Shuster, Yisrael Ruderman, Zelig Kuznitz, Mitzia Friedman from Postov, Hanoch Friedman, Faber Levin from Radishkovicz, Yisraelski from Radishkovicz, Itzhak Einbender from Kurenets, Binyamin Shulman from Kurenets, Shpreyergan from Plashensitz, Faber Rodnik from Radishkovicz, David Glasser from Dokshitz, Menashe Kopilovicz. Honor and glory to their memory. May their souls be melded in the bouquet of living (?). We must remember them in every memorial, and our revenge also will be the revenge of their blood. The revenge quieted for a moment the open anger that boiled in my blood, but late at night, all alone, my soul was restless. I knew nothing of my wife and my little girl was not yet with me. I wanted to leave the town, but I didn't know when or where I would go. I still had a duty there, and I felt that my wife was alive and that she would one day find me. But only after half a year, at the beginning of March of 1945 was I able to leave town.

Meanwhile I continued my work with the NKVD in the town. Slowly there were ten families that returned to town. Some were in Siberia, others in the center of Soviet Asia. Some of the families never returned. Others returned and lived in other areas in the area, but I'm sure others will tell their stories. As they came, everyone had a strong desire to leave the area to go to Poland, which was a gateway to other destinations. There was an agreement with Poland and the Soviet Union that anyone who was a former Polish citizen would be allowed to now leave the Soviet Union to go to Poland, so everyone went there, but no one thought of staying in Poland. It was just a station on the way to other places.

I knew that revenge was not a long term mission for me. At the end of October 1944 (?) I was called to the SlaSoviet, which was the town committee in Dolhinov. The head of the committee gave me a postcard and said, "Segalchik, your wife is alive!" With great excitement and with shaking hands I read the postcard which was written from Stalingrad, and my heart took flight (?). I immediately answered but didn't receive a response and again we were disconnected. At the beginning of December of 1944 I finally received another postcard asking if I was still alive. She was now in Yaroslav and the communication was easier. I started arranging for her to return. As a worker for the NKVD I was given permission to go and I brought her back. I found out that my father-in-law had died in the forest while among a camp of those who had fled Myadel. My daughter, who I left with farmer friends was returned to me. She was returned before my wife came so I put Briana Katz in charge.

Briana Katz, a woman in her 70s, was saved from one of the actions. She succeeded in escaping from town and hid with a Christian woman farmer in the village Miltzia. She stayed there for a long time, but when the woman said that she couldn't take care of her anymore, she came to the forest since she had heard that there were Jews from Dolhinov hiding there. Amongst them there was her nephew Gershon Yoffe. She was amongst the partisans near Malinkowa, and she was ready to go with a big group of Dolhinov Jews past the front lines and into Soviet territory, but the day that they were ready to leave there was a surprise attack by the Germans. Briana was wounded during the fighting and was left amongst the bushes in the forest. The enemy did not see her, and like that she stayed there for a few days.

The partisan atriad retreated during that attack to the forest but returned after a few days. One of our scouts by the name of Dobiniewicz found her and told us about a wounded woman in the forest. Avraham and I immediately went there and found her lying down with a bullet in her leg. Immediately we brought water and we found some first aid materials from a farmer. We washed her wounds and took care of her. She said to us, "If you want to keep me alive and save me, you must return me to a farmer in Miltzia." So we took her that night on a wagon to that village, and told the farmwoman that she must take care of her and keep her alive. The farmwoman made the sign of the cross and swore to us that she would do whatever she could.

After one month we came to visit her and she was in better shape and able to walk. We took her to our base and appointed her to work as a non-combatant cook under the supervision of the partisan Saponov, who had been an officer in the Red Army. And like this she passed her days during the war. Eventually she immigrated to Israel and had about 20 grandchildren. She died at a very old age in a kibbutz among loving children, grandchildren, great-grandchildren, and kibbutz members.

Imprisonment and Trial

Until 1948 I served in the NKVD that was led by Goroshkov. I as well as other Jews were treated very fairly and with much trust by the management of the NKVD in the area as well as in Minsk (the Belarus capital). This allowed us to keep a political reputation that was squeaky clean. On the other hand, the local militia showed clear signs of anti-Semitism, but our relations with the NKVD prevented us from experiencing any direct harm from this anti-Semitism. However, in 1948, Goroshkov left the area when he was appointed to another post, and Kaviljuk became the chief of the NKVD in our area. He didn't have a very strong personality or great influence, but he was still easy to get along with. Since he liked to drink, he delegated most of the jobs to assistants, but he didn't stay in this position for very long. A new head was appointed and after that our situation changed. Slowly they started demoting us. In Minsk, a man from Gruzia (Georgia) named Tzanova, who was an associate of Stalin and Baria, was appointed to the head of the NVD (Ministry of Internal Security) and he was responsible for all of the officers in Belarus. He made trouble for all Jews, but particularly for us, and anti-Semitism flourished everywhere. At the end, this Tzanova was shot after Stalin's death.

With the change of the political climate, I was fired from my job in 1948. I was called to headquarters and asked by the chief if all of the details that I had given when I had to fill out the questionnaire were correct. Then I was asked when my sisters and brothers had left the country, and I told him that they had left before the war. I gave him all the information he wanted. Later he called me in again and said, "Segalchik, you're fired. The last instructions we received from central headquarters were to fire anyone who had relatives outside of the country." Clearly this rule hurt the Jews, especially those in important positions.

Shortly after that, someone instigated another investigation. After I built my house in Radishkovicz, people were envious and suspicious. I saw the house of my father-in-law in Myadel, and as a former partisan I was able to get wood free of charge. To hire people was not expensive at the time, and once in a while I was helped by a German POW who worked for us taking care of horses. Part of the case against me was the abuse of POWs for personal enterprises.

So, my wish to have a decent home caused me to now be a prisoner in the Soviet Union. I lost my freedom, I lost my right to be a free citizen in the state that I gave my life to while fighting the Nazi enemy. After receiving my sentence in Minsk, I was transferred to a prison in Gormel. This was only a temporary holding tank. There were thousands of people there, including many Jews. I was lucky I stayed there for only a short time. From there I was sent to Arkhangelsk, a town near where the Devina River flows into the White Sea, to work in a hard labor camp. Afterwards I was moved to another camp in the area, and we worked very hard. While there, I befriended a prisoner who was a barber who offered to teach me some basic barber skills, telling me that you never know when you might need them. We would take and carry wood pieces from the river in a bridge building project, and sometime later, about 400 prisoners including me were sent to Murmansk.

For a short time I continued on the bridge building operation, but I decided to befriend the barber in this area who was a nice man. I gave him a present and he took me to work with him. I worked with him for a year and a half, so my circumstances greatly improved although I was still a prisoner.

Meanwhile, my wife and my children (now I had a son too) were left without even minimal financial help. They were about to get kicked out of the house I had toiled to build. A sole woman with a five-year-old girl and a three-year-old son. My wife protested and at the end only half of the house was confiscated by the authorities. They let her stay with the children in the other half. But how could she supply the children with food and other needs? Here my loyal friend Leib Mindel helped us a lot. He supported my family through all the years that I was in prison, and always made sure to send me food at the different prisons and hard labor camps where I stayed. My friend, Leib Mindel, could not rest. He kept trying to improve my family's situation. After much pondering he decided to approach Timczok, who had a high position in Minsk (some central planning agency?).

The commissar of Mastitya, a dear friend, saved me. He angrily questioned Mindel on why he didn't come sooner. Immediately he wrote a request for a pardon to the President of the Soviet Parliament (the Supereme/Superior Soviet?) citing my exemplary fighting record while with the partisans during the Great Patriotic War. He also described all the awards and medals that I had received. Timczok received a positive reply shortly after and he immediately called Mindel and informed him of the news. Mindel sent me a telegram and two days later we received the announcement in the camp. I was called to the head of the camp on May 1956 and released from the prison where I had been since 1949. So I returned to my home, my wife, and my children in Radishkovicz. I started bargaining with the people who lived in the other half of the house and finally I got them to leave. Again I was a homeowner and I started working, but very soon we all realized that life there was capricious and that we were always in danger. There was no future for us there, not in Radishkovicz, not in Dolhinov, and not anywhere in this area. Not even the place of my birth and uprbringing, Dolhinov, could keep me there, for at that point I only visited it on days when there was a memorial to the martyrs.

At the end of 1956, once again there was a permission granted for people who were residents of Poland prior to 1939 to return to Poland. Immediately we asked to get permission, but it was not easy. The Belarusian authorities didn't permits to any Jews in the area until 1958. A few Jews left from Radishkovicz and today they are in Israel. I didn't want to wait for my turn so I sold my house in 1957 and moved to Vilna, the capital of Lithuania, since citizens of Lithuania seemed to have had an easier time in leaving. I was not able to receive a permit to live in Vilna, so I registered in Novo Vilejka, which was very close to Vilna. I rented an apartment in the resort town of Volokopa (?).

I started taking care of the needed passports and papers and a Jewish friend helped me receive the appropriate documents from the person who headed the passport division. As you might guess, I had to bribe them. Finally, at the end of November 1957, we were able to leave Vilna for Poland. We stayed for one month in the repatriatza point and then we were sent to Vorstlav/Breslau, where we rented an apartment. To get a free apartment we were supposed to go to Zinov but we didn't want to wander around.

Finally, on October 20, 1958, we arrived in Israel. It would be very difficult for me to express the deep emotions I had when I arrived in the country. A few years later I had a successful farm with cows and other livestock. With the hard toil of my wife and son we were very successful and I was able to give an education to my children. It seems like everything was fine. We were well-established as farmers in the Moshav. It seemed that no dark clouds would come to our lives. We would see happiness in our children and grandchildren. But this was not to be. I became very sick, terminally ill. I had to sell my place and move to a desert climate in Arad. Still, here I will hold to my country until the last day that is given to me. I will continue communicating with my partisan friends, my brothers in arms who gathered here. We will all continue to gather for memorials for the martyrs of Dolhinov, Myadel, and other towns in the area. We will not forget and deny the past. It will be alive in our very beings for eternity and we will plant a seed of its memory that would be grounded in our children and grand children.

PHOTO ALBUMS

The Bernstein Family

Azriel Bernstein Family   **Myadel 1934**
Top Row-left to right:
Chyena Bernstein -Azriel's wife
Azriel Bernstein
Zalman Bernstein
Yoseph Bernstein
his wife - Rivka Bernstein

Middle row: his father -Maishe Nordechai Bernstein
his mother- Chaya Keila Bernstein
Rabbi Zelig Sorasky - grandson of Maishe Mordechai (from his first wife) came from USA to study in Mir Yeshive . He visited his family in Myadel.
Luba Katzman (Bernstein) - the daughter of Shimon and Asne Bernstein
In front: Avram Itze - the son of Yoseph and Rivka Bernstein

Shimon Bernstein family   Myadel 1934
from left to right : Asne Bernstein,
son Shmuel Biran (Bernstein),
Rabbi Zelig Sorasky,
daughter Luba (Bernstein) Katzman
Shimon Bernstein

Myadel 1929 -
Yoseph and Rivka Bernstein and their son Avram Itze

Group Photographs in Myadel

On the front steps of Alperovich family (Shlomo & Rivka) house. The children are dressed in school holiday dresses.

Upper step from left : Dvora Kosczevsky, Yitzchak Alperovitch and Chaya Dvora Dimenstein.
Second step from left: Benyamin Alperovich , Zalman Alperovich (Yitzchak's brothers) and Shepsl Dimenstein (Chaya Dvora's brother).
First step from left: Sima Alperovich (Yitzchak's sister) and Perel Kosczevsky (Dvora's sister)

Estrin family in the early thirties
Sitting from left to right : Chaim Sholem Estrin, his wife Raizl, their daughter Chana Rachel, her husband Tuvya Chadash. Standing from left to right the other 6 daughters: Frieda, Bela, Braine, Pesya , Rivka, and Sarah. The children of Tuvya and Chana Rachel: Dvora Kraiczman and Yoseph Chadash who gave me the pictures.

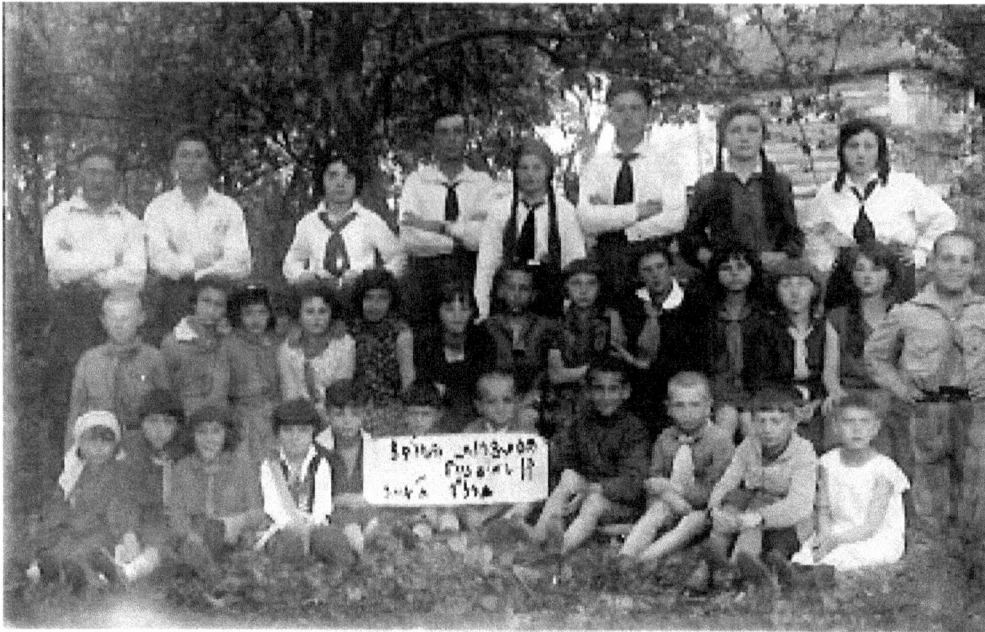

Ken Hashomer Hatzir from 1932 (chet iyar ,taf raish zadi bet)I

Upper row from right: Rivka Estrin (Householder #33) Chaya Gaishe Mindlin (Householder#56) Berl Rubin (Householder #65) Dina Gotkin (Householder #11) David Chadash (Householder #61) Pesya Estrin Householder #33) Itze Vele Friedman (the son of Ester Alperovich) *, Yoshke Roczaisky (Householder #25.

Middle row from right : Hershl Chadash (Householder # 64) Rachel Chadash Householder # 7) Sima Shvimer Householder #12) Hadasa (Hodke) Geller (Householder #18) Ester, the barber's daughter (left Myadel before 2nd w.w.), Chaya Dvora Dimenstein#2, Shilem Chadash # 61, Yente Rubin #65, Malka Shulman (Householder#21) Laike Katz (Householder #38) Dvora Kosczevsky Householder #55) Faige Gotkin Householder # 11) Gershon Finkelstein (Householder #32)

Bottom row from right: Shainke ? , Faigale ? (sisters, surname unknown, father Baruch - the hats-maker, left Myadel before the 2nd w.w.), Alperovich Borech Chaim (Householder #28) Nachman Shulman (Householder #21) Yitzchak Geller (Householder #18) Unknown , Bashe Raichel (Householder #31) Blooma Vitkin (Householder #20) Perel Kosczevsky (Householder #55) Gitl Chadash (Householder #47) Rachel Geskin (Householder #10)

* *house was forgotten in the map.

Meeting of youth from Myadel, Kurenitz and Smorgon on lake Miastro. (in the early thirties)

Photographs collection of Chaya Lupinsky

Chone Menkis - d. 1938.
The photo was sent to his daughter Basia in Canada.

Shulamit Chadash 08.08.1938
2 years old the daughter of Tuvya and Chana Rachel Chadash

Frieda Estrin Enoch -1967

June 12 1934
Chadash Children from left to right: (the children of Tuvya and Chana Rachel Chadash) Yoseph
Chadash (6) and Dvora Chadash (8)
(the daughter of Zusya and Chava Chadash) Shainke Chadash

A Survivor's Story: Silent No Longer

I.   A Survivor's Story: Silent No Longer

Born in Vilna, Poland (now Belarus) in 1935, Linda Schwab spent her earliest years in the lakeside resort town of Mjadel, where her father, Henry Swidler, ran a successful dry goods store. She says that while her father's business prospered, he also became known for his generosity.

"If someone came for fabric – like one woman who needed to make her daughter's wedding dress – but didn't have enough money, he would tell them to take it anyway," Schwab said. "He would tell them, 'When you have money, you will pay me.'" He allowed the hungry and poor to get milk from his cows and to take fruit from the orchards on his property.

The family's serene life ended abruptly in 1941 when Germany invaded Mjadel, forcing the Swidlers and other Jews to leave their homes and move to a ghetto. Though only six years old, Schwab clearly remembers being forced to wear a yellow star on her clothing designating that she was Jewish.

She also remembers watching through a window as Jewish men were tortured, not knowing if her father was among them. And, she remembers her aunts "tearing at their hair" in grief when their husbands were killed.

Henry Swidler was spared and managed to gather his wife, his three children and his sister and her daughter and flee to the countryside. There, a Christian farmer whom Swidler had helped many times risked his own safety to hide the family in his basement. When this arrangement became too dangerous, the family fled to the forest where Swidler, again aided by the farmer, dug a cave in the ground, taking care to dump the extra dirt in the river so it wouldn't be seen, and covering the entrance with trees and brush.

Schwab and her family hid in the forest for two long years. At safe times, the adults told stories – she remembers her father telling Bible stories. Her mother taught the children arithmetic and poetry. Neither Schwab nor her brother, Harold, recall playing. At night, her father would return to the village, foraging for food and returning with bread and potatoes.

Other times were not safe. Schwab recalls once hiding among brush piles and haystacks, listening to the sounds of German soldiers advancing as she lay with her cheek pressed to the ground. Her father spooned rain water from a puddle to quench her thirst while they waited.

Suddenly, she heard an order shouted. "Turn right." The soldiers changed course and the family was spared again.

Soon after, the family learned that the Russians, who they felt would save them, were approaching nearby. Schwab described the jubilant scene in a Harrisburg Patriot News interview in 2001:

"With that, he [her father] ran back to get all of us. Can you picture this? It's April, just getting warm. All of us went running to the road. No one is hungry. No one is thirsty. No one is scared. You forget about everything else. We were liberated."

II.   Making a New Life

After the war and fearing life under Russian rule, the Swidlers again fled, this time taking a train to Berlin, Germany, and hoping to settle eventually in Israel. The family instead landed in Foehrenwald, a displaced persons camp in the American zone of occupation in a small town near Munich. The U.S. Holocaust Museum lists Foehrenwald as one of the largest Jewish displaced persons centers in the American zone and describes it as having had a "rich educational and cultural life." There, Schwab first went to school and learned how to speak Hebrew and several other languages – Russian, German, Belarusian, and Yiddish – as she encountered people of many backgrounds.

The Swidlers spent three years at Foehrenwald before deciding to travel to America where Linda's mother had relatives. U.S. policy required immigrants to have a sponsor, so Mrs. Swidler wrote to her cousin David Schwab in Binghamton, N.Y. He agreed to sponsor them and brought them first to New York and then to Harrisburg, where he had relatives. The Swidlers created a new life in Pennsylvania and Linda eventually married David's son Morris, her husband of 23 years who passed away in December 2006.

III. *Preserving History*

For many years, Schwab was uncomfortable talking about her Holocaust experience. Finally, in the early 1990s, at the urging of educators including professors at Penn State Harrisburg, she publicly recounted her story for the first time – to an auditorium of school children at a Christian school in Harrisburg.

"They were studying the Holocaust," she explains, "and the school wanted someone without a heavy accent to speak to the children so they would understand. How could I say no? After all, I was their age when it all happened. It hurt me to talk about it, but the experience was unbelievable." The children and their teachers listened intently and asked questions eagerly.

Schwab said she began to realize it was important to tell the story of the Holocaust so it would not be forgotten as the generation that experienced it firsthand passes on. In the 1990s, she also participated in Steven Spielberg's Shoah Foundation project to chronicle Holocaust survivor memoirs worldwide. Today, the foundation has compiled an archive of nearly 52,000 testimonials in 32 languages.

Schwab also stresses the importance of young people, Jews and non-Jews, learning about the Holocaust. "They are the bridge to tomorrow," she says.

To that end, Schwab and her husband Morris helped create an endowment fund named Gesher L'Machar, Hebrew for "Bridge to Tomorrow." The fund supports local teenagers who wish to participate in the March of the Living, an annual trip to Poland and Israel to study the Holocaust. The Schwabs also established a Holocaust essay contest in conjunction with The Patriot-News that awards scholarships to winning writers in middle school and high school.

And now, Schwab has made a permanent commitment to telling the Holocaust story. Through a generous donation to Penn State Harrisburg, Schwab and her late husband have supported creation of the Schwab Family Holocaust Reading Room in the college library. To be dedicated later this year, the reading room will be the college's Holocaust and Jewish Studies Center focal point, housing resources and preserving local connections to the Holocaust. Mrs. Schwab said Penn State Harrisburg was the ideal place to establish the reading room because it recognizes their family allegiance to Penn State – Morris Schwab was a 1940 University Park graduate and active alumni volunteer – at the University's campus closest to Harrisburg, where she has spent most of her life.

Schwab's decision to speak and her extraordinary steps to ensure that a history of the Holocaust is preserved in Central Pennsylvania are particularly relevant and timely. As recently as this past winter, Holocaust revisionists – those who believe the Holocaust did not occur – continued to make news headlines worldwide.

Linda Schwab is a witness to history and a survivor.

"I felt I was left alive – I was saved by God," Schwab says, "so that people will remember this really happened."

Testimony from the Swidler Family, By Harold Swidler

What you are about to read is an unusual, but true story. You have heard and seen movies of how people survived WWII. They are all fine, I guess. What you will read here is how an entire family of five, including three little children, did not fall for the German's propaganda. In Europe before WWII, there were various conflicts that caused many countries to change their borders (Poland, Latvia, Estonia, Lithuania, Belarus).

My father, Hendel (Henry) as a young man, lived in Sventzian. He was very intelligent, bright, learned, and especially educated in Torah study. He could recite much of the Sidur prayers by heart. Actually, he was the youngest of 17 children. His father Chaim died when he was very young, and the mother Glila, raised the kids alone. She was called Glila the Chachoma, "Glila the Brilliant Mind." In the olden days arranged marriages were the custom, and that's where a Yenta (the Matchmaker) came into play. Because of my father's intelligence, they fixed him up with the daughter (Rifka) of one of the chief Rabbis of Vilna, Anshul Aronovitch. When we say the chief Rabbis of Vilna, Vilna was one of the largest cities populated by Jews in Eastern Europe, and was known as "Little Jerusalem." There were more than 30 synagogues there. When the Rabbis had problems solving certain cases, they came before a board of rabbis (overseen by my grandfather), for a final decision. My grandfather's other work was overseeing the Jewish printing plant, known as Rhoms Druckerei. Every religious book was checked and signed by him. My parents were married in Vilna, then ended up settling in a small village or shtetl called Myadel, located in Belarus on Lake Narach. My father brought his four sisters (Basia, Henia, Belkia, and ?) to live there too. Before WWII, that little shtetl was a resort town, due mostly to the pleasant surroundings of the lake and rather close proximity to the hustle and bustle of Vilna. My grandparents would come from Vilna, the Aranovitchs, for a visit in the Summer. Approximately half the town consisted of Jews, and the other half was Catholics. Most of the Jewish population in Myadel were in the retail business: the tailor, the shoemaker, candy store, bicycle store, bakery, Kosher butcher, etc. My father Hendel, because of his business success, built a brick house in the middle of the square. Behind the house was a large garden with vegetables for our own use, and another house for the servants who worked in our house.

There was also a large barn to house our horses, cows, carriage and wagon. We made our own cheese, butter and milk. We had our own chickens and as a ritual they would always go to the shochet to kill a chicken for the Sabbath. The village was so dominated with Jews, that one street was the Yiddishe Gas (Jewish Street). On that street was a large synagogue with a Rabbi, and all the rituals that the Jews lived by. In the olden days, when observing Shabbat, the women would start cooking on Friday morning, tzimmes, cholent, kishka, and koogle. The food would be ready to eat on Saturday after the synagogue prayers. The unique thing about my father, was that in those days the government would not allow Jews to own farms and he did. My father had two orchards outside of town that he would visit every week, using a bicycle as transportation because there were no cars and it was faster than going by horse and buggy.

Besides owning two orchards, he opened a large store for the sale of fabric and material. Ready made clothing was not available, so fabric had to be purchased. He travelled often to Vilna to purchase these fabrics wholesale, and as a result, he had the largest and best selection in town. Many of the Christians came to our store to buy from him. If a customer did not have the money to pay immediately, he would trust them and put it in the books and let them pay later. Because of that trust, everyone in the village and area surrounding, appreciated him. After years in business he was able to build up not only friends (Jews and Christian), but also some degree of wealth.

My father's sisters would always complain to my mother that my father worked too hard; it wasn't necessary for him to work so hard. As the sisters entered adulthood, they found husbands in Myadel, and raised families. In general, the Jews of Myadel lived a very nice life. They lived a typical religious life. They had a sizable synagogue (located on the "Yiddish Street"), a Rabbi, a shochet, and they observed the Sabbath. Jewish people were able to raise their kids by sending them to Cheder to study the Jewish religion. Then the war broke out between Poland and Germany. There was little defense from the Polish military where the Germans attacked and the Germans were able to go through Poland very easily. The shtetl where we lived, Myadel, which was partially Polish and Belarussian, didn't feel much of the war in the beginning. But then, one day, two German automobiles with four Germans in each (which they called a patrol car) arrived. That was the first time we noticed the Germans. Many people of the village greeted them with cheers. After that, it didn't take very long for the German Gestapo to arrive in the village. They started organizing people- differentiating the Jews from the rest of the population. The Jews were put into a certain section of town, now known as a ghetto. Then, they made the Jews organize themselves into a Judenrat, which meant that Jews had an office with someone in charge. Anything the Gestapo wanted, they came to the Judenrat to demand it. For example, every week, they came to demand a sum of money or gold; if the sum wasn't met, the Jews would be taken to be killed. Or, they would organize all the Jews and bring them to Lake Naroch, at the edge of town, and make them walk into the water until they almost drowned. One day they took 21 of the most prominent Jewish men, including the rabbi, to an area outside the Christian cemetery. They were herded by German Shepherd dogs who eventually tore the Rabbi apart. Then all the 21 men were shot and thrown into a mass grave.

Luckily, my father was able to hide from this action lead by not only the Germans, but also some of the town's gangsters. That's when my father understood the severity of what was happening. While we were still in Myadel, my father's sister Basia, worked for the two German officers in charge. She became very good friends with them and they liked her very much. One day they told her in secret, that if she and her family wanted to survive, she should run away. With that information, she came home and told us. When my father heard this, he didn't wait. When the ghetto was organized, Pop felt that we should not get involved with that, and as a result we did not go into the ghetto He realized that it was like being locked in a jail. He packed up the family and on that rainy evening (before Yom Kippur), he put his hands on our little heads and blessed us as we took off in a horse and buggy. The buggy was given to the farmer as partial payment for hiding us. My father didn't expect the farmer to help us for free, even though they both realized that if they were caught by the Germans, they would kill us and the farmer's family. Of course my father paid him for hiding us, we were hiding in his basement for several months where they brought us food. We didn't have it so bad. After some time, my father felt that it was time to leave before the farmer asked us to... my father did not to overstay our welcome. From there, we went to another good friend's bar, full of hay. From the barn we could see the Gestapo coming into town. After a short time there, which was too close for comfort, we decided to go into the forest.

The forest where we went was known to be the place where many of the partisans were hiding. Speaking about my father, we felt that he was a visionary, he didn't want to be too close to the partisans and he didn't want them to know we were also hiding in the forest. Once he located an ideal place for us to situate ourselves, he contacted the farmer to help us build a large bunker-style dugout with walls of wood. He disguised the opening with bushes and grass. The door to enter was camouflaged with a bush. The farmer brought his horse to the forest and helped with the necessary digging. After it was finished, the farmer went back to the village and brought my father's sister and daughter to us in the forest. His other sister made contact with the partisans and managed to cross the front lines and go deep into Russia (Uraslav). While in hiding, my father made contact with someone and paid him to go into the Vilna Ghetto in order to bring out my mother's parents. But he returned with bad news that we were two weeks too late, they were taken to Ponar Forest, where the Germans killed over 75,000 Jews. Not much time elapsed before the Germans gathered the remaining Jews in the Myadel ghetto and took them to the nearby forest and shot them all. My father knew that with a family of three small children we should not get involved with the partisans. As it turned out, he was absolutely right again. Some of the families with small children were left behind by the partisans because they couldn't keep up and run when the Germans came into the forest...some of these children were left behind, only to be found by the Germans and killed.

How did we survive without food and clothing? How did we receive news about the partisans and their fight with the Germans? My father left each night to this farmer's house, they shared their bread, milk and potato babkes (a dish made from shredded potatoes, onion, egg, and fried in oil) with him. Sometimes we went into the forest, in "season" and gathered blueberries, mushrooms; basically that is how we were able to survive.

We wore the clothes on our back day and night. Periodically, we went to the farmer's bathhouse, where he had a stove with some stones to make steam and to wash up. While in hiding, to keep us kids occupied and quiet, my father told us Bible stories that he remembered by heart. As a result, to this day, I was very well versed in the Old Testament. Mom, who was a Vilna University graduate, taught us to memorize Russian poems and songs.

The partisans gave the Germans a rough time. They put mines on the railroads to blow them up as well as intercepted a German convoy and opened fire on them. The Germans could not tolerate this. Periodically they engaged in sweeping the forests to find partisans and destroy them. Towards the end of the war, we knew when the Germans would retreat because they would burn everything in their path. In their campaign in the Naroch forest, they brought thousands of soldiers and lined them 20 yards apart in a line, and in this way they combed the forest to find the partisans. We could not stay any longer in our bunker because of this, so Pop framed a shelter under the stacked straw that was gathered for the harvest. In these shelters, Pop put his sister and her daughter in one, Mom and Norman in another. For Pop, my sister and myself he dug a hole, then covered it with a bush. We stayed there for what seemed like 24 hours, and finally we could hear the Germans coming towards us. They came about 30-50 yards towards us, my father heard the order "Ein Shleessen reicht" (make a right turn), so instead of them marching toward our hideouts, they turned right. That was the closest we came to being caught and killed. We went without food for three or four days. I remember that Pop somehow got some smoked pork, to this day I can remember how great it tasted. Then we went back to our bunker where we stayed as another few days passed quietly. We thought the Germans had left and we could go outside, but then we spotted planes in the sky. We realized these were Russian planes and that the Russians were approaching. In a couple of hours when we got to the main road, we saw the Russian soldiers on tanks and personal carriers passing. It was then we knew we were liberated! But the war wasn't over yet because the Russians were still advancing towards Germany. One thing we couldn't understand was why the tanks and trucks had white stars on them; the Russian symbol was a red star. Later, I learned these tanks were American equipment sent to aide the Russians. The stars stayed white because the Russians didn't have the time to change them from white to red.

Somehow we managed to return to Myadel where we lived before the war. But the house was not fit to live in anymore, as they had turned it into a milk house. So we settled into a small, empty house. My father was able to get a job as the overseer of Reicheem LesHoseh, a company that turned sap from maple trees into syrup. He was called "nachalnick Reicheem Leshoseh" by the head of the company. Pop had about 100 people working for him. We had it pretty good; we went to school there and enjoyed a normal childhood. But, I can remember an incident that occurred one day when the Russians caught two Nazis who were responsible for killing many people. A scaffold was built in the center of town and a truck pulled up with the two handcuffed Germans. A band was playing, a speech was given, and then a rope was put around their necks. When the truck connected to the rope pulled away, the two Germans were left hanging for several days before their bodies disappeared.

My father soon came to realize that with no Jews left in Myadel, this was not the place to stay. The Russians had started mobilizing the younger boys into the military and somehow my father made fictitious birth certificates for all of us. He made himself older so he would not be drafted. After escaping another disaster, he arranged a railroad car to transport us to Lodz where we stayed a couple of weeks. By then, the war was over. Pop knew that Berlin was divided into 4 sections, Americans occupied one. If we could get to the American sector, from there we could make arrangements to go to America. Russian trucks were constantly driving through Lodz to Berlin. In order to get a ride, my father knew he needed something valuable for the driver to stop and pick us up. As we were waiting he pulled out a bottle of whiskey, and the driver agreed to take us to Berlin. He dropped us off on the outskirts and from there we made our way to the American sector.

Berlin, in those days, was in shambles because of the bombings. No building was intact, but we managed to find an apartment in an empty building that was deserted when the Germans ran away. Here we stayed approximately 6 months, until it was evident that the Russians were trying to blockade Berlin. We packed up and took a train (with difficulty) to Munich, Germany.
In Munich, Pop found out that there were places for refugees and displaced persons from all countries in Europe. These people were mainly Jews who were liberated from concentration camps, those who were in hiding and those who survived the war. We settled into one of those DP camps outside Munich, in a village called Wolfizhausen. The camp was called Forenwald.

While in Forenwaldwelived we lived a real Jewsh life. We lived in a second floor apartment, with one room that had an old style kitchenette. We had to go to the bathroom downstairs. Meals were cooked and eaten in our apartment. We attended a regular school where everything was taught in Hebrew. Every day we had homework, which was to read a story and recite it the next day in Hebrew. My parents were very "education oriented" and they always had a tutor for us. We spent the rest of the day playing soccer and in the colder months playing table tennis and billiards. We made new friends. My father left for Munich almost every day and did business on the "black market." He made money selling cigarettes, coffee, and other necessities that Germans had difficulty buying. By saving pennies, he managed to save a substantial sum of money. Most of the people from our DP camp immigrated to Israel, along with Pop's two sisters. While we were in camp he was able to locate our two cousins who survived the concentration camps and were now living in Dansig, Poland. He managed to bring them to our DP camp. My father intended to go to Israel, but he felt it would be too difficult to settle there with three small children.

Because my father had a brother, Motel Swidler who came to the USA in the 1890's, and his mom had a cousin who came to America and lived in Harrisburg, PA (there are no addresses, just approximate areas), my Mom decided to write a letter to the Jewish Community Center in Harrisburg in Yiddish, addressed to her cousin (David Schwab). There were very few people who could read Yiddish, but the letter fell into the hands of Rabbi David Silver, Rabbi of Kesher Israel Synagogue. Rabbi Silver read Mom's letter to David Schwab, and the Schwab family arranged for us to be brought to America. We left Forenwald at the end of 1948 to go to the port of Bremen Hoffen and boarded the ship called "General Black". We were at sea about a week and my recollections tell me that this was the first time I saw a black woman. As the ship neared the New York harbor, we spotted the statue of Liberty and were amazed at the number of cars on the New York streets and bridges. We landed at Ellis Island and had to be processed there and all our bags checked. They made us undress and undergo a medical checkup. We were all sprayed with disinfectant powder and our luggage was checked. When they finished processing us, our relatives were waiting outside. They took us for dinner in New York. We stayed overnight and the following day left for Harrisburg.

Upon arriving in Harrisburg, we stayed for a short time with a cousin, Anna Kleinman, who was Dave Schwab's sister. In a short time they bought us a townhouse on 2702 N. 7th Street in Harrisburg. They gave my father a job, as he didn't speak English, they placed him in their business, D&H Distribution Company, where his work didn't require the English language. Anna Kleinman and Mrs. Frieda Spector took us to school where, even though I was one year older than my sister Linda, we both started in the 6th or 7th grade. In a few months summer vacation started, and because I was older than Linda they advanced me to the higher grade the next fall. Through the summer vacation I was able to learn more English. As we moved through the grades my sister made many friends and was totally engrossed in school activities, including becoming a majorette. In high school I made new friends and enjoyed our new life.

In those days soccer was not a popular sport in America. So I joined cross country, and ending up receiving a number of athletic scholarships for running. I ended up attending NYU on a full athletic scholarship, where I graduated with a degree in physical education in 1957. I was selected to compete in the 5th Maccabean Games in Israel and was a successful medalist in the 5,000 and 10,000 meter events. When the team returned to the United States, I decided to stay in Israel for a while. I met a beautiful young woman, Hailla, and in a short while we got married. Upon returning to the US, it was mandatory that I report for basic training in the army at Fort Knox, Kentucky. After six months of active duty, I was promoted to Second Lieutenant. The only place in the area where I could get the bars for this rank was at the Army War College in Carlisle. On the way there, on the Carlisle Pike, I noticed the only building that would fit the criteria for a large discount store. This store, Swid Brothers, was a successful business for 20 years. I did a lot of promoting on the radio and therefore became close friends with the manager of the station and within a short while, the manager got fired. He and an engineer found a frequency known now as AM 1000-W100. As they were working with the Federal Communications Commission to acquire the frequency, they ran out of money. They asked me to invest, and thus I was able to get the frequency for myself. During that time, while my parents were still alive, we talked about visiting Belarus, where we had hidden. But the relationship between the U.S and the Eastern Block was not at its best. My father kept reminding us of our survival story, about the farmer (Alexander) who hid us, and all other relevant information. Unfortunately my father passed away in 1986 before travel was permitted to Belarus.

Ten years later, I decided to go back to Belarus and Lithuania to visit Vilna (where I was born) and to Myadel (where we lived before the war and after). Before we went on this trip, I kept saying that I could still envision the way our village looked when we left. Of course, I was only a boy of 8 or 9. When we finally arrived in the village I could not recognize anything. So I decided to ask an old lady who was walking by if the Jewish cemetery still remained. She showed us the direction and commented that it was as if no one had touched it for years. When we got there, we found one hundred tombstones. After looking for a few minutes, we found a large marble headstone which I recognized because our family had a picture of that headstone (which was that of my grandmother). That discovery made our trip worthwhile. While I was at the cemetery I noticed a woman with two children and asked her if there were any Jewish families living in Myadel. She told us one man remained and she gave us directions to his apartment. We proceeded to visit him and his wife greeted us and called him to come home. He rushed home from his volunteer job at the museum. It was a nice reunion because we remembered each other, although he was 6 years my senior. Mones Gordenwas able to recount where all the Jewish people lived while we went on a walking tour of the Jewish section of town. He showed us where our house was on the square; they had torn it down and built a large government building. We had tea together with his wife, and vowed to return soon so we could spend more time locating our hiding places.

Two years later we returned, this time with a plan. In our conversations with Monis, he said that people thought the Swidlers were in one home but he was not exactly sure. We travelled throughout the area for several days asking the elderly people who might possibly remember my father. We almost ran out of luck, but on our last day, driving along a dirt road we asked a middle aged man, dressed as a farmer. Monis stopped the car, started a conversation and told him we were looking for someone who had known Hendel Swidler. "Oh, my father-in-law always asks about a man called Hendel who once lived in Myadel," he said. So off we went to see his father-in-law. He introduced himself as Alexander! When we arrived in the log house, I couldn't remember Alexander but I remembered the stories that my father told us and the stories that were now being told by him. I knew that this was our Alexander who had helped us. We asked why he helped us even when he knew we were Jewish. His answer was short and simple, "Hendel was a father with children, and I was a father with children, there was no question." Alexander and his wife were quite elderly but had sharp memories...what a reunion! Before leaving them, we gave them watches, coats, money and a promise to ourselves that we would try to continue to be generous to these people for a long time. Also, we were able to take a video of this reunion to show to our family back home.

Upon returning home, my sister Linda and I continued sending them money and corresponding. Our hope was to bring them to the U.S for a visit. But soon after, we heard Alexander had passed away. I have been able to call Mones on a regular basis and enjoy hearing about life in Myadel. Although he is a little rusty, he is happy to speak his mother tongue of Yiddish, and so am I.

Hendel, Basia, Bailka, Glile and Hene Swidler

Above picture of Hendel (Henry) in the USA with his wife, Riva (Aranovitz) Swidler.

Above picture of the Swidler Family in Germany on the River Rhine.

Linda Swidler

Younger brother Norman

About the Authors

Nancy Holden has been researching Myadel Region family history since 1983. Concentrating mostly on the Gordon and Chadash roots in Myadel, she has collected, wherever possible, information that will inter-connect the many Gordon and Chadash families of Myadel Region. With others, she is also trying to trace the many Gordon families to a common root in Lithuania in the late 17th century. A teacher and lecturer, she is retired and lives in Southern California.

Chaya Lapidot Lupinsky was born in Haifa, Israel. She served in the army, studied at the University of Jerusalem with a major in Geography, the Bible and Education. She was a High School teacher in Rehovot and is a certified tourist guide. Her Myadel roots go back to the Menkis and Chadash families. Through this search she has became knowledgeable about the shtetl Myadel and the Myadlers who were born there.

INDEX

Note : This index does not include the names on pages 8 – 9 (Households in Myadel)